Clever Soldiers is 'a thoughtful play about violence' (*The Times*) which attacks the Oxbridge mythology against the background of war.

Hitting Town, a powerful play about incest, is 'a riveting piece of theatre . . . a stupendous achievement.' *Sunday Telegraph*

City Sugar: 'A savage dissection of that pristine slagheap of Our Times – mass culture.' *Time Out*
'A scathingly brilliant play . . . Simply by concentrating on essentials, Mr Poliakoff produces a world of technological nightmare.' *The Times*

Shout Across the River 'traces the progress of a passionate and extraordinary relationship between a young mother and her teenage daughter played against the background of a vast suburb of south London. I know few writers with such a beady eye for the creeping horrors of urban life.' *Guardian*

American Days: 'Into the escapist limbo of a top record company executive's office tumble three teenagers, spotted by an insecure talent scout and now given a hit or miss chance to impress . . . Poliakoff has the dramatic ability to make you care very much . . . a completely enjoyable play.' *Financial Times*

Strawberry Fields is about three young members of the 'lost generation' of the sixties: 'What Poliakoff manages to do as he has done before in other plays, is to make his three principal characters seem like emanations of the world in which they live. That is his great and rare talent.' *The Listener*

Stephen Poliakoff, born in 1952, was appointed Writer in Residence at the National Theatre for 1976 and the same year won the Evening Standard's Most Promising Playwright award for *Hitting Town* and *City Sugar*. He has also won a BAFTA award for the Best Single Play of 1980 for *Caught on a Train*, and the Evening Standard Best British Film award for *Close My Eyes* in 1992. His plays and films include *Clever Soldiers* (1974), *The Carnation Gang* (1974), *Hitting Town* (1975), *City Sugar* (1975), *Heroes* (1975), *Strawberry Fields* (1977), *Stronger than the Sun* (1977), *Shout Across the River* (1978), *American Days* (1979), *The Summer Party* (1980), *Bloody Kids* (1980), *Caught on a Train* (1980), *Favourite Nights* (1981), *Soft Targets* (1982), *Runners* (1983), *Breaking the Silence* (1984), *Coming in to Land* (1987), *Hidden City* (1988), *She's Been Away* (1989), *Playing with Trains* (1989), *Close My Eyes* (1991), *Sienna Red* (1992), *Century* (1994), *Sweet Panic* (1996), *Blinded by the Sun* (1996) and *The Tribe* (1997).

by the same author

Breaking the Silence
Close My Eyes
Coming in to Land
Hitting Town & City Sugar
Playing with Trains
Runners & Soft Target
She's Been Away & Hidden City
Sienna Red
Sweet Panic & Blinded by the Sun

PLAYS: 2
(Breaking the Silence, Playing with Trains, She's Been Away, Century)

STEPHEN POLIAKOFF

Plays: 1

Clever Soldiers
Hitting Town
City Sugar
Shout Across the River
American Days
Strawberry Fields

introduced by the author

Methuen Drama

METHUEN CONTEMPORARY DRAMATISTS

This collection first published in Great Britain in 1989
by Methuen Drama
an imprint of Reed International Books Ltd
Michelin House, 81 Fulham Road, London SW3 6RB
and Auckland, Melbourne, Singapore and Toronto
and distributed in the United States of America
by Heinemann, a division of Reed Elsevier Inc
361 Hanover Street, Portsmouth, New Hampshire, NH 03801 3959
Reissued with a new cover design 1994; reissued in this series 1997

A CIP catalogue record for this book is available from the British Library

ISBN 0 413 62460 9

Printed and bound in Great Britain by
Cox & Wyman Ltd, Reading, Berkshire

Contents

A Chronology

of First Performances

Introduction

The plays in this volume were all written between 1973 and 1979, those grey years when the last residue of sixties optimism was quickly fading and before the harsh divisive upheavals of the Conservative eighties. A period which already seems strangely distant: the years of Heath, Wilson and Callaghan, of Wimpey bars, the Bay City Rollers, punk and the National Front. The plays, to some extent, lasso the atmosphere of that time, but they also look forward to many of the anxieties and desires of the late eighties.

In this introduction I discuss each play briefly on its own, recalling the atmosphere in which they were written, some of the things they were trying to express, and I also look more generally at what I consider are the central tenets of my writing.

Clever Soldiers was written just before I left Cambridge, at the end of my second year, ignominiously failing to take my degree. It is the obvious odd play out in this collection in that it is my first period play, set just before and during the Great War.

Despite the difference in subject matter and setting from the other plays, and the more overtly poetic style, it seems clear to me that I was already working out various attitudes in this play that have dominated my work ever since. The first and most obvious is a reaction to the Brechtian approach to theatre, and in this case history plays in particular. It clearly shows my desire to involve the audience totally, to chart a character's change, to reach an audience through vivid, tactile, emotional theatre: a commitment to visceral writing.

Secondly, it illustrates my belief in approaching events in a play on the same level as the characters. In other words, to give a simple example from this play, not suddenly having the King of England or Field-Marshal Haig popping up, but seeing the whole action through the eyes of the central characters, in this case following Teddy's highly charged, rather hallucinatory journey.

This approach has sometimes been called 'cinematic', but that seems to me to reveal a profound misunderstanding of what that term means. Cinema is generally the wrong medium to try to reveal complex character changes or to attempt to operate dramatically on two or three levels at once. Both are clearly central aspirations in most of my plays. It could be argued that cinema's ability to summon up time and place, to locate people forcibly in a particular world, is very close to what I'm trying to do in the theatre, especially in the urban plays. But, again, I think this is a mistaken view. The plays do, I hope, have a strong sense of place, but this is only their starting point, and the 'landscapes' are never passive or literal as they would be on film, but part of the characters' internal world too, their state of mind. What is more, the settings in the plays are always attempting to be both specific and general at the same time, something that is immensely difficult (some would say impossible) to achieve on film.

It may appear perverse to discuss *Clever Soldiers*, clearly one of my most overtly polemical plays, in purely stylistic terms. But there is no mystery in what this particular play is saying. The urge to write it grew irresistibly stronger as I moved through a classical English education (a prehistoric prep. school in Kent, public school, Oxbridge) and as I gradually came to the perhaps unsurprising conclusion, to put it gently, that not much had changed in the class structure of this country since the Great War.

What I hope now appears fresher and more interesting about the play is the way it shows pre-War Oxford as an intensely violent place (instead of the customary syrup of a golden Edwardian summer) and the attempt at sensual passion in the writing, something that doesn't re-surface in my work so strongly until *Shout Across the River*.

In contrast to *Clever Soldiers*, *Hitting Town* is a very spare play, written on the wing, very quickly.

It has, I suppose, a limpid quality and lack of strain compared to some of the other plays in this volume, but I wish it burrowed deeper into the incestuous relationship between the brother and sister.

As I remember it, I deliberately chose not to do that. It was written in February 1975, soon after the Birmingham and Guildford bombings, that have so recently come back to haunt us. I was living at the time near Selfridges, where all the windows were blown out one day near Christmas, leaving pieces of decorations and clothes scattered all over Oxford Street. It was a time when, as you walked down the street, you expected cars to blow up in front of you.

I became very interested in trying to write a play about a personal reaction to violence and the ugly mood of the mid-seventies, about people growing inward and private and lonely, after the noise and frivolity of the sixties. Onlookers gradually slipping into a type of melancholy as Clare is at the beginning of the play. *Hitting Town* was meant to have the simplicity and compactness of a short story so that the incestuous relationship seemed as fragile and impermanent as the architecture Clare and Ralph were passing through.

Funnily enough, this is the only play of mine that I have ever wanted to write a sequel to. I keep being drawn back to this relationship and wondering what happened to Ralph and Clare during the eighties. I have always found a reason for not writing the play, but the idea regularly re-surfaces. Maybe I will get round to it soon.

City Sugar was written in the summer of 1975. It was the time of the Bay City Rollers. The 'weenyboppers' were pursuing them all over England, and I actually watched these children hurling themselves against the Bay City Rollers' limousine as it did a three-point turn in a street in Kensington. A desperate and rather frightening sight. Of course I'd grown up during Beatlemania, so this was hardly a new phenomenon. But what did seem new was the extraordinary, synthetic nature of what these kids were being offered, their enormous hunger apparently being cynically manipulated.

Reading *City Sugar* now I'm struck that the wheel has come full circle again, we are in an age of bland manufactured sounds, popular culture has plunged further and further down-market, increasingly afraid to offer anything that might stretch the minds or imaginations of the young.

Like all the urban plays in this volume, *City Sugar* is written with very few direct contemporary references (except of course the names of the records, which clearly can be adapted). This was because I was trying to create a world that would not date overnight, that would contain a form of dark poetry that might allow it to resonate for as long as people wanted to perform the play.

In all my contemporary plays set against these concrete inner-city landscapes, the challenge is both to create a recognisable world, but also one that has some universality. To take seemingly bland and everyday terrain and view it with an intensity that makes it reveal something deeper about our lives, and about the modern world.

Many people have latched on to the 'stained desolation' of these plays and found their atmosphere their main subject, the chief centre of interest. But that is not my intention, nor what really happens when the plays are performed. In *City Sugar* the disc-jockey Leonard Brazil's darkening journey, his gradually erupting fury, Nicola's mute defiance, and the suppressed anarchy of her friend Susan fighting against the world she is growing up in, are just as important as the urban landscape that is closing in around them. As in nearly all my plays, the entwining of character and the outer world so they are practically inseparable, is my chief objective.

But something else that is, I think, just beginning to be visible in this play, is an ambivalence about all that urban desolation, a disgust if you like, but also a sense of the writer being drawn irresistibly back *towards* the neon and the concrete.

Shout Across the River was written for the Royal Shakespeare Company in 1978, and is the darkest and most emotional play in this volume. It tells the story of a mother and her teenage daughter during an extremely eventful week in their lives. Again there is the urban world outside, in this case the great sprawl of south London, across the river from St Paul's, stretching out seemingly for ever. And, against this background, a story emerges about two women fighting desperately for some sort of release from their very stunted lives. A form of love story between mother and daughter.

Two things strike me about this play now. It reminds one how the shadow of unemployment and recession was hanging very strongly in the atmosphere then, even though the desperation of these two women seems to belong more to the terrible bleakness of the early eighties.

Secondly, the play unapologetically and quite violently breaks free of any trace of social realism, moving into a more heightened and sensual world than the previous urban plays. It tugs you along on a roller-coaster of emotion, which you either roll along with or resist.

Despite its structural faults (the sprawl of the long pub scene in the second half) it remains the play I like best in this volume. I think it is both one of the boldest plays I have written and it continues to have a considerable degree of contemporary relevance.

When it first appeared some people resented Christine's violence, found her a terrifying and ghastly creation, but after the mass unemployment of the eighties, and the despair felt by so many young people, the fury seems to me to make a lot more sense.

It is perhaps useful to pose some questions in relation to this particular play that are, on occasion, asked about my work in general. 'What on earth is he saying?' This is a recurring refrain from certain quarters. 'What exactly is it about?' 'Is it at all plausible?' 'Where does he stand politically?' 'Is he saying all women are prisoners?' 'What are the themes of the play – that some of the young have no choice but to dive into despair and madness?' etc. etc.

I would reply that my plays are best experienced as an entity. Read it all the way through, or watch it without standing back from it, and the play should speak to you. Search as you go along for particular themes to be carefully enunciated and underlined and you may find yourself writhing in frustration. This is because all my work is a reaction to the sort of playwrighting (fine though a lot of it is) that first takes a theme and then populates it from an Olympian height. My plays are hard to categorise and I am unapologetic about that. To me the best plays are the ones which mysteriously evade being neatly summed up.

This is not to say I do not think long and hard and plan carefully what the central concerns of each play are. But I am trying to reach people obliquely, working on their imaginations, instincts, memories. Indeed my work is often called oblique, but I am pleased that this doesn't seem to stop millions of people responding to it on television. I think if audiences are trusted, not yelled at through a play, or even talked to directly, they will often respond with considerable warmth to work that often seems on the surface quite difficult and elusive. Moreover, if an audience is approached this way, the work often stays with them far longer than if they are addressed more full-frontally. This is one of my most passionate beliefs about playwrighting, and one of my chief aims, to make the plays echo in people's minds for a long time afterwards.

Shout Across the River was written to work this way, a central relationship and a journey that calls out to us and resonates, in a fashion that is sometimes not easy to define.

American Days was written as a reaction to *Shout Across the River*. After such a dark play, I found myself writing an 'entertainment', something quite funny and less emotional, about some kids auditioning for a large record company. After its English première I re-wrote it for the New York production as I was concerned to deepen and strengthen the second half. This explains the odd construction of the play, a short first act and a long second. (Though for those thinking of performing the play and worried about this element, it is possible to move the interval to just before Sherman's re-entry in the second act.)

My chief memory of writing the play is of Thatcher winning the '79 election while I was in the middle of the first act. And, indeed, in hindsight the play seems to encapsulate some of the values of the eighties. The hard-faced kids staring into the future with shrewd commercial eyes, the increasingly ephemeral nature of nearly everything, the importance of fashion and style, of hype, of surfaces and image.

The play was written to show the reverse side of *City Sugar*: young people not as victims, but as avengers, coming out of the mass culture and spitting it back, manipulating it with equal contempt.

The play again inhabits a world close to stylisation, but still remains very tactile, grounded, not surreal. I hope the main surprise of the play is that Sherman is not the real monster you expect him to be. He is, in fact, quite honest, consistent, and even, in a peculiar fashion, honourable. It is Lorraine that is the disturbing and frightening creation, in many ways the true monster of the action.

Strawberry Fields was originally written during the blistering hot summer of 1976. And in fact that is a good way to approach the play, as a summer nightmare. It was the time of the National Front, of racist demonstrations, of a minority Labour government lurching from crisis to crisis.

Reading the play now, perhaps the most surprising feature is how the strong 'Green' views, the conservation streak expressed by Kevin and Charlotte, gives the play an odd and different contemporary relevance. A vision of the potentially dark side of Green issues, raising the possibility of some people reacting with savagery against the urban world they have grown up in, as they try to project themselves into a never-never land where the car can be de-invented and motorways no longer exist.

In one way the play clearly belongs to the mid-seventies in its depiction of the hippy dream turning sour and, in Kevin's case, evil. But with all the incidents of European terrorism both from the Left and the Right since the play was written, *Strawberry Fields* has proved to have one of the busiest lives of any of my plays, being regularly performed all over the world.

This brings me face to face with one of the central questions about my work. Do I share this revulsion with modern life, with the urban world, expressed by some of my characters?

The answer is a simple no. As I grow older I become increasingly convinced that I am at heart a modernist, that I revel in these urban canyons, and cannot stand the idea of retreating into pastoral worlds or into the past as a refuge. I hope my next plays will explore some of this further.

What links the plays in this volume is clearly a passion for character, and the development of character, as the central starting point of all drama that really interests me. And, secondly, a belief in attempting to create a vivid, dramatic world which is both recognisable and also completely original at the same time.

I believe, fervently too, that one can write small cast plays, without the plays themselves being the least bit small. That out of the collision of the characters that inhabit this volume, a large and resonant world of its own can be created.

Stephen Poliakoff
October 1989

CLEVER SOLDIERS

Clever Soldiers was first presented at Hampstead Theatre Club, London in November 1974 with the following cast:

TEDDY	Simon Ward
DAVID	Michael Byrne
HAROLD	Michael Feast
SARAH	Sheila Ruskin
FAG	Sean Bury
PRIVATE ONE	Bruce Bould
PRIVATE TWO	Duncan Preston
ARNOLD	Roger Davenport

OXFORD 1914:
The set should suggest the atmosphere of Oxford. Mellow, warm, and must allow the scenes to melt into each other.
The same basic set should be used for the war scenes.
The two main areas of action in the First Act, DAVID's room and HAROLD's, need only be indicated, not fully represented.
The short opening scene, in the changing room of a Public School, can be played frontstage without scenery.

ACT ONE

Scene One

TEDDY *alone. Spot frontstage.*
TEDDY *starts the action, about eighteen, good looking, striking blue eyes. At first an impulsive excitable manner.*

The changing room of a public school. He is in games clothes. Cut, sweating, muddy, staring at his cut. A suit lies in front of him, with a flower on top.

TEDDY. It looks good doesn't it.

He turns, spot on ARNOLD, *other side of stage.* ARNOLD *thin sharp face, nervous eyes, a year older than* TEDDY, *a watchful, grey manner.*

TEDDY (*surprised*). Arnold . . . ? (*Smiles.*) What are you doing, hanging about the changing room?

ARNOLD. I wasn't doing anything. (*Pause.*) Was the match good?

TEDDY. Yes; yes it was. We won.

ARNOLD. What are they all doing now?

TEDDY. Go and look for yourself if you want.

ARNOLD. No, it's all right. I can imagine it.

TEDDY. They've gone into town. Victory celebrations down the main street in their games clothes – sweaty and cut!

ARNOLD. Why aren't you there?

TEDDY. I don't feel like it. But it was a good game. (*Laughs up close.*) You're not jealous are you? You could have done better if you'd wanted. You're not that bad at games. (*Pulls* ARNOLD's *tie.*)

ARNOLD. Stop it! (*Pause.*) You've made a mess of yourself in the match haven't you. (TEDDY *moves close.*) Careful! You'll mess me up too.

TEDDY. Yes! (*Stabs at* ARNOLD's *clean shirt with his cut arm.*) All dressed up for the end of term. (*Pause.*) Are you sad to be leaving?

ARNOLD. No – not very.

TEDDY (*beginning to change into suit*). Looking forward to Oxford . . . ?

ARNOLD. Yes.

3

TEDDY. Better than this place. Look at those blazers of the bloods. So well starched you could cut yourself on them. This is the real school isn't it. Down among the boilers and rust, and the stench from the lockers. The foul air in this place!

ARNOLD. Yes, it's always so sticky here – so hot.

TEDDY. Fifty feet below ground, used to come here out of school so often to watch the Juniors change. So did you! The terrible things that happened against those pipes – scalding hot!

ARNOLD (*quiet*). Yes.

TEDDY. And a line of boys vomiting in the showers after a cross-country run. (*Kicks floor.*) You know I've had my face crushed into this floor so often I've left a lot of my best skin on it. I think this may well be the worst place on earth . . .

ARNOLD. You can be alone here though. (*Noise of movement – out of darkness.*)

TEDDY. There's something over there! Catch it.

ARNOLD. It's all right.

TEDDY. A rat . . . Arnold it's your fag – (*Catches him by the arm.*) FAG *is smaller than them, good looking, dressed in school suit.*

TEDDY. Got him!

ARNOLD. Spying on us.

TEDDY. Was he (*looks at* FAG) or did you bring him down here? That was what you were doing wasn't it!

ARNOLD. Jenkins! You know this part of the changing room is out of bounds to Juniors.

TEDDY *continues to dress.*

FAG. Yes.

ARNOLD *and the* FAG *face each other, very close.*
ARNOLD's *manner is gentle, suggesting a relationship with the* FAG.

ARNOLD (*quiet*). Don't answer back boy. Come and see me later. I'll have something for you to do.

FAG. But . . .

ARNOLD (*quiet*). Did I hear you say something?

FAG (*close to him*). I . . .

ARNOLD. And again. You're answering back all the time. Touch your toes 1000 times.

FAG. I wasn't . . .

ARNOLD. 2000.

FAG. I won't.

ARNOLD (*smiles*). 15,000. Go away now. . . You can come and do them before I swish you, can't you.

FAG *moves to go.*

TEDDY (*loud*). Come here! You're Jenkins then. It's the last day of term.

FAG. Yes.

TEDDY. Why's your face covered in blisters?

FAG. Don't know.

TEDDY. Did you see me in the match, Jenkins?

FAG. Yes.

TEDDY (*smiles*). He saw me in the match. See I'm bleeding from it. Quite a graze.

FAG. It must hurt.

TEDDY. It does. Your hair's very long, Jenkins, probably too long. You can have my clothes if you like. To keep. With traces of the match on them. Would you like them?

FAG. Oh yes! Can I? (*Gathering them up hastily before* TEDDY *changes his mind.*

TEDDY (*suddenly*). Go on run – he won't try to stop you.

FAG *stands bewildered.*

Run like hell – so he can't get you! Go on – run Boy! For your life!

FAG *exits – zig-zags into darkness – clutching bundle of clothes.*

TEDDY. I bet you brought him down here.

ARNOLD. Of course I did.

TEDDY. What were you doing to him? (*Lightly.*) You're disgusting aren't you. A disgrace to the nation.

ARNOLD. I wanted somewhere to say goodbye. Have to get away from the others. I was only saying goodbye.

TEDDY. Oxford. . . . How do you feel about Oxford? Becoming a total nobody again.

ARNOLD. I won't mind.

TEDDY. No. (*Loud.*) I so want to get away from this! (*Looks at* ARNOLD.) You look very smart.

ARNOLD (*hands him a button-hole*). So do you.

TEDDY. See you there.

ARNOLD *exits.*

Scene Two

Loud peal of bells leading into piano music.

TEDDY. Oxford! In a heat wave. In all its glory!

Lights full. Bright warm light. HAROLD's room. HAROLD tall, very thin arms, long white face, dressed in a smoking jacket. He has a prematurely aged quality about him – ostensibly he is twenty-one but should be played by somebody older.

HAROLD. It's a delightful day to come up on. Almost too much sun. In summer the view out of this window is quite outrageously overdone. Always brings a miniature lump to my throat. Everyone tends to lapse at this time of year . . . don't they . . . into poetry or hay fever. Both disagreeable. I succumbed yesterday – after a mild struggle. EDWARD ROGERS.

TEDDY. Yes.

HAROLD. That is your name?

TEDDY. Yes.

HAROLD. A lovely day isn't it. Intoxicating.

TEDDY. Yes.

HAROLD. Why aren't you ready for your medical examination? Haven't you been informed?

TEDDY. No.

HAROLD (*hands him sheet of paper*). There . . .

TEDDY. What now?

HAROLD. Yes. You should undress here. I have a dressing gown waiting.

TEDDY. Undress here!

HAROLD. Yes – it's the way we do it here. College regulations. Come on, hurry . . .

TEDDY (*undressing fast*). I'm sorry . . . I didn't realize. I went for a walk. I had no idea . . . I'm sorry.

HAROLD. Don't worry. I shall stay here and show you the way.

TEDDY. Is it far?

HAROLD. A fair distance. Here put this on.

Hands him very short gown.

TEDDY. I . . . ?

HAROLD. No, I'm afraid you must use this one.

TEDDY. But . . .

HAROLD. I'm afraid I must insist. Regulations.

TEDDY. Where is it? Next door?

HAROLD. Oh no – in New Court about ten minutes' walk down the street. Come on – we'll be late.

TEDDY. Who are you?

HAROLD. Me?

TEDDY. I don't believe there's any medical exam is there? (*Loud.*) Tell me or I'll . . .

HAROLD. You're quite right there isn't. Whatever roused your suspicions . . . ?

TEDDY (*savage*). You bastard . . .

HAROLD. We play that joke on most freshers . . . But I didn't do very well this time . . . I should have at least got you into the quad. I did last year. (*Smiling blandly.*) Practical jokes are immensely stimulating don't you think. Licensed cruelty which even the victim feels it's bad form to complain about . . .

TEDDY. Just get out of here. Go on . . .

HAROLD. I'm afraid I can't.

TEDDY. What do you mean?

HAROLD. You see I live just across the way. We both share this room.

TEDDY. What?

HAROLD. Yes!

TEDDY. Who are you? We're not going to be able to stand each other – are we!

HAROLD. I think we'll get on rather well. I always do with primitive types. What are you doing . . . ?

TEDDY. Getting dressed.

HAROLD. You don't have to. (TEDDY *looks up.*) (*Approaching him.*) Haven't you heard it's going to be a wonderfully hot summer.

TEDDY. No.

HAROLD. Have you seen your tutor yet?

TEDDY. Yes.

HAROLD. Did you like him?

TEDDY. Yes, a lot.

HAROLD. Did you? Haven't you heard about him?

TEDDY. Heard what?

HAROLD. Haven't you been told the truth about him?

TEDDY. No I haven't. What are you talking about? (*Loud.*) Come on – tell me!

HAROLD. You *must* have liked him.

TEDDY. I knew somebody just like you before.

HAROLD. I'm delighted to hear it. I thrive on competition.

TEDDY. And I loathed him –

HAROLD (*leaning towards him smiling*). I forgot there's a message I've got to give you – it's from your tutor. He wants to see you again at once.

TEDDY. Really. (*Stretches out for the note as HAROLD hands it to him. TEDDY catches him, pulls him down.*)

HAROLD. What you doing?

TEDDY. What does it look like?

HAROLD. Crude aren't you. (*Smokes as TEDDY sits astride him.*)

TEDDY. You're very hot. Are you ill?

HAROLD. I get like that.

TEDDY. And very fragile. Puny. All bones.

HAROLD. Hadn't you better go to your tutor?

TEDDY. Don't start that or . . .

HAROLD. Or what? You'll use more violence will you? Don't think you can frighten me off that way. They're always the same when they're straight from school.

TEDDY. You talk like an old man.

HAROLD. Don't do that – careful – you don't understand I'm nearly blind.

TEDDY. Are you? Really. (*Lets him get up.*) What do I look like?

HAROLD. Delightful.

TEDDY. Come on.

HAROLD. You've got fair hair beginning to brown.

TEDDY. What colour eyes?

HAROLD. Blue, very blue.

TEDDY. Nearly blind! You liar! (*Moves close to him threateningly.*)

HAROLD. I'm only half-blind . . . have difficulty in seeing . . . a little short-sighted. But it's more romantic being nearly blind.

TEDDY. I don't believe anything you say.

HAROLD. Look what you've done to me (*Looking at his arm.*) – wouldn't it be pleasant if people could shed their skins like lizards.

TEDDY. You never told me your name.

HAROLD. It's Harold. But I'm called H by most people. You better hurry up, hadn't you. Your tutor's waiting . . .

TEDDY. I don't believe you . . . (*He exits.*)

HAROLD. It's going to be a good term. Quite unlike any other.

Fade down on HAROLD. Up on DAVID, on other side of stage. The young Don – early thirties. Strongly built but round baby face. Sitting behind desk. TEDDY faces him – some distance from the desk. Very bright sunlight from behind DAVID, shining straight at TEDDY, so he has difficulty in seeing DAVID's face.

DAVID. Rogers?

TEDDY. Yes?

TEDDY moves forward.

(*Nervous.*) I'm late, I know. I'm sorry. I thought it might be a practical joke. But it wasn't. You wanted to see me again.

DAVID. Yes. (*Stares at him.*) It's purely an administrative matter. For you to sign . . .

TEDDY signs it.

DAVID. Thank you.

TEDDY. What is it?

DAVID. Purely administrative.

TEDDY. Is that all you want?

DAVID. Yes. (TEDDY, *surprised, hesitates, moves to go.*) No! What's your Christian name?

TEDDY. Teddy . . . sir.

DAVID. And I'm David.

TEDDY. Yes . . . sir.

DAVID. You needn't call me sir.

TEDDY. All right.

DAVID. Do you think you're going to like it here?

TEDDY. Yes.

DAVID. How can you tell? Have you got a pleasant room?

TEDDY. Yes.

DAVID. With a good view I hope.

TEDDY. It's very beautiful.

DAVID. It's a beautiful day.

TEDDY (*quiet*). It's very wonderful here.

DAVID. So you're not disappointed.

TEDDY. No. (*Pause.*) Are you?

DAVID. What do you mean by that?

TEDDY. I don't know.

DAVID. Why are you looking at me like that?

TEDDY. Why are you staring at me?

DAVID. There's no need to become impudent, boy – that's one thing I won't tolerate.

TEDDY. I'm sorry – sir.

DAVID. I told you, you're not to call me . . .

TEDDY. I know, I'm sorry. (*Pause, staring at him.*) If you don't mind me saying so.

DAVID. Go on.

TEDDY. You're not what I expected.

DAVID. Aren't I? What did you expect?

TEDDY. I don't know . . . now.

DAVID. You're not what I expected either, not really. (*He stares at him.*) So we're both surprised apparently . . .

TEDDY. Yes. (*Turns.*) When I arrived you know . . . just now, I felt so . . .

DAVID. So what?

TEDDY. Pleased . . . but strange. Yes.

DAVID. It's a very strange place. Probably stranger than you think. In fact you may be in for quite a shock.

TEDDY. Am I? I keep seeing people you know that I . . . I was at school with, and many others too, that are so alike, you see, so familiar, immediately I think I know them, you see. It happens on nearly every corner, but I don't, only somebody like them, with the same mannerisms, the same looks. I'm sorry I don't know why I'm talking so much. It seems almost as if I'm completely drunk. (*Quiet.*) I don't know why . . .

DAVID. Do you often get drunk?

TEDDY. Oh yes. Sometimes. Quite often. Never as drunk as this though. I suppose . . . I am pleased to be here. The sun hurts, is every afternoon like this?

DAVID. Nothing changes here – you should know that.

TEDDY. Should I? (*Stares at him.*) Why did you ask me to come here again so soon?

DAVID. Because I felt like it. (*Pause.*) Because I wanted to talk to you, see what you were really like. It's conceivable that you're a little different from the others.

TEDDY. And what if I am?

DAVID. Do you always answer back?

TEDDY. Usually, yes.

DAVID. You're rude as well then. (*Pause.*) I think we're going to get on, you know. I really think we might, boy – don't you?

TEDDY (*quiet*). I don't know.

DAVID. If you turn out to be different to the others that is – which I hope you will.

TEDDY. You put me in the sun so I couldn't see your face – didn't you?

DAVID (*smiles*). I may have done.

TEDDY. Will I do?

DAVID. For what?

TEDDY. For here.

DAVID. Oh yes. (*They look at each other.*) You can go now.

TEDDY. Thank you.

DAVID. For what?

TEDDY (*hesitates*). I don't know.

Quick fade down to spot on TEDDY.

(*Sharp.*) When you walk down through the town the sun dazzles, cobbled streets. All is golden brown. And it is solid! Hard! Unchanging! It doesn't melt when you touch it. There's no place like it.

Blackout.

Scene Three

Music hall song playing on old gramophone. Fade up on HAROLD, *next to gramophone, and with a tea tray in front of him, staring towards* TEDDY *downstage.*

HAROLD. Where've you been? I've hardly seen you all week. I've been waiting furiously for you. Been listening to this tune eighty-eight times. (*Takes record off.*) I thought you'd never come. I had the scout make tea. (*Pause.*) My speech in the debate yesterday was a great success, you'll be pleased to know.

TEDDY (*not looking at him, quiet*). Good.

HAROLD. They say I get better and better with each speech – an alarming situation if it's true, reminiscent of a boiling kettle. To be a success with one's contemporaries is obviously a pleasure but it lowers the chances of immortality quite considerably . . . which is depressing. Are you listening to me, Teddy? My opponent was Oliver Jew Boy Crankshaw. Listening to his speech reminded me of walking barefoot over gravel, not that I've ever done that. He sat there with that smile of perpetual goodness on his face. I find his saintliness almost unbearable, it hangs about him wherever he goes. Like codliver oil. Everything about him you know is more than perfect. I should think even his excrement is snow white and elegantly shaped.

DAVID *enters, stands watching them.* HAROLD *looks up.*

DAVID. Good afternoon.

TEDDY. Hello. (*To* HAROLD.) I've invited my tutor to tea.

HAROLD. So I see. This is an unexpected pleasure. Mixing with Royalty are we.

HAROLD's manner immediately becomes provocative and outrageous.

DAVID. I can't stay long I'm afraid.

TEDDY. This is Harold.

HAROLD (*extending a limp hand*). H . . .

DAVID. I don't believe we've ever met Har . . .

HAROLD. H. I wonder why that is, Mr Jones. Do take a seat.

TEDDY. Tea?

DAVID. Thank you.

TEDDY. Milk?

HAROLD. We'll have to hear that tune for the eighty-ninth time won't we! (*Gets up.*)

TEDDY. Tea, Harold?

HAROLD. No I shan't be having tea today. I've suddenly lost my appetite. (*Staring at* DAVID.) It must be this heat (*suddenly loud*) and the TEDIUM.

They look at him.

(*Smiling.*) As a nation we are far too tolerant of boredom don't you find, Mr Jones – real boredom. We tolerate awful puddings and the Irish just because we consider Civil War an unsavoury alternative.

DAVID. That must have been in your speech yesterday Harold – it came out very nicely.

HAROLD. You have heard about my speech then Mr Jones.

DAVID. Yes I have heard a great deal about you Harold.

HAROLD. You flatter me.

DAVID. Do I? That was not my intention.

HAROLD. Nevertheless you flatter me. (*Pause.*) No in my speech yesterday I stopped short of advocating Civil War, but I did suggest the abolition of treacle pudding.

DAVID. Congratulations! No doubt you won the debate.

HAROLD. Certainly. Nothing wins votes more successfully than intolerance and persecution.

DAVID. I've heard that before Harold.

HAROLD. Nothing I say, Mr Jones, is ever original. I merely borrow selectively. I may even borrow from you.

TEDDY. Biscuits?

HAROLD. I find this present tolerant age very irksome don't you? I've just written a novel on the subject . . . The spice has gone out of life don't you find? Gone. Without public executions and bear-baiting we are left totally impotent. Aren't you . . . ?

DAVID (*staring at him*). It depends on the perversion you indulge in – doesn't it Harold?

HAROLD. Really? I find there are no good perversions left. Most of them now are too unripe for my taste. Of course this place is not quite what it was thirty or forty years ago in that respect.

DAVID. You talk as if you were here then.

HAROLD. In a sense I was.

DAVID. What sense is that?

HAROLD (*pleasant smile*). I shouldn't think it'll make a lot of sense to you. (*With surprising violence leaning forward.*) But this place has definitely declined in a certain other respect too, Mr Jones.

DAVID. Of course it has. It's rotting Harold.

HAROLD. Rotting? It's remarkably beautiful for somewhere that is rotting. But I suppose that can't be helped.

DAVID. Inside. Every day, it rots a little bit more. Biscuit?

HAROLD. Most kind. You dislike this place then, Mr Jones.

DAVID. I dislike some of the people in it.

HAROLD. Ah then we have something in common after all! You dislike it sufficiently I see to carry on teaching here.

DAVID. It depends on whom I'm teaching it doesn't it?

HAROLD. Does it? (*Loud.*) Will you teach me then Mr Jones? That's a superlative idea. I must have Mr Jones to teach me immediately.

DAVID. Teach you what Harold?

HAROLD. Anything that I haven't already learnt.

DAVID. I don't think I could teach *you* anything.

HAROLD. You don't want to teach me!

DAVID. It would be an impossible task, Harold.

HAROLD. You refuse to teach me then. (*Savage.*) On what grounds Mr Jones do you refuse me? Social are they! Political are they! I do believe we have a socialist in our midst. Perhaps we can ask – are you, or are you not, a complete socialist? Why don't you parade up and down the room? Go on! Teddy, you have unwittingly I feel invited to tea . . .

TEDDY (*savage*). At least he was invited.

DAVID (*coolly*). And what are you, Harold?

HAROLD. What am I? (*Pause.*) I'm a socialite I suppose. Unforgivable, isn't it?

DAVID. And what else are you?

HAROLD. What else am I? I . . . I don't see why I should tell you Mr Jones. Who are you anyway?

He moves to the door.

I am here to be taught what to be aren't I. (*Sharp.*) I'm having a picnic tomorrow. Do come.

He exits.

DAVID. You've found a splendid one there, haven't you? (*Loud.*) H . . .

TEDDY. I am sorry about that.

DAVID. Of course you don't know about him do you – he's famous. He can be seen every day lying on a bench in the quad, a blanket over his legs, and his eyes half closed, watching all those that go past, ready to pounce.

TEDDY. Really?

DAVID (*staring at* TEDDY). He devours people you see. Sometimes you catch a glimpse of him with a pair of legs sticking out of his mouth, but usually they slip down without trace. (*Stares at* TEDDY.) And the arrogance, the revolting, unashamed arrogance while he does it. You know, I'm meant to help perpetuate an institution that makes that sort of thing possible. I'd rather be a zoo keeper wouldn't you? A few things really make me angry you see.

TEDDY. Why on earth was he like that?

DAVID. Why? Because that's what he is, isn't he. And because, of course, he knows my background.

TEDDY. Your background?

DAVID. Yes. (*Pause, he watches* TEDDY.) A modest one, to put it politely. You know . . . lowly. In fact about as low as you can get really. Welsh too – the final straw of course. Really Welsh. I am, quite violently so, you see.

TEDDY. I see. I don't think I would have known.

DAVID. No. I don't think you would have done probably.

TEDDY (*slight smile*). You must be rather brilliant then, to be allowed to teach here.

DAVID (*smile*). Possibly. A little. Your hair's wet.

TEDDY. Yes, I've been swimming.

DAVID. I thought it was sweat from all that argument. How are you settling down in this paradise then . . . ?

TEDDY. I'm not sure . . . (*Louder.*) Sometimes I feel . . .

DAVID. Restless.

TEDDY (*looks at him*). Yes – that's right.

DAVID. But this is a special time you see.

TEDDY. Why?

DAVID. Because there's a feeling in the air, even in this stale place. Murmurings. Not very loud yet, but they're there. And it can be quite fun to listen to them. (*Pause.*) I think I like you, you know. You don't mind me saying that, do you? (*Loud.*) It doesn't offend your sense of decency – that you've been so carefully instilled with.

TEDDY. No.

DAVID. You don't mind then.

TEDDY. Should I?

DAVID. You should do what you want, boy.

TEDDY. I shall.

DAVID (*smiles*). We must have a good talk soon Teddy.

TEDDY. There are all those books you gave me – hundreds.

DAVID. There's plenty of time for that. (*Quiet.*) When I came here first I read twenty books a week. For the first three weeks. Then I piled them in the middle of the room, a heap of crisp new books, the sort I'd never owned before, and I burnt the lot. I sat and watched the smoke pour out of the window across the whole college. A huge black column, it was very thick smoke with a particularly revolting, tarry smell. It smothered these buildings, leaving a grease on all the walls, and drove everybody shrieking and coughing outside. I sat up here and watched it all. It was quite a moment. (*Pause.*) Goodbye then and thank you.

TEDDY. For what? (DAVID *smiles and exits left.*)

TEDDY *turns,* HAROLD *is standing watching him, having entered quietly, a moment before.*

HAROLD. Teddy?

TEDDY. So you were listening. (*Loud.*) He's a fascinating man isn't he! (*Loud.*) Isn't he!

HAROLD. A certain grim fascination perhaps. (*Quiet – nervous.*) Don't look at me like that, please.

TEDDY. You should have heard yourself.

HAROLD. Should I? I do often.

TEDDY. You're a disgrace really. (TEDDY *moves close.*) Your days are numbered.

HAROLD. You look as if you intend to hurt me. (*He stares at* TEDDY.) Don't.

TEDDY. Look at your eyes – you're not scared are you? How strong are you? (*Touches him.*)

HAROLD. That depends. You're not to touch me. I hate being touched. You'll bruise me.

TEDDY (*suddenly savage*). How strong, Harold? What if I struck a match now against your cheek.

Sound of distant, drunken singing – TEDDY *turns away abruptly.*

Listen to that.

HAROLD. What?

TEDDY. It's the bloods. They're out tonight. Looking for trouble after some match or other.

HAROLD. I hate this place at night, the evenings are glorious, but then the nights . . .

TEDDY (*excited*). It's extraordinary at night. Different!

HAROLD. You don't come to talk to me as much as you did. I hardly see you.

TEDDY (*close, loud*). That's because your sight's so bad.

HAROLD (*surprised*). Teddy?

TEDDY. I knew all about you, the very first time I saw you. I knew everything.

HAROLD. You astonish me. (*Pause.*) I miss you, you know.

TEDDY. I want to do something shattering tonight. Get outside. Get violently, sickeningly drunk. Listen to the noise they're making – enough to silence the bells! The idiots are looking for a fight. I'm going to see.

HAROLD. Don't go Teddy.

TEDDY. Why not?

HAROLD. You'll get hurt by them.

TEDDY. No I won't.

HAROLD. And I have so much to tell you. Sometimes I could tell you my whole imagination, you know. You must stay and listen. (*Fast.*) I went to see old Goodrich. He lives at the top of a tower. He's an extraordinary shape – completely round – like a huge cheese. And he has the most astonishing voice, as if his mouth was clogged with oysters. He knew Browning very well, and he told me a filthy story about . . .

TEDDY (*loud*). You told me all this yesterday.

HAROLD. I didn't. You lie . . . I couldn't have done.

TEDDY. You did. You're always following me around too aren't you? Everywhere –

HAROLD (*staring at him*). You can't escape me, Teddy, it's impossible.

TEDDY. Can't I? (*Pause.*) Look at you. Why are you so old, so clumsy? I saw you running across New Court, running for your life. You looked so ridiculous, like a vulture. You ought to be careful where you go Harold, for you're the most absurd person I've ever known.

He exits.

Silence. HAROLD *alone.*

HAROLD (*staring out*). I don't know which I find more boring, being with Teddy or without him. I must find a party somewhere. A party where I'll be asked to dance naked. Where people will surround me. (*Loud.*) I will not be left alone. (*Stares out.*) Once this time was the cream of life – now it's just the top of the milk.

Blackout.

Scene Four

Outside. Dark.

TEDDY. Who's there . . . Come on . . . Arnold . . . ?

ARNOLD *keeps his distance.*

TEDDY. I thought it was you. What are you doing out there?

ARNOLD. I was just walking.

TEDDY. Walking where?

ARNOLD. Nowhere – really. (*Pause.*) Did you see those bloods?

TEDDY. Yes – and heard them too.

ARNOLD. Vicious aren't they?

TEDDY. Saw them come out of Christs . . . I did, they were as drunk as hell. Their wounds from the match all bandaged up.

ARNOLD. And riding piggy back on their college porters with some ladies' shoes in their mouths. There's food lying all over the lawn back there too, completely squashed.

TEDDY. Yes! They're stampeding in and out of parties at the moment in fancy dress. Have you seen that? Some of them dressed in a suit of armour or wilting under a pair of antlers on their head. While they line up to urinate in the chapel. The pride of Oxford.

ARNOLD. You can smell their breath from here.

TEDDY. They'll be jumping from roof to roof any moment, trying to fly.

ARNOLD. Of course.

TEDDY. Fly! (*Sharp smile.*) They can do anything can't they after all.

ARNOLD. They've got a lady up there now and they've tied her to a chimney. Soon they'll go ahead and try to light her.

TEDDY. Light her! Oxford at night is always exciting. Always.

ARNOLD. Yes.

TEDDY. They can be dangerous though. They've been smashing glass tonight. You shouldn't be out alone should you. It's not safe.

ARNOLD. No it's not very safe, is it?

TEDDY. Aren't you happy in this paradise then, Arnold?

ARNOLD. No.

TEDDY. Do you often come out here?

ARNOLD. Yes.

TEDDY. You look different.

ARNOLD. Do I? How?

TEDDY. Are you lonely?

ARNOLD (*loud*). No, not very, no.

TEDDY. You're so quiet now, all your spark's gone. I hear you never go out of your room, except at night.

ARNOLD. How do you know that?

TEDDY. How lonely are you?

ARNOLD. I'm not. Just get my room raided a little, don't I, because I won't join in.

TEDDY (*smiles*). Got to plunge in! It's full of our future rulers, Arnold, isn't it. You're rubbing noses with them all the time, every day.

ARNOLD. I hate them you know, I do. I've taken to walking out here at night, so I'm not there when they come to raid my room. I don't get hurt quite so much like that.

TEDDY (*smiling*). And we're part of this Arnold, aren't we!

ARNOLD. Caged!

TEDDY. Yes!

ARNOLD. There's no privacy here, you're always being watched by someone.

TEDDY. We probably are right now! There's too many people on this earth Arnold, didn't you know that. (*Pause.*) There's no room any more.

ARNOLD. I'm not like them, you know. I'm not going to be a success at all – am I? Not like you.

TEDDY. I don't know. You might be. (*Smiles.*) It's possible.

ARNOLD. I won't and you know it. I have to drink myself to sleep every night, did you know that? (*Nervous.*) Please don't come near me.

TEDDY. No. Sssh, don't be nervous of me Arnold, nothing's going to happen, come on. We'll find a big orgy in Balliol where all the celebrities will be, dressed in white, and full of food, the stars of this place, all on top of each other. I haven't been able to find an orgy yet you know. (*Loud.*) Who's that? There's someone over there. You haven't got somebody hidden away again have you?

ARNOLD. No, it's nothing . . . nobody.

TEDDY. Nothing? Who's that then?

SARAH *enters.*

ARNOLD (*pulls her forward*). This is . . .

SARAH. His sister Sarah.

TEDDY (*very embarrassed*). Oh . . . how do you do.

Pause.

I . . . didn't expect.

SARAH. No.

Pause.

TEDDY. I really didn't think . . . you know . . . a woman.

SARAH (*watching him*). No.

ARNOLD. She insists on visiting me here you see.

SARAH. Yes – I do.

ARNOLD. She hangs about me all the time. I don't know what to do with her.

TEDDY. I don't suppose you do.

SARAH. He doesn't . . . no.

TEDDY (*slight smile*). She should be able to look after herself, shouldn't she?

SARAH. Yes – I expect I can.

TEDDY. Were you hiding her in your room?

ARNOLD. Have to.

TEDDY (*laughs nervously*). A woman in your room!

SARAH (*swings round*). Why shouldn't I be?

TEDDY. Why should you be, it's not allowed.

SARAH. So?

TEDDY (*smiles*). Against the rules.

SARAH. What rules? You go by those, do you?

ARNOLD. She snaps at everybody.

TEDDY (*smiles*). An anarchist is she – a young dragon . . . Probably all the men are terrified of her.

ARNOLD. They are.

TEDDY. That's a very peculiar dress. Do you usually dress like that?

SARAH. What's peculiar about it?

TEDDY. It doesn't look very feminine.

SARAH. It's not meant to, is it?

TEDDY. A girl here! Should she be up at this time of night?

SARAH. It's when I'm most awake, isn't it . . .

TEDDY (*nervous*). Are you?

SARAH. What about you?

TEDDY (*aggressive*). I remember now Arnold saying you used to play the piano all the time.

SARAH. I don't any more. Why should all the women play the piano?

TEDDY (*very loud*). She doesn't play the piano any more!

ARNOLD (*teasing, close*). Of course not.

TEDDY (*moving close too*). Your hair's wet – soaked. Do you know that. You've been out all the time in the rain.

SARAH. So have you.

TEDDY. But I like it.

SARAH. So do I.

TEDDY (*aggressive*). But it's disgusting in a woman – mud in your hair.

ARNOLD. Yes – but she is very tough.

TEDDY. Of course she is.

ARNOLD. At home she stays out all night with the gardener's son.

SARAH. Yes – who can kill rats with his bare hands.

TEDDY. A murderer . . . a sadist.

SARAH. Yes he is, amongst other things.

TEDDY (*close*). The gardener's son!

SARAH (*slight smile*). Yes.

TEDDY. Listen . . . they're coming back. Probably with peacock feathers in their hair. You better be careful.

SARAH. Why?

TEDDY. These people can be rough you see.

ARNOLD. Rough!

TEDDY. Tend to tease rather fiercely. They go wild in the night and if they find a lady – they'll think you a prostitute.

ARNOLD (*grins, up close*). Because that's the only kind of woman they know.

SARAH. Just like you.

TEDDY (*smiles*). Prostitutes. (*Catches her.*) Shall we show you what they do, the bloods . . . (*Pulls her up to him.*) Now . . .

SARAH. You can try.

TEDDY. It's like this.

Pulls her head back, ARNOLD *holds her arms behind her back.*

TEDDY. You see it's not a pretty sight.

SARAH. No.

TEDDY. They'll bruise you all right.

SARAH. Is that all?

TEDDY (*holding her head back*). Cheeky, isn't she?

ARNOLD. You'll get hurt you see, all over.

SARAH. I don't mind.

TEDDY. You don't mind? (*He lets go of her.*) You can't want to get hurt.

SARAH. Neither can you.

TEDDY. I shan't be.

SARAH. Won't you?

TEDDY. Anyway you're the one that likes murderers aren't you . . . and gardeners' sons

SARAH. That's right.

TEDDY (*swings round*). Here they come.

SARAH. Yes.

TEDDY. Their noise! We're part of this, aren't we? All right let's see them. (*Taunting.*) Come on! They'll start throwing bottles any moment. They like doing that.

ARNOLD. And they're very good at it.

TEDDY. So you better scatter. (*Loud.*) Go on – scatter.

As noise begins to increase.

This is really a bit of a risk, isn't it. I could get minced up.

Noise increases.

Come on.

TEDDY *alone onstage, facing the increasing noise.*

(*Stamps his foot.*) Let's see it then. (*Loud.*) Let's see it.
Here. (*Smiles.*) Look at these people. What are they for? Why
were they ever born?

Noise full.

Suddenly he shouts with pain, his hands go up to his face.

Blackout.

Scene Five

Noise of bloods, loud, then recedes. Silence. TEDDY's *voice out
of darkness.*

TEDDY. Are you awake?

Fade up. On DAVID's *room. Desk and chair. Jacket on chair.
Really strong, golden sun. Unnaturally bright.*

TEDDY. Good morning – are you awake?

DAVID (*off*). Who is it? (*Very loud.*) Who the hell is it?

Enters, his shirt undone, carrying his tie.

TEDDY. It's me . . . Rogers.

DAVID. What on earth do you want – it's very early –

TEDDY. I wanted to talk to you – before the picnic.

DAVID (*staring at him*). What's happened to you, have you hurt
yourself?

TEDDY (*turning away from him*). No – it's nothing, absolutely
nothing. I'm fine . . . (*Pause.*) You drink – don't you? There's a
terrific smell of drink here. A stench.

DAVID. Yes – there is. I drink a vast amount. If you want to
know. Always have done. Drunk very vigorously. So do you.

TEDDY. Yes.

DAVID. Now what have you done to yourself? (*Up to him.*)
There's some blood, Teddy . . . you have a great gash here.

TEDDY. I was outside last night. There were some very drunk
bloods – I tried teasing them. I provoked them.

DAVID. And they did that? Savages aren't they, you haven't been
outside all night, have you?

TEDDY. Yes – I couldn't stay indoors – it's hot.

DAVID (*looking at the cut*). I'll see to that.

TEDDY. No, don't – it doesn't hurt all that much. I didn't know people like that existed.

DAVID. Didn't you?

TEDDY. It's absurd.

DAVID. Of course it's absurd. So is the whole of this place. Totally absurd – hadn't you realized that yet?

TEDDY. No.

DAVID. Then you may be learning something. (*As he ties his tie – quiet.*) I got my first taste of here very early, my mother brought me when I was small. Out of the dark a fire engine came covered in screaming undergraduates, came straight at us. I could see right into their eyes. They were leaning towards us, cracking whips and screaming 'Get out of the way'. Nearly killed us. And look what they've done to you. You should let me see to that . . . you know.

TEDDY. No, I can take it – the sun'll dry it out.

DAVID. Being brave are you – how do you feel about the people that did it?

TEDDY. Quite angry.

DAVID. How angry –

TEDDY. Enough.

DAVID. Enough for what – (*Pause. He smiles.*) Have you ever thought of committing murder?

TEDDY. Murder? No – have you?

DAVID. Yes. When I was your age I thought about it frequently. In fact it was never out of my mind. I planned several hundred murders quite happily.

TEDDY. But you never – you didn't ever . . . ?

DAVID. Kill? Yes. I killed to get here –

TEDDY (*quiet*). You did.

DAVID. Yes. I killed a bull to get here – there was a bull in the yard of the farm next door – in Wales –

TEDDY. And you killed it.

DAVID. I thought if I had the strength to kill that bull, I'd have the strength to get to Oxford. So I teased it from the fence – and one day it charged straight at the wire. It got its head and

horns badly caught. It started bleeding fast. And it had to be
shot. (*Loud.*) I wanted to get here you see. God I did. Because
it was so excruciatingly beautiful. So I fought my way up – all
the way up.

TEDDY. And you're here.

DAVID. They're very clever of course, they let a few of my kind
in each year so they keep things very peaceful.

TEDDY. And you're part of it now.

DAVID. No, I'm not part of it.

TEDDY. You're teaching here, you're one of them.

DAVID (*loud*). I'm not one of them – I don't even begin, boy!
(*Silence.*) I walked along the river one night you know. And I
saw a river party. I was really very drunk. And I watched them
dancing along the bank, very drunk too. We were all
fantastically drunk. (*Loud.*) But the difference in our
drunkenness! – you couldn't imagine the distance – we were a
thousand miles apart. See –

TEDDY. Yes.

DAVID. Then I went down to the water's edge. There was
something splashing about. One of the party had fallen in the
river. He'd gorged himself. His face was under water.
Amongst the weeds. He couldn't get up. He was drowning in
one foot of water! And I could see his face – and I didn't
believe it. I'd never seen something so grotesquely ugly and
repulsive as that bloated face. That man drowning in one foot
of water. It made me freeze totally inside. I could have watched
it to the end. (*Pause.*) Like a fool of course I helped him out.
(*Loud.*) I've seen a lot of those faces by now, you know.
Everywhere you go, you can see them, grey, scabby, complacent
faces. In this cage, crowding in front of me here, staring back,
full of such confidence, such a certainty of power . . . yes . . .
and suffocating everything else around, saying this is how it is,
the way we like it, and this is how it will always be. There is a
complacency here that is totally savage.

TEDDY (*quiet*). Yes.

DAVID (*smiles*). And the power . . . you have no idea of the
amount of young power here.

TEDDY (*staring at him*). Yes. I've seen them too.

DAVID. I have a magnificent hatred for this place, don't I? That
is undoubtedly why I stay.

TEDDY (*slight smile*). And because of course you want to change it.

DAVID. Do I? (*Pause, he smiles.*) Only something vast will change it, won't it, something immense, powerful, a cataclysm that will affect everything. (*Pause.*) It might just possibly be coming, Teddy, and coming quite soon.

TEDDY. You think you're another Lloyd-George don't you?

DAVID. What if I am? (*Silence.*) Often I have this ludicrous desire to achieve something momentous. A Napoleonic ambition. I love size you see. And sometimes all I want to do is read books, for I'm so lazy, and teach little buggers like you. (*Pause.*) It's good to talk. You're certainly a little different from the others. (*Pause.*) I have quite a few confessions to make you know.

TEDDY. Like what?

DAVID. Like sometimes I can see a lot of myself in you. And sometimes all your public school spills up in those eyes and burns straight at me. Like a different animal altogether. You have a very aristocratic face.

TEDDY. I haven't.

DAVID. You're a very strange boy, Teddy – you know.

TEDDY. Why?

DAVID. You're not one of them, and yet you're perfectly happy being amongst them. Joining in.

TEDDY. Am I? Not now, I don't think. (*Pause.*) Is this what is meant to happen in tutorials?

DAVID. No – I don't believe it is. But then this is not a tutorial. (*Quiet.*) And you're learning something too.

TEDDY. Why do you talk to me like this?

DAVID. Like what?

TEDDY. Like you have been.

DAVID (*loud*). If it embarrasses you, why do you stay?

TEDDY. I don't know. Because we fascinate each other, I suppose.

DAVID. Yes, I suppose we do.

TEDDY. You fascinate me anyway. (*Silence.*)

DAVID. Come on, I'll finish washing that cut, it may hurt a bit you know. How strong are you?

TEDDY. Not very.

DAVID. You have to be. And then we'll go for a walk above the town. (*Touches* TEDDY's *head*.) Nearly tore your head open didn't they – this won't be nice.

TEDDY. Please. (*Begins to murmur with pain.*)

DAVID. Sssh – it's all right.

TEDDY *lets out a cry of pain.*

DAVID. Over.

TEDDY. David –

DAVID. Does it still hurt?

TEDDY (*quiet, stares. Pause*). Yes – it really does.

Blackout.

Scene Six

Spot on HAROLD *sitting midstage.*

HAROLD (*calling as if from a long way off*). Teddy? (*Loud.*) Teddy? (*Facing front.*) Picnic, somebody suggested it. Water picnic. Picnic by the river or in boats. Drifting down the river slowly enough, so one can be admired from the bank. Certainly it has been done before, but it remains unanswerable like strawberries – one should dislike them, if only because some immensely boring people appear to like them too. But one can't. It's glorious weather for our picnic. Ideal conditions for a very big meal – is it not? (*Pause.*) Where on earth is he? (*Loud.*) Teddy?

ARNOLD *and* SARAH *sitting by picnic basket.* DAVID *and* TEDDY *move towards them.*

TEDDY (*nervous, explosive*). I'm sorry we're late.

DAVID. Are we late?

TEDDY. Yes, I think we definitely are. We've been for a walk above the town. I think they're waiting for us to sit down. Come on. (*Pulls at* DAVID's *arm.*)

DAVID. Who's the lady . . . ?

ARNOLD. This is my –

SARAH. His sister Sarah.

TEDDY. So it is. It's hot up here. (*Lying on his back.*) I'm exhausted, aren't you? I'll die of exhaustion probably. They're already flies in my eyes. It must be the hottest day there's ever been.

SARAH. It is, without doubt.

TEDDY (*suddenly loud*). But I'm hungry, aren't you?

DAVID. Yes – ravenous.

TEDDY (*fierce*). Come on – we're hungry.

HAROLD. Yes – the heat is terrible, isn't it. That must be why you're so exhausted Teddy, unless other exertions were involved.

TEDDY (*slight smile*). What can he mean?

HAROLD. We've been waiting here for nearly an hour, do you know that? With astonishing patience. (*Staring at* TEDDY.) In fact I thought I was going to melt before you got here. Waiting for people is one of the most unbearable things to have to do, don't you find, it gnaws such a hole in one's ego, which can get very aggravating, you know. (*Loud.*) But even I have better things to do than watch two people perform in front . . .

TEDDY. Oh shut up, Harold. Just stop it!

Sudden explosion of violence, TEDDY *flies at* HAROLD, *pulls his head backwards and forwards, shakes him fiercely.* HAROLD *sits doll-like, motionless,* TEDDY *smiles.*

TEDDY. That should shut you up.

Silence.

DAVID. I hear you have had something published in a magazine, Harold.

HAROLD. Have I?

DAVID. Yes you have. What magazine was it? What was its name?

HAROLD. Nothing – I don't know. (*Pause.*) It had some extraordinary name. (*Quiet.*) The Barbarian.

They laugh at him.

SARAH. That's what everyone is in this place, aren't they? Far worse than that really.

TEDDY (*looking at her*). Yes . . . us too.

DAVID. Of course, we all are.

SARAH. They're bathing along the whole river today – splashing each other. Why don't we go and push them in. Watch them go under. (*Looks at* TEDDY.) You ought to come with me.

HAROLD (*to* TEDDY). Why aren't you talking to me? What on earth is the matter today?

TEDDY (*lying on his back*). It's a very special day today.

SARAH (*looking at him*). At least it could be.

TEDDY (*looking at her*). It will be.

DAVID. Tell us – do you have talent, Harold?

HAROLD. We all have talent for something, Mr Jones – even the least gifted of us. I have a lot of talent really – for a few things.

DAVID (*loud*). You see: there is one thing we all have in common which we won't admit.

ARNOLD. And what is that?

DAVID. We all deep down want to become immortal, don't we? (*Pause.*) Who's going to admit that? Come on.

SARAH. I don't. (*Smiles.*) I've no desire at all to become immortal.

HAROLD. You soon will want to – everybody does.

DAVID. To do something unforgettable, momentous and to do it quite soon.

TEDDY (*quiet*). Very soon.

DAVID. And what is more, we all believe, in our idiotic fashion, that we're actually going to do it. Achieve it.

TEDDY. Perhaps we are.

DAVID (*smiles*). Not all of us, I don't think. That would be too much to . . .

TEDDY (*smiles*). Just most of us.

HAROLD. Teddy? Will you look at me – please.

TEDDY (*turning away from him*). It's getting savagely hot now. (*Quiet.*) Walking here you know the roses behind Queens looked so very red they'd burn a hole in your skin if you touched them, or tried to smell them even. (*Touches forehead.*) I'm sweating already.

DAVID (*loud*). Everybody's eating too much today. Have you seen? The whole place is covered with people eating. There's hardly room to move back there! Even the scouts are doing it you know.

TEDDY (*smiles*). The scouts . . . my scout'll be there.

DAVID. Yes – all the college servants are being allowed to picnic. (*Smiles.*) But I haven't seen any of them up here.

TEDDY (*smiles*). Of course not.

HAROLD. Why is this a special day? Have I missed something then . . . Teddy, tell me?

TEDDY (*suddenly turns and stares at him*). Why do you think?

HAROLD. I don't know, do I?

TEDDY (*tone, teasing*). Take a look through those then. (*Picks up binoculars.*) Yes, go on. . . . Look at the sun.

HAROLD (*holds binoculars*). Through these? (*Lifts binoculars to eyes, but lowers them quickly.*) You nearly had me doing that. Could have really blinded me . . . Teddy, totally.

TEDDY (*up to him, smiles*). No, not a chance, Harold. You're indestructible aren't you . . . ? . . . aren't you! Here!

He pulls the binoculars away from him.

HAROLD. You're behaving very peculiarly you know . . .

TEDDY. Yes it gives you quite a feeling of power to be up here. To be outside! We've got to stay out of doors now.

SARAH. Of course we have.

TEDDY. Not let them get us back inside. (*Smiles.*) We can see the lot from here, can't we. All of it.

DAVID. The whole place will fall down very soon.

TEDDY. Yes – our college. The City. The whole fortress, tumbled straight down.

SARAH (*smiling*). That would be quite something wouldn't it . . . a real shock.

HAROLD. It's a terrible time to be alive, isn't it.

TEDDY. It's the right moment, Harold. Why are we speaking so quietly?

DAVID. Are we? It's because it's Sunday.

TEDDY. We're whispering. Come on, let's shout it out. It's one of those days. Why don't we try and wake them. (*Suddenly loud.*) WAKE!

SARAH (*picking it up, big grin*). WAKE!

Pause. DAVID joins in. All three shout 'WAKE'.

We aren't doing it loud enough, are we?

TEDDY (*swings round*). COME ON, ARNOLD . . . ! See, he's frightened of opening his mouth, aren't you?

SARAH (*moving close*). Yes he is!

ARNOLD. Can you do this then?

TEDDY. Do what? What is it?

ARNOLD. It's a razor blade. (*Pause.*) Can you chew it?

DAVID (*moves uneasily*). I think . . .

ARNOLD. Can you?

HAROLD. I don't think you need do that. (*Quiet.*) There are other things to eat you know, this is a picnic.

ARNOLD. All right. I'll show you.

TEDDY. Arnold, you're mad, cut yourself in pieces.

ARNOLD. It's one of those days, isn't it?

ARNOLD *stands, sucking razor blade, slowly, deliberately.*

DAVID. Please . . . gently . . . don't.

ARNOLD. See. I did it. You see. I can do it.

Wipes his mouth with his handkerchief. Silence.

Who else will do it? Come on . . .

TEDDY. No.

SARAH. Yes. (*She takes it.*)

TEDDY. Don't let her do it. Take it out. I'm going to get it out.

He follows, gets her mouth open.

Give it here – if you swallow it!

She turns her head away, spits it out.

Pause.

TEDDY. Your blood's hot. Why did you do that?

SARAH. Why shouldn't I?

TEDDY. You did it to get us looking at you.

SARAH. You do that anyway, all the time.

TEDDY. You wear your hair cut short to look masculine, don't you?

SARAH. Oh no, I don't. I like it like this.

TEDDY. Do you? Isn't your mouth all sore?

SARAH. Yes it is. (*Smiles.*) A little.

TEDDY (*smiles, quiet*). You've gone crazy, haven't you? (*Pause.*) If you're interested I'm going to the war – if it's declared this evening, which it will be.

SARAH. Going to the war.

TEDDY. Yes, get away from here and everything. Does that interest you?

SARAH. Yes it does. You're quite lucky, you are. I envy you a little.

TEDDY. Come here. (*Kisses her clumsily.*)

SARAH. No. (*Slight smile.*) Don't do that . . . Not yet.

TEDDY. Come here.

SARAH. No – wait till the war. (*She moves off.*) You'll have to, won't you?

   Blackout.

Scene Seven

Loud peal of bells – excited rasping clanging. HAROLD's *room.* DAVID *faces* TEDDY.

DAVID. Have you heard?

TEDDY. Yes.

DAVID. War. (*He looks at* TEDDY.)

TEDDY. Yes.

DAVID. Are you going?

TEDDY. Of course I am. Yes.

DAVID. I thought so, it was obvious in your face – I am too.

TEDDY. You?

DAVID. I've been declared unfit of course, straight away, but I'm settling that, I'm coming.

TEDDY. You can't, can you?

DAVID. We'll see about that. I'm going to get out there, if it's at all possible. I am. Think, war . . . Teddy, I'm sure we were the last to know – this being the most isolated place on earth. I didn't know it'd come so soon.

TEDDY (*staring at him*). No. You're soaked through, David.

DAVID (*smiles*). Yes – it's even raining out there now. Pouring! (*Pause.*) Of course, it's a tragedy it had to be war. War's horrible and it will be. But it had to come to this, there's no stopping it now.

TEDDY. No there isn't.

DAVID. There's such an electricity in the air – you can feel it, everything's going to be touched. Really shaken.

TEDDY (*smiles*). David . . .

DAVID. Yes. (*Close, smile.*) You see we understand each other, don't we?

TEDDY. Only because you've corrupted me, of course.

DAVID. Corrupted you? What do you mean, how did I corrupt you?

TEDDY. Very easily. But I wanted to be, didn't I? I didn't much like what I was before.

DAVID (*smiles*). So you're corrupted and what else are you?

TEDDY. A little excited. And so are you. (*Slight smile.*) God, you look so bloody excited.

DAVID. Of course, I am. Supremely so. I've longed for this, haven't I, actually hungered for it . . . you know . . . for things to boil up, explode, for any kind of earthquake. I've had such fantasies all the time boy, locked in here surrounded by eccentrics and madmen, and feudal servants, waiting for something big enough to crack this place open. (*Louder.*) And now! Just this moment ago I'm walking along here . . . I didn't know! . . . and suddenly I see people running wildly in the street, sitting on window ledges, screaming with laughter, throwing paint at each other, and suddenly it hits me, it's happened. (*Loud.*) It HAS happened. The end of all this, the chance of freedom for all. War . . . So I am yes, just a little excited. (*He touches his stomach.*) It's been lurking, inside here hasn't it . . . ? I've seen most of my life squashed delicately out of me by this place, from the first moment I arrived here – but not quite all of it! There's still some blood in me. (*Stares at* . . .) There's cream on your face you know. What have you . . . ing?

. . . *is to laugh and wipe his mouth*). There isn't, is

DAVID (*up close*). Greedy. You know for some unknown reason I feel together we could achieve a lot. I do, you know, do you feel that?

TEDDY. Yes, we could. (*Quiet.*) War!

DAVID. There'll be such fireworks tonight. Riots and a great dance. Bursting this place open. We should go down there and shout louder than any of the rest. Because we know what it's really about. There'll never be a chance like this. (*Close to him.*) There's no limit to what can happen now. For us too, boy. (*Touches him.*) I like you, you know. Did I tell you that, I like you quite a lot.

TEDDY. I like you.

DAVID (*close to him, touches him*). There's a lot of power here, isn't there? In you too, inside here. A great deal really. Strong and pretty *angry* – POWERFUL! You can use it now, you can. (*Pause, they stare at each other.*) Yes. . . . I'll give you that Dostoyevsky novel to take with you – it's most remarkable, far more than any English novel. (*Pause.*) You'll enlist tomorrow?

TEDDY. Yes.

Pause.

DAVID. I'll . . . I'll see you before you go then.

He exits.

HAROLD (*calling*). Teddy . . . Teddy.

He enters, lights bright.

TEDDY. Harold. (*They look at each other.*) Listening were you?

HAROLD. Of course. I always do.

TEDDY. Aren't you pleased? What's the matter with you?

HAROLD. What do you think?

TEDDY. I don't know – do I.

HAROLD. A surfeit of happiness of course. You've hardly spoken to me for weeks. Have you? Are you happy?

TEDDY. Just a little, yes.

HAROLD. And this rain is so savagely melancholic, it makes one even happier doesn't it?

TEDDY (*smiles*). Yes – you're right.

HAROLD. Do you like me, do you?

TEDDY. Like you? (*Pause.*) I don't think that matters very much now. (*Quiet, slight smile.*) Look at it, I don't expect it'll ever stop raining, the whole building will probably drown in the rain and we'll wake up . . . and there'll be nothing but water round our beds.

HAROLD (*quiet*). At least it's warm here.

Silence.

(*Looks at him.*) You're really very excited, aren't you?

TEDDY (*quiet*). Yes.

HAROLD. Why, Teddy?

TEDDY (*looks up*). Why?

HAROLD (*staring at him*). Yes.

TEDDY (*quiet*). Come here . . . (*Pause.*) Come on. (HAROLD *moves slightly.*) Don't you realize what this means then . . . this . . . don't you . . . ?

HAROLD. No, tell me. (*Pause.*) Go on.

TEDDY (*quiet, small smile*). I shall . . . (*long pause*) when it's started.

Fade.

ACT TWO

The stage should be set for war — almost bare.

Scene One

Small pinpoint of light, rest of stage dark.

ARNOLD (*voice out of darkness*). FIX BAYONETS.

TEDDY (*echoing him — stretching words out so they become ridiculous*). FIX BAY-ONETS.

ARNOLD. Charge!

TEDDY (*really sudden wail which* ARNOLD *joins in*). Chaaarge!

They rush on stage, wail ends in sudden burst of laughter. ARNOLD has gained in authority — has found a job he feels he can do. Lights come up frontstage, lying on edge two swords and belts of commissioned officers.

TEDDY (*laughing, pushing* ARNOLD). You fool.

ARNOLD. Look, all right . . .

TEDDY. Platoon commander is it, one of the chosen!

ARNOLD (*loud, authoritative*). That's enough now, stop it.

Silence. TEDDY *stops.*

ARNOLD. Come on now, we'll be late. (*They begin to strap on belts and swords.*) Hurry! We'll miss the officers' train if we're not careful, have to go with the troops and stand all the way.

TEDDY (*smiles, teasing*). You wouldn't survive that, would you!

SARAH *enters.*

TEDDY. Sarah, I knew she'd come.

TEDDY *moves over to her.* ARNOLD *watches them.*

TEDDY. I knew you'd come.

SARAH. I nearly didn't.

TEDDY. We're off in a moment.

SARAH. I know you are.

TEDDY. You're *smoking.*

SARAH. You've noticed . . . (*Smiles.*) Why are you going then? You don't want to *fight* do you?

TEDDY. Of course not — but one's got to be there. I'm a correspondent really, aren't I, sent by David. (*Smiles at her.*) To see the full explosion.

37

SARAH (*smiles*). Yes . . . (*Glances at uniform.*) They don't still use *swords* do they? What you doing with that? (*Knocks sword.*)

TEDDY. Yes – it's just for a decoration really, I think. (*Slight smile.*)

SARAH. I hope you don't imagine you look smart.

TEDDY. No.

SARAH. Because you look totally ridiculous in uniform. (*Looks at ARNOLD.*) So does he. It doesn't suit you at all.

TEDDY. Of course not. (TEDDY *looks at her.*) You look very lovely.

SARAH. I didn't *mean* to.

TEDDY (*affectionate*). Naturally.

ARNOLD. Come on – we're late already, you can't start talking now.

SARAH. We've just been tearing down recruiting posters, you know, . . . or covering them with obscene drawings, and hair!

TEDDY. Really – ?

SARAH (*mock*). It seems to be against the law. I nearly got arrested twice for causing malicious damage.

TEDDY (*up close*). Malicious.

SARAH. Yes! . . . But I'm not going to get caught at all, they haven't a chance.

TEDDY (*smiles*). They haven't, no.

ARNOLD. Listen, are you two going to be all day . . . because if so you can't.

SARAH. My family won't speak to me any more of course, which is the first good result of all this. They think I'm diseased. I've left home, I have, soon as this happened. I'm changing my name too, and my looks, cutting myself off completely. (*Looks at ARNOLD.*) He knows about this, but he can't do anything.

TEDDY (*smiling*). Nothing.

SARAH (*smiling, smoking*). I think I'll shave my hair off probably, you know, have a bald head, so they won't be able to trace me, at all. (*Up close.*) I'm starting again, I am.

TEDDY. From scratch!

SARAH (*more serious*). Yes. Most women ought to now. (*Quiet.*) You see things are happening already.

ARNOLD (*loud*). Look – I think we've already missed one train
. . . come on.

TEDDY. Stop worrying!

SARAH (*lightly*). I talked to some soldiers just now. Privates, I
was right in amongst them, and they were really talking to me,
openly, for a long time, and you know, I've been up to the
trains as well and seen the young officers, small buggers, with
voices that have hardly broken and spotty faces, most of them
are so drunk, they can hardly stand up.

TEDDY (*smiling at her*). But I'm different aren't I? I can hold my
drink.

SARAH. Yes, you are. A little. Enough.

She touches his face.

TEDDY. What are you doing?

SARAH: Nothing special.

Kisses him provocatively.

ARNOLD. Look, stop it. (*Pause.*) For chrissake . . . I can't wait
while you . . .

TEDDY (*breaking away*). Sarah –

SARAH *undoes button on his uniform.*

I don't think . . . not here!

SARAH *undoes a second button.*

I mean . . .

SARAH. Why not? What's wrong?

TEDDY. This is a public place. (*Mock.*) People don't do such
things do they?

SARAH. Precisely . . . (*Smiles.*) You're not embarrassed are you?

TEDDY. No. There *are* rather a lot of people, Sarah.

SARAH. Let them watch – the more the better. It'll only make
them jealous. (*Smiles affectionately, undoes another button.*)
Come on, stop wasting time.

ARNOLD. For chrissake.

TEDDY. But . . .

SARAH (*firm but affectionate*). Listen, you don't have to worry
about things now you see! Don't have to hide any more.
(*Smiles.*) Nobody does, that's over. It is. (*Pause.*) You really
need educating don't you?

TEDDY (*smiles*). Yes.

SARAH. But your sword's getting in the way.

TEDDY. Yes, wait . . . I'll take it off. (*Fiddles with belt.*) There's so little time . . . Oh Christ, I can't get this off now.

SARAH. No. It'll have to stay on then, won't it? (*Kisses him, firmly.*)

ARNOLD (*watching*). We've missed all the bloody trains now — see what you've done.

SARAH *finishing long, sensual kiss.*

SARAH. You'll remember that.

TEDDY (*smile*). I will, yes . . .

SARAH (*staring at ARNOLD, briskly. Pause to TEDDY*). And see that one doesn't do anything stupid, won't you. My dear brother . . . He's rather impressionable.

TEDDY. Of course. Right, Arnold. This is the beginning Sarah . . .

They move off, at exit TEDDY turns.

Don't get caught, will you?

Blackout.

Immediate spot up on other side of stage. HAROLD and DAVID sitting opposite each other at small table, front stage.

HAROLD. Could I have a cigarette? (*DAVID hands him one.*) It's so quiet isn't it? People are picking the college roses. I've seen them. And the scouts are sitting sunning themselves on the stairs because they have nothing else to do . . . at least we're rid of the tourists.

DAVID. I was asked to sign a declaration of hate today. A declaration of hatred against the Germans. A move proposed by the more elderly dons.

HAROLD. Did you sign?

DAVID. Don't be absurd boy, my hatred is reserved for the white-faced doctors that declared me unfit. (*Slight laugh.*) It would be a fine thing if my entire war service ended up as being one pathetic scrawl on a petition of hate. Hate is only found among the mindless anyway. You know I've seen men twice my age limping along to enlist, and being accepted! You can watch them from here. Young boys of fifteen too, going just for the excitement, and to get away from Mum, or because they want to ride a motor-cycle. I'm as fit as any of those! They ask permission to enlist and it's granted with just a quick glance and a flick of a pen. (*Pause.*) This isn't a time for Boys. (*Looks at* HAROLD.) And I'm left among the invalids and cowards.

HAROLD. Yes, I was sent a white feather through the post. I'm using it to write with. You're smoking too much.

DAVID. Am I? I've been smoking since I was old enough to cough. Look at the colour of my hands.

HAROLD (*watching him as he smokes*). You're drinking a lot too.

DAVID. Of course I am. To be alive at a time like this and not be able to see it! I've taken to buying every paper there is each day you know. He better write every day like I told him to. He'll do all right I think. There's this fascinating feeling outside now. People walking fast in the streets, hurrying to get indoors, waiting for the explosion. I want to see the real thing you know, rather badly! I refuse to miss out on it. (*Pause.*) There can be no turning back now anyway – there's this marvellous expectant hush.

HAROLD (*quiet*). I'd noticed.

A crash of a field gun. Silence.

What on earth was that?

DAVID (*bursts into laughter*). Only the practice gun down on the playing fields. The practice gun – Harold.

Blackout.

Scene Two

War. Noise swells up, loud, not of gunfire, but whistles, the sound of movement etc. reaches a pitch. Then out of the darkness, excited nervous whispers and giggles.

ARNOLD (*out of the darkness*). OK chaps – fifteen seconds to zero. Make for the Big Shell hole as far as we're going. Keep your head down.

PRIVATE ONE (*nervous giggle*). Piece of cake.

ARNOLD. Ready.

TEDDY. This is it then.

ARNOLD. Now!

ARNOLD, TEDDY, PRIVATE ONE *and* PRIVATE TWO *throw themselves flat on their stomachs with a loud thud*

midstage. Full lighting. Bare stage. Bright warm glow.
PRIVATE ONE is thin, nervous, highly strung. PRIVATE TWO
is strongly built, tough, tall. Large round head. Silence. They lie
for a second motionless, then TEDDY lifts his head, looks
about, begins to laugh. PRIVATE ONE giggles.

ARNOLD (*slight grin too*). SSSH.

TEDDY (*loud*). What next? What next you fool?

ARNOLD. We'll give it fifteen seconds then we'll chuck our Mills
  Bombs as far as we can and buzz back.

TEDDY. Why don't we try to get to the half-way mark, we'll get
  more from there?

ARNOLD. We're going no further.

TEDDY. Come on, to the half-way mark. (*Tugs at his sleeve.*)

ARNOLD. You're out of your mind.

TEDDY. Am I? Come on.

ARNOLD. If you're mad enough to try. (*Snaps.*) You shouldn't
  have come on this raid, you fool. If two officers cop it in the
  same raid . . . Back!

PRIVATE ONE. I'll stay, sir.

TEDDY. See, he wants to stay with me.

ARNOLD. You're out of your mind.

  ARNOLD *and* PRIVATE TWO *roll over, and exit.*

TEDDY. With me, Private!

PRIVATE ONE. Yes sir –

TEDDY. We're going to get to the half-way mark. Then hurl your
  bombs and see what happens. (*Stares ahead.*) What are we
  doing? There's no cover at all. (*Loud.*) Right over!

  They roll over, to frontstage left, then freeze, lying along edge
  of stage.

  We've done it! How's it feel? Wasn't difficult was it? (*Begins*
  to relax.) What're you thinking about, Private?

PRIVATE ONE (*nervous*). I don't know.

TEDDY. You don't know!

PRIVATE ONE. Sir – get your head down.

TEDDY. God, this ground is rough. It stings and makes you
  bleed. I've really done in my bollocks.

PRIVATE ONE. Your what, sir?

TEDDY. My bollocks.

PRIVATE ONE (*grinning*). Mine too, sir . . .

TEDDY. Got grit in my mouth. In my teeth. It'll need a pen-knife to get it out. (*Pokes in his mouth.*) I can taste it. This grass looks almost newly mown, doesn't it? How do you find the war, Private?

PRIVATE ONE. All right sir, so far, sir.

TEDDY. Learnt to sleep in your clothes yet?

PRIVATE ONE. I'm used to that, sir. I done it often.

TEDDY. Writing many letters home are you?

PRIVATE ONE. One, sir. (*Pause.*) – 'alf of one.

TEDDY (*looks at him, slight smile*). Slow writer, are you? (*Rolls over onto his back.*) The sun's very hot, isn't it –

PRIVATE ONE (*nervous*). Yes – we safe, sir?

TEDDY. And there's a large sky isn't there? Do you want a barley sugar, Private?

PRIVATE ONE. What, now sir? Here . . .

TEDDY. Yes, come on, have one. (*He pops it into* PRIVATE'*s mouth.*) That's better isn't it? (*Holding onto him.*) You know there's madness creeping up from behind that ditch, Private. A short burst of it should do the trick, blast everything we knew before out of existence. There's something in this war for you, Private? Excited are you? (*Pause.*) Are you scared?

PRIVATE ONE. Yes. (*Loud.*) Can't we go back now, sir? What are we doing?

TEDDY. Poor kid . . . you're terrified, aren't you? Quivering all over. It'll be all right, Private. You're not going to die this time, don't worry.

PRIVATE ONE. Aren't you scared, sir?

TEDDY. Let's see if I am. I'll take a look at the bastards. We need to know how heavily manned that observation trench is, don't we?

TEDDY *kneels.*

PRIVATE ONE. You'll get yourself killed, sir.

TEDDY. Will I? If they're a good shot I will. (*Begins to stand.*) This is a pretty incredible risk. God . . . (*He stands, stares out.*) Come on.

PRIVATE ONE. Get down.

Shot rings out, TEDDY *falls to the ground, hands up to his face.*

PRIVATE ONE (*slithering over to him*). Sir . . . sir . . .

TEDDY (*loud*). That was a close thing, Private, wasn't it! What are we doing here? Come on. Back. (*Really loud.*) Back.

They roll over once. Lights change, harsher. They jump up.

We did it, didn't we?

PRIVATE ONE. Yes, just, sir.

TEDDY. Pretty stupid wasn't it? I'm going to see you get recommended for this. I'll get you a Military Cross. That's what they give you out here isn't it? Mauve and white stripe. (*Loud.*) Do you want it, boy?

PRIVATE ONE. Yes sir, thank you, sir.

TEDDY. You deserve it.

PRIVATE ONE. But sir, we never threw our bombs.

TEDDY (*stares*). No – nor we did. It'll have to be next time won't it. (*Turns, his tone changes.*) It's extraordinary here, David, walking down a zig-zagging trench covered with field mice and small frogs that have fallen in. Seeing people you knew at Oxford and school, and then just passing them with a small smile and a nod, bright polished faces. They look exactly the same! Everybody's here that's anybody. The Harlequin Club, the Somerset House Company, the Daily Mail Company, the Gamages Company and the South Metropolitan Company. But mostly I meet Oxford men. I know a man from Christchurch, who wants to introduce pythons into the trenches, to get rid of the rats. I receive pâté and copies of *Punch* from my mother. She is furious I write to her so little, that is because I'm always writing to you – isn't it? (*Quieter.*) I saw some of them trying to get across to the Three Beeches to get to the deep shady wood behind – a killer wood. (*Pause. Quiet.*) What a sight it was. There are two birds circling overhead, round and round, and they're mating. They make me really hungry, you know, and it's not for army biscuits. There is a Private Dix standing by me. Not a bad soldier really – are you? I think the men even respect me. I came upon a group of soldiers cleaning their rifles, they looked suspiciously at me. Hostile. I thought desperately of the right thing to say. (*Awkwardly.*) 'Fucking awful weather' I ⌐ᵈ. They all laughed. I had no trouble with them after that. *⌐ns, catches hold of the* PRIVATE.) Your neck seems ⌐st yellow, look at it. It shouldn't be dirty, should it? ⌐ PRIVATE *by the ear.*)

PRIVATE. We've just been on a raid, sir.

TEDDY. So we have. Why did you let me do that to you, Private, why did you? The men are all so accepting. (*Stares at* PRIVATE.) They are. You can go now.

PRIVATE *leaves.*

You're right, David. (*Smiles.*) We're in the grip of something loud and big and soon it'll explode!

Blackout.

Spot on DAVID.

DAVID. You should see this place now. . . . (*Smiles.*) A bloody great tremor has gone through it already. It's quite satisfying to feel that. People are very definitely scared of what's going to happen here. There're a lot of very apprehensive faces, because they at last realise events have grown big and uncontrollable and are beginning to threaten. In fact, I'm living in rather a frightened place – as a result there is some ferocious drinking going on occasionally and a few real verbal fights, which can get very intense and violent. Signs of unrest seem to be appearing in other places too, it could be beginning to spread already. I hope you're not surrounded by too many officious fools revelling in it all, and that life's not too insufferable or uncomfortable. At least it can't be boring. Your spelling has improved in the last few days, so something bloody important is obviously happening! I have much more to tell you. Am waiting to see you. Be careful. Don't let the bastards depress you.

Spot on HAROLD.

Sitting frontstage, in silk dressing gown. Face very pale.

HAROLD (*loud*). Why haven't you written to me? Everybody who is anybody has gone and those that you've left me with are astoundingly tedious. Aggressive invalids with hands like hop-pickers. War really is a very overrated attraction. I had another success in the debates. The audience though was rather too small. Where are you? Up near the action or sitting in some converted château copying out orders for hard boiled eggs and reading Balzac in the tea breaks. I hope there isn't too much fighting. Old Goodrich is dying you know. (*Pause.*) Oh Teddy I dreamt the most monstrous dream. I was climbing a mountain with you and some others. I got my foot stuck in a crevice and couldn't get it out. Everybody else just walked on, getting further and further up the mountain. They didn't hear my cries,

never even looked back. It was snowing and it turned as hard as
stone, and went into my eyes. Very Wagnerian of course!
(*Pause.*) Each day I long for a letter from you. I had a nose
bleed and the blood flowed into my mouth. (*Angry.*) You're
surrounded by people, have to talk to them all the time but I . . .
Loneliness is a slow poison and it is rusting my blood. I send all
my love and more.

Blackout.

Scene Three

PRIVATE TWO *fiddling with something in mud.*

TEDDY (*enters loud*). You! – Over there!

PRIVATE TWO *turns.*

TEDDY. What on earth do you think you're doing out here?

PRIVATE TWO (*picks up object behind him*). Nothing.
(PRIVATE *doesn't move.*)

TEDDY. Come here. (*Loud.*) I said come here. (PRIVATE *moves
towards him, hiding object behind his back.*) I haven't spoken
to you before.

PRIVATE TWO. No, you haven't.

TEDDY. Sir . . .

PRIVATE TWO (*pause*). Sir.

TEDDY. You aren't allowed to hang about here and you know it.

PRIVATE TWO. Yes.

TEDDY. You could have copped it easily. There's been some very
useful sniping tonight. We've already lost three. Are you eating
something?

PRIVATE TWO (*chewing*). Yes, sir.

TEDDY. Finish it quickly. What are you hiding behind your back,
soldier? Come on . . . show me. I said . . . (PRIVATE *doesn't
move.*) . . . Show me!

PRIVATE TWO *reveals object he's been making, strange
mud-clogged shape.*

TEDDY. What on earth's that, soldier?

PRIVATE TWO. Nothink.

TEDDY. Were you making that just now?

PRIVATE TWO. I was only mucking around, sir, with mud and things.

TEDDY. It's not allowed is it, out here. Give me it, soldier. So you were making this? (*Quiet.*) Extraordinary object – it's rather revolting isn't it.

PRIVATE TWO. Yes, sir.

TEDDY. Probably made out of something nasty. It's so bloody cold. I'm surprised you can move your hands. I can't at all. Is this what you do outside, Private? I mean . . . normally – make things.

PRIVATE TWO. No, sir.

TEDDY. Perhaps you will afterwards. Has this got a head? Tell me what it's meant to be, soldier.

PRIVATE TWO. What's it look like, sir?

TEDDY. You're not meant to answer back soldier, are you?

PRIVATE TWO. I know, sir.

TEDDY (*slight smile*). You're being insolent. And this is very muddy.

PRIVATE TWO. You can keep it sir, from me – to you, sir.

TEDDY. Can I?

PRIVATE TWO. Yes!

TEDDY. You may carry on, soldier! (SOLDIER *moves off.*) (*Very loud.*) And take this filthy thing with you – I don't want it!

PRIVATE TWO (*aggressive*). Of course – sir. (*He reaches for it.*)

TEDDY. I'm going on a raid soon, maybe you'll come.

PRIVATE TWO *exits.*

Lights come up harsh on ARNOLD *by table, stove and single chair downstage left. There's a blanket on the chair. Something cooking on the stove.*

TEDDY *enters upstage, carrying snow white uniform folded up.*

TEDDY (*nervous, unfriendly*). You're here! It's so cold tonight isn't it. What's that cooking over there?

ARNOLD. Bacon.

TEDDY. I'm so hungry you know.

ARNOLD. You're bleeding.

TEDDY. That's nothing, only a scratch coming over here. (*Suddenly swings round, into wings.*) Private, stop that.

(*Louder.*) Stop it! (*Turns back.*) I hate it when they pilfer the dead. I can't stand that. (*Sits.*) But that smell is good, Arnold. It's extraordinary how good it seems, French frying.

ARNOLD. Yes – a hamper came in from Harrods yesterday. You're going on a raid tonight I hear.

TEDDY. Yes, trying to get some of those wounded in.

ARNOLD. They've been squealing a little out there. It's a very bright night. It's stopped snowing. You're sure you don't want somebody else to go? Going with that hand?

TEDDY (*shouting*). I tell you I'm going! And I must have something to eat now – so come on!

ARNOLD. You can start with that. (*Drops a roll of bread in front of him.*)

TEDDY. I had to eat some snow on the way here. (*Looking up, fierce.*) You look very smart, Arnold, I think you're actually happy.

ARNOLD. We've got complete ascendancy in no man's land! We're the best battalion that's ever held this position.

TEDDY. You're proud of that aren't you?

ARNOLD (*quiet*). Yes. You know some of the men are quite human if you treat them right. I've seen them actually sculpting figures out of mud! Sculpture! And making crosses out of twigs and earth. Then all they do is leave them lying about, so they just get broken!

Sound of distant, palm court orchestra waltz.

Do you hear music?

TEDDY. Music?

ARNOLD. There's an orchestra playing along the trench tonight. Lull the Fritz to sleep. As they're listening, we're up on the parapet, and giving them everything we've got. We can wipe out a whole trench like that if we're lucky. (*Music continues.*) Strange isn't it?

TEDDY. Not what I would call it.

ARNOLD (*quiet*). It's a messy way to kill people.

PRIVATE ONE *enters, faces them.*

ARNOLD. Yes, Private, what is it?

PRIVATE ONE. Sir – I've been hit, sir.

ARNOLD. No you haven't, Private.

PRIVATE ONE. I have, sir. I feel so sick, sir – just now, I swallowed my vomit. I did, sir.

TEDDY. He's clenched his teeth.

ARNOLD. Yes – mild shell-shock.

Crosses over to PRIVATE.

ARNOLD (*to* TEDDY). Help me put this out will you? (*He takes the* PRIVATE *by the shoulder, swings him to the ground. The* PRIVATE *offers no resistance.*) Blanket!

TEDDY *hands it to him, and* ARNOLD *wraps the* PRIVATE *in it, who moans slightly.*

ARNOLD. Have to be careful, sometimes they bite. Poor chap – he'll stop that noise in a moment. Look at his hands, how long his nails are, and they're full of earth. He wouldn't be able to fire that quickly with those. (*Gets up, goes over to* TEDDY.) Cigarette? We'll let him sleep for a moment. I'm going to issue my men with mouth organs, it should help.

TEDDY (*staring at him*). You're expert.

ARNOLD. Comes with practice –

TEDDY (*loud*). Lots of practice!

TEDDY *swings round, begins to put on snow white uniform over his ordinary uniform.*

God it's cold. It's so bloody cold.

ARNOLD. Yes. (*Stares at him.*) That hand of yours is very raw isn't it. It must burn like hell.

TEDDY. It does.

ARNOLD. I met an officer who told me he was marching a platoon of raw recruits to the front. One of them started causing trouble, so the officer tied him onto the back of a supply wagon and had him towed along the ground. At the end of the march the recruit was just a little bit more raw than all the others.

TEDDY (*staring at him*). You're mad, aren't you?

ARNOLD. And the man's pack was full of books. The officer burnt the lot.

TEDDY (*loud*). Aren't you!

ARNOLD (*loud*). I met an officer. The first one to shoot one of his own men. If they won't go over the top you're ordered to shoot them. Got to keep them under control, otherwise they'll get ideas, and we'll have a revolution on our hands.

TEDDY. A revolution yes. (*Suddenly loud, over to him.*) Why are you here, Arnold?

ARNOLD. Love of country I suppose.

TEDDY. I love this bloody country too, but I don't . . .

ARNOLD. Like it here, is that what you were going to say? You don't like this at all do you . . . do you, Teddy?

TEDDY (*comes up very close*). Shall I tell you where this is leading, Arnold? It's leading where people like you just won't exist. Won't be tolerated at all.

ARNOLD. I just do what I'm told. (*He kicks the PRIVATE gently.*) Wake up man, wake up.

PRIVATE *struggles to his feet.*

PRIVATE ONE. Sir?

ARNOLD. You can go now, Private – you're well now.

PRIVATE ONE *exits.*

TEDDY. Why don't you stop, Arnold?

ARNOLD (*moving towards him*). It's cold isn't it. Too cold for you! You don't like it here, because you're afraid, aren't you? You're so bloody frightened. You're worse than my horse, who won't ride through shell fire. (*Loud, up to his face.*) Just a moment ago you were trying to get out of this raid tonight. You're as scared as hell aren't you, admit it, go on, ADMIT IT!

TEDDY (*shouts loudly*). Private! It's going to be easy, this.

He moves forward, lighting change, ARNOLD in shadows.

TEDDY (*staring out towards the bombardment*). A fairly lively night tonight. The air is full, smacking and kicking. The lights, the Jack Johnsons, the steel boxes, whirring round one's face, like flies, taking a bite or two. And the crackle of frost as it covers the bodies. It's savage tonight. Everything you can see is being torn up out of the ground.

PRIVATE TWO *enters.*

TEDDY. I'm going on a raid now, soldier.

PRIVATE TWO. Course, sir.

TEDDY. Here. Put this on your face – Vaseline. It'll keep out the smell.

PRIVATE TWO. Now! (*Puts it on.*)

TEDDY. Keep close to the snow. (*As PRIVATE TWO wipes Vaseline on, TEDDY stares at him.*) Quite aggressive aren't you? Should be able to take just about anything we throw at you. Just a short raid, Private.

PRIVATE TWO. Of course, sir.

TEDDY. Right now.

Waltz wells up really loud, they throw themselves flat on their bellies midstage, and begin to crawl, incredibly slowly.

TEDDY. Gently – gently, the poor buggers, the buggers even their moaning has stopped. If they send up flares – freeze for your life.

PRIVATE TWO. SSSH. Quiet. Got to be quiet.

TEDDY (*quietly*). Rawlinson is out there somewhere. He was leading the attack. He was in my college. That smell, it's like marzipan, it hits you.

PRIVATE TWO. Must have been a machine gun – mustn't it?

TEDDY. Very clearly killed – neat holes too. Look for Rawlinson, I'm still sweating from when he caught me cheating at cards. We might cop it tonight, Private, in this sludge.

PRIVATE TWO. We could, sir. If you make so much noise – sir.

TEDDY. We're amongst them – tell me this is worth it. David, it better be! (*Whispers.*) Do you go swimming, Private?

PRIVATE TWO. No. Don't talk see! Sir.

TEDDY. I'm lying on something, Private. (*He giggles nervously.*) You'll never guess what.

PRIVATE TWO. No, sssh.

TEDDY. There's something in this war for you, soldier! Have you ever been swimming in a muddy river. And fish touching you and then imagine dead fish touching, brushing against you. (*Fast.*) I crawled into bed with my dormitory leader, and pretended with him, as it was called. He was terribly fat. He knocked me onto the floor for not being experienced enough.

PRIVATE TWO. There. (*Points into darkness.*) Your friend, sir. Rawlinson, sir.

TEDDY. Yes, not messy either, just wanted to look at him, what a huge head pure white. He didn't like to black it up. That smell of marzipan. I'm scared you know soldier, I am.

Burst of machine gun fire, very short, very loud.

Back! Back!

They roll over and jump up at edge of stage.

The raid is over, Williams!

PRIVATE TWO. Yes, sir. It is!

TEDDY. It's over! The war can't kill us now, we're going to get furiously drunk. Get our rum.

PRIVATE TWO. I've had my ration. Not allowed any more.

TEDDY (*loud*). Then we'll drink port shall we? Did you see that dead Scotsman lying there. Huge. His kilt blowing up. How dark his eyes were, weren't they?

PRIVATE TWO. He's been there three weeks – sir.

TEDDY. Private, look at your uniform, it's got splashed a lot more hasn't it – spurts all over it.

PRIVATE TWO. Sorry – I am, sir.

TEDDY. And there's something in your hair. I can't look at it, take it out quickly. (*Pulls at snow uniform.*) I'm going to get these filthy things off. There's nothing on me is there? No. On my hands. Can't get these things off – God they revolt me. (*Pulls off snow uniform, swings round to* PRIVATE.) Why did you let me lead you into that sewer, Private? – that raid wasn't necessary. I knew they were all dead, people had checked already, I just wanted a raid.

PRIVATE TWO. I know, sir.

TEDDY. You know?

PRIVATE TWO. Knew it all the time. All officers do it.

TEDDY. Do we? (*Pause.*) Aren't we astonishing, Private?

PRIVATE TWO. Yes, sir. Like them down there, sir – getting ready for dawn inspection. They're early too!

TEDDY. Brother officers. And I'm one of them aren't I?

PRIVATE TWO. The BIG BOMBARDMENT will start at sunrise, all ready for the battle.

TEDDY. The battle, yes. We're sliding towards it. (*Mimics viciously.*) Let's go on another raid tonight, soldier – one more quick one, before morning.

PRIVATE TWO (*mimicking loudly too*). Of course, sir. Right away, sir! Now, sir!

TEDDY. Won't take a jiffy, keep us in trim.

PRIVATE TWO. Raring to go, sir. Been waiting for it, sir. Wouldn't miss it for the world, sir. Would I!

TEDDY (*swings round*). I mean it, Private. We're going on

another raid, right now. (*Silence*.) You take your punishment don't you?

PRIVATE TWO. Yes, sir —

TEDDY. How much will you take? (*Pulls* PRIVATE's *head back suddenly, by his hair*.) How much? (*Holds him, slight smile*.) Give us a song, Private! Would you let them tread on your face, Private, break it open?

PRIVATE TWO. — I don't think so, sir. Not my face.

TEDDY (*close, loud*). It's all still working see! They're keeping it going, carrying on just as usual. They're all around us. People I know. It's teeming with them, soldier.

PRIVATE TWO (*moves away*). Look, sir — look at that.

He exits.

TEDDY (*turns*). A new battalion coming. Faces very white. Shuddering in the cold. As if they were all barefoot. Row upon row waiting to go into the showers. First time up at the front. They'll be made a mess of soon enough. Officers with narrow, nervous faces, herding them up, their lips very dry, it's teeming with them. (*Loud*.) We're not normal — we're not. (*Shouts*.) Private . . .

Immediately bells begin to jingle. Behind him very slowly, lights come up golden, very warm.

Scene Four

Incredibly warm light — DAVID *standing*. HAROLD *sitting at a desk*. HAROLD's *face is covered with bright make-up. They speak quietly as if to an invalid.*

DAVID. He's here. (*Calling softly*.) Teddy? Teddy?

TEDDY. Yes.

DAVID (*quiet*). We've been waiting all day — how are you?

TEDDY. I'm very well. (*Pause*.) I am. David . . .

HAROLD. You have been our sole topic of conversation, you know.

TEDDY. David, I . . .

DAVID (*close to him, concerned*). How are you really? Are you really well?

TEDDY. Yes.

DAVID. Your hair's a lighter colour you know.

TEDDY. David, I must . . .

DAVID. You must be hungry. We've got a lot of food for you. I've been preparing it for weeks. A dazzling meal. It'll astonish you.

TEDDY. I've eaten already. Everybody's given me food. I want . . .

DAVID. Salmon. And a lot of fresh cider. (*Close to him.*) What would you like to do? You can choose anything. Absolutely anything. A walk along the river or bicycle out to Blenheim.

TEDDY. I must tell . . .

DAVID. I'll get that food shall I?

He exits.

TEDDY (*shouts after him*). David!

Silence.

(*He stares at* HAROLD). You know you have make-up on your face?

HAROLD. Have I? I've been forced to join the war effort, entertaining the wounded, with Gilbert and Sullivan. I had to be a pirate. Shall I sing for you?

TEDDY (*quiet*). You ought to wash it off – you don't know what people might think.

HAROLD. You're not all nervous, jumping from all those guns flashing, in the way I expected.

TEDDY. No – no I'm not.

HAROLD. Not breaking out in a cold sweat.

TEDDY. Do you want me to?

HAROLD. You look just the same, even more the same than you used to.

TEDDY. I am.

HAROLD. And inside?

TEDDY. Inside what?

HAROLD. You, of course.

TEDDY (*turning*). I hate this place you know. I really hate it.

HAROLD. It's very strange being here without you.

TEDDY. I've never left it. You can't escape it. I can smell it out there.

HAROLD. Some people have said I cease to glitter. Often I feel like a stranded whale. I suppose you're growing to despise me, out there. (*Loud.*) Do you think about me?

TEDDY. Yes. There're some sick officers playing in the quad. Hear them?

Laughter and shouts of officers die away.

HAROLD. Often? Who else enters your thoughts, apart from me? Does David?

TEDDY. I don't know.

HAROLD. I sent you a telegram on your birthday. Why didn't you answer it?

TEDDY. What? (*Turns away.*) I've peed in my pants I think. I have, Harold. We get that feeling often. Sometimes it's blood.

HAROLD (*staring at him*). How many times did you write to David?

TEDDY. I don't know.

HAROLD. You're lying. You've been lying all the time. I've seen the letters. He showed me them all. And I wrote to you so often!

TEDDY (*quiet*). And what were in your letters, excrement, dirty dreams, hundreds of drawings of cocks.

HAROLD. I thought that would please you. (*Pause.*) The trenches have made you very sensitive, haven't they. It must be all that undressing in public, that or the sweet tea.

TEDDY. I'm going.

HAROLD. You can't.

TEDDY (*loud*). It's my one chance to sleep. To get any rest at all.

HAROLD (*loud*). You can't go. We have such a little time together.

TEDDY (*shouts*). All my leave is going. It's slipping away. I'll have to go back any moment. Don't you realise, it's the Battle very soon.

HAROLD (*very quiet*). You mustn't be angry with me.

TEDDY (*stares at him*). If you cry all that make-up will pour straight down your face and into your eyes.

HAROLD. I'm cold now, Teddy. (*Pause.*) Sometimes I think if I were to split my head open, the blood would come out frozen. I find myself staring at my middle finger thinking of biting it off, as a practical joke. It's not pleasant. Why did all this have to happen? I sit on the stone steps out there and watch winter come up towards me.

TEDDY. David. (*Loud.*) Where's David?

He moves across stage.

HAROLD. I shall continue to write to you, more and more.

He exits.

Lighting change. Harsher. TEDDY *faces* DAVID *who is leaning against side of stage. He is slightly drunk.*

DAVID. Teddy.

TEDDY. What do you think I've come to see you for, David? (*Pause.*) It's not working you know, what you thought. The war's . . . the war is . . .

DAVID. Horrible.

TEDDY (*loud*). Don't smile. I saw you smile!

DAVID. I wasn't smiling. You better drink something, hadn't you? I think so. (*Hands him glass.*) Your hand's bleeding you know.

TEDDY. Yes – it's just an old scratch. I knocked it open again. (*Sucks back of hand.*) Stings a bit.

DAVID (*moving closer, very quiet*). Gunshot is it?

TEDDY. Yes.

DAVID. Let's see. (*Leans forward.*) That's rather nasty isn't it.

TEDDY (*turning away, quiet*). You don't know what it's like just out there, do you?

DAVID. Tell me . . . go on. Please.

TEDDY. You have no idea – have you?

DAVID. I still want to get out there myself of course.

TEDDY. You do – do you!

DAVID. Yes. I make a very impatient spectator. Want to join you.

TEDDY. Think it will be interesting do you, worth a visit. Take notes. (*Turns.*) I've got to go back very soon you realise, so soon . . .

DAVID. You need some more I feel, Teddy. (*Smiles, pouring bottle.*) Got to indulge.

TEDDY. You're trying to get me drunk aren't you?

DAVID. You're drunk already. You were drunk when you arrived. That's why you've been shouting.

TEDDY. You don't know how many of them I know.

DAVID. Who?

TEDDY. Officers . . . Who do you think? I know hundreds of them – hundreds from here.

DAVID. Of course you do.

TEDDY (*loud*). And they accept it all. We do, you know! (*Loud.*) Everything!

DAVID. Of course they do. That's how they've been brought up. It's what this place makes them. How it wants them, of course.

TEDDY. It's so strong. Unbelievably strong you know. Out there . . . just carrying on . . . doesn't stop . . . and we accept all of it. (*Very loud.*) All.

DAVID. Of course.

TEDDY. And I'm part of it.

DAVID. Of course you are.

TEDDY. Except you tried to teach me to see differently.

DAVID. Yes.

TEDDY. So I really see, don't I?

DAVID (*pause*). Of course.

TEDDY (*loud*). You ought to stop saying that you know.

DAVID. All right! I've stopped, see!

TEDDY (*loud*). Nothing's really changing at all, is it? Absolutely nothing. (*Pause.*) Is it?

DAVID. It's early days yet. You'll see quite soon . . .

TEDDY. You're enjoying this aren't you?

DAVID. What?

TEDDY. You're really enjoying it. You all are.

DAVID. Enjoying what? My dear boy, listen . . .

TEDDY. Don't you dear boy me . . .

DAVID. Teddy, I know it's difficult for you to control yourself. But you're going to . . .

TEDDY (*turns*). After all, what you want most is to get on afterwards, isn't it? Higher and higher till you're master of a college. And it's handy if all the competition gets killed off isn't it?

DAVID. That's unworthy of you, boy.

TEDDY. Unworthy is it?

DAVID. And you know it is. I know it's difficult . . .

TEDDY. You're not the one that's going to get killed are you?

DAVID (*nervous smile*). Aren't I? Stranger things have happened.

TEDDY. Oh yes? Killed eating strawberries on Magdalen lawn . . . sending little boys to war! Spurring them on, waving them off at the station, waiting for their letters, exciting isn't it?

DAVID (*tone hard*). Teddy . . . ?

TEDDY. You don't really lust after them do you, you just live your entire life through them instead. You see yourself in them, don't you, all the time. Pour yourself into them. To make up for what you haven't got and never will have. I wonder how many there are, apart from me. You've probably lost count. (*Pause.*) Haven't you?

Silence.

DAVID (*icily controlled*). Teddy . . . ?

TEDDY *looks at him, keeps his distance.*

DAVID. War or no war you're not going to get away with that, and you know you're not, boy. Come here. (TEDDY *doesn't move. Loud.*) I said come here.

TEDDY. Yes.

DAVID (*staring at him*). Bursting with small hatreds aren't you! Well I won't be on the receiving end, do you hear? You took a liberty and that's dangerous. Don't you ever try to do that again or something unpleasant might happen. Do you understand?

TEDDY. Yes . . . David.

DAVID (*quiet, stares at him*). Good. We must try not to spoil your leave. (*Smiles.*) You're getting quite tough aren't you really – give as good as you get, if not more.

TEDDY. Yes.

DAVID. Your hand's still bleeding.

TEDDY. Yes.

DAVID. You mustn't worry. I do know what it's like out there. Your letters have hit me all right. Very vivid. I could feel it all.

(*Pause.*) I've missed you, you know. Quite a lot in fact. More than you imagine probably.

TEDDY. Have you?

DAVID. Now look at me . . .

TEDDY. Yes.

DAVID. What do you see?

TEDDY. I don't know – do I?

DAVID. Look me in the eyes. I'm selfish yes and rather arrogant too, and apart from that deep down there's also a crust of madness that makes me see very clearly.

TEDDY (*quiet*). I see.

DAVID. Very soon there's going to be such a holocaust you know. The world's biggest battle, bigger than anything ever before, and whatever the outcome, this revulsion is going to start working. This wave of revulsion – and revenge – that is building all the time, is going to reach explosive proportions, and will sweep the country see, and it'll be of such intensity, such sheer colossal size, that it's going to penetrate the minds of every little bastard in the country. Each one . . . even the most sluggish – the most deceived, even the totally passive. It's going to completely slash through this stupor we're in – do you hear boy, and everything will go down before it. This government, this place, and all its assorted barbarism – the whole hierarchy will collapse. Smashed clean open, stunned out of existence. Nobody . . . that was responsible for all this can possibly survive it. It can't. That's certain and inevitable. (*Pause.*) The war has only lasted as long as it has, because of the strength of what it's removing. But you can feel it already, the force of what's coming, for the natural thing is going to happen, boy.

TEDDY. A Revolution?

DAVID. Yes. Socialism – it has to happen.

TEDDY. Yes.

DAVID. It'll happen. There's no stopping it. (*Pause.*)

TEDDY (*very matter-of-fact*). Yes.

Noise of sick officers ragging around, singing growing louder.

DAVID (*close to him*). You have to be careful though, very careful with yourself. (*Smiles.*) Keep out of the way during this battle, in any way you can, because nothing must happen to you, must it?

Pause.

TEDDY (*turns*). Just wait here, I'll be back in a moment.

He exits.

DAVID. Don't be long, boy. Soon now, very soon. . . .

Blackout.

Scene Five

Sounds of sick officers' laughs and shouts reach a pitch and then cut out suddenly. Lights up on SARAH and TEDDY frontstage.

SARAH. You've got a lot more hair on you, you know, now.

TEDDY. Have I?

SARAH. You have, all over. (*Pause, she smiles.*) Would you like to go to bed now?

TEDDY. To bed . . . ? (*Pause.*) Yes. (*Close.*) There isn't much time.

SARAH (*smiles*). It's the least I can do, isn't it, the least.

TEDDY (*up to her, quiet*). Often, really often, I take off all your clothes out there and rub up and down your skin to your other hair . . . you know.

SARAH. Yes. (*Kisses him once gently, then moves away slightly.*) Teddy – there is one thing you ought to do you know.

TEDDY (*quiet*). Yes.

SARAH. I've been waiting all the time to tell you this. (*Pause.*) You ought to wound yourself oughtn't you. Get yourself out of it.

TEDDY. Wound myself?

SARAH. Yes. It'll be done quickly. Very easily, really. (*Slight smile.*) Because you see we need people like you, don't we, you know . . . Those that have changed. People like us, you see. For what's about to happen, after this battle. I think you really ought to, Teddy. (*Pause.*) Now . . .

TEDDY. Now?

SARAH. We can arrange it.

TEDDY (*very quiet*). We . . . who?

SARAH. People I know. Mostly women of course. I know a place it's impossible to discover, completely cut off. It's where I've been all the time. There're a lot of us there. Mostly women. Working . . . you see. Getting ready.

TEDDY (*very quiet, sarcastic*). You mean for what's coming!

SARAH (*quiet*). Yes. And it's there where we'll do it.

TEDDY. I see.

SARAH. Yes. It's not a difficult thing really, and you're quite strong aren't you? (*Up close.*) Aren't you?

TEDDY. Not very, no.

SARAH (*detached but affectionate*). But you're in a state to take it. (*Looks at him.*) It's all right, you are. Thinner but all right. It'll hurt of course. It's nasty but that's rather better than being dead isn't it –

TEDDY. Sarah . . .

SARAH. Come here now. (*Takes his arm, presses down on flesh.*) I'll show you where it'll be, there's no need to be scared, it'll clean, we're not total beginners at this sort of thing.

TEDDY. No.

SARAH. We've done many and we never get caught you see.

TEDDY. I think I'll just go out there Sarah, and ask not to get killed.

SARAH (*sharp*). For Chrissake there's no need to be stupid, there isn't time for that. Now come here.

TEDDY. Sarah –

SARAH (*authoritative, louder*). Listen, this is what's necessary. Necessary – can't you see that? You'll be out of it won't you, safe, able to be here, when things happen. Begin.

TEDDY. You don't understand do you?

SARAH (*calm*). Oh yes I do.

TEDDY (*loud*). You don't understand at all. I want to go back. (*Pause. Loud, sarcastic.*) I love it there. I do. I really love it. I'm part of it. I am.

Silence.

SARAH (*icy*). I see!

TEDDY. Do you?

SARAH. Yes, very clearly.

TEDDY. Goodbye then.

SARAH. Goodbye.

Pause.

TEDDY. Take care.

SARAH. I shall.

She exits.

TEDDY. See you soon maybe. This is it, Sarah – this is going to be the most interesting show.

Scene Six

Lights come up, harsh, grey. TEDDY turns, faces upstage. Mouth organ playing a jarring, jaunty tune. ARNOLD is standing centre stage.

ARNOLD. The second battalion will be the first over the top. Our normal position. Before zero hour there will be the most intensive bombardment of the war. Conditions should be ideal. (*Tone changes.*) About yesterday, I take full responsibility for the premature release of gas, owing to the wind there were particularly heavy casualties in *my* company. A man can never live down a mistake like this.

FAG *enters.*

FAG (*calling from a distance*). Rogers . . . Rogers.

ARNOLD *remains staring ahead upstage.*

TEDDY. Yes?

FAG. Remember me?

TEDDY. Yes, Jenkins. A fag. So they've got you too, have they? Go home you fool.

He turns back to stare at ARNOLD.

FAG. We're out here already. Far quicker training than you were. Cut it down from three months to one month.

TEDDY (*staring at him*). You smell of the changing room – are you wearing your school socks?

FAG. I'm in C company, they're a rough lot, but they're shaping up. They respect me too. Look here, see (*holds out his hand*), we went past a church coming up the line, there was stained glass all over the ground. Extraordinary bright colours, incredible what you find isn't it? Look here, see! Broken carvings too and the head of a stone eagle. I stuffed my pockets with them.

TEDDY. There're other things on the ground you know, too. Things you're never seen before. Don't ever look down – don't try looking at your feet again. (*Turns to stare at* ARNOLD). Our platoon Commander doesn't look the same man. He's broken, but he's still keeping the war going.

FAG. There's one thing I want to ask you – about getting girls. Is it true there's a razzle over a shop in Béthune? Which shop is it? What time is it open? (*Loud.*) Come on Rogers you've got to tell me, you can't wave rank at me any longer!

TEDDY. I'll take you there.

FAG. Will you, Rogers?

TEDDY (*close to his face*). Yes, after the attack . . . IF you've got anything left to do it with. Sssh. . . ,

ARNOLD. Our company, B company, is not only the finest in the battalion, it's the finest in the whole army, on the whole front.

TEDDY. Hurray! God, I can't listen to this.

ARNOLD. I want you to know I'm very proud to be in this battalion.

TEDDY. I just can't listen.

ARNOLD (*tone changes, far quieter*). The first thing I saw when I came out to the trenches was a young soldier, a fat looking soldier, lying across the front of his dug-out with his sock off. He'd shot himself through the mouth. Just now I passed the same dug-out and the same thing had happened. Exactly the same – though this soldier was even younger. (*Loud.*) But at least this man looked an excellent soldier – one of the best. (*Draws a pistol.*) I've had trench mouth for many weeks now – quite severely. (*Places gun against cheek.*) Yes. Are you frightened of pain? My lips are incredibly sore. They burn already.

Into mouth, he shoots himself, PRIVATE ONE *runs on, lies him flat on his back.*

TEDDY. Poor soldier.

Both TEDDY *and* FAG *cross over to him.*

(*Smiles.*) You've made a mess of that all right. Spattered, clumsy aren't you – shot himself through the cheek, not through the throat at all. Cover that side of his face. Jenkins, go and get some stretcher bearers, it'll stop you throwing up.

FAG *exits.*

It looks as if a whole army has walked over his face. Poor bugger. You're going to miss the show because of this, aren't you? (*Loud.*) Private!

PRIVATE ONE. Yes, sir.

TEDDY. Did you respect this officer?

PRIVATE ONE. I did, sir.

TEDDY (*savage parody*). He was a fine officer in every way, loved and respected by his men. He never flinched for a moment, and worthily upheld the tradition of Oxford men. Turn him over. He still believes in the war.

PRIVATE ONE. What, sir?

TEDDY. I said turn him over.

PRIVATE ONE. It'll hurt him, sir.

TEDDY. Do as I say, Private. We're going to make him flinch, I think, if that's at all possible. (PRIVATE *rolls him over towards* TEDDY.) See, he doesn't make a sound. (*Slight smile, tone hard.*) What's going on in there then, what do you see, Arnold? Oriel Street . . . Christchurch in the sun. None of it touched is it, but that face is rather touched – is it not? Broken it open, haven't they, didn't take that long. (*Quiet.*) But you'll be replaced. It doesn't matter how many pistols you stick in your mouth, they'll keep coming won't they, and stay, like the lice crawling over you now. (*Smile.*) You bastard! What have you achieved then? We've just fulfilled our function haven't we, all the time, didn't protest, part of the machine. Why don't we fight it then, look at me. (*Tone teasing.*) You're going to fight it aren't you, aren't you? Come on you bugger, look at me. (*Slight smile.*) You were a friend of mine after all. So what are you going to do about things with a bit of your face shot away? How sore is your mouth now then . . . rather sore, is it?

Silence, he gets up.

Private – we'll move this man ourselves.

PRIVATE ONE. Right, sir.

TEDDY. What are you doing tonight, soldier, before the Battle –

PRIVATE ONE. I don't know, sir.

TEDDY. Aren't you going to the razzle, a last fling?

PRIVATE ONE. Can't afford it, sir.

TEDDY (*hands him money*). Here, now you can go twice.

PRIVATE ONE. Thanks, sir. I won't waste it.

TEDDY (*quiet*). You may even live tomorrow. I've bet two
guineas on your life.

They pick up the body.

PRIVATE ONE. You have to lead the attack now, sir.

TEDDY. Yes, lead it. I came back for it. But it must be like no
other attack, mustn't it, Private?

Blackout.

Spot on HAROLD, *sitting frontstage in silk dressing gown.*

HAROLD. I've heard about it, your nightly encounters. Keeping
watch with a young soldier. Alone together. (*Tone loud, but
sad.*) I do hope you are making the most of each opportunity
and the results are satisfying. The noise of the guns must surely
add to the excitement. The earth exploding all around you. Do
be careful of passing bullets, we wouldn't want you to lose
anything vital. And remember to be discreet won't you, and not
shock the tender minds of our young soldiers. (*Loud.*) For it is
on people like you that this country is counting. Of course you
haven't written to me. Not that I expect that any more. (*Quiet.*)
You will have the added satisfaction of knowing that when in
conversation I need a synonym for despicable I use your name.
I am far from happy, Teddy. (*Quiet.*) There was a terrible fight,
between sick officers on the lawn – then I found them lying
asleep and still by the river, looking so like you. Sometimes
I want to destroy everything of you there is. I stay in my
bedroom in the dark for fear of seeing anything that reminds
me of you. I am beginning to suffocate. I try to forget you, but I
am in pain and very afraid.

Scene Seven

Behind HAROLD *the silhouette of* TEDDY, *the* FAG, PRIVATE ONE *and* PRIVATE TWO. *Spread across upstage. Kneeling with rifles and bayonets.*

TEDDY. Ten seconds. Nine, eight, seven, five, four, three seconds, two seconds, one second, zero!

PRIVATE ONE. You missed out six, sir.

TEDDY (*quiet*). Yes, yes, I did. Ready? (*Screams.*) CHAAARGE!

Four stand up, all shout, lights full, bayonets straight forward. But they remain still.

TEDDY (*moves slightly in front of them, his tone is a fierce parody*). Forward! Forward! This is good. Forward! Well done this is very good. We are going to get there, we are. You fools. You are doing fine. Savage them, savage. (*Loud.*) Savage quickly!

A very loud burst of machine gun fire followed by a whistle. They throw themselves flat on their stomachs. Firing continues then recedes.

TEDDY. That was bloody good. A good advance. (*He lies forward, next to* PRIVATE ONE.) Look at the sun lying across the pitch. We are going to get there of course. Reach their touchline, or at least their twenty-five-yard line. (*He moves forward on the ground slightly.*) We're seeing something that nobody's ever seen before. Except we can't see it, we're buried in grey grass and slush and can only see a few red flowers. And if we lift our head we get a ball quite quickly between our eyes. (*Nervous laugh.*) Balls in our head. It's something rather incredible, isn't it, the sweat and muscle and skin scraped off in the last attack. A company gone down in front of us. Crisp uniforms, pale faces, very freshly killed. (*Louder.*) Just in from ENGLAND. You can see a lemon bomb fall – a young soldier get it, you can pour him out now like a bucket. You can pull the soldiers by their tails, kicking and flapping out of the craters. They never bite and shine in the sun. (*He lies flat, pressing himself close to the stage.*) Every third second the guns go off and smash your teeth into your tongue. If you lie very close to the ground, you can often feel it kick and swell under you. It tugs your body forward. And it's quite a feeling really!

You can watch what is pouring out of them into the sky. Very fast, loud, it'll never stop now – it's going on . . .

Pause.

I am part of this – yes. (*Quiet.*) Across the pitch there is a red rain, quite strong, and it's very hot, and God, that smell when it gets into your clothes. (*Quiet.*) I can taste it.

Whistle blows.

(*Jumps up.*) We're going forward to their touchline! Got to get there! Come on you bastards, I said forward. Charge!

PRIVATE TWO. They're all dead. (TEDDY *turns.*) Aren't they?

TEDDY. Dead, how?

Silence.

Did you speak? (*Loud.*) Which one spoke?

PRIVATE TWO. Me – sir. It was me.

TEDDY. I thought I was alone, Private.

PRIVATE TWO. You'll get yourself killed like that you know, sir.

TEDDY. I knew they were dead actually. Copped it. (*Matter-of-fact.*) Quite clean. In the middle. Sometimes it is clean. Wounded are you?

PRIVATE TWO. Yuh – got it a bit. Not all that much.

TEDDY. So you have. Unlucky. Get that one. (*Points to body.*) Wipe the mud off. (*While he does it.*) Count to ten and then they can all get up again. Get it out of his eyes, out of his hair. (*Suddenly loud.*) Look at you – soldier! Why are you taking orders from me!

PRIVATE TWO. What?

TEDDY (*loud*). Take orders from me!

PRIVATE TWO. Because I have to – don't I? That is what I have to do, sir.

TEDDY. You're not going to any more. I'm no longer your commanding officer.

PRIVATE TWO. Yes you are. You're leading this attack. Got to get to their touchline, sir.

TEDDY. Leave them. . . . See. . . . (*He holds out his hand.*) It rubs off on the back of my hand. The smell of it. Stale and really sweet. Smell, go on.

PRIVATE TWO (*watching him*). Yes . . .

PRIVATE *moves towards him.*

TEDDY. Why are you fighting, tell me why you're fighting, soldier?

PRIVATE TWO. Because I have to, don't I, sir. Got to.

TEDDY. Go back then. Now. Go on. You're going to, that's an order.

PRIVATE TWO. Is it?

TEDDY (*loud*). An order . . . (*Catches hold of him.*) You bastard, don't you see, it's going to make no difference at all, none of this. (*Close to him.*) England's untouched isn't it, it's too incredibly strong . . . isn't it?

PRIVATE TWO. Let go of me.

TEDDY. No. It's all going to survive this. It is. Everything. There'll be no real change. You believe all sorts of things about afterwards, don't you? I've heard you talk about them, but you're mad you know, because afterwards you're going to get nothing you see! Because it's unbreakable isn't it? It's inside me – right through me and it just won't break, will it, not even here? (*Pause.*) And it will give you nothing, Private – nothing at all. (*Silence.*) Don't look at me like that, I don't like your eyes.

PRIVATE TWO. Where do you want me to look, sir?

TEDDY (*moving closer*). How old are you, soldier?

PRIVATE TWO. Twenty-two years old, sir.

TEDDY. You know we're about the same age, soldier.

PRIVATE TWO. Are we?

TEDDY. You should go to Oxford! Have dinner in Hall, that's an idea. (*Loud.*) What's your Christian name, Private? Tell me – your first name.

PRIVATE TWO. I won't tell you, sir.

TEDDY. You're to tell me.

PRIVATE TWO. No.

TEDDY *moves closer.*

TEDDY. Come here. Here. (*Takes hold of him.*) And where's your mouth organ, Private? Why aren't you playing it? Go on, play it. (*Catching hold of him.*) Come on . . .

PRIVATE TWO (*pulls away, loud, aggressive*). Of course . . . (*Begins to mimic.*) Right now of course! Play! Sir!

TEDDY. Yes. (*Loud mimicking too.*) And what do you think of this attack, Private – a good one is it?

PRIVATE TWO (*mimicking loud*). Yes it is. A fine attack, sir.

TEDDY (*also mimicking*). We can smell it already, can't we?

PRIVATE TWO (*mimicking*). Very clearly, sir!

TEDDY. Almost too strong.

PRIVATE TWO. Almost! Sir.

TEDDY. And it's only just starting . . .

PRIVATE TWO. Yes, sir! Best moments, sir! These! By far, sir! (*Loud, smiling.*) Because it's so really easy to cop it, sir.

TEDDY (*swinging round, tone changes*). What did you say? You shouldn't use that tone with me, soldier. (*Pulls PRIVATE's head back by the hair.*) Should you? Come on. (*Pulls his head back further.*) Do I have to pull your gut open to make you do anything to me? Why don't you go for me, soldier? You've got a gun. You ought to try. Come up from behind and strike! You could crush us easily, couldn't you, you don't know how easily . . . you could. (*Stares at PRIVATE.*) That's better. You look as if you want to do something to me – do you?

PRIVATE TWO. Yes, sir.

TEDDY. Want to try to hurt me – break my face.

PRIVATE TWO. May I, sir?

The boy throws himself at TEDDY, dragging cut leg, they fight furiously, on the ground, a real fight, shouts, laughter, and cries of pain.

PRIVATE TWO. For King, sir. (*Hits him.*) For Country.

TEDDY. Oxford!

PRIVATE TWO. For you, sir.

BOY *hits* TEDDY *very hard, again and again. Silence. They face each other.*

TEDDY. You've made me bleed. You've broken my lip, soldier, see, blood. I could have you court martialled for that.

PRIVATE TWO (*quiet*). What you trying to make me do then? (*Staring at him.*) What do you want?

TEDDY (*quiet*). You're going to finish us. Get rid of us, aren't you, soldier? You have to, don't you realise who you're really fighting? (*Staring at him.*) You can do it . . . Come on, soldier. You can!

PRIVATE TWO. But you're here, sir.

TEDDY. You're going to shoot me, Private, aren't you? Pick it up – go on.

PRIVATE TWO. What you trying to do . . . ? What you want?

TEDDY. Up! Your rifle – that's an order. (*Gun between them, both kneeling.*) Now, fire, soldier. Come on, straight through . . . fire.

Silence, gun between them, both kneeling.

PRIVATE TWO (*slight smile*). I can't kill you, can I, sir? They'd kill me twice for it. Wouldn't they – straight away. Burn me in hell too, if they could, wouldn't they? (*Leans forward, smiles.*) But you could do it. Yeh . . . you're mad aren't you – sick inside, you are. You could do it easily. You could, mate . . .

TEDDY (*hits him across the face*). You struck an officer. You threatened him with a rifle. Drew blood. I will have you shot for that, Private, and you know it. Your life's on a knife edge, isn't it? Completely. (*Pause.*) What's the matter with you? (*Pause.*) You've got it, have you?

PRIVATE TWO (*leaning back*). Yes, I've got it, mate. I have. Got it, sir. Right in the middle.

TEDDY. In the chest, haven't you? Bleeding very fast. Really you should have stopped me. Like I told you to. Come here. (*Pulls him slightly.*) My chest's quite full of splinters too. (*His tone is very detached.*) Feel his bones. Quite strong really. Powerful. But draining away rather fast. Not that much left. (*Pause.*) I'm scared, Private. This should not have happened. I'll wait for it here too. Right here.

Pause. TEDDY *lies down next to* PRIVATE.

TEDDY (*quiet, detached*). And don't go yet, Private, you make me warm.

Torrent of bells, loud vicious clanging.

Spot on DAVID *and* HAROLD *frontstage, as backstage blacks out. The bells ringing out behind them.*

HAROLD (*his face very white*). I hate the bells. Why are they ringing them now? My clothes stick to me. It's very very hot. My hair's dirty. I feel . . . not very well. I can't stop dreaming, you know.

DAVID (*speaks very slowly, cracked, harsh*). You'll keep going. It's that or killing yourself. And I don't see either of us doing that. Have to keep going. Silently. Out of the way.

HAROLD. You've been drinking.

DAVID (*quiet*). Yes. I have. Just a little. For my health. (*Pause.*)
The traces are being covered up very quickly. Only the paint is
a little scabby. Everything's back in place. The holiday's over!

HAROLD. My eyes are sore. It's sad here now. I don't think I can
bear it. I'm crying now, David. I'm crying. (*But he is staring
unblinking straight ahead.*)

DAVID (*quiet*). Go on, it won't last long.

Pause.

HAROLD. How lonely and beautiful it is. How like it's always
been.

DAVID. Term starts soon. Then you'll be more yourself again.

HAROLD (*staring straight out*). Yes. I have been waiting a long
time for that. That will be better. Much better again.

Pause. They stare out.

It has been such an odd time recently.

Fade.

HITTING TOWN

Hitting Town was first staged at the Bush Theatre, Shepherd's Bush, London, in April 1975, with the following cast:

CLARE   Judy Monahan
RALPH   James Aubrey
NICOLA   Lynne Miller

Directed by Tim Fywell

It was subsequently televised by Thames Television on 17 April 1976, with the following cast:

CLARE   Deborah Norton
RALPH   Mick Ford
NICOLA   Lynne Miller

Directed by Peter Gill
Produced by Barry Hanson

The action takes place in a city in the Midlands, e.g. Leicester.

The set should be suggestive of an overall precinct-style environment, neon lit, in which Clare's room is the dominant part, a featureless nasty blank box. Other areas and the front stage can be used for the rest of the locations — walkway, precinct, snack bar, and disco — which can be suggested simply by concrete blocks etc., litter bins, and bright striking graffiti.

Characters
RALPH. He is twenty, messy appearance, attractive and with considerable nervous charm. His energy is a mixture of a sharp humour and a dangerous vulnerability.

CLARE. She is thirty and seems old for her age. Very efficient but withdrawn manner, but extremely poised and seemingly in control.

NICOLA. She is sixteen. Totally flat voice, but a very determined manner underneath the quiet, completely blank exterior.

Author's Note
RALPH and CLARE hardly ever see each other as is evident from the first scene. It is important that their tone to each other in the opening moments of the play is totally and only that of elder sister to a highly troublesome younger brother.

Scene One

Blackout. Voices on the telephone.

CLARE. Who is this? (*Pause.*) Who is this speaking?

RALPH (*with a foreign accent*). Hello.

CLARE (*impatient, loud*). WHO is this?

A dim spot comes up on CLARE talking at the sort of telephone box found on landings.

RALPH (*accent*). Want to ask you about your knickers, lady. I mean are they the see-through variety? Can one see through them—if one looks...*

Silence.

CLARE. Oh, it's you. (*Pause.*) Where are you then?

RALPH (*normal voice, terse*). In a phone box.

CLARE. Are you still in Birmingham?

Pause.

RALPH. No. I'm by the station.

CLARE. So you're here at last.

RALPH. Maybe.

CLARE (*annoyed*). I thought you said you'd be here by lunchtime.

RALPH. Well I wasn't, was I?

CLARE. You really shouldn't be so unreliable, you know. I never thought you'd be as late as this. (*Pause.*) You coming now?

RALPH. Probably.

CLARE. Well I'll see you soon then, won't I? (*She replaces the receiver loudly.*)

RALPH (*as she does it*). Could be.

Lights up full on the room area. CLARE's room is a bare wooden box — modern, hideous, with a door leading to a bedroom off. CLARE is tidying brusquely, slightly bad tempered; she is about 30 — withdrawn, efficient appearance.

RALPH *stands in the doorway; he is 20, untidy, unshaven. Both are nervous, but offhand.*

RALPH. I'm here.

CLARE. So I see.

RALPH. Good.

CLARE. You're late.

RALPH. I apologise. (*Leaning against the door, chewing, his manner is unexpected, edgy, but light.*)

CLARE. What you chewing?

RALPH (*continuing to chew*). Nothing. (*He puts his hand up to his mouth, slips something out of his mouth into his pocket, moves past her.*)

CLARE. Are you all right?

RALPH. Yes, tremendous. (*He moves into the room.*) I can't stay long.

CLARE. You look a mess.

RALPH. Do I? I got wet on the train.

CLARE. On the train?

RALPH. Yes, it rained. All the time. (*He looks down at his feet.*) And it got in.

CLARE. You haven't got a hole in your shoes.

RALPH. No, I don't think so. Only a small opening.

CLARE. Why do you let yourself look like that?

RALPH. Like what? (*Slightly aggressive:*) I look fine — people stop me in the street and tell me so. (*He moves round the room — slight smile, edgy. Suddenly.*) Tell you something, on the train there were two people making love on the lavatory. No, honestly, this is true. It's not uncommon now. And the whole carriage was listening. We couldn't help it — we could hear the noise. All of us pretending to ignore it, reading our newspapers as it grew louder.

CLARE. Really.

RALPH. Yes — really. (*He sits on the bench-type sofa. Pause.*) You'd believe anything. I think I'll have a quick nap now. IF I may.

CLARE (*surprised*). Now?

RALPH. You know, sleep.

CLARE. Where?

RALPH (*lying down*). Here'll do. (*He snuggles down with his coat still on, as she watches.*) You don't mind, do you?

Silence. His eyes shut. Long pause.

CLARE (*looking down at him, sharp*). You might take your coat off first.

Lights fade to blackout.
Immediate but slow fade up.

RALPH (*just before the fade up is complete*). Am I awake? (*Pause.*) How long have I been asleep?

CLARE. About two minutes.

RALPH. Oh Christ — (*He turns over.*) — I couldn't think where I was. (*Pause. He curls up again.*) You've grown fatter you know.

CLARE. Thanks.

RALPH (*curled up*). My pleasure.

CLARE (*quiet*). I went through a compulsive eating stage for a bit. Had to have the feel of food in my mouth all the time.

RALPH (*loud, not listening to her*). What's that noise? (*He sits up suddenly, staring at the back wall.*) Sssh.

CLARE. There's no noise.

RALPH. I heard something. (*He lies down again, curls up.*)

CLARE. How's the architecture going?

RALPH (*curled up, grunts*). All right.

CLARE. Have you been doing any work then?

RALPH. Why — should I have been?

CLARE. I was worried about you, you know.

RALPH. Were you — why?

CLARE. You know why. The bombings.

RALPH. Where? What bombings?

CLARE. In Birmingham.

RALPH. Those bombings.

CLARE. Yes, those. I thought you might have been near them. (*Pause.*) Were you?

RALPH. No. (*He shifts his position, turns his back.*) I'm here aren't I?

CLARE (*watching him*). You've got to ring mother.

RALPH (*quiet*). Yes. (*Suddenly loud, sitting bolt upright.*) For chrissake. It's getting *louder!* — the noise. I'm trying to go to sleep for Godsake. Don't people realize?

CLARE. What noise?

RALPH. You must be able to hear it. (*He points to the wall.*) From there. Noise. It's late — he shouldn't be making noise. Who lives there?

CLARE. I don't know. I've never ever seen him.

RALPH (*turning*). You've never seen him!

CLARE. He doesn't come out. Must be nervous.

RALPH. It definitely has got louder! How come you can't hear it?

CLARE. I can just. It's always on.

RALPH. Do you wear ear plugs then?

CLARE. Occasionally.

RALPH. It's not a very pretty picture that. You curled up here, your ears stuffed with ear plugs. (*Facetious smile.*) Are they very big? Can I see them?

CLARE. You're putting mud all over the floor you realize. If you're going to be a nuisance you can leave.

RALPH. Right.

CLARE (*snapping*). And take that coat off for Godsake.

Silence. RALPH *watches her, puts the thing back in his mouth, lies down, chewing.*

RALPH. I got your letter.

CLARE. Did you?

RALPH. It was full of moans.

CLARE (*gets up*). Was it?

Pause.

RALPH (*moves his head, stares up at her*). How are you then?

CLARE. I manage . . . more than manage.

RALPH. Then why did you write to me?

CLARE (*suddenly looks at him*). I don't know. Because I haven't seen you for five months.

RALPH. You never usually write to me.

CLARE. No. (*Pause.*) I'm beginning to wish I hadn't. And stop chewing that . . .

She moves past him — he puts out a hand, catches hold of the beads round her neck.

RALPH. What's that?

CLARE. It's mine — and I like it.

RALPH (*looking at her dress*). And is this one of your firm's — wearing your own products are you?

CLARE. Yes. An old one.

RALPH. It's hideous. (*She moves away.*) Why've you had your phone removed?

CLARE. I just didn't want it in here. I was getting dirty phone calls too. (*She glances at him.*) Like yours just now.

RALPH. That wasn't very dirty — you're a bit isolated, aren't you really.

CLARE. Lonely you mean.

RALPH. Yes.

CLARE. Then say it. I'm not anyway.

RALPH. Do you miss him?

CLARE. Not much.

RALPH. Then cheer up.

CLARE (*quiet*). I'm all right.

RALPH (*suddenly, very loudly*). GO ON, CHEER UP! (*He hits the floor hard, but not aggressively.*)

CLARE. Don't.

RALPH. Why not?

CLARE. You're making me sound like a depressed menopausal old hag. (*She turns.*) Am I?

RALPH. No. (*Slight smile.*) Not menopausal. (*He is still chewing away.*)

CLARE (*staring straight at him*). Thank you.

RALPH. You're still quite attractive.

CLARE. What do you mean still?

RALPH. Still. In a way.

CLARE (*looking up*). What you got in your mouth, Ralph?

RALPH (*chewing*). Nothing.

CLARE. Come here. Come on — what is it?

RALPH. Nothing special. (*Slopping loudly*). An old penny I found on the platform.

CLARE. You didn't. You are disgusting.

RALPH. I've had it in my mouth the whole journey. Tastes rather nice, quite powerful.

CLARE. Take it out. Come on.

RALPH *spits the coin into his hands.*

RALPH. Actually it's only a new coin. You should try it sometime.

CLARE. You could have poisoned yourself.

RALPH (*slight smile*) Do I get a sisterly kiss now?

CLARE. Not in that state you don't. Do you ever change your clothes?

RALPH. Of course.

CLARE. You need to be put through a mangle probably, several times. Why you looking at me like that?

RALPH. Because I was. (*He lights a cigarette.*)

CLARE. I thought you said you'd given up smoking.

RALPH. I have. (*He takes a drag.*) Till this evening. (*He swings round.*) Anyway there're cigarette burns all the way round here.

CLARE. I do that sometimes.

RALPH. It looks as if you've been trying to burn yourself out of here. Doesn't it!

CLARE. Well I haven't.

RALPH. Are things as bad as that?

CLARE (*staring straight at him*). No.

The noise from next door is growing louder.

RALPH (*suddenly swinging round*). Listen! No — ssh — (*Loud.*) Listen! It's getting even louder.

CLARE. He may be waiting for his request to come up.

RALPH (*with sudden energy*). Probably sitting there in a totally bare room, in a high chair. A little scabby man, in black leather and yellow socks, with a streaming nose and a bald head. Do you think!

CLARE (*watching him, slight smile*). Maybe.

The music is getting louder.

RALPH. Oh Christ! This is ridiculous! Can't even hear ourselves speak. (*He suddenly turns and hammers on the wall, incredibly loud.*) Turn it down. Quiet! Down!

Silence. RALPH turns, smiling.

There. That's the way to do it.

The music starts again.

CLARE (*looking at him*). Not much good are you?

RALPH. I've only just started. Haven't I. (*He moves up to her.*)

CLARE. What's the matter?

RALPH. Nothing. (*He looks at her.*) Do you want to come out for a meal with me.

CLARE. Is that an invitation?

RALPH. If you like.

CLARE. All right, I will.

RALPH (*moving to go.*) Right then.

CLARE *turns, goes over to the wardrobe, takes clothes out. Her back to RALPH, she pulls her top off, bare-backed, moves off-stage to the bedroom. RALPH gives a quick glance towards her, as she goes, then turns away, moving about the room.*

RALPH. This is just a box you know. Really badly made — terrible finish. Cheap and nasty. (*He stops, crouches down.*) And look at this. Lots of dead insects here.

CLARE. What?

RALPH. Insects. A whole pile of them here.

CLARE (*calling*). Yes. They get in there. Behind the wood somehow. Get trapped in the night. I hear them knocking themselves out.

RALPH (*standing up with some in his hand*). I've got an idea, Clare.

CLARE. What's that?

RALPH. To shut up our friend. (*He kicks the wall.*) Go up to his door you see, and feed these through the crack. Flick them under the door — so they come at him. Terrifying.

CLARE (*coming back into the room, authoritative*). No, you don't.

RALPH. Why not?

CLARE. Come here, Ralph, give those to me.

RALPH. No.

CLARE. Give those here.

RALPH (*loudly*). Come on — are you ready? (*He moves towards the door.*)

CLARE (*trying to grab insects*). Ralph.

RALPH. Careful, you'll squash them.

CLARE. Look, I'm not having you being childish. (*He moves on to the landing. She follows.*) Leave those here. (*Lowering her voice.*) And sssh — you can't be a menace out here, please . . .

RALPH. It won't take a moment.

CLARE (*loud*). Give those beetles to me Ralph.

RALPH. It will work.

CLARE (*very loud*). I said HAND OVER THOSE BEETLES. (*She giggles, suddenly, then stops herself.*)

RALPH (*drops the lot, then starts*). Hey! one of them was alive! (*Loud.*) You didn't tell me one of them was alive. (*Silence.*) You look quite nice, you know.

CLARE (*sharp*). We're paying compliments now are we?

RALPH (*raising his voice, so the whole building can hear*). BUT DO YOUR ZIP UP.

CLARE (*looking down, embarrassed*). It's not undone, Ralph.

RALPH. Don't argue. Do your zip up lady. You're indecent like that.

CLARE (*hissing*). Stop it. You'll get me a bad name.

RALPH (*even louder*). Just do it up a little further. You're nearly there.

CLARE *is backing away.*

CLARE. You're embarrassing me, you know, Ralph.

RALPH. Good.

Blackout.

Scene Two

The walkway, suggested by a concrete shelf. Behind it the wall is covered in graffiti — of all sorts.
RALPH *is moving about holding a Coca-Cola can.* CLARE *is sitting, drinking through a straw.*

RALPH. GET DRINKING. Go on.

CLARE. I am.

RALPH (*slight smile*). Is this a good start to your evening?

CLARE (*sucking the straw*). Not very, no. (*She looks about her.*) I don't especially like walkways, least of all at night.

RALPH. Why not? (*Facetious smile.*) What's wrong with them? (*He moves up to her, quieter.*) Anyway you've got to enjoy yourself. (*He looks at her.*) You haven't been out for ages, have you?

CLARE. I have.

RALPH. Not properly. Not for a really good time.

CLARE. No. (*He is staring at her.*) Ralph — why do you keep on looking at me like that?

RALPH. Do I?

CLARE. You know you are. Never seen you stare so much at anything.

RALPH. Am I? (*Pause.*) Can't think why I am. (*Quiet, coolly.*) You've been looking at me, haven't you?

CLARE. Not much.

RALPH. I haven't seen you for a long time. Just refreshing my memory I expect . . . (*He swings round.*) Great place now, isn't it? All this new stuff round here. Fantastically well planned.

Pause.

Our home town. (*Loud.*) Get drinking!

CLARE. You haven't started yours.

RALPH (*holding his can over the flame of her lighter*). No — I'm heating mine.

CLARE. Heating it.

RALPH. Yes, to make it warm. To show you something when it's really hot.

CLARE (*beginning to get nervous*). What'll happen?

RALPH. You'll see in a moment. (*He turns the can over in the flame.*) Come on — get hot.

CLARE. What are you doing Ralph? (*She stands up.*) Is that going to do anything? You'll frighten people you realize.

RALPH (*staring at the lighter, turning the can round*). Could be.

CLARE. One can't go anywhere with you, can one, without you . . . causing trouble.

RALPH. Right now, we'll see.

He puts the can down several feet in front of him.

(*Smiling broadly.*) Keep your eyes fixed on that. It's only small . . . but when I pour your ice cold drink over it, it should . . .

CLARE (*getting up, backing away*). No, stop it . . . please.

RALPH. Where are you going? Ready. Watch!

CLARE *backs away*. RALPH *with a very sudden movement pours her drink over his can.*

Silence.

CLARE *stares fascinated at the upright can.*

RALPH. You see. Absolutely nothing. (*He tosses the can loudly at her, smiling.*)

CLARE. For Chrissake, I was about to block my ears! You're an idiot!

Pause.

(*Looking at him.*) It's totally unsafe to be with you, isn't it?

RALPH. Of course.

CLARE (*slight smile*). I'm here at my own risk, I suppose.

RALPH (*looking up at her*). That's right.

CLARE (*slight smile again*). I ought to be insured — shouldn't I?

Silence.

RALPH (*suddenly stops gazing at her, looks at the ground*). Clare . . . look I don't know quite how to put this but . . .

CLARE (*sharp*). Put what?

RALPH. This . . . (*He looks at her, then away.*) It's quite funny . . . but I keep . . . I keep on — (*Slight smile.*) — Christ! . . . Do you know what I'm going to say?

CLARE (*avoiding his eyes*). No.

RALPH (*glancing at her*). Don't you . . . (*Nervous laugh.*) No. Then forget it.

CLARE. What?

RALPH (*jumping up*). Sssh — there're people coming. (*He moves over towards the wall.*) Be quiet. Sssh.

CLARE. What on earth's the matter?

RALPH. No they're gone — you can stop worrying. (*He swings round.*) Have you seen all this — (*Staring at the graffiti-covered wall.*) Some real British graffiti — see what he says . . . (*He looks at it, reads*). 'Even the Queen enjoys it' . . . Yes . . . 'City rules OK' . . . 'Red Killers' — who do you think they are? (*Staring right up to the wall.*) You can learn a lot from this . Some of it is very fresh too. Newly done. The paint's still wet. (*He pulls his hand down the wall, smudging the paint; he grins at her.*) Some fresh graffiti, Clare.

CLARE (*slight smile*). Yes.

RALPH. And really fiercely written too, see. Jagged writing. We must have just missed them, by a few seconds . . . whoever did it! (*Putting the palm of his hand on the wall and smiling.*) Think of people standing up here scribbling away with anything they can get hold of. Pouring it all out. Everything's here!

CLARE (*watching him*). Just kids with nothing else to do.

RALPH (*gazing straight at her*). That's right. So give me a pen now.

CLARE. Oh no you don't.

RALPH. Give me a pen.

CLARE. It's against the law, defacement.

RALPH. That's a lie for a start. This is a public graffiti spot. Purposely put here to encourage it, let things get out. It's reserved for it. So give me that pen.

CLARE. It says 'Prohibited' up there.

RALPH. That's out of date. Give it here!

CLARE (*hesitates, then throws the pen*). You shouldn't.

RALPH (*catching pen*). That's better. (*He writes in red in huge letters, R A L P H.*) And now through the middle. (*He draws a huge 'C' through the middle.*) That's you. (*She moves up to him. RALPH faces her.*) Ralph was here with C.

Pause. He smiles.

So now you're equally guilty.

CLARE (*catching hold of him, slight smile*). Why you so excited Ralph, tell me.

RALPH. Why shouldn't I be — it's allowed. Anyway I'm not at all. I'm perfectly calm. (*He smiles.*) Does it make you nervous!

CLARE (*slight smile.*) A little.

RALPH. That's all right then.

Muzak begins to play.

Listen! The Sound of Muzak. (*He moves.*) We ought to follow it. (*He turns, touches her.*) Don't worry Clare, you're going to have the time of your life. (*He moves again, CLARE catches hold of him.*)

CLARE (*looking at him*). You've got to phone our mother, remember.

Blackout.

Scene Three

In the blackout we hear the voice of LEONARD BRAZIL, *the local disc jockey, loud, authoritative, brash.*

L.B.'s VOICE. Hello there. This is LS — who else — YOUR LOCAL SOUND. And this is Len-Don't-Switch-Off-Brazil on night call saying this is your line all the way through to midnight. This is LS on 55304, that's 55304. So night callers everywhere let's hear those phones ringing . . . as . . . from . . . now!

Muzak comes up — the sort played in a restaurant — and lights up on a Wimpy, where CLARE *and* RALPH *are sitting at a table, no food, only one side plate. Just behind them and to the left is* NICOLA *in her waitress uniform, sitting eating. She is 16 years old. The muzak goes on playing, but quietly.*

RALPH (*quiet, in public*). This is ridiculous. (*Pause.*) This is ridiculous Clare.

CLARE. They'll come eventually.

RALPH. What do you mean, eventually? They haven't even looked at us since we arrived.

CLARE. Probably think we're here for the music.

RALPH. It's all planned. They keep you waiting for as long as possible to lower your resistance, part of their national policy. (*He looks about him.*) Look at it! Think of the people that never eat anywhere else. (*He looks at her.*) I want you to have quite a nice meal.

CLARE. Thank you.

RALPH (*still quietly, but with feeling*). God I hate these places. They're multiplying all the time. Must make millions every day. They ought to be hounded.

CLARE (*smiling, leaning towards him*). Being the rebellious student now are we, continuing your college activities . . .

RALPH *glances towards her with a slight aggressive smile. Then he turns.*

RALPH. Over here! (*He waves his arm.*) Could we have our food. (*Pause. Stronger.*) Please could we have our food. (*He turns back.*) It'll come now.

CLARE. It better.

Muzak playing.

RALPH. Or else what'll you do?

CLARE (*leaning towards him*). Make you listen to this for the rest of your short life.

RALPH. We will anyway. There's no escape. (*Louder.*) There's one woman, you know, one *single, anonymous, lady*, who arranges all this muzak, produces it, by herself, she does, this is true! It just pours out of her, uncontrollably, tons and tons of it! A real madwoman.

CLARE (*watching him*). Really.

RALPH. There are three enormous warehouses of it. This is absolutely true. And they take it away in lorries — tankers . . . Drive it to every corner of England. Everywhere you go you hear her artistry, flowing out. She can rise both to a small cafe and a major airport. The lot. To keep the people 'happy'! And you know something. She lives in this town. Here. She does.

CLARE (*touches him for a second*). Really?

RALPH. We ought to find her, quickly, she's contaminating the whole place.

CLARE *brushes some ash off the table.* RALPH *catches hold of her hand.*

And stop doing that can't you? You're always tidying. It's a dreadful habit.

CLARE. Listen, Ralph, you're not going to make an exhibition of yourself now.

RALPH. NO!

CLARE. Do you hear. You're taking me out. And God I'm hungry.

RALPH. Really hungry.

CLARE. Yes.

RALPH. OK then, we'll make our own food.

He takes some brown sauce, begins to squeeze it out onto the side plate.

CLARE. What? Look, I told you a moment ago . . .

RALPH. No don't worry, this tastes quite good. In fact it's better than what they give you. There's plenty here for both of us.

CLARE. You're being childish now, aren't you?

RALPH (*looking up, loud*). Look will you stop telling me to stop being childish. (*Silence.*) Now do you want to eat something or not?

CLARE. Yes, but —

RALPH. Right, now watch. You put this on first. (*He finishes with the brown sauce.*) Then two portions of this unflavoured mustard. (*He dollops them on.*) Then half a packet of crisps going blue at the edges that I happen to have ready prepared. This is about the only food you can get round here any more. (*Loud.*) And by God it's good.

CLARE. Ralph . . . she's watching us.

RALPH (*not looking up*). Is she? She can have some too. This should be enough. (*He puts the crisps away.*) Then take anything else you have in your pocket, like old sweets, tobacco or nougat, I've saved a piece of Mars bar. (*He cuts it, squashes it in.*) And throw in a few tranquillisers.

He pulls them out of his pocket and drops the pills in.

CLARE. What you got tranquillisers for, Ralph?

RALPH. Why not? They're for you. Stir the whole revolting mess together — (*He does so vigorously and aggressively.*) — and squidge it. You needn't worry, I've done this before. (*He adds vinegar.*)

RALPH *tastes it with his finger.*

Yes; now give me the tomato.

CLARE (*smile*). Look . . . (*She picks up a plastic, tomato-shaped sauce container.*)

RALPH. Come on, quickly — not there, in the middle. (*He puts it in the middle of the plate.*)

CLARE (*slight smile*). I see.

RALPH. Good. (*Pushing it towards her.*) Now you carve.

CLARE (*astonished*). Carve?

RALPH. Yes. Go on. People forget how good these things are.

CLARE (*smiles*). Don't be stupid.

RALPH (*louder, aggressive*). Look, how long have you been here?

CLARE. Half an hour.

RALPH. Then carve it!

CLARE (*picking up a fork and knife, hesitates*). All right — what — like this . . .

RALPH. Yes, go on. It comes open.

CLARE (*shoving her fork into the plastic tomato very hard*). Bloody thing! She's staring at us now!

RALPH (*looking at the waitress, who is staring*). No, she's not. Come on. More attack.

CLARE *drives the fork into the tomato hard.*

CLARE. You sure it comes open.

RALPH. Go on hurt it, more . . . it'll split open. You can do it.

CLARE. No. I can't. (*She pushes it towards him.*) Made enough of a fool of myself.

RALPH (*grins*). Have you? (*He picks up the tomato.*) We've got to see what's inside anyway. We'll open it this way. (*He unscrews the top.*) Yes — there we are. (*He pulls things out of the top.*) Bit of chewing gum — half of a sardine . . . lots of cigarette butts — (*He puts them on the table.*) — and what's this? (*He pulls something else out.*) And a tooth!

CLARE (*turns away*). Oh Christ . . .

RALPH (*wiping sauce off the tooth*). A big one. (*He puts it on the table.*) About what I expected.

CLARE. Did you?

RALPH. More or less. (*Smiling.*) You know each tomato will contain something different. Seriously! You can always tell a town by what's in its tomatoes. All its undesirables are pushed there. It spews out of them. (*He squashes the tomato.*) I'll have a look around. Collect the lot. (*He gets up.*) You'll learn a great deal. See the whole revolting truth. (*He stands up.*) Shall I?

He moves across to the waitress.

Excuse me, can I borrow your tomato?

NICOLA (*looking up from her food*). What?

RALPH. Thanks very much. (*He puts it down, smiles excitedly.*) We need some more, four at least.

CLARE (*catching hold of him*). That's enough Ralph . . . enough.

RALPH (*sitting*). Is it?

CLARE. Yes. (*Slight smile.*) If I was to leave you alone for five minutes you'd cause complete chaos, wouldn't you.

RALPH. Am I embarrassing you then?

CLARE. No — you're not. But you're trying hard enough — aren't you.

RALPH. Could be.

CLARE. Well, you can give up, you understand.

RALPH. Can I?

CLARE. Because you won't succeed any more.

RALPH *moves slightly towards her, stops.*

RALPH. You're quite a tough customer, aren't you.

CLARE. Yes.

RALPH (*trying to throw her, smiling broadly*). Are you thinking what I'm thinking?

CLARE. I don't think so . . . No, I'm not.

RALPH. Then you know what I mean.

CLARE. No I don't.

RALPH. Forget it.

CLARE. All right — I will.

RALPH *looks away* — CLARE *continues to look at him.*

Come here, you've got tomato on your lip. In fact it's all over your face.

RALPH. I know.

CLARE. Come here then.

RALPH *grins, tries to move away as she wipes it. She stops him, wipes his mouth for a moment, then kisses him.*

They kiss.

Complete silence. Silence held.

RALPH (*quiet*). That was all right.

CLARE (*very quiet, looking at the plate*). Yuh.

Pause. She looks at the waitress.

RALPH. She didn't see.

CLARE. Didn't she —

Pause.

Look I think . . . we better not ask questions, OK . . . Just . . . it happened. (*She puts the tomato back.*) Don't know what's got into us really.

RALPH. I knew you'd say that.

CLARE (*nervous*). Did you . . . (*Nervous laugh.*) You realize I'm known round here. I . . .

Pause.

RALPH (*suddenly loud*). Christ — they're still playing the same tune! How long have we been here?

CLARE. Thirty-five minutes — I don't know.

RALPH (*very loud*). Thirty-five minutes. Do you hear that? Look I know this is asking a lot. But could I have one glass of water. Just one glass of your water. We'll pay for it. A good price!

CLARE (*quieter, excited*). Stop showing off — do you hear!

RALPH. I'm not.

CLARE. Oh yes you are — incredibly.

She catches hold of him, sexual kiss. Silence.

Both sit still.

CLARE (*very quiet*). All right I . . .

RALPH (*not looking at her, squeezing brown sauce on to the tomato, very quiet*). Quite exciting, isn't it?

CLARE. Is it? (*She turns, then turns back.*) Christ, she's seen us now. She has.

RALPH. Yes. (*He looks up for a moment.*)

CLARE. I think we better leave, hadn't we.

RALPH (*jumping up suddenly*). Of course. (*He moves towards the waitress.*)

CLARE. Where are you going?

RALPH (*by the waitress*). Here's your tomato back, thank you.

NICOLA (*pushing her plate away*). Yuh.

RALPH (*suddenly very loud*). Are you going to get us anything to eat?

NICOLA. I'm off duty, sir.

RALPH. But we haven't had anything to eat!

CLARE. Ralph. (*She goes up to them.*) Sorry we made such a mess on your table. We were just doing a little cooking. (*To RALPH, very quiet.*) Come on.

RALPH (*looking at NICOLA*). Is she going to report us?

NICOLA. No sir, I've finished for the night.

RALPH. Here. (*He takes out a coin.*) That's for occupying two seats for half an hour in these pleasant surroundings. It's for you.

NICOLA *looks at the money.*

NICOLA (*quietly*). OK then — thanks.

RALPH. What's your name?

NICOLA. My name. (*Pause; she is putting on her coat.*) Nicola.

RALPH. That is a nice name.

CLARE. Ralph. (*Tugging at him. To the waitress.*) I'm sorry. We're a little confused after sitting here for so long.

NICOLA. That's OK.

RALPH. Can we give you a lift anywhere?

NICOLA. You got a car then?

RALPH. No, we haven't. (*He looks at CLARE.*) I don't think.

NICOLA (*slight smile, moving out*). Excuse me. (*She goes out into the precinct.*)

CLARE (*to RALPH*). Stop it . . .

RALPH. I know what I'm doing. She's the only one that saw us, isn't she. Hey, wait . . . Nicola.

He crosses out of the Wimpy, into the precinct, followed by CLARE.

Lights change.

Scene Four

The precinct. Neon light.
RALPH *following* NICOLA *from the restaurant area into the precinct.*

RALPH. Come here a moment. (NICOLA *hesitates, comes up to him.*) There you are, that's for not reporting us back there. (*Nervous.*) Take it. (*He gives her some more money.*)

NICOLA. What? What you giving me this for?

RALPH. I told you, for not reporting us.

CLARE. Ralph. (*She pulls at him, moves him away. In a hissed whisper.*) Look what on earth are you doing? You realise you're drawing attention to us.

RALPH. I'm not at all.

CLARE. You'll make her incredibly suspicious.

RALPH (*loud*). Rubbish! Why should me giving her money make her suspicious?

CLARE. You're going to keep calm, Ralph.

RALPH. Don't worry . . . there's absolutely nothing to worry about.

NICOLA *is undoing a chocolate flake;* RALPH *goes up to her.*

RALPH (*conspiratorial, but nervous*). Actually you see . . . We've been exchanging dangerous substances in there . . . me and her, highly illegal, see . . . you know what I mean.

NICOLA (*silent laugh, knowing he is joking*). Oh, I see . . . OK then.

CLARE. Ralph.

NICOLA *is sucking her chocolate flake centre stage.*

NICOLA. Are you two from London then?

CLARE. No we're not.

RALPH. She went there, but she came back. (*Glancing at* CLARE.) It didn't work.

NICOLA (*looking from one to the other*). Oh I thought you might have been.

RALPH. Sorry no! I've just come from Birmingham.

NICOLA (*eating her chocolate flake, matter-of-fact*). You were one of the ones blown up were you?

RALPH. That's right.

NICOLA (*still matter-of-fact*). Were you nearly.

RALPH (*slight smile*). Yes — very nearly.

NICOLA (*looking at him, slight smile*). Were you?

RALPH (*suddenly*). Hey — did I introduce you? I can't remember . . . this is my *sister* Clare.

CLARE. For Chrissake!

NICOLA (*looking at both of them*). What! Your sister.

RALPH. Yes. (*He glances at her.*) She designs dresses sort of. For a rubbishy firm. (*To* NICOLA.) My *sister* does. Come here. (*He catches hold of* CLARE.)

CLARE (*hissed*). Stop it, Ralph — (*Close up to him, hissed.*) We're forgetting it ever happened, *remember*.

RALPH (*loudly*). Right.

CLARE (*strong*). Please . . . (*Up close to him, quiet.*) You realize what we've done is illegal, don't you.

RALPH. Don't worry. (*He kisses her on the lips.*)

CLARE (*pushing him off*). Stop it. DON'T.

Silence.

RALPH (*to* NICOLA). There you are, you see.

Pause. NICOLA *is leaning against the wall with her chocolate.*

Look at her. Totally calm. Hasn't batted anything.

CLARE (*quiet*). Thank goodness. (*Putting her arm round* RALPH. *To* NICOLA.) She knows you're only my boyfriend . . .

A burglar alarm suddenly bursts out ringing.

RALPH (*swinging round*). What on earth's *that noise?*

CLARE. What?

RALPH. That. Ringing the whole time.

NICOLA. That's a burglar alarm.

RALPH (*loud*). Simply everywhere we go there's noise. We must really attract bells. Look! There it is. Up there, see it. Tiny pink box terrorising the neighbourhood.

NICOLA (*not looking up*). Yes — it's always going on.

RALPH. You know this precinct well do you?

NICOLA. Yes. I'm here every day.

RALPH (*smiling at her*). That's good. You see, Nicola, I'm giving my sister — over there — a night on the town.

NICOLA. Are you? (*She looks at* CLARE.) I see.

RALPH. And we want to have a really good time. You see she lost her dreadful boyfriend a few months ago. She's got to let her hair down. (*Smiles.*) You understand — all the way.

CLARE. What the hell . . . (*Moving towards* RALPH.) Look, please . . .

RALPH. It's all right! Nicola's going to keep an eye on us. (*Smiling at* NICOLA.) Aren't you?

NICOLA (*slight smile back*). Yes.

RALPH (*swings round*). Going to show us round the new appalling precinct, isn't she. Look at it! Totally unsafe, it'd burn like balsa wood. (*Aggressive.*) And full of TV shops, it's just a morgue for them.

NICOLA. Yes, I watch those often. You can stand in front of them for hours watching for free. Till the colours go funny and you feel sick.

RALPH (*to* NICOLA). Whole centre has changed — me and my *sister* used to know a different place. Imagine being locked in here, the rest of your life unable to get out. (*He turns back to* NICOLA.) You know most of the architects of this atrocity are probably in gaol or just about to be. But we're left with it! Something ought to be done.

CLARE (*coming up*). Stop teasing her, for Godsake.

RALPH. I'm not teasing her.

CLARE. Look, we got to be careful, Ralph.

RALPH. I am being careful.

CLARE. What do you mean? You keep on telling her the whole bloody time. (*She turns.*) And now she can hear everything we're saying!

RALPH. Don't worry, she's the only one that knows yet.

CLARE (*snaps*). What do you mean yet? (*Moving towards him.*) Look we don't want to corrupt her, do we?

RALPH. You're the only one that's been corrupted.

CLARE. Is that so?

RALPH. Yes. (*He smiles, touching her hair.*)

CLARE. That's what you think. (*Looking at him.*) You're totally irresponsible, do you know that, Ralph. (*Not looking at NICOLA, she hisses.*) Why doesn't she go away for heaven's sake. She keeps watching us.

RALPH. Because she's interested, isn't she. Look! She's finished her chocolate.

NICOLA. Yes.

RALPH (*going up to her, grinning*). You have one each evening.

NICOLA. That's right. (*Standing by the bin.*) Here — you can see all the ones I've had for weeks. They don't empty them much.

RALPH. Look Clare. You can see all her dead chocolate skins . . . What do you do all by yourself every night, apart from eating chocolate?

NICOLA. Nothing much. Why? (*To herself.*) Sometimes I shout.

RALPH. What?

NICOLA. Nothing.

RALPH. Sometimes you shout. Is that what you said?

NICOLA. Yeh. When it's empty like this.

RALPH. You shout very loudly?

NICOLA *nods.*

Do it now.

NICOLA. No . . . I couldn't.

RALPH *turns.*

NICOLA. Well . . . I

She moves forward. Her face is calm, expressionless. She lets out a sudden short scream. RALPH turns. Silence.

CLARE. What a horrible noise.

NICOLA. Something like that. Don't do it often.

CLARE. Look you better have a cigarette.

NICOLA. No thanks. I don't smoke.

CLARE. And you mustn't believe what he says.

LEN BRAZIL's *voice suddenly pipes up.*

L.B.'s VOICE. That was — (*Title of the music.*) — and this is Len Brazil on night call saying this is your spot. So don't forget folks. More calls please on 55304. Just pick up your phones, and stimulate us . . .

RALPH (*half-way through L.B.'s speech*). Oh shut up, just shut up. Leave us alone. (*He lights a cigarette.*)

NICOLA. Your hand's shaking.

RALPH. Is it? Here have a cigarette, you need one.

CLARE. No — I just offered her one. She doesn't smoke.

RALPH. Rubbish — here take one quick.

NICOLA. No thanks.

RALPH. Come on, take one. (*Loud.*) Go on — take the bloody thing!

CLARE (*loud*). Look everyone calm down. (*Really loud.*) JUST CALM DOWN FOR CHRISSAKE.

Silence. Distant muzak. NICOLA is leaning against the wall between them.

NICOLA. Are you *really* brother and sister?

They look at her.

(*To* CLARE.) I mean are you his sister?

CLARE (*totally thrown*). Me? Oh Christ . . . No, of course not.

NICOLA (*to* RALPH). Are you her brother?

RALPH. Yes — of course I am.

NICOLA (*grins*). I see.

CLARE (*loud*). You've told her now.

RALPH. I'd told her before.

CLARE. But it's for real this time. (*Suddenly loud.*) Why don't you tell everyone. Go on. Put an ad in the local paper. (*Indicating the precinct speakers.*) Why not broadcast it over the loudspeakers.

RALPH. OK I will, shall I.

CLARE (*startled*). What do you mean?

RALPH. Phone him up.

CLARE. Who?

RALPH. The disc jockey. The phone-in. Shall I? (*Over by the phone.*) Why not? It's what they want on their shows, isn't it.

CLARE. Ralph . . . Christ . . .

She leans back as RALPH *picks up the phone. She covers her ears in embarrassment, but is smiling.*

RALPH (*disguising his voice*). Hello, is that the phone-in. I want to speak to Mr Brazil, please. Yes, on this is your spot. Can I please . . . Yes . . . 55304. Jeremy . . . Thank you very much indeed, that's very exciting. (*He puts the phone down.*) They're going to ring back.

CLARE. I thought you were going to do it for a moment.

RALPH. I might.

CLARE. Will you? I don't think so. You're a great one for suggesting things.

RALPH. Am I?

NICOLA (*moving over*). You going to speak to Len Brazil.

RALPH. Yes.

NICOLA. Ah. I tried ringing him once. Didn't get him. He never rang back.

RALPH. He won't ring back now.

NICOLA *begins to move off.*

Where you going now, Nicola?

NICOLA. Going down to the disco.

RALPH (*smiles, moving towards her*). The disco.

NICOLA. Yeh, it's my night tonight, my spot.

RALPH. You got all your friends there?

NICOLA. My friends?

RALPH. Yes.

NICOLA. Yeah . . . a few. It's all right there. Some nights. If you're lucky. Bit of a squash.

RALPH. Better than this place.

NICOLA (*quiet*). Yes.

RALPH. Right then.

The phone rings loudly.

Oh Christ! That can't be him, can it?

CLARE (*turning, smiling*). Won't be anybody else, will it.

RALPH. No. (*He is stranded centre stage.*)

Pause.

CLARE (*loud*). Well, go ahead and do it. If you're going to do it.

RALPH. Shall I?

CLARE. Don't just talk about it. (*He picks up the phone.*) Go on!

LEONARD BRAZIL's VOICE. Hello. Hello, caller.

RALPH. Hello . . . (*Putting on his small boy's voice.*) I want to speak to Leonard Brazil.

L.B.'s VOICE. Go ahead please. Leonard here.

NICOLA. You've got him.

L.B.'s VOICE. What's your name please?

RALPH. Jeremy.

L.B.'s VOICE. Hello Jeremy.

RALPH. I want to ask you something, Leonard.

L.B.'s VOICE. Fine, go ahead. This is your spot. How old are you Jeremy?

RALPH. Eleven.

L.B.'s VOICE. Eleven — near your bedtime isn't it, Jeremy, getting close anyway —

RALPH. I've got a sister.

L.B''s VOICE. Fine Jeremy. That's very good. What's her name?

RALPH. Lucy.

L.B.'s VOICE. Fine . . . Jeremy. That's good. Ask your question — THIS IS YOUR SPOT, night callers everywhere, pick up your phones, for a direct line on to LS and your host — as always — Leonard Brazil. Let's hear your views and blues all the way through to midnight.

RALPH. Well it's about me and my sister.

L.B.'s VOICE. Is she in the telephone box with you Jeremy?

RALPH. Yes — she's right by me, Leonard.

L.B.'s VOICE. Put her on the line, Jeremy, let's say hello to her.

RALPH. Christ — Here.

CLARE (*taking the phone, speaking in her ordinary voice, not young but quiet*). Hello there Leonard.

L.B.'s VOICE. Hello, Lucy. Speak up can you. There're a lot of people listening. How old are you Lucy?

CLARE. Eleven.

L.B.'s VOICE. You're eleven too . . . Tell me Lucy, are you twins, you and Jeremy?

CLARE. No — we're not.

L.B.'s VOICE. Fine, very good. Well it's near your bedtime too. Nice to talk to you Lucy. Can you put Jeremy back on the line, just hand him the receiver.

NICOLA *snatches the receiver.*

NICOLA. Hello Leonard — this is your spot.

L.B.'s VOICE. Are you there Jeremy?

RALPH. Yes, I'm here Leonard.

L.B.'s VOICE. I thought we'd lost each other for a moment. Go ahead Jeremy, ask your question — Three minutes to news time on LS.

RALPH. Well Mr Leonard, me and my sister . . . we just gone to bed together.

L.B.'s VOICE. Hold it there, Jeremy. You're sleeping in the same bed with Lucy. Is it a double bed or have your mother and daddy got guests?

RALPH. No — you see we've just done sex together, my sister and me, sexual inter —

L.B.'s VOICE. Christ. Abort. I said abort. What's happened — have we aborted?

RALPH (*normal voice*). You'd better abort bloody quickly.

L.B.'s VOICE (*really angry*). So you're still on the line you little shit. How old are you really?

RALPH. Twenty-one.

L.B.'s VOICE. Are we off the air yet? — This is Leonard Brazil, this is your spot. (*Muzak comes on.*) So you're twenty-one years old Jeremy. You think this is a funny joke to play on the listeners.

RALPH. It's not a joke — Mr Brazil.

L.B.'s VOICE. Well, let me tell you, we have a lot of people ringing up on this programme with genuine problems. (*Loud.*) I said genuine problems. Don't you ring off yet, I haven't finished with you — just hold on to your receiver if you can, and listen to this Jeremy. (*Getting really worked up.*) We're off the air now, you creep and I'm telling you it's because of shits like you that we have trouble and violence in this city. And now I'm going to tell you something Jeremy which probably nobody's had the courage to tell you before —

RALPH *hangs up. Silence.*

RALPH. We done it.

CLARE. Not bad. You lied a bit.

RALPH. Yes. But we're famous.

Blackout.

In the blackout. LEN BRAZIL's *voice, confident, authoritative, slightly threatening.*

L.B.'s VOICE. Yes — I just want to say to all those upset callers we've heard from, that these people were obviously very sick and very stupid — practical jokers. And the sort of people that you and me can easily do without. It's what gives

phone-ins a bad name, this sort of filth going out on the air.
There're some very nasty customers even in a city like this,
but luckily they're pretty few and far between. And I can
tell you, we're not in the least afraid to take action against
them. If they try to be clever again, we'll trace them, and have
them dealt with accordingly. So rest assured. (*In his normal
voice.*) And now let's change the mood . . .

Scene Five

*Blackout. Music loud. Dancing bubblegum music. In the disco.
NICOLA leaning against the wall.
RALPH and CLARE just a little in front of her. RALPH
dancing — CLARE moving more restrainedly.
The music dips for a moment.*

DISC JOCKEY's VOICE (*loud, trying to sound transatlantic*).
GET DANCING!

> *The music continues but quieter. RALPH moves towards
> CLARE.*

CLARE (*warning*). Don't come too close, Ralph.

> RALPH *is closing up.*

RALPH. I'm not.

CLARE. You are. (*She glances over her shoulder as she moves.*)
It may be my imagination but isn't absolutely everybody
looking at us.

RALPH (*slight grin*). I should think they are. (*He looks round
silently.*) Not many of them are dancing — just standing.

CLARE. We're something for them to stare at, aren't we. Wonder
what they're thinking. (*Pause. She moves, grins nervously.*)
God knows what I'm doing here. Haven't been to a place like
this for years!

RALPH. You look good. (*Moving closer.*) Quite different. You
realize the whole town will be talking about us soon. You'll
have to learn to live with it. By morning we will have caused
a sensation Clare.

CLARE. What you mean? (*She looks up.*) What you expecting?

RALPH. Your guess is as good as mine.

CLARE (*strong*). No, it's better. (*She drinks out of a bottle from the side. With a slight smile.*) We're regressing the whole time, falling backwards, soon we'll be aged three, you realize and have wetted our beds. (*She drinks again.*) It's way past my bedtime.

RALPH (*up really close*). No it's not, you're going to let your hair down, remember.

DJ's VOICE. That was — (*Title of the song.*) — and now here's a really smoochy number for all you smoochers to have a little smooch to. So get to it quietly, as the bishop said to the actress. Whoops, what am I saying. (*He starts the smooching music.*)

RALPH *moves up to* CLARE.

CLARE (*firm, warning*). Stop it!

RALPH (*turning to* NICOLA). This disc jockey's tongue's made out of foam rubber, isn't it. (*He turns.*) God, this is a nasty sight.

NICOLA. It's always like this. Each Sunday. It's all right here.

RALPH (*looking round at* NICOLA). Look, one filthy black room as small and squashed as you can get. Hell on earth. If anything went wrong we'd all be done for — never get out. And the heat, Nicola — it's difficult to breathe.

NICOLA. Yes — it gets like that.

RALPH. The only place you've got to come to! And the kids aren't even dancing.

NICOLA. They don't feel like it.

RALPH. They all look as if they've got glass eyes don't they. Totally glazed . . . (*He looks at them.*) Limp.

NICOLA. Excuse me — got to get ready -- it's my night tonight. (*She takes out a box with glitter make-up in it.*)

RALPH (*turning, looking at her, smiles*). You ought to get away from here, Nicola. Leave town. You're too good for this place. (*Louder.*) I mean what are you doing stuck in this mad hole a hundred feet below a multi-storey car park. Being ordered what to do. (*Smiling at her.*) By total morons.

NICOLA (*smiles*). Yes.

RALPH. Who probably loathe your guts.

He turns, moves forward, suddenly grinning, putting on manager's voice, upper class.

Hello! Good evening. Hold it there please. (*The music stops.*) Nobody move. Just wanted to introduce myself — here I am — and wish you a pleasant evening on behalf of the management. And so, feel at home, let — it — all — hang — out for as long as possible, and spend very freely. That's what we recommend.

DJ's VOICE. Hello there! I think we have a little trouble over in the corner. Come out of there you slinky corner huggers and GET DANCING.

The music starts again.

CLARE. You're going to get us into trouble you realize.

RALPH (*smiling broadly*). We are in trouble, already.

CLARE (*slight smile*). And you'd make it worse, wouldn't you, given half a chance. (*She picks up her bottle again.*) I'm going to get really drunk tonight, anyway, if I'm not allowed to go to bed.

RALPH (*smiling*). You are going to bed eventually.

CLARE (*warning*). You're coming too near. I said not to. (*Suddenly she shouts very loudly.*) GET OFF!

Pause. RALPH *glances startled over his shoulder.*

RALPH. All right then. (*He moves straight over to* NICOLA, *with a seductive smile.*) What you waiting for Nicola?

NICOLA. My spot. It's coming soon. (*Slight smile.*) I've had to wait weeks.

RALPH. Your spot. (*He smiles.*) I see. (*Coming very close to her.*) You don't know what it's like having a relationship with one's sister, do you. It's a tricky business, I can tell you. Can be explosive, as you've seen. (*He touches her.*) Or perhaps you do know . . . you got a brother?

NICOLA. Sort of.

RALPH (*smiling, touching her*). Sort of. I see, and what's he like then.

NICOLA. Don't see him very much, now.

RALPH. Don't you? Why not, Nicola? (*He touches her lightly, nervous laugh.*) Perhaps you should meet him, soon.

CLARE (*suddenly moving over to him, loud*). What you doing with her?

RALPH. Nothing.

CLARE. What disgusting suggestions was he making? (*Slight smile.*) Been making up to you, has he?

NICOLA (*slight smile*). Not really.

RALPH. No!

CLARE. He's a total menace. Can't be left alone with anybody for two minutes without trying something. You have to fight back. (*Looking at the glitter make-up.*) Shall I help you with that?

NICOLA. I can do it myself, really.

CLARE (*close up to her*). I'll do it. You want to look very striking, don't you. (*She touches NICOLA's dress.*) You're wearing one of our bad dresses — an old one. Where do you want these? All over.

NICOLA *nods*.

(*Looking at the glitter.*) You got a lot here haven't you? (*She looks at RALPH.*) What on earth's she going to do?

RALPH. I have no idea! Here, you better have some of this. (*He lifts the bottle up to NICOLA's face.*)

NICOLA. I don't drink. Not usually.

RALPH. Come on! (*He puts the bottle up to her lips.*)

CLARE. She's quite calm.

NICOLA *hands the bottle back, her face very serious*.

NICOLA. I've got to take my shoes off too.

CLARE (*brushing NICOLA's hair, smiling*). You're going to look good Nicola. Really outrageous! Magnificent in fact — like nothing they've ever seen. And very, very sexy! You want to, don't you. (*She puts some glitter on NICOLA's face. As she does so.*) To think I wasn't even allowed to walk barefoot round the house at your age, let alone not wear a bra, and look like you. (*She looks at her warmly.*) But you're not much better off are you, really. You don't look that happy, do you?

NICOLA (*matter-of-fact*). I'm all right . . . It's very soon now.

CLARE (*putting the glitter on*). God, she's pale isn't she. Like some night creature.

RALPH. She probably hasn't seen daylight for weeks. Been living off strip-lighting hasn't she — like you.

He touches CLARE.

CLARE (*slight smile*). Keep your hands to yourself, I warn you. (*Very close to* NICOLA.) You ought to get away from here Nicky, you know.

RALPH (*smiling at* NICOLA). You see.

CLARE. Your face is finished anyway.

They stare at her.

Doesn't she look *good*.

RALPH. Yes.

NICOLA (*staring back*). Are you *really* brother and sister? I mean . . . after . . . tonight. Are you?

CLARE. What do you think?

NICOLA. I don't know.

Pause.

What does he do then?

CLARE. He's a student, isn't he. (*She touches* RALPH's *arm for a moment.*) A total idler — a waste of money.

RALPH. A usual grey, turgid student —

CLARE. Who doesn't believe in anything.

NICOLA (*quiet, staring at them*). No, I mean — what does he do to you?

CLARE. Nothing — we don't ask questions like that. You've to forget all about us, forget our faces.

RALPH. Yes.

NICOLA (*staring straight at them*). I mean, does he touch you and things . . . and . . .

CLARE. Don't be vulgar. Of course not. Don't worry.

NICOLA. Maybe he will.

CLARE. Don't be stupid. He knows better than that, doesn't he?

RALPH. Oh yes! (*He puts the bottle to* NICOLA's *mouth.*)

CLARE. Sssh — you're making her nervous.

RALPH (*grinning*). You're the one that's nervous.

CLARE. Rubbish! (*Trying to take the bottle.*) And give that to me!

RALPH (*smiling, teasing*). No. I think you've had enough don't you.

CLARE. Come on. (*Very loud.*) GIVE ME THAT BOTTLE RALPH.

NICOLA. Excuse me. (*Moving between them.*)

The music stops.

It's my turn now.

DJ's VOICE. And now, we hand over to you. For a moment. Is tonight's lady ready? — Whoever she is? Tonight . . . the brave girl is . . . er . . . Nicola Davies. Good for her. — Of 35 Poole's Road. So let's all give her a chance now.

NICOLA (*moving into the spotlight, she picks up the microphone*). Good evening — it's my turn now. (*She holds the microphone up to her mouth.*) OK — ready. (*She is really concentrating; her face is totally calm, expressionless.*)

The taped music starts; she starts singing along with it, then loses it. The tape stops.

(*Quiet, calm.*) OK, start it again please.

RALPH (*loud*). Go on, sock it to them Nicola!

NICOLA *throws back her head nervously. Her face is totally expressionless, then she launches into* Wheels on Fire — *singing along with the actual tape which is playing quietly. Her concentration is total, her expression remains completely blank, but we feel something building up inside her, a clenched feeling, and during the second verse she gets louder and louder, until after the last line of the verse, a tremendous and shattering scream comes out of that calm face and we feel real danger. The tape cuts out. Silence.*

NICOLA (*total blank stare*). Thank you.

Blackout.

Scene Six

Blackout. A voice.

VOICE. Efforts are being made to trace the two voices purporting to be children who caused a sensation over the air a few hours ago.

The lights start coming up. We see it is RALPH speaking.

They made lewd and outrageous suggestions to the compere, one Leonard Brazil, and claimed to be indulging in incestuous practice. They are still at large and could prove extremely dangerous. (RALPH *is leaning against the door of the room.*)

CLARE. You ought to ring your mother.

RALPH. Our mother.

CLARE. You gotta do it. One phone call, that's all she likes.

RALPH (*staring at her*). It's too late now, isn't it.

CLARE *is turning away.*

She never says anything anyway.

CLARE. God. I'm full of drink. It'll slop out. (*She swings round.*) What are you doing?

RALPH. Only taking my coat off.

CLARE. Yes. Good. So where are you going to sleep then?

RALPH. I don't know. (*He stares at the sofa.*) Down there.

CLARE. Yes. It's the only place. (*She turns, sudden.*) God, I hate this room. Do you know that. I really detest it. I do. What can one do in it? It's a wooden cell. I'm always banging and cutting myself on things. You get room sores from this building . . . you know . . . I got them all over me.

RALPH (*quiet*). Have you? I can imagine, yes . . .

CLARE *looks up, catches his eye, turns away.*

CLARE. I haven't been up this late for months, years even. I'm always in bed.

RALPH. Doing what?

CLARE (*half turns*). Awake. (*Slight smile.*) By myself. Listening to the kids downstairs knocking about in the car park, smashing and screaming. I can never sleep.

RALPH. Remember Nicola. (*He opens his mouth in a silent shout.*) I don't sleep much either now. (*Watching her.*) What you doing?

CLARE (*with her back to him, taking rings off her hands slowly*). Taking these off.

RALPH (*nervous*). Yes. You'll probably get a dirty phone call in a moment. It's undoubtedly the little man next door. It's the only way he can talk to you — sweaty phone calls. He's bound to have a spy hole in this wall — (*Running hand over it.*) — and he watches as you take your things off. All your neighbours have them probably, one there — (*He points.*) — one there, and one directly above. And they watch you . . . like a rat in a cage. They may be watching us now.

Silence.

You're a long time taking those off.

CLARE (*still with her back to him*). Am I?

RALPH. Yes you are. And you're standing like that on purpose, aren't you?

CLARE. Like how?

RALPH. Like that — now.

CLARE. Why?

RALPH (*loud*). I don't know.

Pause.

Have you had lots of men?

CLARE. Men? A few. Not so many. (*Still with her back to him, brushing hair.*) How many have you had?

RALPH. Men —

CLARE. No. Start with the others.

RALPH. Three.

CLARE. Ever?

RALPH. Yes. That's the lot.

CLARE. More than I'd had at your age.

RALPH (*suddenly urgent*). Clare — What's the time? I said — WHAT'S THE TIME?

CLARE. I heard.

RALPH. Well answer.

CLARE. Don't shout.

RALPH. I'll shout if I like.

CLARE. I've no idea. Two, three? I've forgotten all about time now.

RALPH (*very loud*). You see! I don't believe it. Listen. (*Very loud.*) Listen to that!

Silence. Both listen. There is distant muzak and a voice.

(*Very loud, excited.*) At this time! And it's still going on —

(*Moving over to the wall.*) Alone in his room. (*He suddenly shouts.*) Be quiet — or we're coming to get you.

He punches the wall savagely.

CLARE. Stop it — for Chrissake.

Pause.

RALPH. Clare . . . my hand's — gone through the wall.

CLARE. What you mean?

RALPH. It has. Look. (*He tries to pull it out, masking her view.*) I told you these walls were ridiculously thin! (*Loud, angry.*) They're like paper! (*He pulls.*)

And I can't get it out. It's gone all the way through —

CLARE (*quiet*). Oh God . . .

RALPH. It's sticking out the other side — right out. I can feel things . . . in the room. . . I can feel his bald head. I'm touching it now . . . and it's very rough . . . like sandpaper.

CLARE (*realizing*). Ralph!

RALPH *pulls his hand out from behind his body, really excited.*

RALPH. You believed me. You did. (*He shouts.*) You believed me!

CLARE (*moving over to him, excited*). Sssh. Just shut up. (*She shakes him.*) You'll have the whole building up here.

RALPH. What does it matter? (*He smiles at her.*) One ought to live dangerously.

CLARE (*slight smile*). Dangerously? (*Moving up to him.*) You're determined to get us caught aren't you?

RALPH (*nervous smile*). I'm not!

CLARE. You've already done enough to get us burnt, you realize, if this was another century.

RALPH (*loud*). Me! I have!

CLARE. Yes. You have! Except you probably wouldn't have burned. They'd have had to keep on relighting you.

RALPH. What's that meant to mean?

CLARE (*excited, close to him, but not loud*). What do you think?

Pause.

Come on, tell me, why are you like this?

RALPH. Like what?

CLARE (*prods him*). This . . . here.

(*With a provocative smile, touching him.*) You've given up all your rebellious activities . . . at college, haven't you.

RALPH. Yes b-

CLARE. You see.

RALPH (*fast, strong*). Because there's nothing going on any more is there! . . . Except one or two people with tiny minds just in it for their careers.

CLARE (*loud*). Really? (*Smiling, moving up to him.*) Why are students now all so grey and defeated, and miserable and can't do anything? At your age . . . tell me? (*She is staring straight at him.*) You're almost incapable of action, do you know that?

RALPH. Really? And you were different were you?

CLARE. Oh yes. (*She smiles, pause.*) Haven't seen me like this, have you? (*Up close, quiet, touching him.*) Look at you, all that energy and you just don't know what to do with it, all you can do is thrash about and *shout*.

RALPH. Is that so.

CLARE. Yes — it's so. (*She smiles.*) You've always been like this, had energy. (*Matter-of-fact, not seductive.*) I remember taking a huge sticky bandage off you, once, when you were small, only time I touched you probably, and you were just beginning to have hairs on your legs, and I pulled it off really slowly, all the way down, and hurt you like nothing had ever before, and you . . . nearly tore the place down, a whole explosion, almost wrecked the entire house.

Pause.

(*Matter-of-fact.*) But you can't do anything with it.

RALPH (*smile*). We'll see.

Pause.

Are you feeling nervous too?

CLARE. About what?

RALPH (*nervous smile*). For Chrissake!

(*He moves away. Lightly.*) Christ . . . I wish that noise would stop. I really do. (*Facing her again.*) Just for a moment —

CLARE (*smiling*). You're very sensitive to noise aren't you — (*Suddenly more gently.*) Those bombs gave you a scare did they —

RALPH. No. (*Pause. He is looking at her. Lightly.*) You know what we ought to do, Clare, we ought to have one week of total terrible insanity together. When everything will suddenly cease to exist . . . you see — fade right away. We'd get into a car, with a gun maybe, and some music, and set off, just like any film. And probably have a few sudden killings, you know, in the hot sun on the motorway. Through windscreens. And keep moving all the time, be fired at from bridges, and be chased through some big city, and drive on until we were almost senseless, you see, and then get cornered, and caught, and shot several hundred times, very slowly. Coming?

Pause.

CLARE. What a useful idea.

RALPH. Yes. (*He takes his jacket off.*)

CLARE. What you doing now?

RALPH. Taking my jacket off.

Pause.

Want me to go any further. I mean. (*Pause.*) . . .

CLARE. What did you say?

RALPH. You heard.

CLARE. Do you mean it?

RALPH. Mean what.

CLARE (*louder*). That . . . Do you mean it?

RALPH. Half . . . I mean . . .

CLARE (*quieter*). You ought to be careful what you say Ralph.

RALPH (*smiles*). I am.

CLARE. Well what were you trying to say?

RALPH. You know what I meant. I mean . . . (*He begins to giggle.*) FOR CHRISSAKE!

CLARE (*loud, but smiling*). Stop giggling and tell me. Go on. (*She moves forward.*) You think you can suggest things and then just draw back, don't you? But you can't you know, because it just doesn't work like that.

RALPH. No.

CLARE. You've always thought you could get away with everything haven't you — the spoilt little brother . . . (*Moving forward, loud.*) All the time — anything.

RALPH. I haven't always managed it. Because you've been around.

CLARE. Like now.

RALPH. Yes.

Pause.

All right then Clare.

CLARE (*loud*). What you mean — '*all right*'?

RALPH (*smiles*). Come here.

CLARE. You really want to?

RALPH. Yes.

CLARE. You've made up your mind?

RALPH. Yes.

CLARE. That's a change. Good.

(*She casually strokes his hair then gives him a very sexual kiss.*) You're very cold. Why are you so cold? (*Looking at him.*) You've got the same bad complexion as I have — your skin — all spots. (*Touching him.*) You're really rough up here. And you're too thin. Much. (*Slight smile.*) I'll crush you flat probably.

RALPH. You won't you know.

CLARE (*quiet*). Are you clean then, everywhere?

RALPH. Of course I am.

CLARE. Let's have a look. (*She moves his head slightly.*) Not very, no. But you'll do. I think. (*She is staring straight at him, touching him, caressing him.*) Won't you.

Blackout.

Scene Seven

Blackout.
Loud radio murmuring — half heard sounds, talking fast. Then the phone starts ringing. Very dark.
Long loud ring.
CLARE *comes out on to the landing, half dressed.*

CLARE. Oh Christ.

She stumbles about in the dark; the ringing continues.

Yes!

Pause. She grabs the phone. We hear on the line, occasionally, through the conversation, a female voice, only half audible, whining. No words are distinguishable, only her noise.

Hello! . . . Who is this?

Pause.

Look, who the hell is this?

Pause.

Mum — what on earth — do you know what time it is? . . . Oh. What do you want? No I wasn't asleep actually. I haven't been asleep at all. (*Slight nervous laugh.*) Christ! No, I didn't say anything. I . . . It's early morning . . . No, I've just been, I've . . . just . . . been occupied . . . All night . . . Yes . . . I . . .

RALPH *moves into the lighted area.*

No, I'm all right. Just hold on.

RALPH *moves closer.*

Here. There's someone to speak to you. (*She holds it out to him.*)

CLARE (*as RALPH takes it*). It's your mother.

RALPH (*disguising his voice*). Hello . . .

Pause.

Hello there . . . this is Paul. Yes — I'm a friend of your daughter's.

CLARE (*slight smile*). Stop it . . .

RALPH. Yes, this is Paul speaking. I've just become friends with your daughter. I . . . I've been keeping her company. For the night.

CLARE. Come on — we don't want to upset her.

RALPH. She's a nice girl your daughter. Very polite. (*He begins to giggle.*) Christ. No, listen . . .

He is giggling even more, almost hysterically. CLARE *begins to giggle too.*

(*To himself.*) Shut up! . . . (*He puts a hand over the receiver. Loud to himself.*) God, I can't stop it. (*Loud.*) Stop it.

He lifts the receiver.

Hello mother, actually, it's me. Me! It's not fuck, who did I say it was? No, it's Ralph. (*Shouts.*) RALPH!

He starts giggling all over again.

God I can't stop it. Hold on Mum. I'm just — (*He bites his lip.*) No, I wasn't laughing — I was just coughing. Look I'm sorry I didn't phone before . . . I was going to but I didn't. I was busy . . . BUSY!

He bursts into helpless giggles — holds out the receiver to CLARE.

Look you take it. (*Loud.*) Take it, for Chrissake.

CLARE. No, you talk to her.

RALPH *drops the receiver. It hangs between them on the end of its flex.*

RALPH (*to* CLARE). Go on!

>   (*The phone hangs there.*) Oh Christ — this is ridiculous.
>   (*He picks up the receiver.*) Listen Mum. (*Very serious voice.*)
>   It's difficult at the moment to talk. Difficult! (*To himself,
>   as he feels he is going to giggle.*)
>
>   Get a grip — stop it. (*Shouts.*) Oh shit!
>
>   *He puts the receiver back on the rest with a loud thump in
>   the heat of the moment, then he realizes.*
>
>   Look . . . I've rung off now.

CLARE (*serious*). Pick it up, quick, she may still be there.

RALPH (*picking up the receiver*). Hello Mum — you there?

>   *Pause.*
>
>   I don't know if she's there or not. (*Loud.*) Mum? (*He lets go
>   of the receiver.*) No, she's gone.
>
>   *Silence.*
>
>   She probably only wanted the holiday rent. (*Nervous smile.*)
>   Her ringing now!

CLARE. You should have done it before. (*Quiet.*) She's gone
anyway.

>   *She is by the phone.*

RALPH (*swings round*). No, leave it off, I'll ring her later.

>   CLARE *moves back into the room. Greyish white light,
>   getting brighter.*
>
>   (*Suddenly quiet.*) You know it's almost morning.

CLARE. It is morning. It's arrived.

RALPH (*astonished*). Now. Is it?

>   *Pause. He is watching her.*
>
>   Are you all right then?

CLARE. Me? I'm fine. Just cold.

RALPH. You realize we haven't slept at all. Aren't you exhausted?

CLARE. Not much.

RALPH (*nervous grin*). No, not at all. We'll probably start
hallucinating from lack of sleep in a moment.

He bangs the wall with the palm of his hand.

CLARE (*swings round*). Sssh.

RALPH. What do you mean 'Sssh'. I can do that. It's time he was awake.

Pause. RALPH's manner is a mixture of nervousness and dangerous lightness.

It's terrifyingly quiet, isn't it, Clare.

CLARE. For once, yes.

RALPH. Quite eerie. (*He moves.*) It's a horrible light. We're very high up here aren't we . . . (*He looks at her.*) Do you think there'll be anything about us on the radio this morning? Should be.

He watches her.

(*Snaps.*) Why you getting dressed?

CLARE. Because I have to.

RALPH. You don't have to. There's no reason at all to. (*Lightly.*) We don't have to take any notice of morning. (*Slight smile.*) You're not getting ready for work anyway.

CLARE *continues to get ready.*

(RALPH *is watching her; his tone is light.*) Clare . . . you know it was really quite like this, when one of the bombs went off right outside, last week, you know.

CLARE (*with her back to him, quiet*). So you were near them. I thought you were.

RALPH. Yeh, I was. Right on top. All the glass was smashed everywhere. (*He watches her, his tone light, trying to get her attention.*) It's a funny feeling . . . I can tell you, afterwards . . . You know next day I expected every car I passed to go off. (*Smiles.*) I got this idea, rather crazy really, that when I was walking along the pavement if I stepped on the lines a steel mantrap would spring up and get me by the leg, right there — honestly. I was sweating, just walking along. (*He looks at her.*) And you know, the day before yesterday I saw a car parked. And I knew just like that it had a bomb in it, you see. It was a dirty green mini, vicious looking. Are you listening? — And I went up and leant against it, Clare, yes.

It was hot — the metal was — though the air was freezing. And I leant right on it. But nothing happened.

Pause. He continues, trying to get her to turn round.

You know something kicks into place in your mind after a loud bang, it does. The place . . . and things . . . comes into focus . . . everything one's thought. All the streets . . . and buildings begin to look, you know . . . dangerous, all of it. The whole hideous heap . . . Birmingham. You know what I mean? It's a real dump, Clare.

Pause.

You're very calm suddenly.

Pause.

You shouldn't be getting dressed. Did you hear what I said?

CLARE. Yes I heard.

RALPH (*loud*). Then don't.

CLARE. I'm doing what I want.

RALPH (*slight smile*). You're not even looking at me.

Pause.

Are you feeling guilty then?

CLARE. About what?

RALPH. Don't start that. You know what I mean. (*Pause.*) About us doing it — are you?

CLARE. Feeling guilty?

RALPH. Yes.

CLARE. No, not really. Why should I?

RALPH (*slight smile*). You haven't even mentioned it, have you.

CLARE. No.

RALPH. Come here. (*He catches hold of her, nervous smile, light.*) You don't think you're pregnant do you?

CLARE. Of course not.

RALPH. What would happen if you were. If you were really . . . I mean . . . how do you think the kid would turn out?

CLARE. There's no need to talk like that.

RALPH. It'd have an enormous head probably.

CLARE. I said don't.

RALPH (*slight smile*). No. (*He swings round.*) The noise is beginning to come up, hear it?

CLARE. Yes.

RALPH (*quick smile*). Can't have that happening can we? Look at it Clare. (*He half turns towards grey light.*) Great grey mess — starting up again, spilling out. (*Quieter.*) I hate this place now — this town! Quite a lot. Don't you?

CLARE (*matter-of-fact*). A little, yes.

RALPH. What you doing?

CLARE. Shivering.

RALPH (*moves up to her*). I'll stop it.

CLARE. No you won't.

RALPH (*slight facetious smile*). You don't want me.

CLARE. No.

RALPH (*grinning*). Why not? (*He moves away.*) So what are we going to do about it all, Clare . . . We can't let it stay like that. No. (*He tosses a coin, suddenly jokes. Fast.*) We could throw something out of course, for a start. Drop this over, for instance. Would probably make a hole in a traffic warden's head. Right! (*He moves across.*)

CLARE. Stop it! That's dangerous.

RALPH *swings round.*

RALPH. That's better. (*He moves over.*) I don't like you too calm. You've gone all quiet — (*He touches her face casually.*) — and white.

CLARE. Do you want something to eat before you go?

RALPH. Before what?

CLARE. You go.

RALPH (*smiling*). Yes, I thought that's what you said. (*Tossing up the coin.*) 'Before I go'. The only problem you see, is, I'm not going back.

CLARE. Aren't you?

RALPH. No, you see, what's happening instead is — very simple. We're going off together. In a car, like I said. We can go by bus of course if you like. (*Slightly louder.*) But we're going to disappear anyway. Together, untraceable. Live in some very flat empty spot. (*Smiles.*) Marshy. (*Louder.*) That's what's going to happen you see.

CLARE (*slight smile, staring at him*). NO.

RALPH. What do you mean 'No'. It'll happen.

CLARE. I don't think so.

RALPH (*aggressive*). You don't think so. (*Then a broad smile.*) I thought you might agree. You want me to take myself off then, just like that.

CLARE. Yes.

RALPH (*staring at her, loud*). Right! (*He catches hold of her head, moves it towards morning light.*) You ought to look at it — (*Staring at her, with a slight aggressive smile.*) We're bigger than all of it you know . . . Yes. (*He turns, grins.*) I'm just going to make a quick call, OK.

CLARE. Who to?

RALPH. What do you mean who to? Just a call. (*He moves back to the phone.*) You stay there. (*He grabs the phone, moving very fast, flicks through the pages of a directory with the other hand.*) Getting very good at this aren't I. Very fast.

CLARE *is moving towards him.*

RALPH. No, you can stay there.

He dials, smiling broadly.

(*Adopting an Irish accent.*) Hello, is that the Mercury? Well listen to this will you. This is the IRA speaking.

He smiles at CLARE.

(*Loud.*) The IRA, you know —

CLARE. Ralph. (*She rushes onto landing area.*)

RALPH. Are you listening? I'm phoning a warning, you understand, and I will only say it once — Right! There's a bomb somewhere in the Haymarket.

CLARE (*loud*). What the hell do you think . . . (*She pulls at him. He fights her off.*)

RALPH (*very loud*). Did you hear that — I said a *bomb*. Christ this line is —

His voice begins to change.

And it's going off in ten minutes *flat*. (*He shouts down phone.*) Did you hear what I said?

CLARE. For Chrissake Ralph.

RALPH (*swinging round*). You keep out of this.

(*Loud.*) Hello, did you get that.

(*Raising his voice.*) Look you idiot you better get this bloody quickly.

CLARE. Ralph.

RALPH (*turning round*). Oh Christ. (*His voice at first under control.*) For fuck's sake — the pips are going . . . I've only just started. (*He pulls at the flex on the phone.*) What's this phone doing? (*He looks at* CLARE.) Come on quick, give me another 2p. (*Suddenly louder.*) Hurry! It's going wrong.

CLARE *doesn't move. Suddenly* RALPH *really shouts.*

I said give me another two pence. (*Really serious.*) Come on, RIGHT NOW. It's going to cut out. (*Beginning to sound dangerous.*) Did you hear what I said? . . . For fuck's sake. (*He moves, scrambles across the room, looking.*) It's going to cut out.

He stops scrambling, looks at her.

Why didn't you give me one. Didn't you hear me ask. DIDN'T YOU?

CLARE (*calm, but very quiet*). Yes.

RALPH (*screaming*). I asked you for one. I had them on the line. I asked you for one — you heard me.

CLARE (*quiet*). Stop it Ralph.

RALPH. If you'd given it me, I could have done it. Do you *realize that?* You idiot. You stood there. You didn't *even move!*

CLARE. I told you to stop it.

RALPH. And don't look at me like that.

CLARE. Are you going to control yourself?

RALPH (*suddenly screams*). I'm not going back! You heard me —
I'm not going. (*Shouts.*) I have no reason to go. None — *at all.*
And nothing you can do will make me.

CLARE. You're not scaring me one bit you know.

RALPH. There's nothing you can do you understand. (*Shouts.*)
And if you try!

CLARE. You're not a child, Ralph — stop it.

RALPH (*screaming again*). I am not *going back.*

CLARE. Come here.

She moves towards him.

RALPH. *I'm not.*

She catches hold of him.

Let go!

He tries to fight away.

You bloody keep off.

But she catches hold of him.

(*Quieter.*) Keep — off.

CLARE. Are you going to stop it by yourself? Or will I have to
make you.

RALPH (*quieter*). Try — go on.

CLARE *catches his head and pulls it downwards, they fight for a long
moment, he pulls away. Ending in them being clasped tight together.
Silence.* RALPH *is pale but quiet. He pulls away.* Pause.

CLARE (*matter-of-fact*). You really shouldn't have done that
you know, Ralph.

RALPH. Shouldn't I.

Pause.

It was something wasn't it — (*Aggressive.*) — and you didn't
expect it . . .

Pause.

You could have got hurt you know.

CLARE (*staring straight at him, matter-of-fact*). You would have hurt me would you.

RALPH. Probably.

CLARE. But you didn't, did you.

RALPH. No. But very nearly. (*He moves slightly.*) It was something anyway. Would have been quite funny if it had worked.

CLARE. Would it? You'd have only got a few sirens going. (*Slight smile.*) That's not very much is it? And you'd probably have got gaoled.

RALPH. Yes . . . Maybe (*Aggressive.*) Saved by the pips wasn't I?

Pause. He looks up.

I'm thirsty Clare.

CLARE. Are you?

She passes him a bottle.

There.

RALPH *takes the bottle, takes a long drink.*

CLARE. Are you all right, Ralph?

RALPH. I'm fine. I am.

CLARE. It's not going to erupt again.

RALPH. Not for the moment.

CLARE. Good. You can catch an early train then can't you.

RALPH. Yuh — of course. The earliest you like.

(*Suddenly.*) Oh Christ — listen to that racket now.

We hear the rumble of the city.

It comes up quickly.

CLARE. It always does.

RALPH (*he glances at her*). Well, will you be wanting to see me again? I mean . . . you know.

CLARE. Yes, if you pull yourself together.

RALPH. Don't talk to me like that —

Pause.

CLARE. If you do . . . It might even happen again. I mean us. If we wanted.

RALPH. Yuh . . . sometime . . . maybe.

CLARE. Could even be soon, if you liked. It might be worth it. (*Pause. Slight smile.*) I wouldn't mind seeing you. It's up to you.

RALPH. Yuh.

CLARE. You know where to find me . . . You can come anytime.

RALPH. Yuh . . . Just ring . . . I know.

CLARE. And I'm often in.

RALPH. Yuh . . . maybe . . . sometime.

LEONARD BRAZIL *is heard, loud and clear.*

L.B.'s VOICE. Hello early risers wherever you are, it's three minutes to *seven o'clock*. Here's a bit of gentle rise and shine on the LB show. And if we can't have shine then at least we can have . . . (*He fades in some loud muzak.*)

The muzak goes on playing.

RALPH (*flicks the lighter, holds his hand over the flame; quiet, slow, with a slight smile*). He's made of plastic and if I light this under him, he'll bubble and melt into a long black sticky line and flow completely away — taking all the rest with him.

CLARE. Yes.

She picks up the bottle.

When this music stops . . . I'm going to work.

She takes a long drink from the bottle.

Fade.

CITY SUGAR

City Sugar was first staged at the Bush Theatre, Shepherd's Bush, London on 9 October 1975, with the following cast:

LEONARD BRAZIL	John Shrapnel
REX	Leon Vitali
NICOLA DAVIES	Lynne Miller
SUSAN	Natasha Pyne
BIG JOHN	James Beattie
JANE	Hilary Gasson

Directed by Hugh Thomas

The play, in the revised version printed here, was subsequently presented by Michael White at the Comedy Theatre, London on 4 March 1976, with the following cast:

LEONARD BRAZIL	Adam Faith
REX	James Aubrey
NICOLA DAVIES	Lynne Miller
SUSAN	Natasha Pyne
BIG JOHN	Alan Hay
JANE	Hilary Gasson
MICK	Michael Tarn

Directed by Hugh Thomas

The action takes place in a sound studio of Leicester Sound, a local commercial radio station; in the Leicester branch of British Home Stores or Liptons (frozen foods counter); and in Nicola's bedroom in Leicester.

The time is the present.

Characters

LEONARD: in his middle to late thirties, extremely polished appearance, but dresses stylishly rather than ultra-fashionably, considerable natural charm, even when being aggressive.

REX: twenty-one years old, a mixture of eager awkwardness and cockiness. He has a likeable naive manner.

NICOLA: sixteen years old. Totally flat voice, but a very determined manner underneath the quiet, completely blank exterior.

SUSAN: is also sixteen, extremely volatile, attractive manner, with a lot of highly charged violence inside her.

BIG JOHN: small shiny man, in his late fifties, totally accepting manner; tidy, neat, completely dedicated to his job.

JANE: sixteen years old, quite a sharp competitive manner, but also nervous, and completely overcome by her surroundings.

MICK: shy seventeen-year-old, overjoyed to be working where he is.

Author's Note

It is important that Leonard's style as a disc-jockey is not too transatlantic, but his own special blend of relaxed charm, sudden fluent bursts of energy, and barbed comment. He is totally in control of his medium, and his actions round his desk and controls should suggest a master disc-jockey.

The tension inside him which explodes later in the play should build up gradually, both on and off the microphone -- his considerable charm in the first scene, both to his audience and to Rex, getting progressively more and more sour, until eventually it becomes savage.

However, he never allows himself to over-step the mark *completely* when he is on the air, even in his huge speech at the end of the first act.

ACT ONE

Scene One

The studio. LEONARD BRAZIL *is sitting at the record desk.* REX *is in the engineer's box. A pop record fades over a blackout.*

LEONARD (*into the mike*). From 1968, there, Amen Corner, featuring the unmistakable soprano of Mr Andre Fairweather-Low, and 'If Paradise Was Half As Nice'. Welcome back to the LB show . . . LB — the two most important initials in the country. LB on five hundred and fifty waves — that's a lot of water. (*Loud.*) *Five hundred and fifty* medium waves! (*Smiles.*) Sorry. 'You can do better than that, Brazil.' 'Yes Boss.' In a few minutes we have something for you, something special. (*Beginning to open letters on the turn-table desk.*) I want to say hello to those I met in North Street yesterday; people out in their gardens with *Green* fingers, very definitely, and green feet too, so I'm told. And one even with green hair. No, it was very nice meeting you. They have lovely gardens up there, don't they, lovely houses! (*In his more normal voice.*) I have a few letters in front of me — I've been struggling to open. I have one from Mrs Lee, Mrs D. Lee, saying that did I know there was now a topless restaurant in this fine city of ours, and its name is the Aubergine — how's that for a free commercial, you guys over there in the Aubergine — and Mrs Lee wonders, what do I think about it? I think — it's a very classy name, *'The Aubergine'*, perhaps in French it is something more than just a vegetable. I wonder, since we're being blue — or blue*ish*, perhaps we could ask — would any of the ladies like to see bottomless waiters approaching you with your curry? Rex is suggesting a lot of rude vegetable jokes about what that restaurant would be called, which I will ignore. Enough of this smut . . . I went to the cinema yesterday, saw the very excellent *Death Wish*, a lot of rape and gore and blood and guts, for those of you that like your toast buttered that way — me, I prefer the lovely, the scintillating, the mind-expanding Lynsey De Paul. (*Over the beginning of the record, which he has switched on.*) Nobody need fear — Lynsey De Paul is here . . .

He turns a switch, after a few bars so that the music now plays silently while the record goes round; he drops his biro onto the desk.

Pause.

LEONARD. That was execrable. (*He flicks the intercom to speak to* REX *in the box.*) That was a real stinker. A loosener — and a very loose loosener at that. (*Pause. He continues to the intercom.*) Come in here . . . It's the sleepy time for them at the moment, all gorged after Sunday lunch, lying in heaps round the room . . . they won't want to be stirred. (*Pause. Louder into the intercom.*) Get yourself in here, right now!

REX *enters behind him.*

REX. I'm here.

LEONARD. That's better.

REX. I've brought a drink.

LEONARD. How kind . . . (*Slight smile.*) Trying to placate me are you? . . . What is it?

REX. Lime juice; it's a free sample of one of the commercials we're carrying this week. I thought you'd like to try it.

LEONARD. It looks like a congealed shampoo. (*He puts it to one side. Suddenly staring at* REX; *loud.*) Now, why haven't you filled these up?

REX. I was going to.

LEONARD. Going to! Everybody keeps on telling me how efficient you are, how fortunate I am to have you. I have yet to notice. Go and do these now. (*Hands him sheets of record titles to be filled in.*) I warn you, it's a particularly grisly lot. (*Smiles.*) I seem to have played pap for an entire week — might as well have stuck the stylus into cotton wool. (REX *moves slightly.*) And why hasn't my mail been checked . . .

REX (*embarrassed*). Sorry, I . . .

LEONARD (*holding up letter*). I've been asked to open another municipal pleasure pond — which is completely out of the question of course.

REX. Why?

LEONARD (*rifling through his other letters*). The last time — the one and only time I had to baptise a pond — it was in front

of councillors and crowds, and all the rest . . . and I had to
launch it — with a champagne bottle, containing — (*Suddenly
looking up.*) — and this is completely and utterly true —
frog's spawn. A bottleful. I wasn't allowed to smash it against
the side of course, I had to solemnly pour it out, and of course
the bloody stuff got stuck and I had to stand there shaking it,
and banging the bottom, like a ketchup bottle, until of
course I got it all over myself. (*Looks up.*) What I really hate
is somebody that doesn't believe a good true story. (*Loud.*)
Get on with it! (REX *moves slightly. Loud.*) What's more, I've
never seen a single person even *near* that pond — thousands
of pounds spent on a small windswept hole in completely the
wrong place.

REX. I . . . By the way — I've left an item there — (*He indicates
the desk.*) — you might like.

LEONARD. You have, have you. Worse and worse, Rex . . .
You're having a good day, aren't you? (*Smiles.*) I don't like
suggestions very much, you should know that by now.

REX. Yeah but I thought — you could . . . I wanted . . .

LEONARD. No! (*He turns suddenly to the mike, turns on the
record over the monitor speakers, fades it down.*) That was
Miss De Paul. I'm now struggling with another letter on
pink paper — it's from Mrs Joan Parsons saying 'Dear Leonard,
Is it true or false that you were a teacher in another life?'
Well, now, I don't know about another life, Joan, but I was
in this one, yes. I trained as a teacher as it happens, before I
slipped into the record business, and when all that went up in
a puff of smoke, I slipped back into the classroom, until of
course I heard the call of Leicester Sound. I thought that
everybody knew that, Joan. (*Smiles.*) A joke. And a note here
from a theatre group calling itself the Gracious Players,
saying, could I give a free plug to their production of the late
Dame Agatha Christie's *Towards Zero* on Saturday at the
Town Hall, Hinkley, which seats one thousand five hundred
people. No wonder they wanted their free mention. And I'm
now being handed by the ever-dependable Rex, a piece of
paper on which is written 'DON'T FORGET'. And if you
don't know what that means, I do, and I'll tell you in a
moment, for we have a real thriller coming up; but to change
the subject — (*Putting on a record.*) — I have lost some weight.
In fact I've lost so much weight, I'm floating out of my seat,

floating round the studio. They've had to weigh down my trousers with Encyclopaedia Britannicas! (*Normal.*) While our friend Rex is gaining all the time, I'm afraid, he's approaching sixteen stone now, a hunky piece of flesh, can hardly fit into his box. Enough of this gibberish. 'DON'T FORGET' means competition time. We have a stunner for you in a moment . . . till then, let's flash back into the dim distant past of last week. (*He switches on a record; 'It's Gonna Sell A Million'; and turns the sound off after a couple of bars.*) That was better — that was very slightly better.

He gets up, walks.

REX (*entering*). Why do you keep on doing this?

LEONARD. Doing what?

REX. You know . . .

LEONARD. Putting weight on you, you mean — making you an obese lump. It's my rather dismal little joke.

REX. I thought . . . you were the one for the truth over the air.

LEONARD. I allow myself this one slight distortion.

REX. But people will discover, won't they?

LEONARD. No they won't, nobody's ever going to publish a picture of you, are they?

REX. Yes. (*Pause.*) The local press might.

LEONARD (*smiling*). Not with shares in this station they won't. In fact a total wall of silence could be preserved about your real size for evermore. In fact if I wanted I could pump you up steadily to twenty-five stone and then burst you. (*Pause.*) Sorry. (*Smiles.*) Don't worry, I do it to everyone that works for me.

REX. So I've heard.

LEONARD. So there's no need to look injured. You're not, yet.

REX *moves to go.*

REX (*slight smile*). By the way, I've got Capital on the line.

LEONARD (*without looking up*). You'll have to be more convincing than that. Been listening to jabber and gossip, have you?

REX. I suppose so, yes.

LEONARD. Well, don't.

REX (*watching him*). Everybody knows anyway. Are they going to make an offer then?

LEONARD. It's just possible. Everything's possible. I shouldn't bank on it.

REX. For the afternoon show . . . (*Smiles.*) They'll be sending spies up here. They'll be sitting in pubs with transistors and earplugs, listening away. You'll have to give them the whole works.

LEONARD (*looking up*). Will I? Get it ready.

REX. It is ready.

LEONARD (*totally matter-of-fact*). You can have a moment longer than usual, because I'm in a generous mood.

REX. Thanks . . . I —

LEONARD (*cutting him off, swinging round to the mike and switching on the monitor speakers, fading down the end of the record*). And now, a special competition. You heard me — a mind-tingling competition. And by my side is the ever-dependable Rex, sweating slightly, what have we got as a prize, Rex?

REX (*nervous, standing by the mike and speaking into it, putting on an almost BBC voice*). We have *their* latest LP — the Yellow Jacks' latest!

LEONARD (*brash voice*). Tell us the title, Rex — *please* tell us the title.

REX. 'High Up There'.

LEONARD. That's a fine title — is it a fine record?

REX. It's very exciting Leonard, it really is . . .

LEONARD (*to the listeners*). And you can have it a whole two or three weeks before it's in the shops, one of the very first in the whole country to have it. And what is Rex going to make us do? . . . Well, I think he's been fiddling with his tapes.

REX. I have indeed —

LEONARD. Very posh today aren't we, Rex?

REX. Are we, Leonard?

LEONARD. And what have you done with your tapes?

REX. I've slowed them down — rather a lot.

LEONARD. Slowed them down — we're getting even more posh.

REX. Yes.

LEONARD (*loud*). Tell me Rex, what effect does this have on the listener?

REX. What?

LEONARD (*very fast*). What effect does this have on the listener?

REX. What . . . well it . . . (REX *dries completely, stands helpless.*) I . . .

LEONARD *presses the button: a tape of the Leicester Sound jingle cuts off* REX's *floundering.*

LEONARD. Enough of this gibberish. (*Normal voice.*) OK, sweets — this is it. Rex is going to play one of the songs in the Top *Eleven*, and it has been slo-o-o-o-owed do-o-o-own, so it sounds a little different. And you're going to give us the singer and the song aren't you . . . Double five three zero four is the number to ring . . . that's right. (*Bogart voice.*) Play it again, Rex.

REX *back in his box, switches on a tape of 'The Proud One' by the Osmonds at 16 rpm.*

LEONARD (*after a few bars, reducing the volume on the monitor speakers, he talks into the intercom to* REX; *off the air*). Sounds a little more exciting like this doesn't it. I shall always play it like this in future. (*Suddenly loud.*) All records will be played at *eight* rpm, and we'll talk that slowly too.

REX *has come out of the box.*

REX. I'm . . . sorry about messing things up, I didn't mean to . . .

LEONARD. Of course you didn't —

REX. You took me by surprise, I didn't think . . . I'm sorry, I won't do it again.

LEONARD. No of course you won't. You won't get another chance to. Now get back into your box where you belong. (*He returns to the mike; switches it to go live again. Loud.*) Rex — what have you done to my favourite song? How's that for first-degree murder — a fine song slo-o-o-owly tortured to death. OK, sweets, who can be the first caller — race to your phones, dial furiously . . . I'm touching the first prize now — all fourteen tracks of it . . . we're handling the two of them with rubber gloves up here — and forceps, and we're keeping them in an incubator at night, in case we can hatch a third. Seriously now — (*He's put his headphones on.*) — we have a caller; and the first caller is . . .

A GIRL'S VOICE (*on the telephone, amplified through the monitors*). Hello? Hello . . .

LEONARD (*softly*). Hello there . . . what's your name, love?

GIRL. Angela . . .

LEONARD. Lovely. Have we ever talked before?

ANGELA. No, never —

LEONARD. Fine. You at home Angela?

ANGELA. Yeah — I'm at home.

LEONARD. Good — well, let's go straight into it Angela, into the unknown . . . (*Signalling to Rex, who switches on the slowed-down tape again, in the background.*) Who do you think the noise is, this *slo-o-ow* noise?

ANGELA. Is it — 'The Proud One' by the Osmonds?

LEONARD. Did you say —

ANGELA (*about to correct herself*). I . . .

LEONARD. Angela, you're r-r-r-o-o-o-o-ight! Well done! (REX *speeds up the record to the right speed, it plays a few bars.* LEONARD *signals to* REX *and the volume is reduced.*) There we go — clever girl. I'm dropping your prize into Rex's hand, to be wiped spotless, and posted, jet-propelled towards you Angela. Bye, love. Let's have the next one Rex. (*A slowed-down version of 'I Can't Give You Anything (But My Love)' by the Stylistics.* LEONARD *gets up again.*) This is an easy kill for them — they use their record-players so much at home, they all run slowly anyway . . . those who *have* record-players.

REX (*staring at* LEONARD). I really like it, you know — (*Slight smile.*) — *if* I'm allowed to say so, how you always touch something when you're talking about it, even if it's the wrong record, like just now.

LEONARD. Yes. I like that too. It's the actor in me. It's what makes it reasonably good. (*Staring round the studio.*) Where is the nauseating object anyway? (*Sees the Yellow Jacks LP, picks it up.*) Have you read the back, with Ross — (*American*

voice.) — the lead singer speaking *his mind*. (*Normal voice.*)
Take an example at random — and this is a nice lad from
Bolton speaking — 'Ross numbers among his favourite things:
walnut ice-cream, honeysuckle, genuine people, starfish, and
sunburnt bare feet.' (*Loud.*) You realise we're going to have
to play the utterances of this jellied imbecile all this week —
the promoters have sent us a long tape, in a silk case, and the
station's excited too, they want it to be a lively few days; I
keep getting little illiterate messages from Johnson pushed
under the door saying, 'Please remember, *maximum* required'.
(*He switches on the mike suddenly.*) Hello — what's your
name please?

GIRL'S VOICE. Rita.

LEONARD (*slight smile*). Lovely Rita, Meter Maid?

RITA. What?

LEONARD. A reference to years gone by, don't let it worry you,
Rita. Have we talked before?

RITA. No.

LEONARD. You listen often —

RITA. Yes . . . yes I do.

LEONARD (*smiles, soft*). Good, that's how it should be. Let's
go straight into it then love, into the nitty gritty — who do
you think it is?

RITA. I think it's — (*She gives the wrong title.*)

LEONARD. Well, Rita, you're wrong, I'm afraid.

RITA. No I'm not . . . am I?

LEONARD. I'm afraid so.

RITA. You sure? . . . (*Louder.*) I was certain. You —

LEONARD (*cutting her off*). I'm sorry love, you're wrong; keep
listening though, for a very important reason . . . bye for now.
(*Hughie Green voice.*) And let's go straight in to the next
contestant! Coming up to Big John with the news at three
o'clock. One down, one LP to go — round, crisp and shiny.
What's your name please?

NICOLA'S VOICE (*extremely flat, unemotional*). Hello.

LEONARD. A little louder please — what's your name?

NICOLA (*very quiet*). Nicola Davies.

LEONARD. A little louder.

NICOLA (*loud*). Nicola Davies.

LEONARD. Nicola Davies. That's very formal. Are you at home, Nicola Davies?

NICOLA. Yes.

LEONARD (*suddenly interested*). And what are you wearing, Nicola?

NICOLA. Trousers . . . .

LEONARD. A little louder — you've got a very nice voice, Nicola. You're wearing trousers, and anything else?

NICOLA. Yes . . . shoes.

LEONARD. Shoes, that's an interesting picture, she's wearing just trousers and shoes. Only wish we had television phones, sexy Nicola . . . so, to win this LP, that Rex is just slipping into its beautiful see-through tight-fitting sleeve — who is it, Nicola?

NICOLA. It's the Stylistics and — (*She gives the wrong title.*)

LEONARD. I'm afraid, Nicola . . .

NICOLA (*correcting herself*). No, it's 'I Can't Give You Anything (But My Love)'.

LEONARD. Well Nicola — I'm afraid your first answer is the only one I can accept . . .

NICOLA. Oh . . .

LEONARD. But you were very close — and so, as you've given us *all* your name, Nicola Davies — I'm going, actually, to give it to you.

NICOLA. Oh good — thank you.

LEONARD. Just for you, Nicola Davies, but on one condition — and that is —

NICOLA (*nervous*). What is that?

LEONARD. You listen for just one more moment, because I have something rather extraordinary to announce to everyone . . . I'm going to be running many competitions this week for all ages — but one of them is different — for, to tie in with the great Yellow Jacks' concert here in this city on Saturday

we're running THE COMPETITION OF THE CENTURY . . .
and the prize is actually meeting one of the boys. How do
you like that, Nicola Davies?

NICOLA. Yes . . . what do you do?

LEONARD. And not only that — the winner will ride to London,
after the concert, in *their* car, sitting with *them*, and what is
more they will then spend four whole days in London, the
capital of this fine country, at the expense of Leicester
Sound. That's OK, isn't it? — Nicola?

NICOLA. Yes . . . what do —

LEONARD (*cutting her off*). So everybody tune in tomorrow,
for the first stage — you too Nicola — (*His voice quieter,
smiles.*) — you never know — what your luck might be — we
might even speak again. (*He puts down the phone. Drops his
biro onto the desk. Pause. Quiet.*)

We're off.

Blackout.

Scene Two

In the blackout: a radio commercial.

SHARP TRANSATLANTIC VOICE. We are going DOWN!
DOWN! DOWN! Yes, everything's down at Liptons. Shop at
Liptons where eggs are down — (*Echo effect.*) — DOWN!
DOWN! Bacon is down and what's not down's not up.

SONG. LIPTONS MAKES THE GOING EASY, LIPTONS
MAKES THE GOING GREAT!

*As the song continues, there is a sudden explosion of white
light.*
*Supermarket. The music of the commercial breaks into pop
music, playing in the background.*
NICOLA standing by the fridge, staring ahead, pale face.

SUSAN's VOICE (*off-stage*). Nicola?

*NICOLA doesn't react. SUSAN enters, stands at a distance from
NICOLA.*

SUSAN. Nicola? Here . . .

*NICOLA glances up. Suddenly SUSAN crosses over to the
fridge, very sharply.*

NICOLA (*surprised, nervous*). What you doing over here?

SUSAN. What do you think?

NICOLA. You shouldn't have come over. You know you're
meant to stick to your own counter.

SUSAN. Why should I? I hate standing over there, by myself all
the time. I've got to talk to somebody, haven't I — even you!
Anyway, I start thinking funny thoughts, after a bit. (*She
glances up at the strip-lighting.*) If you stare at those lights
long enough, it does that.

NICOLA (*sharp*). You'll be seen any moment, you know.

SUSAN. I won't. (*She feels her tunic.*) Christ, I'm tired after
that rush, and it'll soon be starting again. (*Pulling at her tunic.*)
I get so hot in this all over. What's that — let's see that . . .

NICOLA. Nothing.

SUSAN (*making a grab for it*). What you got a postcard for,
with nothing on it.

NICOLA. Stop it! You'll get it wet. (*She puts the postcard
back.*) Look, if I'm seen talking to you, by the camera —
(*They both glance up.*) — we'll both get it, won't we? You
just have to make a wrong move, and he'll see you, won't he?

SUSAN. Don't worry, I'm watching out. (*She smiles.*) It's coming
now. (SUSAN *ducks.*) You know what happened yesterday?
Something exciting. What do you think — a cat got in here,
it did. Just after you'd gone. Came through the stacks of
Ryvita up there, suddenly there it was. *In here!* You know,
spitting and everything. I thought it was a Giant Rat, we all
suddenly stopped what we were doing and rushed after it,
shouting and screaming our heads off. It really got everybody
going. You should have seen us. Made a change. Didn't last
long — you missed it!

NICOLA. Yes.

SUSAN (*loud*). I wonder if anything else will get in here soon.

LEONARD BRAZIL'S VOICE (*suddenly piping up*). That
was — (*Title of record.*) Don't fear, Leonard Brazil is here. Hello
there, wherever you are, whatever you're doing, and a special
hello to you. (*As if to all the girls, but strangely personal.*)
Yes, you down there, I'm saying hello to *you*.

NICOLA. He's quite loud today.

SUSAN. Yes, he is.

L.B.'s VOICE (*running on*). I've got a lot of goodies coming up, and no bad 'uns. Every sound is freshly picked up here, specially for you, that's why they're so ripe and full of flavour. Juicy! You don't believe me, well, it's true.

The music begins.

SUSAN. He's talking a lot today, isn't he?

L.B.'s VOICE. Very soon that special something I promised, Stage One . . .

NICOLA. Yes.

L.B.'s VOICE. Until then, let's move onto the year 2000 and maybe we'll be listening to this. (*He plays 'Long Haired Lover From Liverpool.'*)

SUSAN (*looking into the fridge*). I'm so hungry, aren't you, can't stop feeling hungry.

NICOLA. Careful, what you doing. He'll kill us if he sees.

SUSAN (*her hand inside the fridge*). It's horrible inside here. We could fuse this fridge, you know — just have to get the right thing. (*She pulls at something inside the fridge.*) Once saw it happen, all the food melts slowly, goes soggy and bad, and it all floats in a big kind of mush, you can pour the whole lot out like a lot of soup. (*She pushes the fridge.*) It moves too, you see!

NICOLA. Don't, please . . . I don't want trouble today, Susan . . .

SUSAN (*pushing the fridge*). It moves easily, we could push it down there if we wanted.

NICOLA (*shouts*). Mind! (SUSAN *springs back as the camera pauses. Nervous.*) He's seen us now. Think. You're going to get us sacked at any moment now.

SUSAN. I wouldn't mind that — I wouldn't. Anyway, he's asleep most of the time, the guy who watches it. Up in the office.

NICOLA. No, he's not! When there aren't many customers, like now, he's watching us all the time.

SUSAN. Yeah, he enjoys doing that. It's his sort of game. Come on — (*She calls to the camera, then ducks.*)

NICOLA. Have you see him yet. Do you know what he looks like?

SUSAN. Yes, I saw him through the door once. He's very fat. I've heard all about him, he sits there all day, with one of his socks off, picking his toes, and eating the stuff, while he watches.

NICOLA. He doesn't do that, does he?

SUSAN. Yes — he used to be a policeman, you know. And when he sees a customer taking something, or one of us, he has them up there, and he says 'he'll let them go'. If he can do what he likes with them for half an hour, puts his hand down you know and that — (*She pushes her hand inside her blouse twice.*)

NICOLA. You're making all this up, like always.

SUSAN. I'm not. It's true! And that's why you stare so much at the camera, isn't it? Because you wanted to get noticed — be invited up there. You want that to happen, don't you?

NICOLA. I don't. Well, it might be interesting. But I don't just wonder about him!

SUSAN. Maybe he's staring at us, right at this moment, smacking his lips — about to jump. (*She looks into the fridge.*) Have you taken anything yet, then?

NICOLA. No.

SUSAN. Have you stopped taking things, then?

NICOLA. No, but they've started searching us, haven't they?

SUSAN. Yes. My mum doesn't believe they search us. She can't think why they should have to, except for bombs, in case we had bombs! (*She puts her hand into the fridge.*)

NICOLA. It's coming round again. Careful!

SUSAN. Nicola . . . let's take something now, right now.

NICOLA (*astonished*). What?

SUSAN. Come on — take that! (*She throws* NICOLA *some food.*) And that . . . and that . . . (*Throwing a huge bundle of food at* NICOLA.)

NICOLA. Look, stop it, Susan. Stop it, it's coming . . .

A large can drops out of her hands and rolls along the floor. At the same moment, the music cuts off.
Silence.

NICOLA *turns, frightened and bewildered, and rushes out in front of the fridge to pick up the can.*

ROSS's VOICE. Don't move, folks, stay right where you are, because yes, it's me. See you Saturday.

L.B.'s VOICE. Those few words were spoken by you know who, Ross. I'll be playing some more of his dulcet tones tomorrow.

NICOLA. Shhh! I want to really listen now.

L.B.'s VOICE (*strangely gentle, as if half-aimed at her*). So have you got a lead pencil ready — is it in your hand — are you gripping it — hold it — tight — won't you — because we've come to that moment you've been waiting for since yesterday . . .

SUSAN (*loud*). You're not going in for that competition, are you, you can't . . .

NICOLA. Sssh! Be quiet.

L.B.'s VOICE. Come on, now then, are you ready, because I'm only going to say it *once*, so pin back those ears of yours, and listen . . . ready . . .

Sudden silence.

NICOLA (*loud*). What's that . . .

Just silence.

They've switched it off.

SUSAN (*smiles, teasing*). Yes — they must have known what you were going to do.

NICOLA. They would switch it off then!

FAT MAN'S VOICE (*silky, nauseating, menacing*). Can Miss Lyle come into the office please . . . Could Miss Lyle come here immediately, please . . . immediately . . .

SUSAN (*loud, defiant*). It's not us . . . it's that old bag, seen her nicking . . .

NICOLA (*moving backwards and forwards*). They were only going to say it once, weren't they? How can I find it out?

SUSAN. You can't go in for *that* competition. You won the record yesterday. They wouldn't even let you start.

NICOLA. I must find it out, probably won't be something like this for ages — where's the building that it comes from?

SUSAN. No idea. They'd never let you in, either.

NICOLA. No. (*She turns.*) I'll phone them up then. I know the number.

SUSAN (*smiling*). Can't use that phone. Only for supervisors.

NICOLA. I don't care. (*She moves.*)

SUSAN (*loud*). Mind! Nicola! (*The camera stops . . . the camera pauses . . .*) You'll never get over there without being seen. He's watching now. (NICOLA *stares across at the phone.*)

FAT MAN's VOICE. Miss Lyle . . .

NICOLA. It's worth a try. I'm going to. (*She moves in front of the fridge, sideways, crouches, dashes furiously for the phone; one second pause, then she immediately starts dialling furiously, bending to keep her head down.*)

SUSAN (*calling across to her*). Keep down . . . down. You haven't got long now. Hurry!

We hear a very loud 'engaged' tone. NICOLA *slams the phone down and immediately starts dialling again.*

SUSAN. Probably hundreds of people trying — everybody. You won't get to speak to *him* again.

NICOLA. Sssh!

The very loud 'engaged' tone. NICOLA *slams down the receiver. Immediately she starts dialling again.*

SUSAN. It's coming round, Nicola. (NICOLA *is dialling furiously.*) You're going to get seen! (NICOLA *glances up, freezes as the camera passes.*) It's on you!

NICOLA (*staring up*). Go away . . . (*She finishes dialling: very very loud 'engaged' pips.*) I hate that noise. (*She moves back to the fridge, not caring if she's seen or not.*)

SUSAN. There you are. I told you.

L.B.'s VOICE (*suddenly piping up*). What about that, then? What did you think of that. *Super, dooper* as they say in Russia. That was only the start, remember, wasn't it?

NICOLA. It would happen, wouldn't it?

L.B.'s VOICE. Of course I've been asked to repeat it, say it again for *you* that weren't listening, yes — I mean *you*. Which is against the rules, and I'll probably be fined an enormous sum of money and get banned for life, but I'm going to, just for you.

NICOLA. Hear that?

L.B. OK, sweet-s. Here's Stage One again. The First Great Stage, and it is: if you could go anywhere in the world you can think of, with one of the Yellow Jacks, which one would you choose, where would you go, and why. (*Jokey voice.*) You're not allowed to choose me, and the *thirty* best ones get through to Stage Two. That's not so difficult is it, in fact it's the easiest I could make it for you — isn't it? And now . . . (*Music starts. He cues the record.*)

SUSAN. Now you know, don't you?

NICOLA. Yes, leave me alone now.

SUSAN. Your postcard's filthy, you know.

NICOLA. Yes, but I can still write on it, can't I?

L.B.'s VOICE. Are you OK then? It's over to you. (*The music coming up loud.*) I'm waiting for you, aren't I? (*Music loud.*)

Blackout.

Scene Three

The studio. LEONARD BRAZIL is standing by his desk. A record is playing silently.
A spool of tape is going round — and we hear LEONARD's personal jingle over the speakers.

JINGLE. LB . . . LB . . . LB . . . LB . . .LB . . . (*He turns the volume up.*) LB . . . LB . . .

Behind him, MICK, 17 years old, nervous manner, is dragging in four large sackfuls bulging with postcards.

LEONARD (*flicks off the jingle, swings round*). What are you doing with those?

MICK (*nervous*). I . . . I'm carrying them in here . . .Mr Brazil.

LEONARD. Nothing is allowed in here, you know that.

MICK. Yes . . . Mr Brazil.

LEONARD (*staring*). What are they?

MICK (*very nervous*). They're bags . . . I . . .

LEONARD. Yes?

MICK. Replies from the listeners. Rex is finishing sorting them . . . you see . . . and there're so many we thought you'd like to see ther

LEONARD (*casually*). Did you. (*He puts his hand into one of the bags, pulls out postcards.*) All these are replies, are they?

MICK. You really got them to write in all right, didn't you . . . Mr Brazil.

LEONARD (*slight smile*). I had a ridiculous dream about these girls last night, do you know that?

MICK (*nervously*). No . . . Mr Brazil.

LEONARD (*lightly*). I was in a small park. There was a whole line of them coming towards me — about twenty of them, and they said they wanted to give me a present — a new pair of trousers, but could they first have my old ones to burn. They must have my old ones to burn immediately. (*He looks at* MICK.)

MICK (*bewildered*). Yes?

LEONARD (*turns, sharply, businesslike*). Come on, take these all out again — the whole lot at once.

MICK (*struggling to pick them up*). Yes, of course.

LEONARD. This place is meant to be the nerve centre of the city, isn't it. And you fill it with all this clobber. Go on, we have very little time.

He brings up the record volume and goes on the air. As he does so, REX *enters, stops* MICK *picking up the bags, and they both stand and watch* LEONARD *from the side. At the end of* LEONARD's *piece over the air* MICK *leaves silently.*

That was Peters and Lee and 'Welcome Home'. And now I've got something to say, folks. (*Gentle tone.*) To all of you, I have a message from our little friends, the Po-Leese. They say a lot of people in this fine city of ours have been taking what doesn't belong to them. In plain full frontal language, *stealing* and our little friends in blue have had to go into schools and shops, and put down the deadly purple dye . . . so they can catch them purple-handed. So seriously now, I know times are hard, but keep out of trouble — you will, won't you? (*Tone changes.*) Very soon on this Wonderful Wednesday we have Big John with all the News In The World — till then, let's explode with a raving cataclysmic ditty from 1968, the Rolling Stones and 'Street Fighting Man'.

Explosion of sound. LEONARD *listens for a moment, sees* REX *and cuts it out suddenly.*

What you doing?

REX (*standing staring*). I was watching you.

LEONARD. That's not permitted, especially the amount you do. Your ogling is getting on my nerves. Why do you do it?

REX. Because it really interests me, doesn't it. (*Smiles.*) Have you heard anything from Capital? (*Fast.*) Do you think they're listening now and going to . . .

LEONARD (*sharp.*) That, Rex, is a forbidden subject, and you know it is. Come on, we have three minutes to go.

REX (*still standing there*). Yes, Leonard . . . I wondered if . . . I just happen to have an item here I thought you might like or perhaps even . . .

LEONARD. You could have a quick spot and read it yourself? That's what you were going to say, wasn't it? You're pushing, aren't you lad. I do believe you're beginning to *push*. I've never ever seen somebody begin so early.

REX. I'm not . . . I. (*Quick.*) I'll just read it, shall I? (*He takes out a black notebook.*)

LEONARD. That's the little notebook with all of Rex in it, that you keep hidden in your box.

REX. It's an absurd news item. (*He reads.*) 'And we've just heard that in a Walls factory in Luton, a severed leg was found in a vat of raspberry ripple ice cream. The authorities are checking to see if they've got a cone big enough for it.'

Silence.

LEONARD. Even from somebody like you, that is quite diabolically dreadful. You're a disgrace to this microphone. (*Suddenly looks him straight in the face.*) You are!

REX (*startled*). What do you mean? What's wrong with it? People like black jokes now — I've some *much* blacker ones, you know. They love them — can't have enough. It's what they really want.

LEONARD (*sudden*). You don't have to tell me what they want, Rex.

REX. No, of course not. (*Genuine admiration, quiet.*) I *know* you know.

LEONARD. That's better.

BIG JOHN *enters; a shiny, red-faced man.*

JOHN. Hello there, everyone. (*Smiles.*) Two minutes to go.

LEONARD. The lad's being pushy.

JOHN. Is he? That's no surprise.

REX (*nervous suddenly*). I'm sorry, I didn't mean . . .

LEONARD. We've got to go on to Stage Two in two minutes,
go on . . . get out! (*He switches onto the air without a break,
fading down the record.*) Hello sweet-s — stand by. Very soon
now you'll have you know what — till then, here's . . .
(*He plays something very cheap and nasty. As soon as he's
faded out, he swings round and cuts back like lightning into
his talk with* REX, *who has left the studio.*)

LEONARD (*loud*). And you make one mistake, Rex, and you're
fired — do you hear that? (*Quieter.*) That boy makes me
nervous.

JOHN. I didn't know that was possible.

LEONARD (*flicks round, stares at* JOHN). You look particularly
cheerful today, don't you, John?

JOHN. Thank you. I'm in very good form, yes.

LEONARD. As usual, you've probably got a train disaster and a
couple of mass murders there — (*Tapping* JOHN's *file.*) — and
your cheeks are positively glistening — Bright and Rosy.

JOHN. Thank you. (*Smiles.*) But I haven't got anything really
spectacular now — maybe by tea-time something will come in.

LEONARD (*slight teasing smile*). Good.

JOHN. What's this I've just heard about approaches from the
Big Wide World, from the actual Capital Radio. Are they
going to . . .

LEONARD. You didn't hear anything of the kind. (*Loud.*)
Nothing of the kind.

JOHN (*startled*). I'm sorry, I didn't realize . . .

LEONARD. No, you don't, John. You see this. (*He picks it up.*)
This piece of paper – that is the COMPETITION OF THE CENTURY.
(*He holds it up.*)

JOHN (*looking at it*). Yes, it's a real cash box week, this week,
isn't it? One minute, fifteen seconds to go . . .

LEONARD. And you know what . . . (*He pauses.*) I've done something which I've never done before, John. I've picked out an average girl for this competition. Yes, I picked out her voice. I home in on her each time I go on the air, home in on that voice. And I imagine her face. It would be funny if she knew, wouldn't it?

JOHN (*hardly looking up*). Really?

LEONARD. In fact, each time I pass by the window, I half expect to see her — a small dot standing right down there, staring up towards here, her spectacles flashing — if she wears spectacles. (*He glances at* JOHN *who is not listening.*) You're the only one that knows that yet, John.

JOHN. Yes. I've got no tongue-twisters today, luckily. One minute to zero. Peppermint? (*He sucks one himself.*)

LEONARD. If there was an earthquake today, or a full-scale revolution, those girls wouldn't notice, not a chance. (*Abrasive.*) I taught kids that age once, years ago! But they weren't like this. (*He taps* JOHN's *file.*) Got any earthquakes locked in there?

JOHN. No thank goodness. Nothing like that.

LEONARD. Perhaps you should have.

JOHN (*suddenly looks up*). You must be enjoying all this anyway — it's your greatest week ever, isn't it?

LEONARD. Oh, I am. I am.

JOHN. After all, you've always been wonderful at whipping people up, getting them to TUNE IN. You only have to say the word . . .

LEONARD. Yes?

JOHN. Just have to breathe over the air. They're all waiting for you now.

LEONARD (*standing over controls*). That's right, John. Got your little furry mascot ready, have you? Go on, *hold it up!*

JOHN (*holds it so that* LEONARD *can see*). Yes, of course I have. Ten seconds to zero . . .

LEONARD. You dropped it yesterday in mid-sentence. Hold on to it very tightly, John. (*He flicks on the switch, fades out the music.*) That was the cuddly sound of — (*He gives the*

name of the record. His tone changes, becoming personal.)
We're coming to you very soon now, love, so don't fret, don't
worry . . . It's three o'clock and here's Big John with all the
News In The World.

BIG JOHN *starts reading the News, world items of extreme
unrest, mingled with local items. As he reads,* LEONARD
*crosses to the far end of studio, out of microphone range, and
calls out remarks to him, trying to put him off.*

LEONARD (*smiling*). You know, John, I don't seem to be able
to believe anything you say today . . . I'm talking through the
News, John . . . I think your mascot's going to fall . . . (*He
begins to cross over towards him.*) Perhaps you need a tickle.
(*He crosses to* BIG JOHN *who's reading the News unwaveringly
and begins to tickle him under the chin, and then under the
arms, in the ribs.* JOHN *shifts in his chair, but keeps reading.*
LEONARD *crosses to his desk. Sharply.*) It's got no life in it.

JOHN (*on the air*). And now back to Leonard, and that
Competition of the Century.

LEONARD. Our thanks to Big John for reading the News so
nicely and so firmly. Stand by, love, any moment. (*Music
plays. He fades it down.*)

JOHN. Somebody'll hear you one day, Leonard. Always jealous
of people taking away your microphone, aren't you . . .
even for a moment. Always trying to put them off . . .

LEONARD. Rubbish! Anyway, I never manage to . . . (*Suddenly,
really abusive.*) *Competitions have an effect on me.*

REX (*entering loudly and suddenly with a trolley completely
smothered in objects*). Here you are!

LEONARD (*facing him*). What are those?

REX. They're your bribes.

LEONARD (*sharp*). My what?

REX. Your bribes, Leonard — from the girls.

LEONARD (*completely surprised*). They sent all those? Why?

REX (*scrambling over the trolley*). There're hundreds of them.
A watch – nicked from her dad, probably. A T-shirt with your
initials on it, some cheese, some socks with toes, a whole cake
with *you* on it, a walking stick, and lots of photos of themselves.

LEONARD (*staring at them, quiet*). All for me . . . ? (*He picks up the photos, stares at them.*)

JOHN (*moving over to the huge stack of bribes*). You're doing very well out of this, aren't you? I don't know what you're worrying about. You're in the middle of a glorious week. (*Feeling objects, poring over them.*) We've never had a response like this. Could live off this for a month. (*Casually.*) I wonder if there's anything there for me. (*He picks up the watch, or the cheese.*) I could do with this. (*He pockets it.*)

LEONARD. John! Go and find some more *News*. Something worth listening to, for once.

BIG JOHN *goes*.

(*Urgent.*) We're very late now. (*He glances down at the photos, then throws them on his desk.*)

REX (*looking at the photos*). What were you looking for?

LEONARD (*sharp*). Nothing. I wasn't looking for anything. (*Slight smile.*) What am I going to make them do next, then?

REX (*astonished*). *I* don't know. (*Excited, smiling.*) It could be so many things . . . It's got to be something they can photograph for Saturday's front page.

LEONARD. Christ! Look at you, grinning all over your face. You're as bad as Johnson and all the rest upstairs — not that they ever are upstairs, given half the chance. They'd have the kids tunnelling under the motorway, or buying eighty 'Leicester Sound' T-shirts each before being allowed to win.

REX. Yes — they will do absolutely anything, those kids. They're desperate just to get into the studio and meet you, and then the Yellow Jacks and everything as well!! The last concert the Yellow Jacks did here, a girl asked Ross, begged him to sign her lip. I saw it, and he did and I wondered if she was going to cut that bit off and keep it in a jam jar, so the signature wouldn't come off.

LEONARD. Stop that — you're not going to talk like that in here — understand! *I don't like it.* (*He switches on music, goes onto the air.*)

REX (*as LEONARD does so*). I'm sorry, Leonard.

LEONARD. Hello, sweet. How are you then? Good. I wish you

could see the sight up here. The studio is brimming with your answers, they're hanging everywhere. Rex is just handing me the postcards — perhaps *your* postcard, enabling you to get through to Stage Two. Hurry, Rex! Had a hard job sorting them, have you, Rex?

REX (*entering into the double act*). Yes, Leonard. We've been simply wading through entries.

LEONARD. Up to your knees, were you?

REX. Up to our stomachs in some places, up to our mouths, Leonard . . .

LEONARD. You nearly drowned our Rex, love. Pity you didn't send a few more. (*He begins to read the cards briskly.*) Diane Williams of 30 Sutton Road says she'd like to go to Scotland with Peter and climb mountains with him because he's afraid of heights. Quite a sadist, aren't you, Diane. Thank you for that. Pam Lawrence of 10 Rosendale Avenue says she'd like to go to London with Ross, because that's what the real prize is. I like that, a real realist, there. Pam will go far, won't she. Linda Perry of 18 Horseley Road says she'd like to go to the moon with Ross, that's a long way to go, Linda. Because he looks so like an astronaut, and Nicola Davies of 35 Poole's Road — rather a grubby postcard isn't it, Nicola — says she'd like to go to Kenya with Ken, that's a Nicola-type joke, and go on safari because Ken looks so good in a suntan and so I'm sure, would you, Nicola. You're through *all the way* to Stage Two now, love, and a list of all those that have qualified. Get your lead pencil ready . . . (*Music is playing.*)

REX (*nervously*). What happens if we don't think of something, Leonard?

LEONARD. What indeed, Rex. (*Slight smile.*) Disaster.

REX. Perhaps some sort of race . . .

LEONARD. There is of course something staring us in the eyeballs *right at this moment*! Isn't there?

REX (*staring at the desk*). What?

LEONARD. It isn't original. It's been used in America several times. (*He picks up the T-shirt.*)

REX (*excited*). What is it?

LEONARD. And it's rather cheap, not what they're used to.

REX (*louder*). What is it?

LEONARD. They might just enjoy it. *Just.*

REX. What is it, Leonard?

LEONARD (*swings round*). And it is: they have to make a portrait dummy of Ross, or any of the others, *life size*.

REX. What?

LEONARD. A model, effigy. A dummy of one of the Jacks, out of old clothes, like a guy, stuffed full and life size. That's the idea, Rex.

REX. That's . . . that's pretty good, in fact, it's brilliant. (*Loud.*) It is.

LEONARD. It's not at all. It's not even good, but it'll *just* do.

REX (*quiet*). It's great.

LEONARD (*by the controls*). Christ — listen to that.

REX. What?

LEONARD. You can almost hear all their small ears pressed against the radio waiting for it. The Competition of the Century. (*He brings up the theme music really loud.*)

REX. You knew the answer all the time, Leonard, didn't you?

LEONARD. Rex is coming over with all of Stage Two in his hands.

REX. Here it is, Leonard — all of it. (*He hands him nothing.*)

LEONARD. Thank you, Rex. (*His tone suddenly personal, almost gentle.*) OK, *love*, what we want — what I want you to do *love*, is very simple and a little special, for the next stage of our remarkable obstacle race to get to the Yellow Jacks and London Town, where everything is still possible. I want you *love*, to make in the next two days, a model of one of the boys — (*Laughs.*) — one of the great Yellow Jacks, a model of Ross, or Dave, or Ken, or Pete. 'What do you mean, Leonard, make a model, a dummy, how on earth do I do that, Leonard — that's impossible!' Well, *love*, what you do is you get some old clothes, and paper and stuff it up him, right up and copy his face from a picture, and use some wool for his hair, or go to a gentlemen's hairdresser, or even a ladies'. (*Gentle voice.*) 'Please could I borrow your shavings?' No, seriously, *love*, don't spend any money on it, and get it to me at Leicester Sound by five o'clock Friday. Do you

understand now, love? And the two who make the most
wondrous accurate models will become the finalists, and come
up here. That can't be bad. It's not. So do your best, *love*,
and hurry, won't you. Good hunting.

A blast of music, as he brings in a record.

(*Very abrasive.*) I DON'T LIKE COMPETITIONS!

Music up again.

Blackout.

Scene Four

NICOLA's *room. Radio playing in the background.* NICOLA
*pulling out a pile of magazines methodically from under the
bed and from the side of the room, and a pile of cans, packets,
etc. that she's taken from the Supermarket.* SUSAN *watching.*

SUSAN. I don't want to stick around. Don't know why I
should.

NICOLA. You said you would. (*She continues to pull stuff out
into the room.*)

SUSAN. What you doing with all of this?

NICOLA. There's not much time.

SUSAN (*suddenly grabbing a poster from the pile*). Hey! you've
got one of these. Who's it of? (*She unfolds an enormous pin-
up poster of a star, holds it up and looks at it.*) Oh, him!
You haven't done it, have you? Don't you know the point?
(*She lays it out on the floor.*) Got it at shop, did you, off the
market . . . They're from America . . . Don't you know what
to do? You have to wet it. (*She lies down on top of it.*)
Wet it with anything you've got and rub it all over. Rub.

NICOLA (*moving over to her*). Yes. (*She rubs hastily too.*)
We haven't got time, really.

SUSAN. And the top should sort of peel away. (*She is lying on
top of the poster.*) And you see all the hair underneath, and
you see *everything.* (*She rubs, still lying on the poster.*) It's
not really his body, it's somebody else's and they cut his
head off. (*Loud.*) Come on! (*She rubs frantically.*) It's too
old! (*Loud.*) It doesn't work! (*She rubs again. Loud.*) Why
not. I *wanted* it to.

NICOLA. Probably never did work. Come on — I've lost time now. Hurry!

SUSAN (*lying on the poster*). I took one of these to sex education class, she was new then, Miss Booth, thought she'd be interested. She hit me across the face! Right there! Girls shouldn't have such things and all that. Why not? I saw her flushing it down the toilet, she talked like a dalek, anyway. I couldn't hear any of her sex education lessons, the traffic noise right by me. (*Loud.*) I never heard *anything* at school.

LEONARD BRAZIL's VOICE (*on the radio*). That was — (*Name of record.*) How are you doing then? Yes, I mean *you*, whoever you are, wherever you are, you with the sticking out ears. That's right, keep it up, you haven't got long.

NICOLA. Yes. (*She works even faster collecting all the objects together ready for the stuffing.*)

SUSAN. He's hurrying you now.

L.B.'s VOICE (*continuing straight on*). Rex's bulky shape is beside me here in the studio as always. (*Sudden mock surprise.*) Hey, he's moving away now, don't leave me, Rex, don't leave me. He's going. How can you do this to me, he's left me. I'm alone and afraid Raindrops might start falling on my head — (*Tone changes.*) — and yours too.

Music begins. 'Raindrops Keep Falling On My Head.'

NICOLA. You know, I think he liked me a bit or something when I rang in . . . He spoke to me longer than the others, different.

SUSAN. He only spoke to you different from the others because he was waiting for the News to come up.

NICOLA (*to herself*). Ready now! (*Worried.*) I'm running out of time, come on! (*She suddenly pulls the dummy out from under the bed, all in pieces, the huge torso, the decapitated head, the hands, the feet, the arms, etc.*)

SUSAN. Look at it! You'll never finish that in time.

NICOLA. Got to. Got to fill it up, make it stiff.

SUSAN (*picking up some of the supermarket objects*). What are these?

NICOLA. Things I've taken from the shop, things I've nicked. They're all going inside. No use to me. I'm sending them all in this.

SUSAN (*picking up a pot of paint*). How did you get all this paint?

NICOLA. Saved lunch money.

SUSAN (*startled*). What have you been eating?

NICOLA. Haven't. Don't need to. So I go for days without eating if I have to. And can.

SUSAN. You'll starve to death, you will. (*Suddenly she picks up the head and a foot.*) Is this Ross?

NICOLA. Yes. He's the easiest to do, his face is very simple.

SUSAN (*suddenly loud*). He's very big.

NICOLA. Yes, I made him big. So he'd notice it.

SUSAN. We can do anything we want with him, now all his bits are here. We can stand on his face. (*She stands on it.*) Can't we? Pull his tongue out. (*She picks up the torso.*) Pull his knickers off . . .

NICOLA (*loud*). Don't do that, Susan. You'll tear him — it'll tear.

SUSAN. Yes! (*Firm.*) You're really stupid, do you know that? Even if you get this ready and Leonard just happens to pick it out, which he won't, even then you haven't really started. He can go on forever with you if he likes, *on* and *on* and *on*.

NICOLA (*determined*). I know that . . .

L.B.'s VOICE (*suddenly piping up*). Hello, how are you doing. Yes, I mean *you*, yes you, with the popping eyes and sticking out ears.

They both suddenly stop and stare at the radio.

I hope I'm not interrupting *you*, am I, because a lady wrote to me to say she had the radio on when, lucky lad, she was giving birth to a baby son, Dominic, and the first sound Baby Dominic heard on this earth was yours truly's ugly grating tones pouring out. I'm getting worse and worse, aren't I? Stop polluting British steam radio — Great belches of grey filth pouring out of my mouth, straight at you down there. In a moment I'll be talking to John Robinson, who's just come out of the army and Northern Ireland and all the old troubles, and he's come home to talk to me.

During this speech, SUSAN *has crossed to the wireless and picked it up right at the beginning of* LEONARD's

*speech and turned the volume down. Then she sings loudly
above it.*

SUSAN. Hear him. (*She holds the radio up with* LEONARD's
voice pouring out of it.) That's the nearest you'll get to him . . .
this! It is not any nearer than that! (*She puts the radio down
next to* NICOLA, *having turned the volume up.*)

L.B.'s VOICE. And now *you, you* down there who have entered
the Competition of the Century, time is running out. Here's
some music for you. (*Music begins.*)

NICOLA. Yes! Quick. (*She speeds up the stuffing of the dummy
with the Supermarket objects.*) You're going to help now.

SUSAN. No, I don't think I want to, now.

NICOLA (*swings round*). *You've got to!*

Pause.

SUSAN (*loud*). Why?

NICOLA. Because I'm going to get there. Into the building and
see him.

SUSAN (*quiet*). You won't . . .

NICOLA. Come on, there's no time at all now. Paint that yellow,
quick!

SUSAN. If I have to . . . (*She takes a big brush and splashes huge
dollops of yellow paint on the dummy's body.* NICOLA *stuffs
the legs.*) Your room's too small, it'll stink of paint for
evermore. You won't be able to live in here any more.

NICOLA. Good. I want that. Hurry . . . paint.

SUSAN (*sploshing bright yellow paint on the torso. Gradually
her paint strokes get faster and faster.*) When they played at
Coventry, Ken had a blue belt, the others had yellow as usual.
I don't like this colour, sort of sick-looking. They ought to
change it. You know I had to get back after the concert — it
was twelve or after in the night.

NICOLA (*to herself*). Come on . . . (*She stuffs the legs and the
head.*)

SUSAN. I didn't think I could get back. It was raining really
hard, straight in your eyes. I got onto the road, started hitching
— all these huge lorries went past, enormous. Looked much
bigger in the dark. And you know, they all had their radios

on. Yes! I could hear. It was Leonard Brazil. It was. He was coming from every single lorry. But none of them stopped.

NICOLA (*quiet, determined*). Come on, quick.

SUSAN (*painting fast*). So I *stood straight* in front of one of them and waved, and he *had* to stop, or flatten me, and he stopped all right, and he opened his door, all smiling and everything, and I got in, and you know what, the seat next to him was still warm, it was all covered with chocolate. Somebody had been sitting there just a moment before — *a girl.*

NICOLA (*to herself*). Faster.

SUSAN. I knew he was going to try to kill me then, yes, on the motorway, in the dark, on the side, where nobody could see, you know, get me on my back and jam a stick of lipstick down my throat, and I'd hear Leonard Brazil on the radio, and suddenly it'd stop, and I'd be dead, and they'd find me in pieces like this — (*Indicating the dummy as she paints.*) — in a bundle, in the mud, been assaulted, flies in my eyes, and all that. And pictures of me on the telly, me being lifted up and wrapped in a sheet, you know. (*Lightly.*) But nothing did happen. Nothing at all. (*Pause. She stops painting. Lightly.*) I wanted it to.

NICOLA (*suddenly very loud*). Oh! Look Susan, it's still not nearly full. (*She stares at the legs and then into the torso.*) We've got to fill it up now . . . (*Moving about, agitated.*) Now!

SUSAN. Put this in anyway. (*She crumbles the huge centrefold picture of the pop star. As she does so, they both suddenly look up with a jolt and stare at all the posters and ornaments in the room. The same idea hits them both.*)

NICOLA (*loud*). Yes! Come on. Everything . . .

They suddenly tear down all the posters and ornaments — everything in the room — and throw it into the stomach of Ross. The action begins swiftly and ends furiously. It lasts under a minute.

NICOLA (*as they do it*). Come on down.

SUSAN (*joyful*). Yes. It's coming down. What's that poster? Come on. (*And SUSAN rips it down.*)

NICOLA *takes everything off the chest of drawers, all her furry ornaments . . . everything.*

NICOLA. He's got to *be* full.

SUSAN (*loud*). Yes.

> SUSAN's *pent-up violence comes out in her attack on the posters, whereas* NICOLA *is more methodical, but also very fast. The music on the radio ends. They strip the room.*

L.B.'s VOICE (*his tone very personal*). Hello there how's it going, then . . . Yes, *you*? You down there. Keeping at it, are you, *love*, that's good. (*He brings up more music or a commercial.*)

NICOLA (*throwing in objects*). Go on . . . in . . . in . . . in . . .

SUSAN. Come on down. (*She pulls the lightshade off and throws it in.*)

> *They are both exhausted. The outburst ends, the torso is full.* NICOLA *lifts it up. They both stare at it.*

NICOLA. It's finished.

> *Blackout.*

Scene Five

The studio. Night. A phone-in programme. The voice of a caller, JIM, about forty, on the telephone, coming out of the monitor speakers. The receiver of the telephone is off, lying on the desk. LEONARD BRAZIL is standing some distance away, at the back of the studio, smiling and listening.

JIM's VOICE (*heard first in the blackout*). . . . I mean, don't you agree with me Leonard, about these vandals, hooligans, whatever you like to call them, I mean, everywhere I go I actually *see* things being smashed up, I see them doing it, and writing things on walls and everything. I mean, I saw some young thugs – I don't want to use abusive terms, especially on your programme, Leonard, and I certainly won't do so, but these men – they weren't just boys, they were grown men, and they were standing round this flower bed of red tulips, and they pulled up every single one, they were pulling them out, by the roots, and treading them into the ground . . . the whole lot . . .

LEONARD (*flicks off the switch to cut off the caller in mid-sentence. Silence. He smiles*). Why do they ring me, explain me that, why don't they phone each other . . . ? (*He flicks the switch on again.*)

JIM's VOICE . . . and even more. And apart from that, I don't know if you find this, I mean as an important person, and obviously on the air — but I mean — these filthy phone calls — people ringing me up.

LEONARD (*turns the volume down, speaks to* REX *again through the intercom*). Is he going to start being rude — I think he is. Thank God I only have to do this twice a week — (*He turns the volume up again.*)

JIM's VOICE. . . . you see what I mean, I don't want to mention anything filthy over the air of course — (LEONARD *holds his finger ready to press the cut-off button.*) — and I'm not going to, but I'm always getting wrong phone calls, people talking to me about things I don't know *anything about!* You know the feeling of course, being a famous person Leonard — somebody rang me the other day, started talking about my horse, how he wanted to buy it, get hold of it, I mean I don't have a horse. (*Loud.*) What would I do with a bleeding horse? (*Suddenly very loud.*) What would I do with a fucking horse in this fuck- (LEONARD *cuts him off.*)

LEONARD (*smiling, very calm*). I'd like to say goodnight now, Jim, thanks for that call, it was a Jim-type call. The time is 9.23 on the LB night show on this Competition Friday in Competition Week, so *hold on tight, love.* It's raining up here, raining black buckets just outside, so let's take a dip into the soft inside of Nostalgia Corner, go back to the golden days of 1967 when London was alive and wriggling and bursting at the seams, remember? Or perhaps you don't. And we were listening to this — some of us were —

Music. 'See Emily Play' by the Pink Floyd. The volume is turned down after a few bars. LEONARD *takes off his headphones.*

LEONARD. That's enough. I don't want any more calls — you've already put through too many. (*He gets up.*) I hate that smell of new paint from the corridors.

REX *enters from the box.*

(*Loud.*) And *also* I've decided I'm not going to do my spot tonight.

REX. What do you mean? Why not?

LEONARD. I have reasons. Got to cope with stage three. (*Loud.*) I'm not doing it. That's final!

REX. Some people tune in specially for it. I mean you *must* do it this week of all weeks . . . we've never had so many calls, so many entries . . . if you would . . . it would . . .

LEONARD. I should, should I? No. (*He gets up, starts searching for something.*) I've never liked them . . . has anyone ever shown you this? The secret of phone-ins! Where is it . . . this . . . (*He starts pulling something out of a drawer.*) When we started, a colleague made these . . . (*Loud.*) Come on out!! (*He pulls really hard. A huge mass of tapes, tangled, without their spools, in an enormous ball, comes out of the drawer.*) Tapes. (*He pulls more out.*) Of the phone-ins, hundreds of them — see? (*He holds them up — a vast amount.*) There are a lot more around us, cupboards full, we should tie ourselves up in it, miles and miles of complaints and shouts and whimpers. (*He holds a piece of tape tight.*) And *frustration!* (*He runs his finger down the tape.*) You half expect to get scalded by them. He edited them, of course, to make them even more comical, more juicy — this disc jockey did.

REX (*smiling*). Great . . . I must listen to them sometime.

LEONARD. The usual Rex response. Take the whole lot — (*He tosses the mass of tapes at him.*) — they can become your bedtime listening, can't they.

REX (*taking armful of tapes*). There —

LEONARD (*pauses. He suddenly stares at* REX). You realise we're almost alone in this building, we're surrounded by empty corridors. You and me. That's a terrifying thought. I usually have my rest from you at this time.

REX. I know. I asked to do extra time specially.

LEONARD. Did you. (*Staring at him.*) You know, you're the most ambitious thing on three legs I've ever seen.

REX. That's not true. I only want to hang on to my job, don't I? I only want to become good at it.

LEONARD. Only that? I don't believe it?

REX. And I enjoy working on your show, of course.

LEONARD. Don't try to tell me that's the only reason for this fantastic obsessional attempt at efficiency.

REX. Yes, of course.

LEONARD (*smiles*). No it's not.

REX (*quiet*). Of course, eventually I want to get on . . . that's natural, isn't it? (*Smiles.*) I want my voice up in lights, eventually.

LEONARD (*quiet*). That's very good, Rex . . . for you.

REX (*unblinking*). It's your expression.

LEONARD (*surprised*). Is it?

REX. I heard it over the air, before I was working here. I *still* listen to you all the time. I even sit and listen to you at home, on my days off, when you're on.

LEONARD (*astonished*). You don't really do that, do you?

REX. Yes. (*Smiles lightly.*) There's nothing you've said that I don't remember, nothing! I've noticed everything that you've used up here. (*Smiles.*) I'm sort of photostating you really — all the time.

LEONARD (*slight smile*). So that's what you're doing. I wish you'd stop it. (*Moving away from him.*) You know what you are, Rex, you're reptilian.

REX. Yes.

LEONARD. Don't you ever let yourself go — go for a night on the town?

REX. No, neither do you. Do you?

LEONARD. You ought to get yourself another job — I mean that — and quick.

REX. Why should I? This is better than anything else I could be doing. I'd be out of work if I was down there. I want to be different, not a crime is it? And after all you're good aren't you? You are. In fact, Leonard, you could actually be the greatest, the best DJ there's ever been. Couldn't you? Yes, I mean singers become famous one day and are gone the next, but DJs go on and on. You will Leonard — I wonder what the people from Capital are thinking. You must have got it.

LEONARD (*loud*). I told you not to. (*He flicks a switch.*) 9.26 on the LB night show in Competition Week. We all had a great time the open air concert last week, didn't we — it was a true festival, a celebration if ever there was one — the greatest. But I've been asked to point out by the little man in blue — we did leave rather a mess, didn't we. It was six feet high in some places; the farmer couldn't find his sheep, or his bullocks — they were totally smothered, and he had a

job locating his lady wife, found her under a pile of toilet
paper and cigarette ends. Seriously, friends, let's try to be
cleaner next time, it'll save a lot of hassle. It's black and soaking
wet out now, pelting towards us. Next, the results of Stage Three
— stand by, *love*, this is it, now, after something from the summer
of '67 when those topless young things with shining kneecaps
bounced down the hot streets of our glorious London.

*Music: 'A Whiter Shade of Pale' by Procol Harum. It continues
to play under dialogue, quietly.*

Come on. Bring them in. We'd better get this over.

REX. Yes. (*He doesn't move.*) You're playing a lot of oldies tonight.

LEONARD. Yes. (*Abrasive.*) I'm in a sentimental mood, aren't
I? You're much too young to remember, of course.

REX (*smiles, looks innocent*). Too young to remember what, Leonar

LEONARD. What do you think? (*Abrasive*). Remember before
the rot set in. I'm not in any way nostalgic about that time.

REX (*smiling, watching him*). Oh no?

LEONARD. No I'm not. I'm certainly not one of those mooning
leftovers wallowing backwards all the time. .

REX. No. Of course not.

LEONARD. I know exactly what it was like. (*Loud.*) Exactly.

REX. Yes.

LEONARD (*staring straight at him*). But it's undeniable, Rex,
that the music we were producing on that label, seven or
eight years ago, was *alive.* That is incontestable. It had gut, it
was felt, and it kicked, sometimes savagely. (*He smiles, more
flip.*) Because, of course, everything seemed possible. (*Pause.
He smiles.*) I was even quite militant in a quiet way. (*Smiles.*)
We thought things were changing and all that romantic crap.

REX (*smiles*). Of course you did.

LEONARD. Don't stand there with that idiotic grin on your face!

REX (*doesn't move*). No.

LEONARD (*smiles*). You'd better get on with it, hadn't you,
before I decide to take revenge.

REX *goes.* LEONARD *talks to him as* REX *prepares offstage.*

You should have been at the open air concert at the weekend.

It was vile. It was a perfect example. (*Smiles, slightly mocking.*) A grey shabby echo of the time when festivals really were celebrations. Everybody was lying about in lifeless heaps, mumbling apologetically, and getting bitten by horseflies. A few of them were even fighting with each other in the mud. You felt you could have turned them over with your foot, and they wouldn't have been able to get up. I saw one girl, a large girl, with a very big face, she wasn't very young, wandering through a patch of long grass. Her face and also her lips were sort of swollen, and completely ashen, almost blue, in fact, as if she was actually physically dead. I almost wanted to go up and touch her; I felt that if you touched that face it would probably flake into nothing. (*Smiles.*) In fact I haven't got that picture out of my mind yet.

LEONARD *puts on another record in the current top ten. The sound of the record explodes through the speakers as the dummies are brought in.*

REX (*enters smiling with twenty-five dummies on a trolley, piled high*). You've got to make the final choice.

LEONARD. I don't believe it. (*Pause.*) I just don't believe it!

REX (*smiling unconcerned*). What's the matter?

LEONARD. You mean they did it — they actually made them?

REX. Yes, of course.

LEONARD. Dressed and everything?

REX. You didn't expect them to give us nude models, did you? Though they would have if you'd told them to.

LEONARD (*picks one up*). We could be in Los Angeles, couldn't we — except it's even worse. Christ, look, they've even painted fingernails on them, bound to be toenails under that. (*He pulls at their shoes, pulls at their hair.*) Probably their own new clothes too — or their little brother's. They must have worked all through the night on these obscenities. They're burrowing like moles to get up here! Why do they do it — tell me, why?

REX. Because you told them to do it.

LEONARD. You could drop anything over the air into that pool and they'd gobble it up. (*He feels one.*) What have they got inside them — feel this — feels as if it's stuffed with cans, and packets of frozen food! And all their magazines — clogged with them! How many of these ghastly objects are there?

REX. Twenty-eight. Two of them by people we'd eliminated at Stage One, but they still went and made them.

LEONARD (*has picked up another*). This is rapidly becoming a madhouse. We're being invaded by all these. Are they all there?

REX. All the best ones. I put some in the canteen — they're propped up in chairs — as a joke when people come in tomorrow

LEONARD. AS a *joke*? (LEONARD *looks at the labels on the dummies, looking for* NICOLA's.)

REX (*innocent smile*). Nothing wrong with that is there? I've put two in the ladies' toilet as well, sitting on the pan. So which two are you going to have — these are the best. Don't mind the paint on some of them, it got into their hair as I was pulling them along the corridor.

LEONARD. What?

REX. Which two are you going to choose . . . ?

LEONARD. These two'll have to do.

REX (*looks at the cards*). Louise Prentiss and Jane Harris. A good choice.

LEONARD. All right, get hold of them quickly, get this dealt with and . . . (*He suddenly looks up.*) Whose is that one?

REX (*looks at the card*). Nicola Davies.

LEONARD. Really — Nicola Davies. I thought so. Well let's have her instead shall we. Scrub that one.

REX. Why — you chose the other one.

LEONARD. Do as you're told.

    Pause.

REX. Have you got a thing about her or something?

LEONARD (*looks up*). No! Of course not. (*Pause.*) I picked her voice out, that's all. I've been using it. (*He looks at the dummy.*) They look more and more like home made corpses — take them away.

REX. They'll make pretty good photos in the paper tomorrow, anyway.

LEONARD (*looks up*). I don't like that.

REX (*looks up*). What?

LEONARD. I don't like it do you hear? You ought to have stopped me thinking of it.

REX. *I* should have . . .

LEONARD (*really working himself up*). What do you think you're paid for? I mean this idea was trash. It was unpleasant!, incompetent, lazy — (*He throws the dummy down.*) — it's trash.

REX. Why?

LEONARD. If you can't see that there's no hope for you!

REX (*smiles*). No hope for me is there?

LEONARD. I need somebody that's going to think, *think*, don't I —

REX. Yes, Leonard, I —

LEONARD. Not just a callous, unquestioning, secret police vegetable . . .

REX. It isn't my fault . . .

LEONARD (*carrying on — a real outburst*). You'd be one of the first to come and take us away, wouldn't you. *Wouldn't you.* Come here.

REX. It was your idea Leonard.

LEONARD. You're an abortion really, aren't you — with absolutely no imagination. Nothing! A complete abortion.

REX (*loud*). I didn't think of it, Leonard, did I — it wasn't me —

LEONARD (*cutting him off*). You're a bloody idiot aren't you.

REX. It wasn't me, Leonard — was it.

LEONARD. Get out of here, go on.

REX *doesn't move.*

Go on, get out.

REX *moves out quickly.*

(*Shouting.*) You're fired. Fired! You really are this time. I don't want to see you in this room again. You leave tomorrow. (*Complete silence for a moment. He faces the record desk and fades out the record.*) That was the Loving Spoonful and 'Summer in the City', and *this is* the Competition of the Century. And now we have come to that solemn moment — the finalists — the two people who are going to come all the way up here. Gauleiter Rex has written the two names out in red ink — you all did so well — showed enormous determination — the greatest in England. But the two who got through — the two names on the card are — Jane Harris and Nicola Davies. Jane and Nicola have won through to the Final. (*Fanfare. It fades down.*)

REX (*quiet, matter-of-fact, over the intercom*). I can only get one of them, Mr Brazil, the other one has gone to bed, she must have been very confident . . . I've got Nicola Davies for you.

LEONARD. Put her through then, Rex. (*He fades out the fanfare.*) Hello there Nicola Davies.

NICOLA's VOICE (*over the monitor, quiet*). Yes, hello.

LEONARD. Hello there Nicola — I don't know if you've been listening to your radio — but I've rung to tell you, in front of the listening thousands, that you have reached the Final, the final round, of Competition of the Century —

Pause.

NICOLA (*flat, unsurprised*). Have I . . . Oh good.

LEONARD (*louder*). Did you ever think you could make it, Nicola?

NICOLA (*matter-of-fact*). No.

LEONARD. Are you tall or short, Nicola?

NICOLA. Not tall, quite short.

LEONARD. That's funny. Rex said you were tall, I said you were short — you've got a short voice. What are you wearing now, love — what is Nicola wearing?

NICOLA. I'm wearing . . . I'm wearing a belt and top and trousers . . . and no shoes.

LEONARD. No shoes. (*Pause.*) I see. Ross'll like that. I'm looking forward to meeting you, Nicola Davies, tremendously. Aren't you?

NICOLA. Yes, I am. I am, Leonard . . . (*Flat.*) . . . very much.

LEONARD. Good . . . that's good. Nicola's going to be coming up here — I'm sure we'll get on. Tomorrow's going to be an extraordinarily good day, isn't it? There'll be some big surprises, I'm sure, and there's a big surprise now — do you usually stay to listen to the LB spot?

NICOLA. Oh, yes.

LEONARD. Well, Nicola, I have news for you. You are in it, you are in the LB spot. For each week, for those of you who have never listened before, and if there are any they'll be hung, drawn, and fined — LB has his spot, when he unleashes a few things. Are you still there, Nicola?

NICOLA. Yes. I'm here.

LEONARD. Well, you're high up, high up in the LB spot — high in the clouds. And the first — the first LB moment is, it's my birthday today, so I'm told, which is a lie because it's at least two years until my next birthday, and our friend Rex — who is definitely getting ideas — has made a cake. A cake out of melted down records. I have in front of me — (*He puts a book in front of him.*) — a pile of records squashed together with a cherry on top, thank you Rex, that's just the type of cake I deserve. (*Loud, runny voice.*) I deserve it — what am I saying? (*American.*) What's gone wrong with him? Seriously, folks I've been thinking about London, for a number of enormous reasons — London, capital of this fine country of ours. And of course it's the prize in the Competition of the Century. (*Fast.*) I was walking along Carnaby Street the other day, Nicola, it shows how old I am, I can pronounce that name correctly, yes I was there — I was Lord Kitchener's Grand-daughter — the street that made the world swing — you should see what it looks like now — it looks like a museum street, it needs its glass case — especially as half of it has been knocked down. The Americans, I hear, are going to ship it off soon across the seas — it'll be our last export, our swinging relics. They're shipping it off to Texas to stand in the desert somewhere, where it'll ooze away under the midday sun. (*Smiles.*) We mustn't get bitter! (*Funny voice.*) Your mouth tastes bitter, Brazil, it's going black round the edges. Remember where you are. You can't let the side down like this, Brazil. It's an important moment. Brazil, what are you doing? (*Quieter.*) What does he think he's doing? No . . . seriously, everybody, London's still an exciting place — the most exciting place. The only place to be. It's still brown and beautiful. Why brown — why not? Mustn't get obsessed by all our yesterdays, they're gone thank goodness, must get obsessed by all our tomorrows. (*Like a machine.*) Hear hear. Hear hear. Hear hear. Don't spit on the animals. I said, don't spit on the animals — where's Nicola Davies — where is she? Still there, Nicola?

NICOLA. Yes, Leonard, I'm still here.

LEONARD (*smiles*). The rain is slashing at the window. I'm afraid,

Nicola, if it gets to me I may melt . . . I'm afraid. Hear that, Nicola?

NICOLA. Yes. I heard.

LEONARD. No need to fear, Nicola is here. I have a note here, what do DJs really do while they're playing records? That's a good question. I hate to tell you. Some read the papers, some play the stock-market, call up their stock-brokers between records — that's true, folks — some call up their lady friends, and some just play with their stylus. (*Smiles.*) And some long to scream obscenities over the air! The mad DJ. And they all use words so sumptuously for your pleasure. Do you ever listen to your words, Brazil? Never, thank goodness, but never mind. Everybody needs us, after all — (*Lightly.*) — we're the new jokers of the pack, we're the new clowns, we tell it how it should be. And we're going to lick the blues. Each week I try to lick the blues — this time with a flysprayer, I have it out, I'm spraying it, I'm spraying them now, they're falling to the ground, curling up black and dead, legs in the air — we've done it. Don't spit on the animals. We're going to make it aren't we, get through to the other side, of course we are — and if you've just seen some horrible things, on the television, bomb blasts, unemployment, politicians, and all that part of our good old England, and you've switched it off to listen to me, sensibly! Then remember, no need to fear, we're going to lick it, so Shout it out! Things can only get better and better — so Shout it out! We have the greatest day of the century tomorrow, so there's something to look forward to, so let's Shout it out! Yes, you, madam, get out of the bath, and *Shout it out!* And you, love, take your hands away from there and Shout it out! Throw that away, lad, and SHOUT IT OUT! Come on Grandad, SHOUT IT OUT! You too, Nicola Davies, SHOUT IT OUT! Let's have some real music. I said SHOUT IT OUT! LOUDER! I can't hear you, don't spit on the animals — this is nineteen hundred and seventy eight, this is Len Brazil — this is Crazy Competition Week — be there tomorrow — and once more SHOUT IT OUT!

Music stops after crescendo. REX has entered, stares at LEONARD. Total silence, long pause.

Shit. I wasn't going to do that.

He flicks a switch. A record comes on, incredibly loud. The lights fade.

End of Act One.

ACT TWO

In the blackout we hear two girls' voices singing 'I Can Give You Love' — one of the Yellow Jacks' songs (the words and music appear at the end of the play). They sing the whole of the first verse loudly and slightly harshly to a piano accompaniment, woodenly played.

Scene One

NICOLA's *bedroom. Saturday lunchtime.*
NICOLA *sitting on the bed, brushing her hair.* SUSAN *moving round the room, munching some cheese puffs. A packet with one sandwich in it is on the dressing table.*

SUSAN. You ought to eat something.

NICOLA. I don't need to. Not hungry.

SUSAN (*turning away*). You won't do very well if you don't eat. Here.

She tosses NICOLA *some cheese puffs.* NICOLA *doesn't bother to catch them.*

NICOLA. No don't want anything. (*Smiles.*) Good sort of diet, this competition, I lost a lot. See — it's come off. (*She feels her waist.*)

SUSAN. You don't need to lose any. (*Pause.*) You're getting skinny. (*Pause.*) You look a bit pale, you know.

NICOLA. I want to look pale.

SUSAN. They coming for you in a car?

NICOLA. No, I'm going there.

SUSAN (*turning round the room*). They can't even be bothered to fetch you. Not much left in your room, is there. (*Smiles.*) All this has sort of cleaned it out, hasn't it. I mean the competition . . .

NICOLA. Yes, I put most of it in, didn't I. It all came in useful.

SUSAN (*to herself*). Anyway, there's the concert tonight. (*Smiling, looking at her.*) Is that the lipstick I bought with you — it made my lips so sore, and they itched like anything. (*She rubs her lip.*) Still itch all the time, if I think about them.

I want to get some white lipstick. I'm growing old, do you know that? (*She looks at* NICOLA.) Yes! How do you feel then . . . about it?

NICOLA. OK   . . . Fine . . . (*Quiet.*) I'm going to be all right. I've been preparing for it. Sat here by the record player all night, listening to records, really quietly so *no one* could hear me.

SUSAN (*very lightly*). It'd be more exciting, wouldn't it really, if you were going to be shot if you lost, or something like that. I mean, then you really would be nervous. If they were going to put you in the electric chair, tie you up in a black chair, and press the button, and – (*Smiles.*) – instead they'll just give you a consolation prize if you lose . . . that's not very exciting, is it? (*She picks up the packet of cheese puffs.*) You're very lucky anyway – you could be going to London. Never been out of this town have you?

NICOLA. Not really, hardly.

SUSAN. And you've already won that LP –

NICOLA. They haven't sent it yet.

SUSAN (*excited*). Going with them to London, Nicola, you can't do much better than that.

NICOLA. Well I've got into there anyway – into the radio building. (*Slight smile.*) I'm going there.

SUSAN. If you go with them – You'll have to be careful of the heavies – they'll still have their heavies with them, they go everywhere with them . . . when they were playing in Coventry in March or whenever it was, and I went, you know . . . and you know what happened, somebody I saw . . . she was throwing herself down on the carpet the whole time at the exit, after the concert, and when they picked her up, she just threw herself down again, and they got angry, the heavies did, so they kicked her – not that hard – they kicked her, *one* did, and so anyway, after a bit, she got up, and went and lay down somewhere else . . . and she made herself sick or something on the floor, in a pool . . . so this heavy, he wasn't one of the biggest, but he came over to her . . . and he said something, I couldn't hear it, and she didn't move, so he got her by the hair, not very hard, but he got her by the hair and rubbed her face in it, like that. I saw it. Gave her a quick rub – (*She demonstrates with the head of a teddy-bear by the bed.*) — just once — to stop her doing it.

NICOLA. You've told me before. That's not going to happen to me.

SUSAN (*fast*). I didn't tell you . . . didn't tell you this. That same time, by the place, I was walking along, and I saw this policeman, he wasn't very old for a policeman, he can't have been that old, he was standing in a doorway, I saw him, he was all by himself and he was swearing his head off, he was, with his teeth kind of clenched. And he had water in his eyes, he was crying, well I don't know if he was really crying but his face was all screwed up and red, and really vicious looking, and there was stuff coming out of his eyes. Down his face. He wasn't old. I saw him anyway, it's true. I remember it more than anything else.

The phone rings. NICOLA *moves out of bedroom area to the phone. She picks it up and answers it.*

NICOLA. Yes . . .

REX's VOICE (*on the phone, very soft, we hardly hear it*). Nicola, Nicola Davies?

NICOLA. Yes.

LEONARD's VOICE (*on the phone, very suddenly*). Hello there, Nicola, this is Leonard here, sorry to drop in like this, we're on the air, love — (*Funny voice.*) — in front of the listening thousands, at this moment. I've just been talking to your fine opponent, Jane, and I wanted to know love, are you OK . . . ?

SUSAN (*shouts*). What's he ringing you up again for?

NICOLA. Yes — I'm very well thank you.

LEONARD. Getting a good lunch, are you — what have you had?

NICOLA. For lunch — some water.

LEONARD. Some water — is that all?

NICOLA. Yes. I'm fine thank you.

LEONARD. You must have something else, Nicola, to get really ready for it.

NICOLA. Yes, Leonard.

LEONARD. The reason I've called, love, is so that we both can tell all the people listening that DON'T FORGET, it's the Competition of the Century today.

NICOLA. Yes.

LEONARD. And don't *you* forget that you're having your
photograph taken.

NICOLA. No I won't Leonard.

LEONARD *(slight pause)*. OK love . . . we'll be seeing each other
very soon, so till then, 'bye, love.

NICOLA *(quiet)*. Goodbye. *(She puts down the receiver.)*

SUSAN. Can't leave you alone, can he?

NICOLA. No . . . that's good, isn't it. I think he likes me. I'm
going to meet him. *(Smiles.)* I am.

SUSAN. Yes, you really are, aren't you, Leonard Brazil. Do
your Mum and Dad know about this . . . ?

NICOLA. They've gone out. I told them — don't think they
believed me, or they didn't hear properly — *Mum* would have
listened to the programme — they might have got excited
— but they don't like me doing that much.

SUSAN *(hardly listening)*. You wearing just that . . . ?

NICOLA. Yes.

SUSAN. You should put this on. *(She pulls out another dress.)*
You want to look a bit sexy don't you . . . get him excited . . .

NICOLA. This is OK.

SUSAN. He'll probably give you a bit of a squeeze, quick squeeze
at your tits.

NICOLA. No he won't — don't be stupid.

SUSAN. You know what to do don't you, tell him you're deaf
in one ear.

NICOLA. Why?

SUSAN. So you can ask for every question to be said twice. Also
it'll get him on your side, won't it? You got to try everything
you can think of to win. And you'll have to be really on the
lookout won't you — he'll try to put you through a lot for
something as big as that — he's not going to give something
like that away easily, is he? — come on, I'll do that. *(She
snatches the hairbrush, begins to brush NICOLA's hair.)* He'll
probably hold up pictures of Ross in the nude, to put you
off, you ought to put spikes on your shoes — so you can kick

him under the table — that's what you've got to do — give
'em their money's worth!

NICOLA (*quiet, determined*). I'm going to win, you know.

SUSAN. Yes; well if the other one wins we'll really do her won't
we? We'll finish her. (*She moves away.*)

NICOLA (*sharp*). Why don't you ever keep still?

SUSAN. Because I don't.

NICOLA. You're always doing that. (*Nervous.*) Please . . .

SUSAN. Why shouldn't I? What's the point of keeping still — I've
never kept still *ever* — (*Moving up to* NICOLA.) Come on,
you're going to eat something now. (*She picks up the
sandwich.*) Come on.

NICOLA *doesn't take it.*

(*Suddenly very loud.*) Come on, YOU GOT TO EAT! YOU
MUST! Now open your gob. (*She pushes the sandwich into*
NICOLA's *mouth.*) I might come to London with you, you
know — if you ever get there. Which you probably won't.

NICOLA (*chewing*). You going to be listening?

SUSAN (*slight smile*). I expect so. You ought to stay in London,
don't you think . . . if you get there. We both ought to. Yes.
Get out of here! (*She pushes the sandwich into* NICOLA's
mouth.) Come on — eat it all, get it down. Swallow it,
Nicola. (*Loud.*) YOU GOT TO! RIGHT DOWN.

Long pause. NICOLA *swallows.*

Now you're ready.

Blackout.

Scene Two

The studio. BIG JOHN *sitting.* LEONARD BRAZIL *standing.*
MICK *sweeping up the studio.*

LEONARD (*moving about, speaking to* REX, *who isn't there*).
I want these seats adjusted . . . could I please have these seats
adjusted . . . Where is he . . . (*He swings round.*) And if that
phone rings once more I will have it decapitated. (*Slight pause.*)
It's that oily sod Johnson, he —

The phone rings. LEONARD *picks it up fast. We hear a slimy nasal voice speaking fast on the other end. We catch a few words . . .*

VOICE. Leonard . . . a few words again . . . congratulations . . . just want to remind you . . . Studio A . . . security . . .

As he speaks, LEONARD's *replies are brusque.*

LEONARD (*on the phone*). Yes . . . yes . . . yes . . . Quite . . . Yes . . . All right . . . (*Louder.*) OK . . . Fine! (*He slams down the phone.*) Keeps congratulating me on how things are going. That one was to tell me the precise arrangements for Ross's visit to this building — and not to forget to plug the rest of their tour — and remember you're carrying a bumper lot of commercials —

JOHN (*smiling*). It's going very well isn't it. I haven't seen anything like this for a long time. I like this atmosphere tremendously.

LEONARD (*by the coffee machine*). Yes. (*Quiet, looking at the machine.*) Do you think if one kicked this machine it'd start playing music?

JOHN. Is what I hear true?

LEONARD (*taking his coffee from the machine*). What do you hear, John?

JOHN. That you've been made an offer — that you-know-who have made a whopping big offer —

LEONARD (*matter-of-fact*). Yes. (*Pause.*) It appears I have been offered the job —

JOHN (*smiling*). What? You really have. Congratulations! That's wonderful news isn't it! (*Smiles.*) The station must be really pleased — when you've just started making us a profit. (REX *enters.*) Have you heard? He's been made a firm offer!

REX (*smiles*). He hasn't! Have you, Leonard?

LEONARD (*matter-of-fact*). Nice, isn't it?

MICK. Er — can I just say Mr Brazil how pleased I am that . . . I mean can I congratulate you . . . I mean . . . It's really great isn't it — really great, you'll show them in London.

LEONARD. Yes Mick.

MICK. They won't have seen anything like it, you must be feeling great now, I would be.

LEONARD. That's right Mick thank you. (MICK *grins nervously and leaves.*)

JOHN. When do you take up residence — after this holiday?

LEONARD (*smiling*). I'm not sure, John, that I'm going at all.

REX. What?

JOHN. What do you mean, you don't know?

LEONARD (*smiles*). We'll be seeing about that.

JOHN. Well there's a lot of money there, and the size of the audience — you'll be playing to an audience of millions — you've always been good at that.

LEONARD (*smiling at him, his manner dangerously light*). That's right . . . that's very true John . . .

REX *moves around the studio, getting ready.*

(*Fast to* JOHN.) I think we should put some music behind you today — don't you? Behind the News. A french horn perhaps, sounding your approach — so you seem to gallop in here on horseback, and a banjo under you for lighter parts —

JOHN. Don't think we quite need that . . .

LEONARD. You were a good idea of mine, you know, John.

JOHN (*slight smile*). Of course I was.

LEONARD. My stroke of genius — saying we must have live news and not network.

JOHN (*to* REX, *as he tidies*). It's the best thing that's ever happened to me — I'd been cut back, one of the many to be lopped off the paper; I was lucky.

LEONARD (*laughs*). And I've never been able to take the news seriously since. Like most newsreaders, of course, you have no idea what you're saying — when you read it out. Have you?

JOHN. Of course I do.

LEONARD (*loud*). Rubbish. Last week, I wrote items of total schoolboy gibberish — announcing that the Third World War had just broken out and was due to arrive in five minutes and that the entire Royal family had contracted rabies — and I asked the girl downstairs — Carol — to slip them in. You came in here, sat down, and read them straight out without a blink. (*Grins.*) Without any comment. (*American voice.*) You're highly dangerous, John.

JOHN (*startled*). You didn't do that . . . ? When was that? You had me for a moment. (*Smiles to* REX.) He can take in anybody really if he wants to. (*Smiles.*) This man's rather good, you know . . . he's rather good.

REX. Yes, of course. (*He has collected a tray covered in letters and small parcels wrapped in coloured paper.*) Here's two letters for you. (*He drops them in front of* LEONARD.) And all these presents and good luck cards have come in for the two girls. They've been pouring in all the time before they were even chosen. Some are from old age pensioners, shows how wide our audience is, and some are really aggressive and jealous ones from other kids.

LEONARD (*glancing briefly at his own letters*). Make sure they get one letter each — a pleasant one, Rex. And get this place tidy — we're going to have guests.

REX (*not moving*). Look at that, he hardly glances at his letters. His mother could have died for all we know, or his lady friends could have started eating each other — (*To* BIG JOHN.) — a different one each week — and he'd never show anything.

LEONARD (*putting letter away*). Yes.

REX. And have you heard about his flat? It is totally bare, almost, except for hundreds of books.

JOHN. Yes, I know.

REX. And you know he's hardly eaten all week — so I hear. Gone off his food.

JOHN. The nervous strain — with his offer hanging over him. (*Smiles.*) I hope you're going to give us a great show, Leonard — for all the family.

REX. Of course he is.

JOHN. It's a specially cold day, freezing, out there. Wonderful, isn't it? Everybody'll be indoors, you've got them sitting there already. Probably going to get the biggest audiences we've ever had.

LEONARD (*looking up*). Well, Rex is not going on the air today, is he? He's not going near a microphone.

REX. What?

LEONARD (*lightly*). He's having no part of this competition.

REX (*startled*). What do you mean by that? (*Getting excited.*) What on earth . . .

LEONARD. You're not going on the air, that's what I mean. You've been fired.

REX. What? You didn't mean that, did you? But I've been working things out for it . . . What do you mean. (*Working himself up.*) I've worked all week on this competition — I have, haven't I?

LEONARD (*matter-of-fact*). I think you'd better leave us alone, John, the boy's getting excited. Go on, go and find some really juicy news. (*Slight smile.*) Must have something good, mustn't we?

JOHN (*getting up*). And what if there isn't any?

LEONARD. Use your imagination, of course. Write some.

REX (*as soon as* JOHN *has gone*). What do you mean I can't do anything?

LEONARD. You can't . . . I've decided.

REX. But I must, don't you see . . . I . . .

LEONARD (*dryly*). No. It's not good for you, is it?

REX. What do you mean it's not good for me? (*Loud.*) Why have you decided to do this?

LEONARD. I've told you.

REX. I mean when everything's going so well for you. (*Loud.*) Why?

LEONARD. I don't think you should be let loose, Rex. So I've fired you.

REX. You don't really mean that, do you? Do you? (*No reply; he changes tone.*) Look, please, Leonard, *please*. I've prepared something specially. I have. Just for today please. I've been waiting all week for this. (*Loud.*) I am *asking* you, Leonard. I've worked well for you, haven't I? HAVEN'T I?

LEONARD (*smiles*). You're not going on the air, Rex, and that's final. You're going to run things more efficiently than you've ever done before — for the last time. And you're not going to make a single mistake. Go on.

REX (*doesn't move*). No.

LEONARD *looks up*.

I've got to do something.

LEONARD (*looks at him*). Why have you got to?

REX. Because I want to — (*Matter-of-fact*.) Because I'm determined to. (*Pause*.)

LEONARD. You're determined, are you?

REX. Yes, Leonard.

LEONARD (*matter-of-fact*). You worry me, you know, Rex.

REX (*quiet*). Do I?

LEONARD. You can have just one minute. Sixty seconds. I shouldn't let you, of course — you're still fired. You're leaving after the competition.

REX. Thanks. Thank you, Leonard.

LEONARD. I should keep your thanks till afterwards. You've got a job to do, do it. (REX *is moving off*.) You know this equipment is about to expire don't you. When it gets hot, it smells really tired — probably give out today.

REX. It'll last. It doesn't matter what it looks like.

LEONARD. One wouldn't want to do an operation with rusty instruments would one? (*He looks at the equipment*.) This is all really tawdry.

REX *comes back in quickly*.

REX. There's one of them out there.

LEONARD. One of them?

REX. One of the girls.

LEONARD. Well bring her in of course. Don't let her wait out there.

REX *goes out*.

(*Matter-of-fact*.) Better see what we've netted, hadn't we.

REX (*coming back with* NICOLA). Here.

LEONARD. Hello. (*Pause.*) Which one are you?

REX. Nicola.

LEONARD (*gently*). Let her speak for herself.

NICOLA. Nicola Davies.

LEONARD. Nicola Davies. (*Pause.*) I . . . thought you'd look a little different . . .

NICOLA (*embarrassed*). Oh . . . Did you?

LEONARD. Do I look different?

NICOLA. No — not really.

LEONARD. So you're in the studio now. (*To* REX.) Have they checked her downstairs?

REX. I don't think so — she just wandered in — after they'd done the photo outside.

LEONARD. You better do it. (*To* NICOLA, *gently*.) I'm afraid it's ridiculous, but everybody that comes up here has to be submitted, that's what they call it, to a bomb check. I'm sorry . . . it ought to have been done downstairs.

NICOLA. Oh . . . yes. I didn't know.

She opens her bag.

LEONARD. Rex'll do the honours. (*As* REX *searches her.*) We get hoaxes all the time — twice as much at night. Last week somebody phoned in to say there was a purple bomb, whatever that meant. (*To* REX.) That's OK. Thank you. (*He smiles at* NICOLA.) You like to sit down — careful where you sit . . . Do you want something to eat? We'll try to get you anything you like.

REX *crosses over to the box.*

NICOLA. No thank you.

LEONARD. We're nearly ready for you. (*He puts his headphones on;* REX *is in the box.*) OK, *stand by.* Where's the other one? (*He presses a button. There is a roar of music, really loud.* NICOLA *starts.* LEONARD *fades the music down. To* NICOLA.) Don't worry, nothing in the world to worry about. (*The music fades down; the red light goes on. Into mike.*) Stop where you are! Don't switch off! For I, LB, am here.

This is Crazy Competition Week. This is the final programme
— how are you all? On this savage cold day . . . it's warm up
here, though. So this is the Big One. For me, too. We've
all got to it, and we're going straight into it, folks. (*Slight
accent.*) Get the bleeder over and wrapped up. Both girls are
smiling, just a little bit tense; we'll be meeting them in a
moment. Right now, let's hear one of the prizes in full flow —
and he'll lead us into a few bubbling commercials —

ROSS's VOICE (*on tape*). The things I don't like — that's a
difficult one. I like most things.

LEONARD (*cutting off the tape. Looking at her*). Know that
voice?

NICOLA. Yes — it's Ross's voice.

LEONARD. Rex — we're minus one girl. (*He smiles, flicks a
switch.*)

ROSS's VOICE. I don't like violence — of any sort, of course,
or people that provoke it, create it, you know, exploit it,
they're criminals really, aren't they?

LEONARD (*switching it off*). He's in fine form, isn't he?

NICOLA. Yes.

LEONARD (*calm, smiling*). They're waiting for the Competition
of the Century down there — (*Looking at* NICOLA.) — and
we may not be able to give it to them. (*He flicks the switch
on again.*)

ROSS's VOICE. I mean *we* don't use violence — I know
people, some morons and journalists, have said so, but everybody just has a party when we play.

LEONARD. Got a good voice, hasn't he?

NICOLA. Yes.

ROSS's VOICE (*in the background as they talk*). And I don't
like parasites, journalists, reporters, people that criticise.

LEONARD (*calm, smiling*). Rex — come here.

REX *immediately comes down from the box.*

ROSS's VOICE (*as* REX *comes down*). And write malicious
things about people . . . and also I don't like people that get
above themselves.

LEONARD *switches him off.*

LEONARD. I was thinking, we'd better give them something to drink, something a little strong, so they don't worry.

REX. That's a good idea.

LEONARD. Go and arrange it. (REX *moves.* LEONARD *still very calm.*) And you'd better find the other one, hadn't you, wherever she is, we need her in one minute —

REX (*smiles*). Right, Leonard. (*He goes.*)

LEONARD (*to* NICOLA). You OK?

NICOLA (*quiet*). Yes.

LEONARD *flicks the switch again.*

ROSS's VOICE. I'm not a prude — Christ, you've only got to ask Ken or Dave, or any of my friends, but I really don't like sex where it doesn't belong, I mean —

LEONARD *switches it off.*

LEONARD (*matter-of-fact*). You better come and sit over here love . . . please. Plenty of time, there's nothing to worry about. (NICOLA *moves over to the chair by the microphone.*) Looking forward to it? (*Pause.*) Are you?

NICOLA. Yes . . . I am.

LEONARD (*as* NICOLA *crosses*). Good. Don't suppose you ever thought you'd be here.

NICOLA. No — I sort of hoped —

LEONARD. And you are. You're here. (*Quiet.*) This is the big one, Nicola. You want to listen to him, do you? (*He flicks on the switch as he settles* NICOLA *into the chair, adjusts its height, tests its distance from microphone.*) Are you comfortable?

NICOLA *nods; as this happens,* LEONARD *stares at her,* ROSS's *voice booms loud from the speakers in background.*

ROSS's VOICE. I mean I agree with that too, and I don't like women who swear. I like them to be — I know this is corny — I like them to be feminine, I'm afraid so, and . . . I know this list's getting kind of long, but you know one thing I really don't like is dirty cutlery. I mean it happens in England, it's much better in the States, but you book into a really good hotel, and you wake up in the morning for your breakfast, and the first thing you see is dirty cutlery, really filthy cutlery, I mean people don't work in this country, I mean that's the trouble really, isn't it, and somebody really has got to do something . . . I like cheerful music.

LEONARD *switches him off as* REX *enters*.

REX. She's here.

JANE *enters*.

And she's been checked.

LEONARD. Hello, I'm Leonard — cut it fine, didn't you?

JANE. I'm sorry. I couldn't find it. I am sorry — it's not easy to find.

LEONARD. It's OK, love, you're here now. We're ready to go. (*To* REX.) Have you got the drink?

REX. Yes I have. (*He produces a bottle, moves to get glasses.*)

LEONARD. Come and sit here — do you want a drink?

JANE. I don't know.

LEONARD (*pours some out*). Come on, have some, it won't bite you.

NICOLA *drinks*.

REX. Jane doesn't want any.

LEONARD (*jocular*). Don't know why we don't give them vitamin injections as well. Nothing to worry about, girls, I'm just going to ask you a few questions, don't worry about anything I might do, I'm not going to sit here, I may roam about . . .

REX (*producing roses from a tray on the side*). I thought they'd like a rose each — a present from Leicester Sound — two white roses, make them look nice —

LEONARD (*lightly*). They look nice anyway — don't you. Do you want to wear them? Rex's little gift.

JANE *nods*; REX *pins a rose on her*; LEONARD *hands a rose to* NICOLA.

(*To* REX, *referring to* JANE.) She needs to be a little higher —

REX. Yes . . . That was a low-key start.

LEONARD. Of course — this is a family show. (*He puts on his headphones.*) OK, that's enough, stop fiddling with her —

(REX *stops fiddling with* JANE *and returns to his box.*
LEONARD *smiles. To* GIRLS.) Now don't worry, nobody's
going to get hurt, are they? (*Flicks switch.*) Before the
commercials that was the one and only Ross, who'll be
entering this building very soon. We have the two lucky and
lovely girls with me — Hello Nicola.

NICOLA. Hello.

LEONARD. And now Jane — who's looking very composed . . . (JANE
says 'Hello'.) Rex has just given them a couple of roses — one of
course white, the other is red — we have a real War of the Roses
coming up here. I wish you could smell them, breathe into the
mikes, girls. (JANE *leans forward, he restrains her.*) Here come
the questions, glistening on a silver tray. (*He picks up some
white cards from desk.*) Thank you, Rex.

REX (*loud, excited, important*). We've got one of the biggest
audiences we've ever had — it's a great sight. The studio's
looking very fine. The competitors are in perfect condition,
sleek and healthy, and there's traffic jams for miles —

LEONARD. Enough of this gibber! You're going to make some
noises, aren't you?

REX. I am indeed Leonard — I'm going to make this noise for a
right answer . . . (*Loud bell.*)

LEONARD. That's a nice noise for a right answer.

REX. And this noise for a wrong answer . . . (*Loud vicious
buzzing noise.*)

LEONARD. That's a grisly noise for a wrong answer.

REX. And I'll be making this noise for 'Don't Knows' . . .
(*Funny, irritating noise.*)

LEONARD. Yes, girls — *No* 'Don't knows' — have a guess. If
you say, 'Don't know', — (REX *makes the 'Don't Know'
noise.*) you lose a life; if you lose three lives, you're out of
the game, and if it's a tie —

REX. If it's a tie —

LEONARD (*quiet*). We want *you* to vote, ladies and gentlemen,
for who put up the best show — so keep your ears skinned,
or peeled, or however you like your ears done.

REX. Where are the other questions, Leonard?

LEONARD. In my head, Rex.

REX. And —

LEONARD (*cutting him off suddenly*). And this now — this
here — is — The Competition of the Century. (*Quiet, matter-
of-fact.*) Jane and Nicola are the contestants; I, Len Brazil, am
putting the questions. (*Quiet.*) 5, 4, 3, 2, 1, ZERO! And the
very first question is for Jane . . . And the question is: Jane —
(*Quick.*) — How old is Ken?

JANE. Ken? He's . . . twenty-one.

Bell rings loudly.

LEONARD. Correct! The lady is correct. Do you know how
many months?

NICOLA (*fast*). Six.

LEONARD. It's Jane's question, Nicola.

JANE. Six months.

Bell rings again.

LEONARD. One point to Jane. (*Suddenly loud.*) Jane has one
point! (LEONARD's *manner begins to quicken, his DJ
instinct coming out despite himself.* LEONARD's *highly
charged inner state during the competition should be underlined by his constant movement away from his chair and his
total absorption in* NICOLA *to the exclusion of* JANE. *He
stares at* NICOLA, *touches her chair, stands over her during
her long speech.*) And the first question for Nicola is — the
question in Round One for Nicola is, and she's looking very
calm . . . is — What is Dave's favourite food — and when does
he like to eat it?

NICOLA. Dave's favourite food . . . it's fresh . . . it's home-made
bread, and he likes it in the morning — (*Silence, nervous.*) —
at sunrise, I think.

Bell rings loudly.

LEONARD (*staring at* NICOLA). That's correct, Nicola. That's
the answer that was wanted. You're doing fine, Nicola. So is
Jane, both of you are doing fine. (*He has got up, is moving
around past his mike.*) Round Two of the Competition of
the Century. Another Nicola question . . . Tell me, Nicola,
which famous historical and Shakespearean character is
traditionally associated with Leicester?

NICOLA. What? (*Pause.*) I . . .

LEONARD. A famous character by Will Shakespeare, associated with this fine city of ours. Have to hurry you —

NICOLA. I'm sorry, . . . I . . . I don't know.

Very loud buzz.

LEONARD. You mustn't say that, Nicola, I'm afraid . . . it's not allowed. So you have to lose a life, don't you. (*'Competition' voice.*) Nicola has lost a life. Do *you* know, Jane?

JANE (*about to reply, then decides not to*). I . . . I . . . (*She shakes her head.*)

LEONARD. Careful . . . NO 'Don't knows'. (*'Competition' voice.*) Neither of the girls know. Which is a surprise! The answer is King Lear — the man with the long beard. (*He moves, picks up the next question. Loud.*) And now Jane, what is the name of the new office block near the prison?

JANE. That . . . it's called . . . I think it's called The New Walk Centre.

Bell rings.

LEONARD. Correct. She has given a right answer. Well up on this fine city of ours, aren't you. Good. (*Funny voice.*) It's completely changed since I was a lad here. It's been torn up and re-planted. You've got two points now, Jane. You're doing well. You're both doing well. Here's another question for you, Nicola Davies — wait for it — when was the Haymarket Centre opened? — Nicola — the great Haymarket Centre. What was the year when its full glory was seen?

NICOLA. I . . . I . . . (*She bites her lip.*) Was it about ten years ago?

Loud 'Wrong answer' noise, repeated twice.

LEONARD. That's the wrong answer, I'm afraid, Nicola. It wasn't ten years ago, no.

NICOLA. Sorry, I — I don't know these sort of questions.

LEONARD. You mustn't say that, Nicola — must have a go, got to have a go at everything — the atmosphere beginning to get a little tense here — not to worry. Nothing to worry about. The year was — (*Loud.*) — 1971. Of course. And our great thanks to Alderman Townshend for setting those questions. There are a lot more I may use later. The score is three points to Jane, and Nicola Davies is trailing behind with one point. Round Three now folks, of the Competition — which is carrying the greatest prize we have ever offered. My questions start here, girls, this is the first one. I'm going to say some words now . . . rather fast. I want you to tell me six of them. Ready Nicola. I'm going to say them very very fast, so be on the look-out. (*He fires the words out sharply.*) Killer, Bottle, Junk, Rifle, Tune, Cheeseburger, Sickroom, Commercial, Knife, Disaster, Stereo, Limousine, Tube, Scar, Women's Lib, Cash Quickie, Needle, Platform, Pill, Dungaree, Snowball, Lump, Oil, Rape, Fire, Neddy, Assassin, Cardboard, Vegetable. (*Pause.*)

NICOLA. Assassin . . . Bottle . . . Needle . . . (*Pause, she begins to panic.*)

LEONARD. That's only three, Nicola . . . Three.

NICOLA (*biting her lip*). Oil . . . Pill . . .

LEONARD. Have to hurry you now . . . Something you ought to know about, being a woman.

NICOLA (*pause*). Women's Lib.

Bell rings loudly.

LEONARD. Well done Nicola — well done. You now have two whole points, yes you do. (*He turns to* JANE.) You thought I was going to do the same to you, Jane, didn't you?

JANE. Yes.

LEONARD. But I'm not! (*Fast.*) Yes I am. Six please of the following. (*Very fast, even louder.*) Chocolate, Wire, Ratings, Tank, Plastic, Movie, Goldfish, Shares, Black, Judge, Union, Red Grass, Steel, Sniper, Index, Trash, Hit, Disco, Chart-climber, Bomb, Cell, Beans, Hook, Barrier, Kite, TV, Kennel, Motorway.

Silence. JANE *stares at him.*

Six please, Jane, quickly —

JANE. Chocolate . . . Motorway. (*Silence. She panics, head in hands.*)

LEONARD. Quick Jane, I have to hurry you, I'm afraid. (*Pause.*) You're running out of time.

JANE (*panicking*). I don't know.

Very loud 'Don't know' piercing noise.

LEONARD. I'm afraid you lose a life too, Jane. (*'Competition' voice.*) Jane loses a life! Both have lost a life now. Neck-and-neck. That's OK, nothing to worry about. Doing very well, Jane. (*He stares at* NICOLA.) Nicola is sitting very still. This is the Competition of the Century. What I want you to do now Jane, is, in your own words, talk about a subject I will give you for *one whole* minute. And the subject is — Jane is smiling, she's straining at the leash — and the subject is . . . folks . . . 'Why do I want to go to London', if indeed you do. It is of course just one of the prizes of this Competition. From now!

Silence.

JANE. I . . . I . . . want to go there . . . to London because I've always . . . (*She stops.*) Are you, are you allowed to repeat things, words?

LEONARD. Yes. You're allowed that. Come on.

JANE. Because, because, I've always wanted to go there . . . and there's a shop in a street, I don't know which street, I saw it . . . this shop, late at night . . . when I was there once, in London, it's the only time I've ever been, and it was open at that time, I mean when shops aren't open, really, and so I wanted to go there, it had big posters in it, very very big posters, some of pop stars, some of politicians, and things, and one of a very fat woman with no clothes on . . . and it had flags all round, the shop did, I mean, and pictures, and names of streets, and souvenirs, cigarettes, and everything. And there was music coming out of it, very loud . . . right out into the street . . . be good to go and shop there. And I mean go and see things, that you know are famous, always been told about, and buy clothes, and look if you can't buy, because there are clothes shops everywhere, not like anywhere else, and see everything, all the night life . . . and I want —

Bell goes.

LEONARD. Well done Jane, thank you for that. That was very well done, wasn't it? Very good Jane. Excellent. I'll give you three out of five for that. So now Jane has six whole points all to herself. 'Six — points — Jane!' And now Nicola Davies, the subject for you is — (*Pause. He stares at her.*)

NICOLA. Yes?

LEONARD. The subject on which you've got to talk for not less
and not more than one minute is — wait for it — (*Loud.*) —
the last pop concert you went to. (*Pause.*)

NICOLA. The last . . . the last pop concert I went to . . . it was
here in Leicester — (*She swallows.*) — and Ross and the group
were playing, and I queued to get in for a long time . . .

LEONARD. How long? How long did you queue for, Nicola?

NICOLA (*completely thrown by his interruption*). I . . .

LEONARD (*staring at her, quieter but matter-of-fact*). How
long did you queue for, love?

NICOLA. I don't know, not . . .

'Don't know' noise, very loud.

LEONARD. No sorry. We don't count that! Rex is a little trigger-
happy, watching out for 'Don't knows'. Come on Nicola.

NICOLA. We queued for a day and a night, I think . . . it was
a bit wet . . . you see, and the stone, the pavement, was very
hard and cold, much harder than you think — because we
slept there you see . . . it was all right and . . . and then a man
came up, it was late you know then, dark and everything,
and he'd come to sell us hot dogs and things, he came out
there and he set up along the side of the queue, it was a very
long queue, and then soon another . . .another came up out of
the dark, and then there was another one, till there were
lots and lots all along the line, really close. (*She looks up.*)

LEONARD (*staring at her, very close*). Go on Nicola! Keep going.
You're doing fine. You've got to keep going.

NICOLA. Oh! I thought it was enough.

LEONARD. I'm afraid it's not.

NICOLA. Oh . . . and . . . (*Lost for words, she is extremely
nervous.*) — and then we went inside . . . and the concert . . .
and it was them of course, and it was, you know . . . well it
was all squashed — and some people rushed up and fought to
get close — and there was a bit of biting, and that sort of
thing, when they called out to us; they seemed a long way off —
a very long way away, in their yellow and everything. They
weren't loud — but they made you feel — I felt something
come up, you know, a little sort of . . . (*A second of slight*

clenched feeling.) I got, you know, a bit worked up inside . . . they were moving very slowly on stage like they'd been slowed down, made me feel strange — then they held things up, waved them at us, smiling and everything, they waved yellow scarves, Ross had a bit of yellow string he waved, I think it was, a bit of yellow rope, and I half wanted to kick the girl in front of me or something because I couldn't see; all the way through I had to look at her great back, pressed right up against it. I remember I half wanted to *get at it.* Move it. And I nearly dropped a ring (*She pulls at her finger.*) I'd been pulling at, put it on specially. (*Very nervous, she smiles.*) If you drop anything it's gone for ever you know — can't bend down if you're standing — (*Smiles.*) — and if you drop yourself . . . then you'd be gone. When you rush out at the end, you can see all the millions of things that have been dropped shining all over the floor, nobody gets a chance to pick them up. And then it was finished — you know, the concert, and I came outside. It was cold, I was feeling a bit funny. Just walked along out there and I thought maybe I was bleeding. I looked but I wasn't. Some people like to be after a concert . . . but I wasn't.

Pause. Bell rings.

LEONARD. Well done Nicola! That was very very nice. Fabulous, wasn't it, folks, fabulous. I'll give you five whole points for that. The very most I'm empowered to give. You now have seven whole points. Now what we want you to do is to sing a song, one of the Yellow Jacks' songs, and you must try not to get any of the words wrong. Rex knows the words, and he'll be watching . . .

NICOLA *gets down off her chair, moves away.*

(*Sharp, still his DJ voice.*) Where are you going, Nicola . . .

NICOLA *half turns.* LEONARD *presses a button; covering music bursts out, the volume then dips.*

(*Louder.*) Where are you going?

NICOLA (*turns, faces him*). I was . . .

Pause. Music playing.

LEONARD. Where on earth do you think you're going?

NICOLA. I . . . I wanted a glass of water.

LEONARD (*calm*). You don't walk away like that, do you —

you can't leave the room, Nicola — we're in the middle of a competition, don't you realise —

NICOLA. I know.

LEONARD. You've got to stay here, till we finish. (*He stares at her.*) Haven't you . . . (*She doesn't move.*) Haven't you?

NICOLA. Yes, I . . . just wanted for a moment —

LEONARD. Come back here. We're on the air. Rex will get you something afterwards. (*He flicks the switch, the music dies.*) We're here, never fear. Nicola's just had a little accident, went for a walkabout — (*'Competition' voice.*) in the MIDDLE of the Competition of the Century! Extraordinary, but she's back now. The question is, Nicola, Nicola, now sing a song, and the song is 'Yellow Blues'. Stand up Nicola will you; Nicola is standing up, and remember the words must be right.

NICOLA. Yes.

Pause. She is standing, begins to sing, almost finishes a verse,* then very loud 'Wrong Answer' noise.

LEONARD. You've gone wrong, I'm afraid, Nicola. No points. Jane now, it's your turn. Your song is 'I can give you love' by the Yellow Jacks. Like to stand up for it? Jane is standing up now! (*Fast.*) Rex is sweating, we're all sweating, the girls have been chewing our fingers down to the bone. Ready Jane.

JANE *begins to sing*; very quiet. It lasts longer than* NICOLA's; *eventually the 'Wrong answer' buzzer goes.*

Jane, you're wrong this time, I'm afraid. No score for that round at all. But I think I'm going to give her a point, because she lasted quite a long time. Well done Jane. The girls have nice voices, don't they, pity we couldn't hear more of them. And now . . .

JANE. Can I . . . can I change places, I can't really . . . I mean I can't concentrate here . . . because of the lights up there, and him up there. (*She looks upwards at* REX's *box.*)

LEONARD (*fast*). Jane's asked to change places, we'll allow that, but what we'll do is — I'll ask you a question and then you both have to change places, run round the table, and the first one there, will have their microphone switched on, and will be able to try to answer. (*He looks at* NICOLA; *smiles.*) Ready

* Words and music at end of play.

to run, girls! And the question is — what were the names of the
four Beatles. Ready — steady — GO! (*They rush round the
table, the long way. As they do so.*) The girls are running now
— running round . . . and it's Jane who's there first, Jane who
gets there. Now the Beatles.

JANE (*she struggles*). Paul McCartney, John . . . John . . .

LEONARD. Have to give their surnames too.

JANE. John . . . and Ringo . . . John . . .

LEONARD. Have to hurry you.

JANE. I can't . . . sorry.

LEONARD. You must know the names of the Beatles. (*He
smiles.*) Now Nicola Davies, it's your big chance.

NICOLA. John . . . and Ringo . . . I can't remember the other one.
(*She looks at him. Deliberate.*) I don't know the other name.

Very loud 'Don't know' noise.

LEONARD. Nicola's lost another life because of that. George
Harrison, of course, was the answer. Nicola's only got one more
life to her. Nothing to worry about. Now quick round we go
again, we'll run before the question. Now! And they're off
again, it doesn't take them long, panting and (*Loud.*) —
round they go. (JANE *rushes round, but* NICOLA *walks it,
not trying at all.* JANE *easily gets there first.*) That was about
equal that time, I think — so we'll move on to the next
question. (*He looks at* NICOLA.) To the final question of the
Competition of the Century. And the great question is . . .
(*Pause.*) Wait for it, who can do the loudest scream for Ross
and the boys? Who can do the very loudest scream? Right now . . .
watch the windows, Rex! And you at home, watch your radio,
because they may break your sets, in fact they probably *will
break* them. And shatter all your ornaments. Nicola Davies is
first. You do a scream for us now, Nicola. (*Silence.*) Come on
Nicola, do a scream. That's all you have to do. (*Funny voice.*)
I'm sure she can do it. (NICOLA *sits still. Silence.*)

Come on Nicola. (*'Competition' voice.*) You can do that,
can't you, used to doing that. (NICOLA *looks up, opens her
mouth slightly, swallows hard; no noise.*) You can scream for
the boys, can't you. A really loud one. That's why you're here
isn't it? (*Louder.*) Isn't it! You haven't got long, Nicola.
(NICOLA *looks up, lets out a half-hearted scream.*) There!

She's done it! That wasn't a very loud one, was it, but now let's see what Jane can do. Ready Jane, just a scream for them.

JANE *sits up straight, lets out a very long scream — which starts loud, gets louder and louder and very very long.*

Jane wins that. Jane wins that point. That is the end of the Competition of the Century, and what is THE SCORE?

REX (*calls*). Very close, Leonard, very close indeed.

LEONARD. The scores are very close, so we are in fact going to invite you to cast your votes for the winner of our prize, going off with the Boys, to the centre of the universe, London Town. So ring us, on 55304, 55304, as quick as *you* can, as from NOW. Just say 'Jane' or 'Nicola', that's all we require, if it's engaged, just dial again at once. And hurry, we're waiting, high up here, in our little box; put us out of our misery.

REX (*shouts*). He's here. Ross has arrived!

LEONARD. And we've just heard, Ross is here, in the building, we've just felt the tremor go through it, and so, while we wait, butterflies swarming in our stomachs, let's have some proper music, a snatch of Rossini's 'Thieving Magpie', followed by a razor-sharp commercial or two. (*He puts on the music. They sit as it plays loudly. A long pause. Total stillness. To the GIRLS.*) You can get down now girls, if you want. (*He calls.*) Rex — get the girls a cup of tea. (*He looks at them.*) Do you want a cup of tea?

JANE *nods.* MICK *enters, grinning happily.*

NICOLA (*quiet*). No thanks.

LEONARD (*his manner suddenly very quiet, withdrawn; to REX*). Get Jane a cup of tea. And Nicola a glass of milk. You must have something, Nicola. And also wipe the spit off the mikes. (*He runs his hand along the desk.*) And wipe this too, it's filthy.

REX (*coming down from box*). Len — that was . . . that was incredible.

LEONARD (*fast*). Was it? I can do without your comments.

MICK. Yes it was, Mr Brazil — really great.

REX. Yes it was. It really was? It was a knockout. (*Smiles.*) I.ve got Carol and everybody standing by. Everything's waiting.

BIG JOHN *enters.*

LEONARD (*turns*). What are you doing there?

JOHN. Tremendous, Leonard. (*To* REX.) Wasn't it? (*He looks at the girls.*) You OK, girls — bearing up? I've got some News for you now.

LEONARD (*turns*). I wasn't expecting the News, I thought it had moved.

JOHN (*smiling, unaware*). No, same schedule as always. Of course — (*Smiles.*) — life must go on.

Off-stage, one telephone bell starts ringing faintly; it's answered.

REX. There we go. That's the first, they've started!

LEONARD. Get their drinks, Rex.

REX *goes.*

LEONARD. All right, girls, keep still where you are. Everyone keep still and don't speak. (*He moves to the mike, stops the record.*) And to interrupt there! For believe it or not, Big John is here with the local, national and international news.

BIG JOHN *sits, begins to read the News, at first mundane items.*

(*From the back wall in his strong DJ voice.*) They call this News. (*He looks at* NICOLA.) Waste of time, isn't it. (BIG JOHN *is still reading. Louder.*) Do they call this news?

The telephone bells are growing louder, more numerous. BIG JOHN *starts reading more violent items. Suddenly* LEONARD *moves over to the table, presses a button, music bursts out.*

(*'Competition' voice.*) This is the Final here. Thank you, Big John, for reading the news for us. Now keep ringing . . . Keep those bells going ting-a-ling-a-ling, ring us, *please*. And while I wait, I'll spin another circle of happiness and pour a little more sugar over the city.

Music continues.

JOHN (*astonished*). I was only half-way through, Leonard.

LEONARD. That was enough News, wasn't it? I haven't spent a whole week whipping up the audience to lose them — let them drift away because of this. (*He picks up the news bulletin.*) It can wait an hour, can't it. (*Loud.*) It's going to, anyway.

JOHN (*picking up the bulletin*). All right then — if that's what you want. (*Smiles.*) If *you* say so, first time that's ever happened. But since it's all going so tremendously — (*Smiles.*) — you can't let much get in your way right this moment, I can see that. Certainly I've never heard you in better form. Never. (*He smiles again.*) Are you going to make a lot out of the announcement of the result then . . . ?

LEONARD (*sharp*). All right John.

REX *enters with the drinks.*

JOHN (*smiles*). He's given me the chop, the News has got the chop for the first time.

REX. Yes, I heard — (*He gives drinks to the* GIRLS.)

JANE. Thank you. (*She tries to drink; it's very hot.*)

JOHN. But worth it just this once I think.

LEONARD (*not unpleasant*). Look, get out of here, John, go on — (JOHN *goes.*)

REX. Very soon now, girls, it'll be all over won't it? Leonard.

LEONARD (*back to him*). Yes?

REX. I wondered — I wondered if . . . *my minute* . . .

LEONARD. Did you? (*He cuts the music.*) Hello again — this is the control room, Competition Week — Leicester, England. Jane and Nicola are a little tense, aren't they, a little pale, but they're smiling bravely. Jane's rose is drooping slightly, Nicola's is bulging —

REX. Leonard . . . my minute . . .

LEONARD. Young Rex is here — calling out to me — he's very eager to have a chance to speak to you. Come here. (*He pulls* REX *forward.*) Here's your chance now, young Rex, how's it going?

REX. Hello — it's cracking along, Leonard, cracking. It's a great contest, isn't it, it's a fabulous contest, we're all agog back there — agog.

LEONARD. Are we. (*Staring at him.*) I see, Rex.

REX (*his voice getting louder, more confident*). The voting's very very close — the phones are jumping and ringing back there —

LEONARD. Jumping and ringing?

REX. Yes, Leonard — like they've got toothache. Want to hear it, folks? Want to hear them ringing folks? (*He bends the mike towards the bells.*)

LEONARD. We're not that posh any more, are we — ?

REX. No — this is *my* voice now Leonard — this is a Rex-type voice. And I just want to say 'Hello' to the listening millions with it. (*Fast, smiling.*) We really seem to have stirred the whole population, Leonard, like soup, we had callers of all ages back there, all sorts, from nine to ninety, all kinds of voices. The machines are over-loading back there — it's terrifying, it's wonderful.

LEONARD. The machines are so busy back there, they're going to explode.

REX. That's right Leonard. Back there we really need six hands and six feet. (*Grins.*) And six tongues! The girls are looking very happy at the moment, waiting for the result, didn't they do well — put up a great show.

LEONARD. We're making the most of things, aren't we Rex — of our chances.

REX. That's right, Leonard — got to, haven't I. And it's a great feeling up here, a whale of a time — except the tension is killing me — stop the tension Leonard — please . . . stop it, don't leave me, Len, don't leave me! You must stop the tension, it's killing me, my left foot's already gone dead.

LEONARD. You're a bit of a joker, aren't you, Rex. (*Louder.*) A bit of a joker.

REX. That's what we all are, Leonard. (*Imitating* LEONARD's *voice.*) That's why we're here folks — sitting up here, that's how we've been made, Leonard, isn't that right.

LEONARD. A bit of an aper, aren't we, Rex?

REX. That's what I am, Leonard.

LEONARD (*smiles*). And no questions asked.

REX. Of course not. No questions! That's all I can do, isn't it. I can't be any different. Play it again, Leonard.

LEONARD (*staring at him*). Play it again Rex. Rex likes the sound of his own voice, doesn't he?

REX. Yes! (*He laughs, standing over the mike.*) I like the sound of my own voice all right. And I'd just like to say to the listening millions, it's intoxicating up here, folks. I'm flying with it, really flying. (*He looks at* LEONARD.) That's what we enjoy, folks, isn't it! No need to fear, Len and Rex are here. (*Sudden change of tone. Exuberant, brilliant.*) And look . . . look at this Leonard — see what's happening — I'm losing a little weight, Leonard, see it's slipping off, it's starting to slip off, getting more now — see, reels and reels of fat are dropping off me onto the floor, they are! That's right, at this very moment, I wish you could see it folks, Rex is losing the fat, it's just fallen off, whole streams of it coming away all over the studio, some's even gone over the controls, look at it Leonard, have you ever seen anything like it — have you — But seriously folks —

LEONARD. All right. That's enough, isn't it? (*He pulls him away from the mike.*) His hand is still gripping the microphone, he has to be torn away. Go and silence those bells — Rex, the girls can't wait any more.

REX (*smiling broadly*). I'll go and silence them right away. (*He calls into the mike.*) Last calls please! (*He goes.*)

LEONARD (*into the mike*). Rex has gone for the result . . . has even dressed like me today, folks. Don't worry, girls, we're there now!

NICOLA. Where do you want me to sit?

LEONARD. Sit here please, Nicola Davies. The girls are sitting by me now, I'm holding their hands, one each. They're sitting very straight very calm. 'They're tough girls you've got there, Brazil, they can take it!' Rex is bringing in the result — smiling proudly; that's a big envelope you're holding, Sound Engineer Rex.

REX. Yes, it is . . . Leonard. (*Handing small card.*)

LEONARD (*his tone is very quiet*). It has the word 'Winner' on the front in red ink. I'm opening the envelope, this is the moment we've hoped for — (*He looks at the card.*) And the words on the card are — (*He glances at* NICOLA.) — Jane Harris. (*Booming voice, repeating like a machine, fast.*) Jane Harris is the winner, Jane Harris is the winner, Jane Harris is the winner. Let's have some applause. (*He brings up*

tumultuous applause on tape.) How do you feel, Jane?
(*Applause dies away.*)

JANE (*very quiet*). I feel . . . I feel . . . I feel . . .OK . . .

LEONARD. You must be very happy.

JANE (*quiet*). I am, yes.

LEONARD. How does Nicola feel? No hard feelings, I hope?

NICOLA (*quiet*). I'm OK.

LEONARD. Sound Engineer Rex is now going to take you, Jane, to where Ross is waiting. OK Rex, take her away.

REX. What? You mean me?

LEONARD (*not looking at him, with papers on desk*). Yes, you.

REX (*quietly, watching him*). You're not really letting me handle it all, are you?

LEONARD (*matter-of-fact*). Yes. It's what you want, isn't it?

REX. What? You're going to let me take her up — her up there, and deal with Ross and all that?

LEONARD (*not looking up*). That's right. Go on.

REX (*suddenly loud*). Christ — that's incredible. That's really incredible! (*He takes* JANE's *hand, pulls her towards the door.*) Come on, you're coming with me. (*He stops by the door.*) That's fantastic of you, Leonard. I'm not fired then.

LEONARD (*matter-of-fact*). No it doesn't seem you are. There's no stopping you, anyway.

REX (*looking at him*). I suppose not. (*Slight smile*). Not now.

LEONARD (*not looking up*). Go on, get out of my sight.

REX (*smile*). Right, Leonard. (*He waits for a moment, then goes out with* JANE.)

Music in the background, allowing LEONARD *to speak when he wants to.*

LEONARD. Rex . . . an unimaginative kid, isn't he . . . but going places! (LEONARD *glances up at* MICK, *who hastily leaves.* LEONARD *glances towards* NICOLA.) We'll be getting you a car, I hope, to run you back home. (*He is still pent up, brings music up slightly, switches onto air, red light on, sings along to the record. DJ voice, very quiet, very tense.*) Any moment we'll be switching to Studio A, so wherever you are, whatever you're doing, *don't* go anywhere near the switch-off knob, because any minute now you'll be hearing the voice of Rex spreading out towards you — and just a reminder, the great group are going to Nottingham and Manchester, next Wednesday and next Saturday. (*He brings up the music.* NICOLA *touches the red lightbulb;* LEONARD *continues looking towards her.*) Don't touch that, it's hot.

NICOLA. Yeah — it is. (*She takes her hand away, picks up her glass of milk.*)

LEONARD (*red light on again*). I, Leonard Brazil, am taking a break now, a quick *snap*, a brrrreak. (*Calling.*) Come in, Studio A, come in there. Hello — come in Rex with the furry voice, it's all yours then!

REX's VOICE (*on the intercom, booming over the loudspeakers*). Thank you Leonard for that introduction — Rex with the furry voice — there, we all liked that! And I have with me Jane, the lucky winner of the Competition of the Century, and the voice you've all been waiting for, in fact he's sitting in front of me and Jane right now, not only his voice, but *all of him,* the whole of the one and only, the greatest —

LEONARD *clicks it off.*

LEONARD. There.

NICOLA. Yes. (*Silence.*)

LEONARD *gets up, crumples a piece of paper.*

LEONARD. You OK?

NICOLA. Yes. (*She drops the full glass of milk; she hasn't drunk any of it.*)

LEONARD. Don't worry about that — it's a horrible mess in here anyway, isn't it?

NICOLA (*stares round the studio*). Yes.

LEONARD (*beginning to put on his jacket, and get his papers together*). Disgusting leftovers everywhere — the junk that's been sent in here, been pouring in, crammed away in every corner and going bad, probably; it's a nasty room, this, isn't it? (*He rubs at the milk on the floor with his foot.*) This milk'll go grey-blue in a moment, hasn't been cleaned for months in here. (*Loud.*) It doesn't *look like* the nerve-centre of something, does it?! Are you all right? (*He stands ready to go; looks at her.*)

NICOLA. Yes, I'm OK.

LEONARD. Don't worry! We probably couldn't have let you win anyway — could we. Because you won that LP. It wouldn't have looked very good if you'd won both, would it. Might have smelt, as they say. (*Pause.*) So you couldn't really have won.

NICOLA (*quiet, blank*). No . . . I know.

LEONARD. And you've done all right, haven't you, fought your way up into here for the final. You've been quite lucky really . . . (*Pause. Louder as* NICOLA *doesn't react.*) You have, you know.

NICOLA. I know that, yes.

LEONARD. Good. Not much to see in London anyway. You mustn't believe what I've been saying about it, it's dead. (*Pause.*) She's not going in *their* car anyway, she's going in the second car of the convoy with the cook and the luggage. Half an hour's chat at midnight with them in a motorway cafe and that's all she'll get. (*Pause.*) Here — (*He picks up a tape.*) — there's the tape of Ross, we've been playing, you can have it, if you want. (*Then quick change.*) No, I think it's got to be returned, *they* want to use it again. Stop us cutting him up. (*Suddenly loud, changing tone, straight to her.*) You can't really like this shit, can you, do you really, deep down inside, like this music?

She doesn't reply.

Do you!

NICOLA. A bit.

LEONARD. A bit — what does that mean? Either you do or you don't.

NICOLA. Yes, I do.

LEONARD. Right! (*Pause.*) You know, Nicola, if, ten years ago, five years ago even — (*Mock voice.*) — when things were very different, I'd been told that I'd be doing this job, playing this mindless milk chocolate pap, or manufactured synthetic violence endlessly to kids like you, I wouldn't have thought it remotely possible. (*Loud.*) Not at all, it's not exactly what

I imagined happening, not even in my greyest moments. It's extraordinary really that things have resulted in *you!* Do you know that?

NICOLA *is in front of him, silent.*

I've been offered a job, too, Nicola, to do some more, a much much bigger job, to chatter and gibber to many more people, lots of them, all waiting for it. And they want a decision. Quick answer.

NICOLA *watches him; he stares straight at her.*

This competition has been a great puller, you'll be pleased to know — the most successful of all, you're the only lucrative corner of the market left, that never fails, do you know that —

NICOLA (*staring straight at him*). Yes.

LEONARD. All you have to do is just stop buying, don't you, as simple as that, just stop, refuse to lap it up any more. Spit it out. *I mean that.* (*Suddenly loud.*) Do you — understand a word I'm saying?

NICOLA. Yes . . . I do.

LEONARD. I don't often meet any of my audience this close. I picked you out, do you know that, homed in on you . . . I picked out that voice, that slightly dead, empty sort of voice. Picked it out as Miss Average — which in fact you probably are not, and I followed that flat voice, each announcement was aimed at it.

NICOLA. Oh I see —

LEONARD. I let it get through each stage, let you clamber up here, because I wanted to see it . . . *meet you*, face you. (*Loud.*) And now you're here.

NICOLA (*quiet*). Yes.

LEONARD (*louder*). Is monosyllables all I'm going to get?

NICOLA. Yes.

LEONARD. What did you think of the Competition, then? (*Pause.*) Come on . . .

NICOLA. I don't know. (*She looks straight at him, cold.*) I don't know what I thought of it . . .

LEONARD (*abrasive*). Got a little out of hand — though it'll have sounded all right down there. Is that how you'd put it?

NICOLA. I don't know.

LEONARD. There was a touch of revenge, don't you think . . . I must want a little revenge . . . I glanced at you before the first question and saw that stare, that blank, infuriatingly vacant gaze, and then it just happened. I wanted to see just how far I *could push you*, how much you'd take — I was hoping you'd come back — that something would come shooting back, that you'd put up a fight Nicola. That you'd explode Nicola, you'd explode. Do you see, why didn't, why don't you . . .? (*Suddenly very loud.*) What's the matter with all you kids now, what is it? Come on, answer me, you know what I'm talking about, you're not a small child, you know what I mean. (*Pause. Abrasive.*) Are you going to talk to me?

NICOLA. No.

LEONARD. Why not?

NICOLA. I . . . (*Slight pause.*) I don't want to.

LEONARD. You don't want to. (*Pause.*) Come here. (*Loud.*) You're not hoping to get away with that, are you? Come here — come on Nicola. (*He pulls her to him, holds her by the arm.*) There — After all, I brought you up here for this meeting — (*He stares down at her — slight smile.*) What are you going to do now, Nicola? (*Pause. She doesn't move.*) You don't even look startled! Nothing!

NICOLA. No.

LEONARD (*really loud*). COME ON! (*He takes hold of her and shakes her really violently for several seconds.*)

After a pause.

Had no effect on you at all.

NICOLA (*slightly louder*). No.

LEONARD (*still holding her*). You almost feel, Nicola Davies — as if you're from another planet, do you know that?

No answer. He turns.

I would give you a lift, love, but I'm going for a walk. Got to work things out. (*Very matter-of-fact.*) What are we going to do, *love.* (*She looks about her.*) Are you all right? (*He looks*

about the studio.) You won't do anything silly — will you?
No. (*He flicks on the switch:* ROSS's *voice booms out.*)
There! (*He goes.*)

ROSS's VOICE (*on the speakers*). The receptions we've been
getting have been fabulous, *really* fabulous. You know, really
warm, and we've had no bother, no trouble of any kind,
everything's been calm and nice . . .

NICOLA *picks up her bag.*

. . . which should put a sock in all those critics who've written
about us. And to see those faces in the front row, they're
always a special sort of face in the front row. I don't know
how to describe it, but in the front row the faces are always
different.

NICOLA *fastens her bag, moves out of the studio.*

REX's VOICE (*on the speakers*). I know what you mean. I've
noticed that myself.

NICOLA *moves into the shop area.*

ROSS's VOICE (*on the speakers*). And also English front rows
are very different, totally different in a funny kind of way
from American front rows.

ROSS's *voice fades into the noise of the loud hum from the
shop's fridge, as the lights go down on the studio and up on
SUSAN in the supermarket . . .*

Scene Three

The supermarket. NICOLA *stands facing* SUSAN, *who is standing
opposite her holding a dustpan and brush. The shop has closed
its doors for the evening. Silent and dark except for the light
shining up from inside the fridge.*

SUSAN (*standing by the fridge*). Why are you so late? . . . I
wondered if you'd show up at all.

NICOLA. I got delayed.

SUSAN. I've been hanging around for a long time. Everybody's
gone, almost. Had to do this corner all by myself, and there
was lots of it, bloody place. Done most of it now anyway.
So you lost, didn't you.

NICOLA. Yes . . . that's right . . . I lost. (*Pause.* NICOLA *smiles slightly.*) You're right. (*She turns, bites her lip. Her mood is of contained violence.*)

SUSAN. You OK?

NICOLA. Yes, I'm OK. (*Louder.*) I'm all right. (*Pause.*) Did you hear it?

SUSAN. Yes, some of it.

NICOLA (*suddenly loud*). What do you mean, *some* of it?

SUSAN (*surprised*). No, I heard it. Quite a lot.

NICOLA (*very loud, savage*). Why didn't you hear all of it? (*Shouts.*) YOU SHOULD HAVE HEARD IT ALL! ALL OF IT! (*Pause, suddenly matter-of-fact.*) You'd only have been able to tell if you'd seen it. Been there. (*Pause.*) What did you think?

SUSAN. You were OK.

NICOLA (*pulls a fish-fingers packet out of the fridge, lets it drop*). OK?

SUSAN. Ought to have won, really.

NICOLA. Yes, I know. (*Pause.*) It was very hot up there.

SUSAN. They really put you through it.

NICOLA. Yeah — they did. (*Sudden smile.*) Hey, look at that. (*She pulls a leg of the dummy out of her bag.*) It fell off! That's what they made me make . . .

SUSAN. That's right. (*Smiles.*) Should do it to it all.

NICOLA *drops the bag with the dummy in it into the fridge. She smiles.*

NICOLA. Could put it in here, watch it go hard, freeze it, then pull it to bits easily. (*She pulls out the bag, stares into the fridge.*) Not much left in there, is there. (*Suddenly louder.*) Not much left!

SUSAN. Yes. (*She is bewildered by* NICOLA's *aggression.*)

NICOLA (*fast*). It was interesting really seeing him, seeing the DJ there, that was interesting! (*Suddenly louder, quite clenched.*) It was all interesting — *everything.* (*She pulls more packets of fish-fingers out of the fridge.*) Lot of these left, anyway.

As they talk, NICOLA *keeps pulling more packets out, undoing packets and dropping them.*

SUSAN. You going to queue for the concert?

NICOLA. Don't think so. I don't want to. They're all right, I s'pose. But I'm not going this time.

SUSAN. I might go. I don't know.

NICOLA. We're too late — *because of this.* Never get a good place in the queue. We'd never get in.

SUSAN (*suddenly relaxing*). No we wouldn't, would we.

NICOLA. Anyway it's not worth it. It really isn't!

She is holding the bag very tight, with the dummy inside; clenched violence inside her.

SUSAN. Are you *all right,* Nicola? Not ill or anything?

NICOLA (*louder*). Yuh, I'm fine. I told you. There's nothing wrong with me. (*She glances behind her.*) It's all different here when it's dark. (*By the fridge again.*) Nobody's watching. We could throw all this out if we wanted. And all the rest, spread it all over the shop — first thing they'd see Monday morning. They'd never know who'd done it.

SUSAN (*excited, uninhibited violence*). We can do the whole place, if we wanted, the cameras are off, dead, it wouldn't take long. The shelves come down easily, just fall off, and the stacks of cans, just have to pull one and millions come down, all pouring down. Could make them all do that. We could finish the whole place. It would be very easy really . . .

NICOLA. Yes. (*Loud.*) TEAR THROUGH IT IF WE WANTED. (*Pause.*) But it's not worth it really. I don't think it's worth it. Maybe next time. We'll see next time. (*Savage.*) I'll see next time.

SUSAN. What do you mean, next time?

NICOLA (*biting her lip*). I don't know, I don't know, do I?

SUSAN. You're in a funny mood, aren't you?

NICOLA (*clenched*). Yeah, that's right. I s'pose I am.

SUSAN. You are — never seen you like this —

NICOLA. No, that's right.

We hear the distant noise of a radio voice.

SUSAN. Sssh — hear that — listen to that.

NICOLA. What?

SUSAN. There — hear it now? That talking, that voice —

NICOLA. Yes.

SUSAN. Where's it coming from — somewhere near — very near. Can't see.

NICOLA. Don't know — but it's him all right.

The girls freeze.

The lights go down on the supermarket and cross fade to the studio . . .

Scene Four

The studio. LEONARD *is standing over controls. He stops his own noise.*

LEONARD (*his tone is quiet, sharp, he takes the speech slowly*). Hello. That was of course LB's jingle, and this is a very special moment, for which I'm standing, I really am, all alone in this studio, standing above the controls, which are hot and steaming. Thank you to Rex for his first great solo over the air. Very smooth, very good. That was a Rex-type interview. (*His tone changes.*) I've got to tell you something now which is quite a big surprise, because today I was offered a very big job in London, with the very splendid Capital Radio — and they offered me a lot of money and a large, large audience, in London, the capital of this fine country of ours, and a fat programme, to do my very own thing. They offered me this job earlier today. 'We must have you,' they said. 'We must have him.' And I have thought about it. (*He smiles; loud, jubilant.*) And I have accepted their offer! Yes I have. I'm going there. I, Len Brazil, Lennnnnn Brazil, am leaving you for Capital Land, London! I hear it'll need four people to fill my job here, which is nice, but I'm going to London where all the action is — where I'll be giving a few jokes and all the hits and more, all the sounds and more, all the luck and more, where I'll be seeing us through our present troubles, obliterating the bad times — that's a Big Word — and remembering the good times, oh yes — and letting people remember and letting them forget. Drowning all our sorrows, yes I said drowning, till

we're emerging out of the clouds, of course. And now I hope
my voice is reaching out, spreading to the four corners of our
area — across the whole city, through the blackness, swooping
into cars on the motorway and down chimneys, and through
brick walls and across pylons. (*His DJ voice.*) Over the whole
domain, until it reaches you. Because I want to say, I'm
sorry folks, but there it is. I'm sorry to leave you folks; but it's
how I've always wanted to do things of course. (*Smiles to
himself.*) What I wanted! Don't spit on the animals. I'm
speaking to *you* now, I am, remember this, when you're in
London, don't forget to give us a ring, want to hear from you,
over the air, at the very least don't forget to tune in. Yes tune
in! What are you doing Brazil — tell us — what on earth is he
doing — He's saying *Goodbye* and *don't forget*. We're going
to lick it, of course we will. No need to worry, no need to be
sad. Shout that out. So tune in, I said tune in. Because I'll
take your mind off things, oh yes. I will. (*He brings the music
in louder.*) Hear that — some music! Music for Len's farewell.
Tune in, I said. (*Very loud.*) TUNE IN. This is how we like
it. I've got some great times for you, oh yes. You know I'll
never let you down. That was Competition week. This is Len
Brazil. Be seeing you.

Fade.

YELLOW BLUES
Slowly

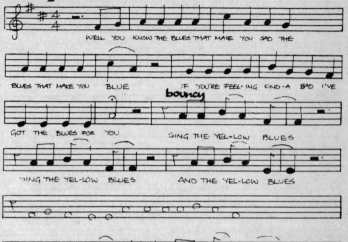

WELL YOU KNOW THE BLUES THAT MAKE YOU SAD THE BLUES THAT MAKE YOU BLUE IF YOU'RE FEEL-ING KIND-A BAD I'VE GOT THE BLUES FOR YOU

bouncy

SING THE YEL-LOW BLUES SING THE YEL-LOW BLUES AND THE YEL-LOW BLUES WILL MAKE YOU SMILE A-GAIN SING THE YEL-LOW BLUES

I CAN GIVE YOU LOVE
slow ballad – lilting beat

I'LL GIVE YOU AP-RIL SHOW-ERS DAFF-O-DILS IN MA-

-Y I'LL GIVE YOU JUNE-TIME FLOW-ERS RO-SES EV-ERY DA-

-Y DON'T YOU THINK THAT MA-Y-BE YOU COULD BE MY

BA--BY MY SWEET LIT-TLE ANG-EL FROM A--BOVE 'CAUSE I CAN GIVE YOU

LOVE*(YES! I CAN) I CAN GIVE YOU LOVE*(BE YOUR MAN) BE MY LIT-TLE

BA-BY DON'T YOU THINK THAT MAY-BE I CAN GIVE YOU LOVE

I LOVED YOU IN DEC-EM-BER----

*(These lines are sung by two singers on the record at the
beginning of Act Two, but not by JANE in the competition.
She leaves a pause, and beats time nervously with her foot.)

SHOUT ACROSS THE RIVER

Shout Across the River was first performed by the Royal Shakespeare Company at the Warehouse Theatre, London on 21 September 1978, with the following cast:

MRS FORSYTHE	Lynn Farleigh
CHRISTINE	Gwyneth Strong
MARTIN	Andrew Paul
LAWSON	Nigel Terry
MIKE	David Threlfall

Directed by Bill Alexander

The play is set in one week in summer, south of the river, on the edge of London.

Characters

MRS FORSYTHE. A good-looking woman in her mid-thirties. Long straight hair, keeps herself smartly and well dressed though her clothes are not expensive. She has sharp intelligent eyes, her manner is quietly nervous. Mild South London accent.

CHRISTINE. She is fourteen. Long blond hair, bright blue eyes. Capable of enormous energy and also moments of extreme stillness. South London accent. Very appealing smile, also a dangerous directness.

LAWSON. A tall impressive-looking man in his late thirties. Balding very slightly. Extremely efficient manner.

MIKE. He is eighteen, also blond and blue-eyed. Relaxed manner, good-humoured self-aware smile, tall thin body. A deadpan manner making it difficult to tell if he's joking or not. South London accent.

MARTIN. A large chunky boy of sixteen, aggressive, almost fierce appearance but intelligent eyes. South London accent.

Author's Note

It is important that MRS FORSYTHE's initial nervousness and loss of confidence are portrayed gently. She has a quiet humour and an ability to laugh at herself, even after moments of genuine panic. CHRISTINE's vibrant alacrity and humour are as important as her moments of darkness and danger.

ACT ONE

Scene One

A large office desk with a swivel chair behind it, and a plain metal and cloth chair facing it. The desk is covered with elaborate stationery. A large shiny stapler. Piles of crisp white paper and files. And an office ornament, wire branches with plastic balls on the end. We hear the steady tick of an unseen clock. The lighting is very bright. MRS FORSYTHE is sitting on the metal and cloth chair. She is alone on stage. She is a handsome woman in her mid-thirties, tidily dressed and wearing smart new boots. For a few seconds she sits completely still. She lifts the back of her hand up to her mouth.

MRS FORSYTHE (*very quiet*). Oh God . . .

She gets up and moves over to the desk, her movements are very preoccupied. She picks up the stapler and puts it down in a slightly different place. She gives the office ornament a casual flick, one of its branches snaps away in her hand. She looks at it for a second in surprise then tries to put it back on. It won't go.

MRS FORSYTHE (*muttering*). I only touched you. Get back you bloody thing.

She is bent over the desk, pushing at the object. LAWSON a man in his late thirties, dark black hair, a smart jacket and trousers, stands looking at her.

MRS FORSYTHE (*looking up, she smiles*). I was just waiting. I wasn't looking at anything – I was just – holding this.

She smiles nervously puts down the broken piece and moves from desk.

LAWSON (*looks at her in surprise for a moment then moves behind desk*). I'm only a minute late I think. I was in a departmental meeting that overran. Please sit down.

MRS FORSYTHE. Here?

It is the only chair on her side of the desk. She sits on it. LAWSON looks down at desk, at the mess she has created.

LAWSON. Just have to get things reorganised.

MRS FORSYTHE (*watching him – trying to smile*). What an enormous stapler.

LAWSON. Yes. (*He is tidying desk briskly.*) This desk is completely scratch-proof, graffiti-proof, it's the only one in the building *like* that and I guard it jealously. (*He smiles at her.*) You couldn't scratch it with a pneumatic drill. I'll be with you any second.

He lays out biros along the desk.

MRS FORSYTHE (*watching nervously*). That's a very loud tick that clock's got.

LAWSON (*smiles*). Yes, it keeps me company when I work late.

MRS FORSYTHE *rubs her leg with a rhythmic movement.*

MRS FORSYTHE (*nervous smile*). This room looks like where they take people to torture them – in films. (*Embarrassed.*) I mean . . . no windows and . . .

LAWSON *looks up, gives her a sharp quick smile. He is ready, he finds the right file.*

LAWSON. Now where are we?

He opens file – looks at MRS FORSYTHE – she has been rubbing her leg with the same rhythmic movement.

MRS FORSYTHE. These boots are rather tight. I haven't worn them before. They're very new. I expect you can smell the leather.

LAWSON (*surprised smile*). They look very nice. So you're (*He reads off the file.*) Mrs Forsythe?

MRS FORSYTHE *nods*, LAWSON *looks up.*

MRS FORSYTHE. Yes. That was a nod . . . Yes.

LAWSON. You're Christine's mother?

He turns page. Silence. He looks straight at MRS FORSYTHE.

MRS FORSYTHE. Yes . . . Sorry I didn't realise that was a question. Yes of course I am.

She winds end of her hair round finger nervously.

LAWSON. You're going to find the next few minutes rather shocking I'm afraid.

Silence. MRS FORSYTHE *swallows very hard.* LAWSON *reaches for another piece of paper.*

MRS FORSYTHE. Is there time to light a cigarette?

LAWSON. Go ahead.

MRS FORSYTHE (*cautiously*). Is there – an ashtray, or shall I use . . .

LAWSON (*looks round*). They tend to disappear.

He begins to look in drawer.

MRS FORSYTHE. No please . . . don't. I've decided I won't have one. (*Loud.*) I really don't want one.

LAWSON (*paper in front of him*). This is simply a list. It's taken from my report as her form master.

MRS FORSYTHE *holding a cigarette packet in her lap, fiddling with an unlighted cigarette.*

LAWSON (*more gentle smile*). And it may be disturbing. Your daughter Christine has been continually rude to members of the staff.

He glances up at her.

She has been found with semen on her clothes, on her tights and skirt, after break on at least four different occasions.

MRS FORSYTHE. Oh God . . .

LAWSON. She has used obscene language at Assembly – she has been known to push human excrement inside somebody else's gym shoes.

MRS FORSYTHE (*involuntarily nervous smile*). This is Christine you're talking about?

LAWSON. (*looks up*). Yes – these are not necessarily in any special order you understand. Just as the typist typed them. (*He continues.*) She has consistently played truant as you must be aware.

MRS FORSYTHE. No I . . . I mean I thought she was . . . No.

LAWSON. She has wandered about in areas which are strictly out of bounds including an episode on the school roof. She has been found with a number of offensive weapons on her person.

MRS FORSYTHE (*incredibly embarrassed*). I'm terribly sorry about this – I know that sounds so stupid.

She gets up and moves away from the chair across the room.

LAWSON. Wouldn't you prefer to keep sitting down Mrs Forsythe?

MRS FORSYTHE. Couldn't I stand. I just find it difficult sitting down. I know that sounds a little ridiculous. (*She smiles.*) But I really need to stand up. (*She leans against wall.*) I am listening. Go on. (*She smiles, embarrassed.*) I mean, *please* go on.

LAWSON. She has destroyed school property, she has smoked blatantly in every part of the school.

MRS FORSYTHE *glances down at her cigarette.*

Pornography has been found on her desk, and on her person.

MRS FORSYTHE (*quiet*). Pornography? (*She smiles helplessly.*) I don't know what to say – except I'm terribly sorry. You probably think I knew . . . I . . .

LAWSON (*carrying on*) She also . . .

MRS FORSYTHE. I'm sorry I thought you'd finished. (*Nervous jokey smile.*) I don't know if I can take much more.

LAWSON. She has refused to take detentions – and she has assaulted other children smaller than herself.

MRS FORSYTHE (*swallowing*). Assaulted!

LAWSON. Attacked – smashed their heads against walls and on the floor . . . She's a very violent girl.

He looks down the list.

I think that'll do.

Silence.

MRS FORSYTHE (*very quiet*). She doesn't seem to have left much out. (*Pause.*) I am really sorry . . . about all this . . .

LAWSON. She ought to be expelled of course – but we try not to expel anybody if humanly possible – (*He smiles.*) – which means we're turning our other cheek. Your daughter has been suspended, not surprisingly, for the rest of term, which is not long enough. She must report to this address –

He puts card down on table.

every other day, absolutely with fail. This is her school report.

He puts envelope on desk.

It's just been finished a few moments ago. If she really does behave herself we'll see if we can have her back next term. Now if you could sign here . . .

He suddenly looks straight at her. MRS FORSYTHE *is standing against the wall, her face turned away from him.*

LAWSON (*loud*). Mrs Forsythe?

MRS FORSYTHE (*turns*). Yes.

LAWSON. Are you listening to what I'm saying?

MRS FORSYTHE. Yes . . . yes of course.

She comes up to the desk – she has forgotten.

What do you want me to do?

LAWSON (*patiently*). Could you sign here?

He gives her biro.

LAWSON (*as she signs*). Is there a Mr Forsythe?

MRS FORSYTHE (*straight at him*). A husband you mean? There was. There still is – somewhere I expect. (*Embarrassed.*) We don't see each other –

Slight pause.

LAWSON. Right. You'll need that and that. (*Smiles.*) Our orange and green cards so you know who to contact in case of trouble. She must report every other day.

MRS FORSYTHE. She's always been very quiet at home. I suppose everybody who stands here says something like that. It must annoy you. (*She smiles.*) And she hasn't really – (*By desk, suddenly loud.*) Could? (*Pause.*) No.

LAWSON. Yes?

MRS FORSYTHE. No – I've changed my mind –

She moves her arm slightly.

LAWSON. At the end of term we . . .

MRS FORSYTHE (*suddenly, completely abrupt*). I think I'd like to go now.

She moves back to chair.

I really have to go now you see . . . I know all this must seem very peculiar – me jumping round the room and everything – and I know saying this now makes it sound probably twenty times worse, and you must think me rather, but it's just . . . I . . . it's . . . (*She swallows.*) Anyway . . .

Pause.

LAWSON. You don't seem to ever finish any of your sentences Mrs Forsythe.

MRS FORSYTHE. No. I had finished really . . . I . . . (*She moves across room.*) I just must go home – right *now*.

She moves straight to exit and then suddenly stops.

MRS FORSYTHE. I hate to ask this but how on earth do you get out of here. Out of the building.

LAWSON (*watching her closely*). Here, have a card, there's a map on it. (*He smiles.*) This room is kept locked twenty-four hours a day and is extremely difficult to find, there are no notices at all pointing to where it is, but the kids still manage to get in here. You find their spore marks all over the floor in the morning. (*He smiles.*) So to speak.

MRS FORSYTHE (*looking hard at card*). Yes . . .

LAWSON (*patient tone*). Just follow the map out – the other way up. (*He watches her.*) You sure you can manage?

MRS FORSYTHE. Thank you. (*At door.*) I don't want to keep apologising to you, but I am really terribly sorry about . . . about Christine, I will do everything in my power.

LAWSON (*smiles*). Yes . . .

MRS FORSYTHE *is half-way through door.*

And Mrs Forsythe.

She stops.

The biro. Please could I have my biro back.

MRS FORSYTHE (*smiles*). Oh God . . . Of course. I didn't mean . . . I didn't take it on purpose. I really didn't, I'm very sorry. (*She puts biro down.*) I . . .

Blackout.

Scene Two

The room. Small box sitting room. Cupboards, chairs, very sparse, and incredibly clean. CHRISTINE, fourteen years old, long straight hair, sharp blue eyes, is sitting with a pair of scissors cutting the TV Times into long thin strips. She does not look up at all. MRS FORSYTHE is standing leaning against the back wall looking at her.

MRS FORSYTHE (*clears her throat*). I've just been out.

CHRISTINE *doesn't turn, sound of scissors.*

Christine . . .

CHRISTINE *doesn't react – continues cutting.*

(*Loud.*) Christine.

CHRISTINE *does not react.*

MRS FORSYTHE (*suddenly fast*). I've just been out and I've been hearing, *Christine are you going to look at me?*

CHRISTINE *doesn't turn.*

And I've been told about these things you've done.

Pause.

Christine I can't talk to your back, it's difficult enough anyway.

CHRISTINE *continues cutting.*

MRS FORSYTHE (*shuffles with pieces of paper she's been given*). I've been to see Mr Laughton and he . . .

CHRISTINE (*without looking up*). Lawson . . . his name's Lawson.

MRS FORSYTHE. Mr Lawson. He told me everything. I had no idea at all that you'd been . . . Of course he didn't believe me. (*She swallows.*) He gave me your report. I don't even dare open it. It's still in its envelope. I've got a list here. They gave me a photo-copy to study. It's like reading something out of the Sunday paper. I'm going to read it to you.

CHRISTINE. I don't need to hear it. I know what I've done.

MRS FORSYTHE (*stops*). You really did *all* of these things Christine, I . . .

CHRISTINE. Yes that's right. (*She suddenly looks up. Loud.*) Except I did NOT assault smaller kids. That's a total lie. They put that one in. They liked the sound of it.

MRS FORSYTHE. But everything else – they really did find . . . things on your skirt and . . .

CHRISTINE (*getting up, totally matter-of-fact*). Yeah. Everything. OK. (*She moves across room.*) I'll say goodbye now. I've got to go out now.

MRS FORSYTHE (*confused*). Where're you going?

CHRISTINE. Out. I'll see you sometime – OK.

Just as CHRISTINE is about to pass her MRS FORSYTHE suddenly slams the door and locks it very hastily. She leans against it.

MRS FORSYTHE. You're . . . You're not leaving this room until I say you can.

CHRISTINE *stops and stares at her in astonishment.* MRS FORSYTHE *very nervous, standing against the door.*

CHRISTINE (*quiet*). What on earth are you doing?

MRS FORSYTHE. I locked the door.

CHRISTINE. I can see that.

MRS FORSYTHE. You're staying here in this room until we've
. . .

CHRISTINE. Until we've what? Who told you to do this?

MRS FORSYTHE. Nobody told me to do anything.

CHRISTINE (*louder*). Don't you realise I've got to go out now . . .
I have to be somewhere.

MRS FORSYTHE *looks nervous but doesn't move.*

MRS FORSYTHE. I ought to hit you really – oughtn't I.

CHRISTINE. I don't advise you to try.

MRS FORSYTHE. But I'd probably get maimed for life. (*Looking
at her.*) I don't think I'll take the chance.

CHRISTINE. Are you going to move? I need to leave in one
minute.

MRS FORSYTHE. Neither of us are leaving this room until I say
so. Not even into the rest of the flat. (*Nervous smile.*) I'll
swallow the key if necessary.

CHRISTINE (*begins to move round the room*). This is fucking
stupid.

MRS FORSYTHE. And don't use that language.

CHRISTINE *stops and stares straight at her.*

CHRISTINE. You know this is against the law.

MRS FORSYTHE. It certainly is not.

CHRISTINE. I'm telling you it's against the law. You aren't
allowed to lock me in. You'll get into terrible trouble. You're
not allowed to do anything to me – not even to touch me.

MRS FORSYTHE (*nervous*). You're staying here . . .

Pause, CHRISTINE *prowls round.*

CHRISTINE (*loud*). The windows aren't open! You realise we'll
run out of air in a moment. They'll find us lying on the floor
with our mouths open.

She is holding scissors, her tone sharp.

This is the worst thing you could do.

MRS FORSYTHE (*still up against door*). Don't try to threaten
me with those . . . I'm not going to have scissors waved at me
like that.

CHRISTINE. I'm not threatening you at all . . . (*She clicks the
scissors.*) I'm using these.

CHRISTINE *moves across room, holding scissors, touches top of sideboard.*

CHRISTINE. It's so clean here isn't it. You can hardly touch anything it's so clean. You've wiped this so much, you've rubbed a hole in the formica. Must have taken you hundreds of hours to do that.

Tone suddenly changes.

I've got to go to the toilet – Right now!

MRS FORSYTHE. I was wondering when you would try that.

CHRISTINE. You mean you don't believe me.

MRS FORSYTHE (*nervous*). No – and don't you dare try to prove me wrong.

CHRISTINE *moves over to the sideboard,* MRS FORSYTHE *watches her every move.*

CHRISTINE (*has picked up a packet from the sideboard*). GLUE. (*She reads off packet.*) Super Glue Three. Handle with care. Sticks for life. Amazing strength – bonds skin tissue in seconds. (*She looks up.*) Keep out of the reach of children.

MRS FORSYTHE. Don't play with that, Christine, it really is dangerous.

CHRISTINE. If you get this on your fingers you have to have them cut apart in hospital. You can stick pigeons on trees with this and they can't fly away. You can stick two lorries together, and they can't drive apart.

She begins to dab the wall with the glue.

It's true. (*She looks at* MRS FORSYTHE, *dangerous.*) Are you going to let me go?

MRS FORSYTHE. Are you threatening me with glue now! Because it won't work . . .

CHRISTINE *begins to cover top of sideboard with glue.*

MRS FORSYTHE (*becoming agitated*). But *please* don't make the flat dirty Christine.

CHRISTINE (*not looking at her, continuing*). Why?

MRS FORSYTHE. Because I'm asking you – because I really don't like it. *Please don't.* (*Tone changes.*) Please.

CHRISTINE (*stops, turns*). Just open the door.

MRS FORSYTHE. No.

CHRISTINE. Open it just for a second, I won't do anything. Just for a moment.

MRS FORSYTHE (*hesitating*). If I unlock this – you'll just rush straight out.

CHRISTINE. No I won't. (*Quiet.*) Of course I won't. Open it.

MRS FORSYTHE *turns struggles with door.*

MRS FORSYTHE. I can't get it unlocked.

But she manages, opens door and turns and looks at CHRISTINE. *They face each other for a second. Completely still. Then* CHRISTINE *makes a very slight movement and* MRS FORSYTHE *slams the door shut with a reflex action.*

CHRISTINE (*slight smile*). I was only . . . (*She completes the movement of her arm.*) going to have a scratch.

MRS FORSYTHE. I don't believe you.

She opens the door. She looks at CHRISTINE.

MRS FORSYTHE. You haven't moved.

CHRISTINE (*staring straight back*). Not yet.

MRS FORSYTHE (*quiet, staring at her*). That's a surprise.

Pause.

Don't stare at me like that.

CHRISTINE *stands very still.*

I've decided I'm not going to let you out of my sight during this time. I'm going to keep a watch on you Christine.

CHRISTINE. That may be difficult.

She suddenly with a sharp movement crosses the room.

Why don't I do something for you. (*She picks up a bundle of dirty clothes from side.*) I'll take these down the road for you?

MRS FORSYTHE (*taken by surprise*). What?

CHRISTINE *has collected the clothes.*

(*Agitated.*) Christine – I'll come.

CHRISTINE *crosses to leave,* MRS FORSYTHE *has moved,* CHRISTINE *looks back at her.*

CHRISTINE (*sharp*). What are you doing over there then?

MRS FORSYTHE *looks strange, rubbing her arm.*

MRS FORSYTHE. I told you. I'm coming. (*Nervous smile.*) You don't understand.

CHRISTINE. No.

MRS FORSYTHE (*swallows, nervous smile*). I'm coming. Please don't look at me. (*She looks away from* CHRISTINE.) Just go and I'll be right behind you.

CHRISTINE (*suspicious*). No, you go first. (*Impatient as* MRS FORSYTHE *moves.*) Come on.

MRS FORSYTHE (*tenses*). Don't look.

She passes CHRISTINE *and exits.*

Blackout.

Scene Three

The laundrette. One machine – new type without window. Three chairs. Soap powder. CHRISTINE *is standing leaning against the wall by machine.* MRS FORSYTHE *is sitting on chair. On the chair furthest from her are some neatly folded clothes. Evening sunlight. The machine is on and making a whining noise.*

MRS FORSYTHE. Stay where I can see you, and don't move around.

CHRISTINE (*standing still against the wall*). It's a fantastic evening out there for once. Really hot. What I'm missing . . .

She keeps her eyes on MRS FORSYTHE.

MRS FORSYTHE. Don't stare.

CHRISTINE. I wasn't sure at first – but I am now. You're twitching. See – you twitched then.

MRS FORSYTHE *hasn't moved.*

MRS FORSYTHE (*quiet*). I asked you not to stare.

CHRISTINE (*quiet*). I'm not even allowed to look at you now. (*Lifting the lid of the machine.*) You know people come in here sometimes, and put their unwanted kids inside these. It's a very easy way to get rid of them. They drop them in with the soap, and watch them go round and round.

MRS FORSYTHE (*looking straight at her*). What a disgusting thing to say. I wouldn't like to be a child of yours – it wouldn't last a week.

CHRISTINE (*quiet*). It's true.

She looks up at ceiling.

I've never seen so many notices as they have here. It's because this is a new kind of machine all in symbols you see, in case we can't read — we can do it by colours. But you have to be able to read the notice to understand the colours. They're trying them out all over South London. I saw it on the tele. It's an experiment and if you kick them —

She suddenly gives the machine a violent kick.

— it screams back at you. It ought to —

She kicks it again — the machine stops.

MRS FORSYTHE. What have you done now?

CHRISTINE. It's all right — we were nearly finished. It's only Mike's filthy clothes anyway.

MRS FORSYTHE. They're not at all filthy. He's a tidy boy. (*Cautiously looking at* CHRISTINE, *brisk.*) Do you — would you like a piece of chocolate? It's white chocolate, you might remember I used to buy it when . . .

She suddenly stops.

CHRISTINE. No. (*Smiles lightly.*) I think I'd better tell you now, I've stopped eating. I'm not eating *anything any more*. As a protest. Against unlawful suspension. Have you taken that in.

MRS FORSYTHE. Yes. (*Smiles.*) — How very convenient.

CHRISTINE *suddenly moves over.*

CHRISTINE. Do you think he's coming back?

She is by the chair.

MRS FORSYTHE. Who?

CHRISTINE. Him. These clothes here. Where do you think he is?

MRS FORSYTHE (*terribly startled*). You mean there's somebody here with us?

CHRISTINE (*looking at the clothes*). No — he's not here at the moment. (*Looks at how they've been folded.*) He's very neat. Smells of after-shave. (*She lifts shirt.*) It's really strong — they must be able to smell him for miles.

MRS FORSYTHE. Now don't touch them.

CHRISTINE (*feeling under the pile of neatly stacked clothes*). He's tucked something underneath, right underneath here.

She pulls them out — with a sudden flourish.

Dirty magazines!

MRS FORSYTHE. Oh my God Christine . . . Put them back at once . . . Don't mess them up.

CHRISTINE (*who is glancing at the titles of the plush, fat Mayfair-style magazines*). I don't like these ones. They're so glossy – they almost slip out of your hand. (*Looks at one large photo.*) She looks as if she's going to melt.

She produces her scissors and cuts out the page with fast sharp movements.

Why does he have to be so secret about it? Have to cure that.

She produces the glue.

MRS FORSYTHE (*apprehensive*). What are you doing now?

CHRISTINE (*suddenly lunges across with picture and sticks it on the man's sweater on top of pile*). Sticking it where it ought to be. (*She presses it down.*)

MRS FORSYTHE. Christine . . . for goodness' sake!

MRS FORSYTHE *grabs sweater.*

CHRISTINE. Too late – it's set.

MRS FORSYTHE *manages to tear it free of sweater.*

MRS FORSYTHE. That was a very close thing. Go back against the wall at once – you've done enough damage.

She has refolded sweater beautifully on top, tucked magazine back.

I hope he doesn't notice there's a page missing.

CHRISTINE (*leaning against wall watching MRS FORSYTHE's every move*). Last term I cut out several male parts and stuck them on my arm. I had seven. See! (*She rolls back her sleeve.*) There's still two there left.

She holds arm out – with two pieces of photos stuck on it.

MRS FORSYTHE (*staring back at her as CHRISTINE holds out arm*). Your pornography. It's not very impressive.

CHRISTINE (*quiet slight smile*). But they won't come off – they'll be there for the rest of my life.

MRS FORSYTHE *is looking down again.*

CHRISTINE (*watching her – an unwavering stare*). You twitched again, then. Can't you feel it when you do that?

MRS FORSYTHE. Christine you don't understand.

She is folding and unfolding the cardigan on her lap.

I'm going to have to tell you, and you just have to accept this, because it's rather strange. (*She swallows.*) I find it impossible . . . (*Sudden.*) I can't go out-of-doors Christine, I can't make myself go out of the flat. Even coming here, only a few hundred yards needs an incredible effort and I won't be able to stay here long. I'll have to go in a second . . . I will.

CHRISTINE (*slight smile*). I don't believe this.

MRS FORSYTHE (*slight smile*). I had the school today . . . (*She smiles at herself.*) It took me THREE HOURS to get there – I had to turn back twice. And that was fast for me. I'd given myself four hours. (*Nervous laugh.*) I wasn't taking any chances. And then when I got there, I went up to the door seventeen times before I got through it. I counted them.

CHRISTINE (*quiet*). Seventeen times?

MRS FORSYTHE (*Smiles*). Like one of those horses that keeps on refusing. I think everybody watching thought I was completely crazy.

CHRISTINE. I shouldn't worry about that, I told you everybody thinks that anyway.

MRS FORSYTHE (*nervous smile*). I wouldn't be able to go into the middle of London if I was paid a thousand pounds per minute . . . I can't take a bus now at all. I have to walk everywhere. Six months ago . . . about six months ago this is just one thing that happened . . . A bus conductor asked me for my fare, this is a tremendously silly story, but it happens to be true. And I said eight p although I knew it might be more – and he said where are you going? He was rather ugly, he had fierce red hair and I *LIED* to him. I don't know why, and all the time I was in the bus, I thought he was going to come up to me and shout at me, in front of all those people. And it went slowly – the bus – crawling down the road, almost inch by inch, and I could feel him breathing behind me, and when I got out I was shaking like this – (*She hunches her shoulder.*) – and I ran all the way home, like the devil was after me. And when I went to bed that night, I felt there was somebody down in the street, outside the window waiting and watching. And I looked outside and I'm SURE it was him. Jangling these coins in his pocket.

CHRISTINE (*watching her*). Frightened of a bus conductor. I can't believe it.

MRS FORSYTHE. I told you it was a ridiculous story. (*She looks at* CHRISTINE.) I can't be the only person who has such thoughts.

CHRISTINE. I shouldn't bet on it.

Their eyes meet.

MRS FORSYTHE. Stop looking at me like that.

She suddenly turns away, and puts on her cardigan, getting up.

Now don't get alarmed Christine . . .

CHRISTINE (*who's standing very still against the wall*). Alarmed?

MRS FORSYTHE (*voice tense*). But I just have to go now . . . I'm beginning to find it difficult. (*Suddenly louder.*) I can't stay here any longer.

CHRISTINE (*watching her with interest*). You can't go now, you haven't finished the washing . . .

MRS FORSYTHE. I've got to Christine, you can't meddle with this. (*Suddenly, loud.*) I need to be HOME. (*Moves.*) At home. (*She moves up and down.*) Get the clothes out quickly . . .

CHRISTINE (*standing, not moving at all*). Stop rushing about. You're making me giddy.

MRS FORSYTHE (*much quieter, seemingly calm*). I thought I was getting better –

She suddenly bursts into tears. CHRISTINE doesn't move or seemingly react. Just stares at her from wall. MRS FORSYTHE is on the chair again – crying.

CHRISTINE (*after watching her*). You're making a terrible noise – worse than this machine.

MRS FORSYTHE *continues to cry.*

CHRISTINE. And stop rubbing yourself or you'll make a hole in your arm.

MRS FORSYTHE (*through tears*). This just happens Christine you can't . . . (*She continues.*)

CHRISTINE. If you make that noise much longer alarms will go off.

She watches MRS FORSYTHE from wall.

Are you going to stop it or will I have to make you . . .?

MRS FORSYTHE *doesn't turn.*

CHRISTINE (*looking down at glue, reading off it*). Bonds skin tissue in seconds. (CHRISTINE *moves closer to* MRS FORSYTHE.) If you don't stop now I will seal you up with this.

MRS FORSYTHE *does not react.*

CHRISTINE *forcefully pushes glue straight towards* MRS FORSYTHE's *mouth.*

MRS FORSYTHE (*springs upwards and away, in amazement*). For Chrissake – you were really going to do that.

She stares at CHRISTINE.

You were going to put that stuff on my mouth.

CHRISTINE. Of course. I always mean what I say. Haven't you noticed that yet.

MRS FORSYTHE (*much quieter*). That's a terribly dangerous thing to do.

CHRISTINE. It stopped you.

MRS FORSYTHE (*reaching for her handkerchief, which is on chair, near clothes*). I didn't mean to get upset. It just comes. I haven't seen *you* cry since the age of three-and-a-half.

She pulls at handkerchief, it is stuck to the chair, she pulls at it hard.

I really can't move it – (*She pulls.*) It's stuck. Your glue . . .

CHRISTINE (*moving over to her, slight smile*). Here, you can have mine for a moment.

MRS FORSYTHE *is sitting on chair,* CHRISTINE *right by her.*

CHRISTINE. You're dribbling soap – it's all over you –

She brushes soap powder off MRS FORSYTHE's *clothes.*

It's in your ears too.

She takes back handkerchief.

Christ, the water that came out of you was really hot.

CHRISTINE *stares down at* MRS FORSYTHE – *who is sitting still, very tense.*

You *really can't* go out, can you.

MRS FORSYTHE. No.

CHRISTINE (*looking at her*). You're a real mess you know.

MRS FORSYTHE. All right Christine.

Pause.

CHRISTINE (*slow, deliberate*). You know I could do something about that since it seems I have to be with you all this time.

MRS FORSYTHE. What?

CHRISTINE. I could so something about you.

MRS FORSYTHE (*sharp*). How? In what way?

CHRISTINE. (*smiles*). I don't know. We'd have to see.

Pause.

You'd have to do exactly as I say of course. In everything.

MRS FORSYTHE. Don't be stupid Christine, you can't play with these things.

CHRISTINE. Can't you.

She is back against the wall staring at MRS FORSYTHE.

I've made you an offer and you're very lucky. It doesn't make any difference to me if you say yes or no. You won't get another offer like this.

MRS FORSYTHE. I'm not going to bargain with you Christine.

CHRISTINE (*slight smile*). It could make a very big difference to you but maybe you don't want that.

MRS FORSYTHE (*looking at her*). What's that meant to mean?

CHRISTINE. You've got precisely fifteen seconds to make up your mind. No point looking over there – there's nobody to ask. (*More steely.*) If you refuse – I'm going to go.

MRS FORSYTHE (*startled*). Go? Go where?

CHRISTINE (*smiles*). Time's running out . . .

MRS FORSYTHE. What's that smile for?

CHRISTINE. What smile? I didn't smile.

MRS FORSYTHE. I don't trust you at all.

CHRISTINE (*innocent*). I wonder why.

MRS FORSYTHE (*watching her closely*). What happens if you misbehave yourself – you're quite capable of driving me to the madhouse.

Pause.

CHRISTINE (*smiles*). That's a risk you'll just have to take.

Silence.

CHRISTINE. Your time's up. The offer's closed.

MRS FORSYTHE (*bewildered*). Christine . . . I don't . . .

CHRISTINE (*cutting her off*). Give me your keys. Go on. Then I could do some proper shopping for you tomorrow.

Staring at her, quietly, firm.

Give me the keys Mum.

MRS FORSYTHE *hesitates.*

MRS FORSYTHE. Just for tomorrow – just for then.

She gives her the keys.

CHRISTINE. Thanks.

MRS FORSYTHE (*very quiet*). I want them back already. You've got to report tomorrow.

CHRISTINE. That's right.

She looks down at the keys in her hand, slight smile to herself, puts them away quietly and turns to the machine.

Here. I'm sure it does squeal if you kick it in the right place.

She kicks the machine.

Just have to find the right place.

She gives it a terrible kick. The machine starts again.

Blackout.

Scene Four

The room. The phone ringing, starts in blackout and continues as the lights come up. The television is on, flickering in a corner. The volume is off. CHRISTINE enters through the front door. She is standing in long black dress as worn just after First World War – it doesn't fit her – and carrying an enormous bulky carrier-bag and a shopping basket. She places them in a corner.

CHRISTINE. Stop. Go on, stop.

The phone stops, she takes it off the hook.
She turns and moves over to the chest of drawers. Very carefully she opens the top drawer a few inches and glances in. She turns swiftly and closes it silently as MRS FORSYTHE enters from bedroom, and stops in doorway. She stares at CHRISTINE, she rubs one eye slightly, as she looks at her. It is obvious she's been asleep.

MRS FORSYTHE (*staring at black dress*). What on earth are you wearing that for?

CHRISTINE. I found it in your room.

MRS FORSYTHE (*quiet*). It was my grandmother's. It's not meant to be worn any more. You didn't walk down the High Street like that . . .

CHRISTINE. Yes.

MRS FORSYTHE. You were a terribly long time.

CHRISTINE. I took as long as it took.

CHRISTINE *is standing very still.*

MRS FORSYTHE (*switches the tele off – slightly embarrassed*). I leave this on sometimes, just playing to an empty room.

She looks up, manages to look CHRISTINE *in the eye for a second. Her manner is expectant, waiting for* CHRISTINE's *next move.* CHRISTINE *still.*

MRS FORSYTHE. So . . .

She looks away quickly and CHRISTINE *immediately moves over to chest of drawers.*

MRS FORSYTHE. Christine – don't open those drawers.

She moves backwards slightly nervously as CHRISTINE *pulls open the top drawer – it is crammed to overflowing with Green Shield Stamps, not in books, but loose-leafed streams of them.*

CHRISTINE (*lifting an armful off the top*). What are these?

MRS FORSYTHE. You can see what they are.

CHRISTINE *pulls out more and more.*

MRS FORSYTHE. I just collected a few.

CHRISTINE (*pulls them out in a long tangled stream*). I don't think they'll ever stop. I had no idea they were here.

She drops them unceremoniously all over the floor.

MRS FORSYTHE. I was trying to save a hundred thousand. Then I could have got a motorcycle for your brother. There were a lot of adverts, save for your family. It takes thirteen years on average. I haven't nearly got there.

CHRISTINE (*looking down into drawer*). They smell horrible.

She throws the last lot out and crosses over to cupboard, very clean white cupboard about four feet high. MRS FORSYTHE *is really very tense, rubbing her arm, as if in slight pain.*

CHRISTINE (*smiling to herself*). I've always wanted to look in your cupboards.

She looks up just before opening it and sees MRS FORSYTHE *rubbing her arm.*

CHRISTINE (*sharp*). What are you doing . . .?

MRS FORSYTHE (*trying to remain quiet*). It's just I would much rather if you didn't move anything of mine Christine – please.

CHRISTINE *opens cupboard doors and a deluge of magazines thumps onto floor.*

CHRISTINE (*looking up*). And what are these?

MRS FORSYTHE (*quiet*). Don't be absurd – you can see what they are.

CHRISTINE (*staring down at the floor*). You haven't read all these!

MRS FORSYTHE. Yes. All of them.

CHRISTINE. And you've probably got hundreds more stacked underneath the floorboards.

MRS FORSYTHE (*slight smile*). They give one a little pleasure. *You've* never read them.

CHRISTINE (*casually reading off the first one that has fallen open*). 'If you could have plastic surgery which part of the body would you choose: a) breasts b) nose c) ears d) knee-cap.' You didn't *really* read these did you!

She turns, reaches into cupboard.

Why have you got so many nail clippers?

She holds out a large fistful of clippers.

MRS FORSYTHE. I won fifty of them in a competition. I think it was only meant to be five, but they sent fifty by accident.

CHRISTINE (*pulling more out of cupboard*). And all these diets . . . (*Neatly folded stacks of diet pages out of magazines.*) In piles.

MRS FORSYTHE (*watching her, brief smile*). Are you going to leave me with anything at all may I ask?

CHRISTINE (*looking at diets*). You could have dieted yourself into any shape on earth.

MRS FORSYTHE. I often did.

CHRISTINE. I'll show you how to try out a diet.

She lifts first diet page to mouth and eats it, she crunches paper and swallows – MRS FORSYTHE *swallows.*

Not too bad a one. I'll try the others later. (*She turns to face rest of room.*) Now . . .

She looks up. MRS FORSYTHE *has flinched as* CHRISTINE *moves.*

CHRISTINE (*staring at her*). You flinch every time I touch something in the room.

MRS FORSYTHE. I don't flinch. Don't be silly.

CHRISTINE. If I move this.

She suddenly moves ornament on top of chest of drawers.

CHRISTINE. Look at you!

MRS FORSYTHE *has tensed again – she smiles nervously.*

CHRISTINE (*loud*). What are you holding your stomach for!

MRS FORSYTHE. It's just – it makes me feel very odd – anything being moved. You moving my things, I can't explain . . . (*Nervous smile.*) – but I come over queasy. I'm not used to it.

MRS FORSYTHE *picks up some magazines.*

CHRISTINE. You can't even move around in your own room! (*Slight smile at her.*) You're almost a vegetable in many ways, you know.

MRS FORSYTHE *is picking up magazines.*

MRS FORSYTHE. Thank you – that makes me feel a lot better.

CHRISTINE. And stop putting any of them back.

MRS FORSYTHE. I've got to.

CHRISTINE (*suddenly*). You will do as you're told. I FORBID YOU TO PUT THEM BACK.

MRS FORSYTHE (*amazed smile*). Forbid me?

She stops, CHRISTINE *is still.*

MRS FORSYTHE (*quiet*). It's so strange seeing you wear that dress – I keep on getting a shock every time I look at you.

CHRISTINE *turns and moves to last drawer in room.*

MRS FORSYTHE (*much louder*). Please not in there Christine.

CHRISTINE *has pulled out last drawer slowly.*

CHRISTINE. What on earth are these?

MRS FORSYTHE. Those are your father's. Some things I kept.

And they're important.

CHRISTINE (*peering into drawer*). It's like a kind of shrine for him in here – bad enough having his snooker pots in your bedroom. One of his socks. (*She tosses it out.*) One of his handkerchiefs. And some of his hair.

She holds up handful of human hair.

MRS FORSYTHE. I always cut his hair. I cut it just before he left – before he left me. He had lovely curly hair. You haven't got it, or your brother.

CHRISTINE. I remember. (*She drops hair.*) It's still greasy.

MRS FORSYTHE (*looking at hair*). Don't be silly. It was never greasy.

CHRISTINE (*looking at her*). You probably still smell of him don't you.

MRS FORSYTHE (*feeling the hair*). Christine – it's not still greasy at all. You lied.

CHRISTINE *is looking at her intently.*

CHRISTINE. That's a hideous dress. Take it off.

MRS FORSYTHE. What . . . (*Looks down at dress.*) Why?

CHRISTINE (*quieter*). Come on, take it off Mum. Go on, don't worry.

MRS FORSYTHE *takes off her dress. She stands in her bra and pants shyly, body exposed.*

CHRISTINE (*takes dress, sudden smile to herself*). Thank you. I think we'll burn this.

She moves towards exit.

MRS FORSYTHE (*her arms round herself*). Did you eat anything when you went out . . .

CHRISTINE. No of course not.

MRS FORSYTHE (*looks down at shopping bags – her voice anxious*). Christine – what are these?

She looks into giant carrier bag.

CHRISTINE (*totally unabashed*). Toasters –

MRS FORSYTHE (*her voice going very quiet*). What are you doing with six toasters?

She fumbles in the bag.

And an electric carving knife.

CHRISTINE. I've acquired them.

MRS FORSYTHE (*lifting one out and then dropping it*). Oh my God! They're completely new – they've still got their prices on.

She stares very worried into bag.

There's over one hundred pounds of electrical goods here.

She looks up, CHRISTINE *is standing quite still, smiling.*

You've taken them haven't you! I mean . . . (*She swallows.*) – without paying . . . (*Louder.*) Why on earth did you do that . . .?

CHRISTINE (*slight perverse smile*). I just took them. I don't want them – particularly.

MRS FORSYTHE. You PROMISED me that if I gave you the keys . . .

CHRISTINE. I never promised you anything! And you know it!

MRS FORSYTHE. I don't want these toasters in my flat . . .

CHRISTINE. You can make lots of toast now. You can make toast for the whole of Croydon. You could drown in it.

MRS FORSYTHE (*who's been moving the bag a few feet*). It's still a terribly stupid thing to do when you've been suspended.

CHRISTINE (*loud, animated*). You can go into any shop in the High Street, nobody is BUYING anything – there's no one anywhere near the cash desks! Everybody in the shop is squashed into corners having a quick grab. Even the store detectives! It's true. You can watch them.

MRS FORSYTHE. That's no reason for you to. I'm . . . I'm not having you acting like a criminal.

CHRISTINE. I don't mind if you phone the police right now. (*She watches her.*) Go on . . . I really don't mind.

Silence.

MRS FORSYTHE. You're going to take them back immediately . . . leave them on the doorstep.

She moves towards CHRISTINE *and the bag.*

CHRISTINE. Don't try to come near me.

CHRISTINE *waves the electric carving knife at her.*

MRS FORSYTHE (*quieter*). Don't . . . wave an electric carving knife at me Christine . . .

CHRISTINE (*looks round*). Where's the plug?

MRS FORSYTHE (*instinctively moving towards her – but nervous*). You took advantage of me Christine.

CHRISTINE (*really loud*). I DID *NOT* take advantage – can't you realise I've made no sort of bargain with you *at all*.

MRS FORSYTHE (*louder*). Stop waving that thing at me!

MIKE *is standing in doorway. He is eighteen, blond hair, bright intelligent eyes. They both look up, startled.*

MRS FORSYTHE (*relieved*). Mike!

MIKE *surveying the devastation across the floor.*

MIKE. Has somebody broken in then?

MRS FORSYTHE (*very embarrassed*). No, I, I was just trying to tidy up . . . Give me back my dress Christine.

CHRISTINE *doesn't move.* MRS FORSYTHE *trying to regain her composure.*

I don't like the phone being off the hook – it's unlucky.

CHRISTINE (*suddenly very steely*). Leave it off. I said leave it off.

MRS FORSYTHE *leaves it off.*

CHRISTINE (*taking a quick look at* MIKE). Look at him, he's so covered in mud it looks like they've been using him for the ball.

She folds dress which she's been holding across her arm and leaves. MRS FORSYTHE *stands in her bra and pants, embarrassed, with* MIKE. *Her arms round herself for a moment.* MIKE *not looking at her – moves to go.*

MRS FORSYTHE. Mike! – I'm so glad you're here now. (MIKE *stops.*)

MIKE. Why?

MRS FORSYTHE (*confused*). I'm not sure . . . I hadn't really seen you for a bit.

MIKE (*not looking at her*). That's nothing unusual.

MRS FORSYTHE. No, but you're here now.

MIKE. Yes, that's right.

MRS FORSYTHE *has moved backwards and is feeling with her hand in one of the open drawers – while still looking at* MIKE.

MIKE (*glances at her in surprise*). What are you doing?

MRS FORSYTHE. I'm just looking to see if Christine's hidden any food in here. (*She smiles nervously.*) I don't *know* if she's been eating or not, I know it sounds odd . . .

Silence. MRS FORSYTHE *looks down at her body.*

I was just changing . . . I'm sorry. (*Her hands go round herself again.*) I expect you're wondering why the room is in such a terrible mess . . .

MIKE (*who has been watching her with bewilderment*). No. I wasn't.

MRS FORSYTHE. You weren't.

She moves nearer, MIKE *is very embarrassed – as she is close to him.*

You're all covered in mud Mike.

MIKE. Yes. I had noticed.

He's not looking at her although she's very close to him.

And I want it washed for tomorrow because we're playing again.

MRS FORSYTHE. Of course. (*She looks at shirt, touches collar.*) Let's have a look at it.

MIKE (*hunching slightly in corner*). It doesn't have to be really spotless this time. You don't have to wash it five times or whatever you do so it shines. But it *must* be ready by tomorrow.

MRS FORSYTHE (*genuine*). Of course. I'll do it without fail tonight. There won't be a stain to be seen. Did you win?

MIKE (*surprised*). Why do you want to know?

MRS FORSYTHE. I don't . . . (*Nervous smile.*) I mean I don't have to know.

Slight pause.

MIKE. We won of course. Is my tea ready then?

MRS FORSYTHE. Not quite yet. It will be in a minute. I must have forgotten. You know I never usually forget.

She reaches up.

You've got some mud in your hair Mike – just there –

MIKE (*not looking at her*). Yes. (*Turning away slightly, she's very close to him.*)

MRS FORSYTHE (*reaches for the mud in his hair*). I'll take it out for you.

MIKE (*awkward, uneasy*). Could you just not –

She pulls at mud in his hair.

Don't do that it hurts. You'll pull the hair out.

MRS FORSYTHE (*smiles*). It just spoils your hair.

MIKE. You really hurt me. Couldn't you . . .

He moves slightly away from her in the corner.

MRS FORSYTHE (*moving close*). Your sister and I . . . have an arrangement while she's been suspended – an arrangement for her own good, so don't wonder about anything.

MIKE. Good. Fine.

MRS FORSYTHE. Why are you looking away all the time?

MIKE. It's just . . . Why are you so close? (*Embarrassed by her undressed.*) OK. Just stop creeping up on me like that. And touching me.

MRS FORSYTHE. I'm sorry. (*She glances at him.*) Could you promise me something Mike?

MIKE (*not looking at her*). What?

MRS FORSYTHE. I know it sounds strange . . . but could you make sure not to leave me alone with your sister. Just for the next forty-eight hours. Can you promise me that . . .

MIKE. What on earth for?

MRS FORSYTHE (*pause, looks away*). Because she can be very violent. Just look at me for a moment.

She turns his head.

MIKE. I asked you to stop touching me.

MRS FORSYTHE. Just look at me.

MIKE *looks for a split moment.*

Promise me.

MIKE. I'll have to see.

MRS FORSYTHE. Please.

CHRISTINE *is standing in doorway. She's holding a second black dress.*

CHRISTINE. Why are you poking him?

MRS FORSYTHE *moves away from* MIKE.

Now put this on. It's the other one.

She holds out second black dress to MRS FORSYTHE.

MRS FORSYTHE. I can't wear that. It'll make me look really idiotic –

CHRISTINE (*really sharp*). You're going to do what you're told –

MRS FORSYTHE *glances towards* MIKE.

MRS FORSYTHE (*tensing in front of* MIKE). Christine – you're not to talk to me like that –

CHRISTINE (*even sharper*). Are you going to put it on or not?

MRS FORSYTHE *puts it on.*

(*Slight smile.*) That's right. There. And then you're going to be given your second lesson – you're going to go out in it.

MRS FORSYTHE (*quiet*). Out. Don't be absurd –

She picks up telephone receiver trying to regain her composure.

MRS FORSYTHE. And I don't want this off any more.

She replaces the receiver – the phone immediately starts to ring.

(*Staring at it, totally bewildered.*) Oh Christ . . .

She automatically glances at CHRISTINE.

Who is it ringing?

MIKE (*watching them both*). Why don't you pick it up and ask –

CHRISTINE. I haven't told her to answer it yet.

MIKE. They mean business whoever it is.

MIKE *moves, exits.*

MRS FORSYTHE (*loud after him*). Mike! What did I just ask you . . .

MIKE *exits. Phone still rings.*

CHRISTINE. What did you just ask him?

Pause – phone ringing.

I've decided, you can answer it. And if it's about me because I haven't reported, tell them I'm not here. That I've gone away.

MRS FORSYTHE. No. I'm not going to lie for you . . .

CHRISTINE (*totally matter-of-fact*). It's your choice.

MRS FORSYTHE. I am *not* going to lie.

She picks up telephone.

(*Very nervous.*) Hello . . . Yes . . . speaking . . . who . . . (*Trying to sound surprised.*) Oh my daughter. Yes. She's . . .

She looks at CHRISTINE *against wall.*

She's . . .

She looks at CHRISTINE.

Yes I know she's . . . (*She swallows.*) not here. No.

CHRISTINE *slight smile.*

She's . . .

CHRISTINE. She went to Manchester.

MRS FORSYTHE. She went to Manchester. No, I don't know for how long.

CHRISTINE. For seven days.

MRS FORSYTHE. For just a couple of days. No . . . I've just remembered that.

CHRISTINE. She's with her boyfriend.

MRS FORSYTHE. I, I believe she's gone to visit relatives. I mean I know she has . . . I didn't know beforehand, I mean she just went. (*Trying to put receiver down.*) I'm afraid that's all I know.

She puts her hand over the receiver.

God he's persistent! No, I don't. Yes I realise . . .

CHRISTINE (*suddenly moving near phone, really loud*). Tell them that they're *complete LIARS*, I did not assault kids.

MRS FORSYTHE *holds receiver behind her back.*

MRS FORSYTHE. Christine! For goodness' sake. (*Into phone.*) No, I just dropped the phone, but I've caught it now. I must go now. She'll definitely be back. Yes. Yes. Goodbye!

She slams down phone. Her hands go up to her face.

MRS FORSYTHE. I'm blushing Christine. I feel I'm covered in blushes all over – and they'll probably never go away.

CHRISTINE. I've never ever known somebody lie so badly. It really was terrible.

MRS FORSYTHE. You'd *better* take these things back.

She looks at CHRISTINE *quiet, bewildered.*

Why did I do that Christine?

CHRISTINE *just smiles.*

I'm protecting you now.

Scene Five

Ice-cream parlour, three bright white chairs, a white table and a poster for ice-creams. CHRISTINE and MRS FORSYTHE in their long black dresses. MIKE in a black suit. CHRISTINE holding two ice-cream cones, and a large ice-cream tub. MRS FORSYTHE is standing a little distance from chairs – warm evening sun.

CHRISTINE. Come on you can manage it.

    MRS FORSYTHE moves towards table.

    (*Handing out ice-creams.*) There's one for each of you and some more when you've finished.

    MRS FORSYTHE by chair.

CHRISTINE. It's safe to sit down.

MRS FORSYTHE. This is the furthest I've been for six months – I haven't eaten ice-cream since I bought it for you. There were hundreds of people in the High Street who could have spotted us –

CHRISTINE. Let them.

MRS FORSYTHE. You mustn't be seen. (*Smiling nervously.*) I can hardly look up without getting giddy.

MIKE. We're not very high up.

MRS FORSYTHE. I can only stay here three minutes –

MIKE. This place wasn't here when I passed last week.

CHRISTINE. It's just grown.

MRS FORSYTHE. Eat yours too Christine.

    But CHRISTINE isn't eating.

MIKE. It's changing round here all the time. It's changing while we sit here. (*He smiles.*) Every half-an-hour. You know they're trying new things out on us all the time round here. Experiments with them. (*He points back.*) That road safety poster back there, the one with the head covered in broken glass, they're trying that out this side of the river first – to see if we can take it. If we can, they'll release it to the rest of the world. New types of pedestrian crossings to see how many of us get killed. They try new foods out all the time all over the suburbs, new music in the discos, it's true! If they invented the third sex they'd try it out here first.

MRS FORSYTHE (*smoking nervously*). I remember when there was a stream near here with sticklebacks in it –

CHRISTINE *looks at her.*

Big ones — as fat as sausages.

MIKE. That was still here a year ago.

CHRISTINE (*moving up to* MRS FORSYTHE). There's still the view, come on look at it, look up.

She moves MRS FORSYTHE's *head.*

MRS FORSYTHE (*hunching up*). No I'm all right . . .

CHRISTINE (*glancing over her shoulder*). I walked down the railway line back there once, and saw a dead fox. It was a really strong colour, bright red and orange. (*Smiles.*) I was going to bring it home to you.

MRS FORSYTHE. You must let me go home Christine if I need to. (*Quiet.*) It'd be dangerous to try to stop me.

Sound of phone ringing.

MRS FORSYTHE. Oh Christ! It's the phone again.

Looks over her shoulder.

CHRISTINE (*animated*). Don't be really stupid! We're not at home now — that won't be for us!

The phone continues to ring.

MIKE. We hope. Where's it coming from? (*Looks down.*) Maybe from under the floor.

He pulls at his suit.

MIKE. I wish you hadn't got me to wear this — I might burn under this glass roof.

The phone stops.

MRS FORSYTHE. It's stopped.

MIKE. You know it's getting hotter and hotter, I mean everywhere, all over the world, even when it doesn't feel like it.

He is leaning back in his chair smoking.

I read somewhere the Arctic is going to melt quite soon and the whole of Europe is going to be drowned. Completely covered in four hundred feet of water.

MRS FORSYTHE (*quietly smoking*). I thought you said everything was going to become terribly hard.

CHRISTINE. He reads all those disaster books and he never finishes any of them. He's never got to the end of a book in his life. I think he'd be ill if he really finished one.

MRS FORSYTHE (*looking at* CHRISTINE). But you don't read anything.

CHRISTINE (*smiles*). No, I'm never going to read a book again.

MRS FORSYTHE (*looking at* CHRISTINE's *ice-cream*). Why aren't you eating that?

MIKE (*lying on his back, staring up*). And if that doesn't happen, the Arctic melting, something that is definitely going to happen will be the Thames. It's going to overflow. It's bound to happen. It's been proved. And the whole of the centre of London will just disappear or float about, millions of people will just be wiped out in half-an-hour. It might even reach us here. We could be just on the edge of it. (*He smiles.*) That could happen next year you know – or the year after. (*Quieter.*) We may never be here again.

He stares at the ceiling.

There's a new disease too! From Africa. A fly or something that eats through your skin – eats all the way through, and there aren't enough birds left to kill it, so it's spreading to Europe, eating its way through hundreds.

MRS FORSYTHE. Could you please stop this Mike. I think we know what's going to happen now . . .

She looks up.

Oh my God there's somebody watching us.

CHRISTINE (*glancing behind her*). Who?

MRS FORSYTHE. He's looking at us. He's coming over here Christine – you will get rid of him. (*Quieter.*) I wish you hadn't made me come.

MARTIN *enters, sixteen years old, thick-set, dark hair, big broad smile.*

MARTIN. Christine. (CHRISTINE *turns*). Thought it had to be you . . .

MARTIN *moves forward. The three of them sitting in black round the table.*

MRS FORSYTHE (*looking down at floor*). You know him?

CHRISTINE (*sharp, to* MARTIN). Why are you out of school?

MARTIN. I had to get out. Even though it's so near the end of term. (*To* MIKE.) It's my last term, going to be free in a few days. But each day gets more and more difficult. I just can't sit still any more.

CHRISTINE. They should nail you to the floor.

MARTIN (*broad grin*). Nice to see you anyway.

CHRISTINE. You haven't met my family have you? This is my brother Mike – and this is my sister Marian.

MRS FORSYTHE (*looks up astonished*). What did you say?

MARTIN. Very pleased to meet you.

CHRISTINE. Marian's my big sister. (*Looks at* MRS FORSYTHE.) It's a nice name, Marian.

MARTIN (*smiling broadly at her*). Have I seen you down at the disco at all with Christine . . .

MRS FORSYTHE (*wildly embarrassed*). I . . . no . . . I . . .

CHRISTINE. My sister has difficulty answering certain kinds of questions, she's saying no.

MARTIN (*looking at them suddenly*). You're all in black.

CHRISTINE. Are we? You noticed.

MARTIN. You look as if you've been to a funeral.

CHRISTINE. We have. We've just been to my mother's funeral.

MIKE *giggles.* MRS FORSYTHE, *who has been fingering the bowl of ice-cream nervously, looks stunned.*

MRS FORSYTHE. I . . . I think I'd like to go.

MARTIN (*to* CHRISTINE). Sorry, I didn't know. I'm . . .

CHRISTINE. Nor did we. She went very suddenly. (*To* MRS FORSYTHE.) Didn't she?

CHRISTINE *sudden slight smile to herself.*

She was cremated – we've still got the ashes with us.

She puts an urn-like object onto the table next to the ice-cream.

MRS FORSYTHE (*jumps up*). Oh my God! Christine what on earth . . .

CHRISTINE (*simply carrying on*). She wanted to be scattered up here. She didn't go out much you see, so we're about to scatter her . . .

MIKE (*slightly worried*). What is that Christine . . .

CHRISTINE (*broad smile to* MRS FORSYTHE *who isn't looking*). You can reach these through the cemetery wall, it's falling to bits.

MIKE (*looking at urn*). What is that?

MARTIN (*bewildered*). So you've just come from there have you?

MRS FORSYTHE. I really am going to faint.

CHRISTINE (*sharp*). Marian behave yourself. (*To* MARTIN.) Do you want to have a look at her?

She begins to take top off it.

MRS FORSYTHE (*very quiet*). Please Christine.

CHRISTINE (*unscrewing top*). She was quite a plump woman. She took ages to burn. She wasn't very healthy. She had a big nose. (*Top comes off.*) We may still see it.

MIKE *stares at it uneasily.*

MARTIN (*a bit shocked*). You're sure you're meant to take the top off?

CHRISTINE (*looking in*). There she is – that's all that's left of her.

She pulls the ashes out.

She won't be missed much. (*To* MARTIN.) Do you want to hold some, you can if you like.

MRS FORSYTHE (*suddenly really loudly*). I SEE WHAT IT IS. (*Pointing at urn.*) That's your father's, of course! Your father's snooker prize.

Silence.

MARTIN (*getting up*). I think I'll get myself an ice-cream.

MRS FORSYTHE. You HORRIBLE GIRL –

MIKE (*feeling ash*). And this is just burnt newspaper.

CHRISTINE (*grinning, holding pot*). I was worried you'd see me carrying it. I was going to produce it on the bus where there would have been more people. But I couldn't wait.

She stares at pot.

It's a really hideous thing.

She rolls it across the floor.

MRS FORSYTHE. That was a very nasty idea Christine.

CHRISTINE. It worked.

MRS FORSYTHE (*fast to* MIKE). I bet you knew about it.

MIKE. I didn't!

MRS FORSYTHE (*looking back at* CHRISTINE). I never know how to tell when you're about to try something like that, you look so normal.

MARTIN. Sorry. I'm a bit behindhand. You haven't been to a funeral then!

CHRISTINE. Not yet. (*She smiles broadly.*) One day you'll all be at my funeral. (*Straight at* MRS FORSYTHE.) Do you remember Marian when we went rollerskating outside the flat one day when you were about twelve – and I was about six, *look* at *me*, and we rollerskated all the way back through the front door, past Mum and Dad's bedroom, and they had left their door open, and we slid up to it, and there they were doing it, right in front of our eyes, and we watched, we were a bit interested, and he was really rather rough with her, like he was in a terrible hurry and she still had her shoes on and her face was all squashed up and miserable.

MRS FORSYTHE. You *didn't* watch Christine! I don't believe you. You couldn't have done.

MIKE. I expect she did.

CHRISTINE (*to* MRS FORSYTHE). *You* were there. I remember the shoes Mum was wearing – her flat brown ones. (*Fast.*) And do you remember one day at tea when you and me made Mum a worm sandwich and she was really going to eat it, she never noticed anything but unfortunately it crawled away while she was stirring her tea.

MIKE. Where was I all this time?

CHRISTINE. I never saw you at all.

MARTIN *is looking from one to the other very bewildered.*

MRS FORSYTHE (*not looking up*). I've got to go now.

CHRISTINE (*powerful*). You will stay where you are!

Smiles more gently by her side to MARTIN.

We're going to take my sister Marian into London one day, she hasn't been there since she was a small girl.

MRS FORSYTHE (*very quiet – not looking up*). Don't be stupid – it's not nearly so long as that.

MIKE. It's several years ago.

MRS FORSYTHE (*very, very quiet*). It's just so very expensive now . . . and your father sends me very little.

MIKE. You know it can take as long to get to the centre of London from here as it can to fly to New York – including the walk to the bus.

CHRISTINE. It can take even longer.

MIKE (*broad smile*). Soon it will only take an hour to fly to New York. They've already invented a plane with different shaped wings – and you won't be able to get into London at all because it'll cost too much.

MARTIN (*smiling*). I went down the West End not so long ago. It was great!

MIKE. It's dying you know – the centre of London – it's true.

MARTIN. I watched through the huge window of this hamburger restaurant first. That's where they pass heroin – I was told about it. Because it's so bright and clear there, so many lights. The least likely place in the world. I watched for hours through this window.

MIKE (*smoking*). By 1995 nobody will be living in the centre – it will just be full of rotting streets and businesses and garbage. And then quite quickly it will start spreading towards here, pushing people further and further out – for miles and miles. We could watch it coming from here –

MARTIN. I saw these three girls when I was there, walking arm in arm. They were quite young you know. They were like identical twins except there were three of them and they all had long white hair. I followed them for ages. I had some good times there. (*Grins.*) Lots of action! (*Smiles.*)

CHRISTINE. And you showed them all didn't you! I went there once. All the men were covered in ash and smelt of drink.

Looks at MRS FORSYTHE.

And she hasn't been there since the age of six.

MRS FORSYTHE *is sitting very still, hunched up.*

Why haven't you finished your ice-cream?

MRS FORSYTHE *starts to shake and a noise comes out of her.*

MIKE (*quiet*). Is she laughing or crying . . .?

CHRISTINE (*quite gentle*). I think she's laughing. She can't be crying because she's not allowed to . . .

MRS FORSYTHE *makes noise – we genuinely can't tell if it's laughter or tears – her shoulders really shaking.*

CHRISTINE. Come on you're laughing aren't you. I think she is. There she smiled.

CHRISTINE *turns to* MIKE, *quite sharp.*

Better find her a taxi Mike.

MIKE. We'll never find one here.

CHRISTINE. Do as you're told. (*Looks at* MRS FORSYTHE.) She's gone quiet.

MIKE *exits.* MRS FORSYTHE *looks up, moves her hair.*

CHRISTINE. That's better!

The two women move away – in their long dresses.

MARTIN. Christine. (*Moving up to her confidentially.*) I just want to mention something to you (*Broad grin.*) since you haven't really been to a funeral.

CHRISTINE. I think I know what that sort of smile means. You mention it in front of my sister or not at all.

MARTIN (*surprised*). In front of her?

They both look at MRS FORSYTHE.

MRS FORSYTHE. I think I'll just go and wait for you outside Christine.

CHRISTINE (*sharp*). I want you to stay here. You're meant to keep an eye on me always.

The two women stand next to each other, staring at him.

MARTIN (*really embarrassed*). I can't really mention it in front of her.

CHRISTINE. Then you don't get to mention it at all.

MARTIN *is nervously fingering his shirt.*

Why are you doing your top button up all the time?

MARTIN (*glancing from one to other*). It's just I heard . . .

CHRISTINE (*innocently*). You heard what?

MARTIN. Rick told me – that you will, that for eighty p you will . . . you – (*Grins.*) – well you know what you do!

CHRISTINE. What do I do?

MARTIN. Christ. (*Embarrassed.*) You know . . . (*Makes a rude gesture.*)

CHRISTINE (*staring at him*). You mean sex – do you?

MARTIN (*broad grin*). Yes. Everybody knows about you Christine, you never stop doing it do you, you get through so many. People are in and out of you like a yoyo. You'll do it everywhere, I've heard, anywhere at all. (*He smiles.*) You'd do it on the moon if you got the chance.

Silence. Evening light dying.

CHRISTINE. (*very slight smile*). They told you I did that did they
– and for *eighty* p.

Phone starts ringing. MRS FORSYTHE *instinctively looks over
her shoulder.*

CHRISTINE. It's all right Marian that won't be for us. And don't
smoke too much will you . . .

MARTIN. I wanted to ask you now you know, because I'm not
likely to be getting another chance am I – after this week. (*He
grins.*) You might not be so readily available. *I mean everybody
knows where you're heading Christine.* It's obvious, you'll be in
some sort of clink one day, and probably very soon, everybody
can see it coming. (*He grins.*) I mean the way you carry on.

Pause.

CHRISTINE. Is that what people say? I'm glad to hear they know
so much about me – what else do they know?

MARTIN (*grins*). They know what you are Christine.

CHRISTINE. You ought to change that grin of yours – it really is
rather greedy.

MARTIN. Will you? – Will you . . .

Pause.

CHRISTINE (*she smiles at him*). My price has gone up since I've
been suspended. I'm much more expensive now, inflation and
everything. It's eight quid for now.

MARTIN (*swallowing*). Eight quid. So!

CHRISTINE. That's without extras. Another quid and you get
those and my sister here thrown in for free.

MRS FORSYTHE *tries to open her mouth but no sound comes
out.*

MARTIN (*looks at* CHRISTINE). Is that true?

MRS FORSYTHE *tries to shake her head – but it will hardly
move, she stands still.*

CHRISTINE. I told you, my sister doesn't like questions.

MARTIN. I'll see what I can raise Christine.

CHRISTINE. And you'll have to be quick won't you – because as
you say, I may not be around for very long –

She moves towards him, smiling to herself.

He knows everything this man – he knows where I've been
heading ever since he set eyes on me – ever since he heard me

speak. He could tell just like that Marian. And you'll have to clean yourself up a bit – (*She touches him.*) – get rid of some of those spots, they're really showing up this evening.

She touches his hand.

What big hands he's got, huge flopping things, you could walk for miles on those – (*Gently.*) and try to look a little sensible.

MARTIN (*uneasy*). OK. I'll . . . get the money.

CHRISTINE. The ice-cream's melted. (*She moves.*) Marian, say goodbye to our friend here, we may be enjoying his company soon. Go on.

MRS FORSYTHE (*tries to open her mouth*). I . . . I . . .

CHRISTINE. Yes?

MRS FORSYTHE *is totally speechless.*

MARTIN. Is she all right?

CHRISTINE. She'll be fine.

Blackout. The phone continues to ring in the distance.

Scene Six

The phone in the distance stops ringing, and immediately the phone on stage begins to ring as MIKE, CHRISTINE *and* MRS FORSYTHE *come through the door into a darkened room.*

CHRISTINE (*coming through door, looking at phone*). Kick it – go on.

MIKE (*staring down at phone*). They'll be coming round soon and banging on the door and the window at four o'clock in the morning . . . looking for you Christine.

MRS FORSYTHE *suddenly moves over and picks up the phone without prompting.*

MRS FORSYTHE (*quiet*). No my daughter is not here. No she isn't.

CHRISTINE (*loud, by phone*). Ask them why they're phoning so late – it's after hours.

MRS FORSYTHE *about to replace receiver.*

CHRISTINE. No leave it off so he can listen if he wants. It's probably Lawson.

CHRISTINE *leaves receiver lying there without having rung off.*

MRS FORSYTHE (*she smiles with relief*). We're back.

MIKE (*leaning against the wall slightly uneasy*). We're all together in one room you realise at the same time . . . (*Matter-of-fact.*) Can't remember that happening . . .

MRS FORSYTHE. I could hardly open my mouth Christine just now out there, like it was completely frozen. I *couldn't talk*.

CHRISTINE. You'll do better next time.

MRS FORSYTHE. What next time. I'll never be able to go out again after that.

MIKE. It's very quiet tonight isn't it?

CHRISTINE. And what are you staring at me like that for?

MRS FORSYTHE. You rollerskated round here when you were small and spied on me and your father?

CHRISTINE. That's right.

MRS FORSYTHE. What else did you watch me doing and store up for later?

CHRISTINE. Things you'd never begin to guess.

MRS FORSYTHE. You probably saw all my secrets – like when I hid one of your father's shirts for three years because I'd spilt coffee over it. I moved it from hiding place to hiding place.

CHRISTINE. I remember everything, starting much earlier than you imagine. When I was one.

MRS FORSYTHE. You probably even remember that I didn't breast feed you.

CHRISTINE. I won't warn you again, you're not allowed to talk about the past.

MRS FORSYTHE *moves towards* CHRISTINE.

What are you doing?

MRS FORSYTHE. I want to know if you're really not eating now.

She tries to catch hold of her.

I'm going to see what you look like under there.

CHRISTINE. Don't you dare try to touch me.

MIKE. You shouldn't take risks with her you know.

MRS FORSYTHE. I just want to have a look at you under there, see if you're really losing weight.

CHRISTINE. I shouldn't try to pull my clothes off, that wouldn't be very wise.

MRS FORSYTHE. They're not your clothes.

CHRISTINE. You're not allowed to look at me I'm afraid. Do you understand? Don't, keep away.

MIKE. She'll probably produce a flick knife in a second, you have to be careful.

CHRISTINE. You keep out of this.

MRS FORSYTHE. You're staying here with me Mike, remember. (*To* CHRISTINE.) Just keep still.

CHRISTINE. You've got to calm down now, you're just over-excited.

MRS FORSYTHE. I'm over-excited! Am I!

CHRISTINE. Yes because it's such a long time since you've really been out. It's gone to your head.

MRS FORSYTHE. All right then. You're going to eat something for me Christine right now, and I'm going to watch you do it. You can damage your brain if you don't.

CHRISTINE. No.

MRS FORSYTHE. Come, on eat this for me, one bite for me.

CHRISTINE. If you try to force that down me – I will make you eat all of this stuff – (*Kicks magazines.*) – for a whole month, and you will never recover ever.

MIKE. You really had better be careful of her, I'm not joking.

MRS FORSYTHE. Come on, it's just chocolate. I want to see you do it.

CHRISTINE. I told you – YOU CAN'T TOUCH!

CHRISTINE *grabs hold of her arm, and pulls her round trying to rip the chocolate out of her hand and throw it away. They both fall over on the floor,* MRS FORSYTHE *grappling back – trying to stop* CHRISTINE *attacking her.*

MRS FORSYTHE. Stop it Christine – *please you're hurting me.*

CHRISTINE *pulls her arms back.*

MRS FORSYTHE. Don't just stand there – help me Mike! She's really hurting me.

MIKE (*shrugging*). What can I do if you want to kill each other. (*He picks up* CHRISTINE'S *diary.*) I've got your diary here Christine – I'll read it.

CHRISTINE. Go ahead.

Sits astride MRS FORSYTHE who is lying on floor.

I told you *not to disobey me*.

MRS FORSYTHE (*really quiet lying underneath her*). I'm sorry Christine – I didn't mean to . . .

She stares up at her.

CHRISTINE (*staring down at MRS FORSYTHE, quiet smile*). You look like the road safety poster like that.

MRS FORSYTHE. You're so strong. (*Smiles to herself.*) You obviously are eating something.

CHRISTINE. Don't try to do anything like that again – you could get yourself badly hurt. And I mean that.

MIKE. Do I get my food soon? I'm waiting. And I want it.

MRS FORSYTHE. Yes. I must get Mike's food. I really must.

She doesn't try to move.

You're very heavy Christine.

But CHRISTINE doesn't move.

I'm not going to protect you for ever you know. I've lied for you so much already and I'm someone who doesn't lie. (*Quiet.*) I won't.

CHRISTINE (*sharp*). You will do as you're told.

MRS FORSYTHE (*very quiet*). Yes Christine, I know.

CHRISTINE (*sitting astride her, smiles*). You don't exist any more – only my version of you. You're my creation, I invented you this week – sent electric shocks through to that brain. And you can't stop now because you're only half-finished. (*Quiet.*) You'd be left a sort of cripple if you did. (*She turns MRS FORSYTHE's face.*) I can do anything I like with you if I wish.

MRS FORSYTHE (*very quiet*). I hate you when you say things like that. You look almost evil – and it frightens me. (*Quiet.*) But I can't do anything. (*Shifting under her.*) You are very heavy Christine. (*Looks at her anxiously.*) You're not just playing around with me are you – promise me that Christine. (*Pause.*) Just promise.

CHRISTINE (*on top of her*). I told you I don't make promises – ever.

MRS FORSYTHE (*quiet, no urgency*). I must get Mike's food. He's waiting.

MIKE. You must.

MRS FORSYTHE. In a minute. (*Very quiet.*) I don't know what you've done to me Christine.

MIKE (*leaning against wall*). If I do it – try to cook – I'll probably cause an explosion. I often expect the gas just to go up, rip through the house, rip the roof off, break up the whole road.

MRS FORSYTHE (*her tone very different*). Christine . . .

CHRISTINE (*still astride her*). Yes.

MRS FORSYTHE (*she laughs very quietly to herself, lying under* CHRISTINE *on the floor*). You won't believe this . . . but I think . . . I think I've wetted myself.

CHRISTINE. That's bad.

MRS FORSYTHE. I have you know . . . (*She smiles to herself.*) It's terrible . . . (*Very quiet.*) I'm sorry Christine.

CHRISTINE (*looking down at her, quiet*). I may have to give you a bath in a moment.

Pause – the two women staring at each other.

MIKE (*leaning against wall suddenly reads slowly out of* CHRISTINE's *diary*). 'July 15th 1978. The weather is strange. It's been strange all these last days, strange shaped clouds and a big sticky haze making things a funny colour.' It's all about the weather! 'Took some toasters – there's a bad new record playing out of every shop in the High Street. I've probably not got many days left. I'll have to see. Won't I. Me and Mike and Mum are going out. I don't know where. I'm *thin* . . . really *thin*.'

MIKE *puts the book down and leans back against wall.*

I can't read the rest of it.

Fade.

ACT TWO

Scene One

Early morning – the room. CHRISTINE *stands alone in black dress. The television is on – blank screen and hum.* CHRISTINE *looks very pale and white, but her hair is brushed. She's holding large scissors. She moves over to the chair and sits down placing the scissors beside her. Takes out diary and begins to write very slowly, speaking as she writes quietly. Early morning light.*

CHRISTINE. 'Thursday July 22nd 1978. Quarter to five in the morning. Somebody's left the tele on all night . . . It is the last day of term . . . I have hardly slept at all but I feel even better than usual.'

She suddenly looks up, drops diary, moves over to the phone. She takes out of pocket chewing gum packet on which she has written something – she glances at it – then dials number.

CHRISTINE. Is that 761 8649? (*Slight pause.*) Is that Mr Lawson? (*Slight pause.*) This is your 4.45 alarm call . . . No. As requested, you're sure you're awake now. Good. And you're going to stay that way.

She puts down the phone and walks back to chair. The phone rings back. She swings round with scissors, approaches the phone and severs the lead in two with a quick cut of the scissors. The receiver of the phone drops off, and it stops ringing. She sits down again and continues to write.

CHRISTINE. 'All the people leaving school will be going on the rampage tonight. Screaming and shouting and drinking, and emptying themselves all over the street. I can hear the first trains running into London. It's the only noise. It doesn't feel like summer. I may not see another one! I don't feel the effects at all so far. I haven't eaten anything for seven days – and haven't drunk anything for two! (*She smiles to herself.*) I'm going to bury this diary I think on Streatham Common – let them dig it up in a hundred years' time.

Suddenly noise and pictures come up on the television – some sort of newsreel. CHRISTINE *starts in amazement, stares at tele apprehensively.*

CHRISTINE. But it's only five o'clock! (*To herself.*) What are they showing things now for?

She stands right up to screen, lifts her hand up to screen and touches the glass. She holds it there for a moment. The picture disappears. She steps back from the screen, glances at television.

CHRISTINE. Where's it gone?

She moves round the television and then sees MRS FORSYTHE *is standing in the doorway.* MRS FORSYTHE *is also wearing long black dress. They stare at each other for a split second, both surprised.*

MRS FORSYTHE. You're up early.

CHRISTINE. So are you.

MRS FORSYTHE. Yes. I couldn't really sleep.

CHRISTINE. I haven't slept at all – not even for half an hour.

MRS FORSYTHE. Your brother's not in his room.

CHRISTINE. He's disappeared again has he. He likes slipping away. He'll be somewhere dreaming about the end of the world.

MRS FORSYTHE *is staring at her.*

What's the matter?

MRS FORSYTHE. You look strange standing there Christine. There's something different about you this morning.

CHRISTINE. No there isn't.

She starts putting on black lipstick.

MRS FORSYTHE (*staring at her warily*). You look very pretty for once.

CHRISTINE *doesn't even react.*

When you look like that you could make almost anybody in the world do what you want. (*Pause.*) For a few hours at least.

CHRISTINE (*putting black lipstick on*). I know.

MRS FORSYTHE. So why are you putting that black mess on your lips?

CHRISTINE. Because I feel like some. (*She suddenly turns very animated.*) You know I've seen some tele! (*Points at screen.*) On there at this time in the morning! It was left on all night and then suddenly these pictures appeared, without any warning, they flashed up, just now.

MRS FORSYTHE. I don't believe you.

CHRISTINE. I *saw them*! I never lie. You should know that by now.

MRS FORSYTHE (*slight smile*). That hasn't been proved yet, Christine. (*Looking at TV.*) So why isn't it still here?

CHRISTINE. It just went. (*Loud.*) Must be for politicians and people like that, things the rest of us are not meant to see. That we just don't know about, all sorts of experiments and secret business. They run them now when nobody else would think to look. I only discovered them by accident didn't I.

MRS FORSYTHE (*slight smile*). What was on it?

CHRISTINE. People in helmets. Lots of them. (*Carrying straight on.*) I saw something yesterday! History on there. About Hitler and all that. About Hitler when he went to America.

MRS FORSYTHE. It can't have been about that Christine – because Hitler never went to America.

CHRISTINE. I saw it! It was a history programme, I can tell what it was. They were old news reports. It all happened, they were showing it. He'd just invaded. And they showed Hitler driving down the main street in New York in a line of cars, with his ambassadors behind him. And all this paper was pouring from the skyscrapers, coming out of their windows, pouring down their sides like water. And they gave him a twenty gun salute. And he climbed the Empire State Building, and when he was on the top helicopters flew all around him, and jet planes flew very low and painted the German flag in the sky.

MRS FORSYTHE. You've got a lot of things muddled up, Christine, you ought to watch the good programmes properly.

CHRISTINE. Don't talk to me like that. (*She stares straight at her.*) And then they showed him on a tiger hunt, it was another time when he was hunting tigers in India or somewhere. Hitler and a lot of the German generals and they were wearing white sun hats, and they were on elephants. (*Loud.*) Stop shaking your head like that because I saw it on here, in this room! They shot so many tigers they were all over the ground. And he'd shot a few people as well, their bodies piled up high in these clumps, and he had his foot on one pile holding his gun, while his photograph was taken, and then they started chopping the bodies up and cooking them for him on campfires . . .

MRS FORSYTHE (*cutting her off*). Don't be repulsive Christine. You make it all sound like a cartoon.

She suddenly moves towards her angered as CHRISTINE *gives a slight smile.*

And don't smile like that about it!

CHRISTINE (*quiet but dangerous*). Don't try to touch me – I won't warn you again. I was just telling you what I had seen.

Silence.

MRS FORSYTHE. And when was this happening?

CHRISTINE *looks straight at her, surprised.*

When did Hitler happen Christine – about how many years ago? I asked you a question.

CHRISTINE. When I was small.

MRS FORSYTHE *watches her.*

A hundred years ago.

MRS FORSYTHE. Do you know who Hitler was?

CHRISTINE *looks at her.*

CHRISTINE (*smiles*). You aren't allowed to ask me questions.

MRS FORSYTHE. I don't think you really know.

CHRISTINE *doesn't react.*

Don't they ever tell you anything at school. You shouldn't let programmes slide together like that.

CHRISTINE (*loud*). I told you! I saw it on here. On *this*.

She has moved over to the television and pulls the back off it.

MRS FORSYTHE (*very urgent*). Christine! Don't touch it while it's on – it's very dangerous, especially when it's hot.

She switches it off.

CHRISTINE. Yes – it's almost burning here. (*She peers into the back of the television.*) All sorts of things in here we didn't know about. I don't understand how it all works. (*She pulls out another piece of television.*) There's some mould growing here too . . .

MRS FORSYTHE (*smiles to herself*). I've watched that machine by myself for hours and hours. They have special programmes for us in the afternoons – people like me. I've just read your report Christine.

CHRISTINE *looks up.*

CHRISTINE. So you finally opened it.

MRS FORSYTHE (*smiles*). It isn't one of the better reports that I've read.

MRS FORSYTHE *looks straight at her, quiet.*

A lot of it is very true.

CHRISTINE. Of course.

MRS FORSYTHE. They'll be coming round here very soon –

ringing the doorbell. This is going to be our last day together.

CHRISTINE. I will decide that.

MRS FORSYTHE (*quieter*). It will have to be.

CHRISTINE. I'm going to take you out again tonight. It's time for your third lesson. We're going up West. Right into the centre.

MRS FORSYTHE (*suddenly nervous and vulnerable again*). No I can't Christine.

CHRISTINE. You will do what you're told. Come here. (*She beckons.*) Come here now.

MRS FORSYTHE *moving automatically towards* CHRISTINE.

MRS FORSYTHE. What are you going to do?

CHRISTINE (*lifts black lipstick up to* MRS FORSYTHE's *mouth*). Keep still.

MRS FORSYTHE. No. I don't want that ugly stuff on me.

CHRISTINE (*quietly but firmly*). Come on. Just keep still.

She puts black lipstick on MRS FORSYTHE, *standing there together.*

(*As she does so.*) People don't realise you're my mum you know. They think you look far too young.

MRS FORSYTHE (*pleased*). Do they? I remember when I . . .

CHRISTINE (*quiet*). You're not allowed to talk about the past. (*She continues with make-up.*) I've stopped drinking you know. Drinking anything at all.

MRS FORSYTHE *tries to say something.*

Don't move. I haven't drunk anything for forty-eight hours which means . . .

MRS FORSYTHE (*moving away, touching her black lips*). Really, then why are you still here? (*She looks at her.*) You should be dead by now in that case.

CHRISTINE. That's right. I just thought I'd let you know.

MRS FORSYTHE (*quiet*). That's a very evil smile Christine.

MIKE *enters. His clothes are covered in mud – and his hair is bedraggled.*

CHRISTINE (*loud*). Where've you been?

MIKE *leans against the wall.*

MIKE. I've just been for a walk. (*He half closes his eyes.*) I've just been out . . . and . . .

CHRISTINE. What on earth's the matter with him?

MRS FORSYTHE. Mike!

MIKE. I've just been mugged that's all.

MRS FORSYTHE (*startled*). What do you mean?

MIKE (*louder*). I went out for a walk – I couldn't sleep, and suddenly there was this enormous crack on the back of my head. Like that.

He indicates his neck.

I thought I was coming apart.

MRS FORSYTHE. Who were they – what happened?

MIKE (*leaning against the wall*). I don't know. I didn't see. There were these guys coming towards me on the pavement. And they had this really stupid look in their eyes. I could see they had been looking for somebody to do over all night.

MRS FORSYTHE. And you didn't try to avoid them?

MIKE. Of course I bloody did. I told you there was this sudden crack from behind me.

CHRISTINE. From *behind* you?

MIKE (*sudden, loud*). Does it matter where it *came from*? (*Suddenly much quieter.*) I'm all right. (*Very quiet.*) It's just that I feel a little . . .

CHRISTINE. It's not that bad – you can see that . . .

He slips down the wall.

MRS FORSYTHE. Mike.

CHRISTINE *moves over fast.*

MIKE (*quiet*). I'm all right.

MRS FORSYTHE (*suddenly more concerned as* MIKE *winces*). Mike are you hurt badly? (*She turns very urgent.*) Go and get a taxi Christine – we've got to get him to hospital. We could ring for one. (*She moves over to the phone – which is cut off.*) Christine – look what you've done! It's useless. (*She throws the receiver.*) Go and get a taxi then.

CHRISTINE *doesn't move.*

CHRISTINE. He probably wanted this to happen.

MRS FORSYTHE. Go on. *He's hurt.* He's bleeding. Christine it's all your fault this has happened. It's all to do with you.

CHRISTINE (*outraged*). My fault! Why is it *my fault*. It's nothing to do with me.

MRS FORSYTHE. Don't stamp like that. (*Then pleads more nervously.*) Go on *please* Christine – please fetch one.

CHRISTINE (*moving to exit*). I'll send one here but I'm not coming back with it.

She exits.

MRS FORSYTHE (*moves over to* MIKE). Let's have a look at you now –

MIKE. You don't have to – I'm all right.

MRS FORSYTHE (*by his side, she smiles*). Don't squirm like that. (*She looks at his arm.*) It's not at all that bad I don't think.

MIKE *looks at door.*

(*She smiles.*) Don't worry about the mess, you're bleeding over the *TV Times*. (*She smiles gently.*) Why didn't you go straight to the hospital you stupid boy . . .

MIKE (*looking back at her – he is half sitting half lying against the wall*). Because I came here. I'll be fine. I can be quite brave when I want to be . . .

MRS FORSYTHE (*who has started dabbing the cut on his arm and on his lip with her handkerchief*). Does it make it better – me doing this?

MIKE (*leaning his head against the wall*). I'm not sure it makes any difference. I was very lucky. I could be dead. (*Slight smile to himself.*) I could have been blinded. In America seven hundred and fifty people are stabbed every day of the year. Yes . . . Some of them just walk out of doors to get some cigarettes and are never seen again. Just swallowed up. And in the morning they find pieces of people on the pavement and it's just swept up like litter. (*Suddenly.*) That hurt!

MRS FORSYTHE *has been dabbing his wounds.*

MIKE (*really shouts*). That hurt me! That really hurt.

He winces and holds her arm.

I think you can stop dabbing me now.

MRS FORSYTHE. It looks better now.

MIKE. You should have heard how loud I sc-reamed when it happened. I really did sc-ream, I must have broken some windows – could have been heard for miles around.

MRS FORSYTHE. You've broken your promise.

MIKE. What promise?

MRS FORSYTHE. You know what promise. You were never going to leave me alone with Christine. Remember. And you broke that. You went for a walk. You *promised* me.

MIKE. Did I? But that time is up now.

MRS FORSYTHE. I see. We were all going to have a night out together tonight. I was going to be taken out – let loose again.

MIKE (*tone changes, serious*). You'll have to be careful of her you know, because she can do some really strange things, when you don't expect them. (*Looking away.*) And *she's stronger* than you.

MRS FORSYTHE. You don't need to worry. I'm not going anywhere   near her again. I'm staying with you.

MIKE. It may be her last night – because she's in trouble now.

MRS FORSYTHE. She'll have to spend it on her own. I'm taking you to the hospital, and if they keep you in there, I'll sit and eat grapes with you. (*She smiles.*) I've got to be with you.

Blackout.

Scene Two

The Entertainments Pub. Sense of size and of a huge Pleasure Palace. Music playing current hits, mingled with more lush, light orchestral music, bursts of silence between records. Coloured lights around walls. Loud and bright atmosphere, occasional bursts of sharp applause. CHRISTINE, in her black dress, is leaning against the wall. She's holding two bottles, one of vodka, one of whisky. She is wearing dark glasses. As she leans against the wall her face is terribly pale, totally composed. We suddenly see how frail she is. MARTIN, wearing his school suit, now spattered with drink and ash, enters.

MARTIN. I've been looking for you. I thought you hadn't turned up. There are so many different bars here – I've been wandering into all of them. (*He grins at her.*) I haven't got it all yet.

CHRISTINE. Got what?

MARTIN. I'll have collected it in a few minutes. (*Smiles.*) Your fee. Somebody owes me a lot and he's just about to cough up. And there's going to be no trouble of any kind . . . or he knows what to expect.

He hits the wall with the palm of his hand, really hard.

CHRISTINE (*slight smile*). I'm sure he does.

MARTIN (*aggressive grin*). It'll hurt him to lie down for a fortnight. He'll have to sleep on his feet.

CHRISTINE *is leaning against the wall. For a split second she seems to totter but in an instant she looks her composed self.*

MARTIN (*watching her pale face*). You OK then . . .?

CHRISTINE. I'm fine. (*She takes off the dark glasses.*) I'm busy. I've got somebody coming. My partner for the evening. (*She looks around.*) But they haven't turned up yet.

Music playing in the background.

MARTIN (*concerned*). Your partner for the evening? Who?

CHRISTINE (*smiles*). Don't worry, you'll get your bit. It won't interfere – I'm not fully booked yet. (*She moves up to him.*) Why is your shirt undone?

MARTIN (*grins*). It must have come undone in this heat.

CHRISTINE (*gently*). Have you washed yourself then?

MARTIN. I have. Several times.

CHRISTINE. Cleaned yourself up for me. Not very well.

She dusts ash off him and then slowly does the buttons up on his shirt.

You've left school now, haven't you? It's the biggest night of your life tonight. How do you feel?

MARTIN. I don't feel anything right this moment. It's just about to hit me. I can feel it coming. (*Looks at her.*) It'll be incredible soon.

CHRISTINE (*finishing buttons*). You've already drunk too much. And you're not used to it. It's beginning to dribble back out of your mouth. (*She puts her finger up to his mouth.*) I'll have to push it back down again.

MARTIN. I've hardly had any yet – all my form are back there and they're already floating in it. They're going to drink the night away.

CHRISTINE (*suddenly turns*). Is Lawson here?

MARTIN. Haven't you seen him! He was sitting right there – a few moments ago. (*He points to table.*) There are all his drinks.

He points to line of glasses on table.

CHRISTINE (*looks at them*). Right there.

She tosses up her keys and holds them in her hand.

MARTIN (*grins*). I'm really surprised you wanted to meet here. With the staff all around, watching everybody.

CHRISTINE. Are you?

MARTIN. But you don't care what happens to yourself, do you? You never have.

CHRISTINE (*looks at him*). You can read people's minds, Martin.

MARTIN. Yes. I don't think you'd really mind if they put you away tomorrow. (*Grins.*)

CHRISTINE. I may not be alive tomorrow.

Pause. Music playing. CHRISTINE *leaning against wall. Her face is pale.*

CHRISTINE. You're staring at me.

MARTIN. Yes. I was just taking a look. I hadn't realised what you looked like before. I mean you look quite nice Christine. You don't care what you look like usually but tonight you look different.

He reaches out to fondle her.

CHRISTINE. You can't touch yet, I'm afraid.

MARTIN. Why not? The whole world's touched there already. And mostly for free.

MRS FORSYTHE *stands there, wearing a long coat.*

CHRISTINE. She's here.

MARTIN. Your sister! You were waiting for her!

CHRISTINE *staring across at her.*

CHRISTINE. She may not come over while you're here.

MRS FORSYTHE *moves over. From the moment she enters,* CHRISTINE'S *energy begins to flow back, and build and build.*

I knew you'd come.

MRS FORSYTHE. I don't know how you could have done. I nearly didn't. I can only stay a minute. I've just come to tell you that Mike's all right, I think. And I must get back to him. (*She nervously nods at* MARTIN.) Hello . . . (*She moves* CHRISTINE *a few feet.*) It's that same boy again.

CHRISTINE. I know.

MRS FORSYTHE. Does he have to be here – in this corner?

CHRISTINE. He'll keep quiet till he's spoken to. (*Louder.*) Won't he?

MARTIN (*knowing grin*). Yes. Definitely.

MRS FORSYTHE (*looking round her, animated*). Everything's so loud suddenly. It took me half an hour to get through the door Christine. (*Smiles straight at her.*) So you see you've made very little difference, haven't you?

CHRISTINE. Of course. (*Private smile.*) That's right.

MRS FORSYTHE (*grins at* MARTIN). He must think I'm mad. (*Louder.*) And then I couldn't find you anywhere! I looked for you in the Pacific Bar and in the Texan and in the Dungeon Bar, and the others too.

CHRISTINE (*suddenly loud, vibrant*). There's a disco underneath here too. (*She taps the floor.*) It's pounding now – you feel the floor shaking, see. There are hundreds of people down there, squashed together. We're standing on them.

MRS FORSYTHE. This is the biggest pub I've ever seen in my life – I had no idea they'd become so large. When I was still going out, they had small ones – with carpets.

CHRISTINE. And it's growing all the time – every day it grows a bit more. There're great chunks behind here. (*She taps the wall.*) They haven't even opened yet. It eats other pubs too. It does. You can watch it happening. In one gulp they're gone.

MARTIN. It's the biggest pleasure centre for twenty miles. There're five different levels . . . You can find anything here . . . you want.

CHRISTINE (*to* MARTIN). You're not allowed to talk. Soon it will have its own underground station, all for itself. The trains will run right into its inside, and people will be carried up here in enormous lifts.

Suddenly a voice is heard in the distance. As the music stops a firm brash voice.

VOICE. . . . And now the next lovely young lady we have for you is Linda. She's going to dance to (*Name of record.*) but I shouldn't think you'll be listening to the music. Linda likes milk-shakes, black underwear and Frenchmen. Thank you, and her measurements are thirty-eight, twenty-four, thirty-six.

MARTIN. That's one of the non-stop topless go-go dancers. They have those . . . too. (*He smiles.*) They never stop. (*Grins.*) Have to keep on dancing . . . even in private.

MRS FORSYTHE (*to* CHRISTINE). You're not meant to be here. You're under age.

CHRISTINE. Yes. (*Grins.*) It's what I've got to look forward to in a few years' time. Take your coat off now.

MRS FORSYTHE. I think I'd like to keep it on. (*She covers herself up.*)

CHRISTINE. No, you'll burn to death inside there. Take my sister's coat off please, Martin.

MARTIN. Of course.

MARTIN *does so.* MRS FORSYTHE *takes her coat off shyly – she stands embarrassed, still in black dress, her arms across her chest, almost as if she was naked. Both women in long black dresses.*

MRS FORSYTHE. There're just so many people here – and a lot of them are drunk.

CHRISTINE (*to* MARTIN). Thank you, Martin. Leave us alone now.

MARTIN. Yes. (*He smiles.*) You'll call me. (*He exits.*)

CHRISTINE. Now drink this, come on. (*She lifts vodka bottle.*) Take one swig of this and then one of this *immediately* afterwards, without a pause. (*She indicates whisky bottle.*) If you drink them close enough together and drink enough you don't get at all drunk, however much you drink – almost. That's true!

MRS FORSYTHE. Do I really look that foolish? (*She almost touches* CHRISTINE.) You won't get me to believe that.

CHRISTINE. You've got to do it.

MRS FORSYTHE *takes a swig of vodka obediently, and immediately a swig of whisky.*

MRS FORSYTHE. I must get back to Mike! You shouldn't be making me drink and in front of him as well. I know why you've got me here.

CHRISTINE. I don't think you could possibly guess . . . come on.

MRS FORSYTHE (*up against wall. Through following exchanges she twice lifts both bottles to her lips and takes quick gulps*). I drank a lot when your father left me you know. Lots! And then I got this phone call. (*She smiles to herself.*) I'm in Germany he said and I feel lost, come and get me back. He'd chased a girl out there of course. I'll meet you at the airport, he said.

CHRISTINE. I know what you're going to say.

MRS FORSYTHE. I arrived and I wandered round the airport and all the time I was holding this huge armful of duty free things that I bought for him, trying not to drop any, with this sort of music blaring away.

CHRISTINE. And of course he wasn't there – anybody could have guessed that.

MRS FORSYTHE. Of course. (*She smiles.*) You can imagine me can't you, tottering round this airport with all these bottles like this (*She's clutching the two bottles in her arms.*) holding on to them so tight as if my life depended on it. I've never wanted to scream so much in my life. And I dropped every single bottle too, by accident, one by one they dropped away – crash! behind me.

She's turned against the wall.

CHRISTINE (*loud, dangerous*). For Christ's sake you're not starting crying about that now.

MRS FORSYTHE (*leaning her head against the wall*). No, no, not this time.

She's smiling, she turns back. LAWSON *has entered during the last line and is sitting down at his table.*

MRS FORSYTHE. Oh my God! It's him.

She pulls CHRISTINE *away.*

Christine, we can't stay here, we've got to leave right now. It's him.

LAWSON *is seated only a few yards away.*

CHRISTINE (*equally loud*). Don't be stupid. He can't touch us tonight. It's all right.

MRS FORSYTHE. Us! You mean *you*, don't you?

CHRISTINE. We're safe tonight. There's nothing he can do. Tomorrow will be different.

MRS FORSYTHE (*loud*). It doesn't bear thinking of. (*Glancing at* LAWSON.) Don't you see, I couldn't possibly meet him again. I made such a complete fool of myself when I was with him before. I broke everything in his room – he probably hasn't got any furniture left. And he's seen us now!

CHRISTINE. Of course he's seen us, he's not blind. Just stare back at him.

They both look at LAWSON *who is sipping a pint of beer cautiously, the froth on his moustache.*

I've stared at him so often in class and taken his clothes off.

MRS FORSYTHE. Taken his clothes off! Ssshh! He can hear every word you're saying.

CHRISTINE. He stands up there in front of you for a whole year and you have to stare so hard at every piece of him. You can't help it.

She is staring straight at LAWSON *and not lowering her voice.*

I know every inch of him off by heart, what his fingers look like, how small his feet are, where his hair is beginning to thin. After a bit you stop thinking of them as people. Suddenly, just like that, they become more like small buildings or machinery.

MRS FORSYTHE. You disgusting child.

CHRISTINE. It just happens. Come on.

She pulls MRS FORSYTHE *towards* LAWSON.

LAWSON (*nods up at her*). Hello, Christine. We're seeing you for the last time, I should think.

CHRISTINE. Yes you're right first time.

LAWSON (*looking at* MRS FORSYTHE). I would offer you a seat but I probably need it more than you do. This is our end of term ritual when a few foolish teachers like myself are brave enough to face an uneasy drink with the leavers. Though they're all under age of course – to be in this place.

CHRISTINE. It makes them happy I'm sure.

LAWSON. Kids lean over towards you, drink pouring out of them and tell you some rather savage things about what you've done for them. Sometimes they remember to buy you a drink. (*Music playing in the background. He looks at them.*) You must be very hot in those dresses.

CHRISTINE. I believe you two have met already. This is my sister, Marian.

LAWSON (*looks up*). Your sister!

MRS FORSYTHE (*catching hold of* CHRISTINE). Don't you dare try that now, Christine.

CHRISTINE. I'm just giving him something to think about – he's all alone.

LAWSON. That makes sense. You do look like her sister. (*Looking straight at* MRS FORSYTHE.) When we met before I didn't think you seemed very sure who exactly you were.

MRS FORSYTHE (*sharp*). That's because I was terrified of you. (*Quieter, surprised at herself.*) I hadn't been out of the house very much before.

LAWSON (*watching her closely*). I sincerely hope you're not terrified of me now.

MRS FORSYTHE. No, I don't think so. (*She smiles.*) You look different when you're not behind your desk. (*Smiles.*) When you're not hiding behind that armoury of stationery.

CHRISTINE. He's smaller out of school, isn't he? Like all teachers, he shrinks when he's out of class. See! He's shrinking now. (*She points at his legs.*) Just watch him. There go his legs. They really do become smaller, you know.

LAWSON. So who are you?

MRS FORSYTHE (*rather too loud*). I'm her mother. Of course I'm her mother.

LAWSON. And you're sure now. It won't change again in a few minutes.

MRS FORSYTHE. It hasn't changed at all – so it can't change again.

LAWSON. Nothing surprises me any more. (*Smiles.*) It hasn't for several years.

Announcement as distant applause rings out.

VOICE. . . . Next, we have for you a glorious redhead – if we've got the right one, Cathy. Yes, Cathy likes middle-aged American men and singing in church. In that order, I'm sure. Big hand for Cathy, she'll be dancing to (*Name of record.*).

LAWSON (*as the announcement is tailing off*). They used to have really good shows in the pubs round here, before this pleasure palace appeared. Really raunchy acts. I remember women belting out songs so loud you could hear them several streets away. Drag artists in spangled ostrich feathers singing rugger songs. Now it's all plastic girls done up in cellophane, don't touch written everywhere, Hamburger Sex. It's all become safe again. I've decided tonight, I was born into the wrong age. A hundred years too late. (*He scratches his ear.*) Excuse me, there's always this ringing in my ears at the end of term. (*Suddenly looks straight at* MRS FORSYTHE.) So you've been protecting your daughter, Mrs Forsythe.

MRS FORSYTHE. I lied very badly for a few days, yes.

LAWSON. That wasn't terribly wise, was it?

CHRISTINE (*to* MRS FORSYTHE). He can't touch us tonight, remember.

MRS FORSYTHE. I wasn't a terribly wise person at the beginning of the week but I'm glad I did it.

LAWSON. Tomorrow I will take action. I'm not going to spoil my night tonight, if it is spoilable, by official business.

MRS FORSYTHE. Tomorrow? (*Suddenly apprehensive*.) I wish people would stop mentioning tomorrow like that.

LAWSON. God knows what'll happen to her. (*Slight smile*.) It depends on the extent of her villainy. It's her last night tonight.

MRS FORSYTHE (*very sharp*). I know it's her last night.

CHRISTINE (*to* LAWSON). I'm going to end up in Borstal. And you're going to end up in the madhouse. So we can visit each other, can't we? I'll bring you some fruit.

MRS FORSYTHE (*standing over* LAWSON *at the table*). You're the man who wrote those reports about her.

LAWSON. I imagine so.

MRS FORSYTHE (*suddenly, rather loud*). Of course, she's infuriating, and idiotic, and *plain horrible sometimes*, BUT SHE'S NOT STUPID! She's a bright girl, my daughter. You didn't mention that, did you?

Both women enormously animated.

CHRISTINE (*amazed, excited grin*). You're doing incredibly well. Isn't she doing well?

LAWSON (*sharp smile*). She is idiotic, but not stupid?

MRS FORSYTHE. Keep still, Christine. I remember my last day of term. They said about me . . . This girl will never be a clever person but she will be a pleasant one. And I believed them for really a long time, which just shows how stupid I was. I don't think that's a very polite smile and rather an obvious one wasn't it? (*She smiles at him*.) It may surprise you to hear this but I would probably have gone *insane* if it hadn't been for this girl here. (*Smiles still*.) But she appears to have managed something. You really have perfected that smile, haven't you? It keeps on creeping out of you. You don't disguise your thoughts well, do you? But it does happen to be true all this, and I am in fact, perfectly normal. If that means anything, which it doesn't.

CHRISTINE (*who has been standing by her side, grinning broadly*). She's doing this without a fee. I hope you're taking notes.

MRS FORSYTHE. Will you stay still! (*She holds on to* CHRISTINE's *arm. Then she whips round to* LAWSON.) What?

LAWSON. I didn't say anything. (*Smiles.*) Unless it crept out of me without me noticing.

CHRISTINE (*who is being held – they're standing side by side*). We're like Siamese twins . . . joined together by one piece of skin. (*She puts on her dark glasses.*)

MRS FORSYTHE (*smiling*). I'm twitching now because I'm just a little nervous – but getting less so all the time. She has, believe it or not, taught me one or two things, which may or may not work and she's going to behave herself now and *prove* that she is really capable of something. (*She hits the table.*) I know she is. (*She spills* LAWSON's *drink which pours all over him.*) I'm sorry about that.

LAWSON. Please don't apologise. I'm used to that happening.

MRS FORSYTHE (*picking up glass*). You've drunk enough, anyway. You're beginning to have that misty look in your face, just like my husband used to have. It doesn't suit some men to drink heavily, the intelligent ones, it makes them look helpless.

She is moving glasses, trying to wipe it up.

CHRISTINE (*smiles*). Isn't she being really good?

LAWSON. I'd rather you didn't try to clean it up, please.

MRS FORSYTHE. Rubbish. I'll do it.

She produces out of her pocket the blood-spattered handkerchief that she wiped Mike's wound with.

MRS FORSYTHE. Oh, I meant to leave that at home.

LAWSON *stares in amazement at the really blood-soaked handkerchief.*

I know this looks strange, but my other child, my son, is in hospital. He was in a fight. I ought to be with him now, of course, but for some reason I'm not – anyway, it may be covered in blood but it'll do to soak up your drink.

CHRISTINE. Wear these.

She has put on her dark glasses . . . passes some to MRS FORSYTHE.

MRS FORSYTHE. Just keep still, Christine.

LAWSON. Tomorrow I will file my report and everything will be out of my hands.

MRS FORSYTHE. I asked you not to mention tomorrow.

LAWSON. I don't believe you are her mother.

MRS FORSYTHE. That's unfortunate. But you can believe what you like.

LAWSON. I'm not even sure that you're her sister . . . but whoever you are, you better be careful, because girls like that are the most dangerous nowadays. Of anybody, the most trouble.

MRS FORSYTHE. Christine's going to behave herself . . . she is —

CHRISTINE (*puts a huge fistful of dark glasses on the table*). Go on take one.

MRS FORSYTHE. *Christine!* Where did you get those?

CHRISTINE *moves away from* LAWSON, MRS FORSYTHE *follows.*

What are you doing with all those dark glasses? Are you trying to make a total fool out of me? (CHRISTINE *smiles.*) Because you've just succeeded triumphantly. You appalling girl. How many have you got there? . . . what else have you taken? . . . show me . . .

She tries to get at CHRISTINE's *bag.*

CHRISTINE. You can wear some.

They face each other.

MRS FORSYTHE. You've really sealed things with that, haven't you? And with him watching, too! You appalling girl.

She gives a quick glances at LAWSON *sitting upstage drinking his beer, then moves towards* CHRISTINE.

The telephone on the wall just by them rings. Both women swing round and shout at it.

CHRISTINE ⎱ Oh, shut up!
MRS FORSYTHE ⎰

MRS FORSYTHE (*looking at the phone ringing*). It can't be Mr Lawson, anyway, because he's over there. (*She glances at him.*) Unless he doesn't dare speak to us in person any more.

CHRISTINE (*produces her scissors and advances on ringing phone*). Just shut up! You can terrorise them with these. (*She holds scissors above phone.*) They're worried about having things cut off and they stop.

The phone stops.

MRS FORSYTHE. Come here a moment, Christine.

CHRISTINE (*loud*). There, I saw it grow! (*She points at the wall.*) Just there! I saw it move a little. (*She presses her palm flat against the wall.*) It definitely is. You can feel it stretching under your hand.

MRS FORSYTHE. Come here now.

CHRISTINE. You've really done very well so far – everything that's required of you.

MRS FORSYTHE (*surprised*). Have I?

CHRISTINE (*warning smile*). Come on, drink some more.

She hands her the two bottles. MRS FORSYTHE sips first one, then the other.

You still can't disobey me, you realise. You haven't had your fourth lesson. I could just say, '*I'm going to get you a drink from the bar now, Marian*', and go through those doors, out into the night and you would never see me again.

She holds the scissors between them as they stand close together.

Like Siamese twins, remember. All I have to do, is lean down with these (*She moves scissors.*) and clip the join, the skin, and cut us apart. Blood would go everywhere, and where would you be?

MRS FORSYTHE. Now we have to wait while you try to be totally revolting for the next few minutes, do we? But I'm not going to. And you're to have some of this now – I don't see why I should be the only one made to drink in this highly suspicious way.

CHRISTINE. I told you I'm not drinking anything. Or eating. I haven't drunk now for three days.

MRS FORSYTHE (*music playing*). Then why're you still here? (*Smiles.*) Why aren't you dead!

CHRISTINE. I'm completely empty now.

MRS FORSYTHE. It would be terrible to think of you really fading away, in front of my eyes – slowly disappearing.

Pause. Music playing.

CHRISTINE (*suddenly serious*). YOU'LL SEE.

Pause.

MRS FORSYTHE. You were going to take me into London, remember . . .? Right into the centre of everything. Instead you've enticed me here – I'm losing my chance. We're the only two women on their own here, too.

MARTIN *enters.*

CHRISTINE. Here he comes.

MARTIN. How are we doing?

CHRISTINE. What does that mean?

MARTIN (*sees* LAWSON *sitting upstage*). Hello, Sir.

LAWSON *lifts his head in cursory greeting.*

CHRISTINE. Who you nodding to? (*She glances at* LAWSON.) You don't need to bother about him. (*Moves to* MARTIN.) Do you think, Marian, he had anything to do with Mike getting done? Did he beat Mike up, do you think?

The two women both look at MARTIN.

MARTIN. Your brother? Don't be crazy.

MRS FORSYTHE. I don't think he looks the type.

CHRISTINE. He's very strong – look at his muscles, and I know he sometimes likes to crack a bottle over people's heads when they walk past.

MRS FORSYTHE. Does he really? I wouldn't have guessed that.

MARTIN. Not often. Not done it that often.

CHRISTINE. We're nearly ready for you. Your patience is about to be rewarded.

She moves away from him.

MARTIN. Good.

CHRISTINE (*to* MARTIN). You better just not open your mouth. (*To* MRS FORSYTHE.) I've given up sex now, so you needn't worry. They don't really know how to do it round here. (*Looks straight at* MRS FORSYTHE.) They've been very badly taught. (*She turns.*) I think he's brushed his teeth you know, specially. (*Very pointedly at* MRS FORSYTHE.) *I'm going to get you a drink from the bar now, Marian.*

MRS FORSYTHE (*looks straight back at her*). Go on then.

CHRISTINE *exits. Pause. Mrs Forsythe stares after her.*

Music playing in distance. MARTIN *is standing by the wall, banging his palms against it incessantly.*

MARTIN (*disconcerted by* MRS FORSYTHE's *stare*). Don't mind me. I'll just wait here for your sister.

MRS FORSYTHE. You have to be careful with her. She's not to be trusted. She may not do what you want.

MARTIN. She'll be all right. She'll want to enjoy herself tonight.

She won't get many more chances! They'll put her in an approved school somewhere.

MRS FORSYTHE. Will they? And what will you do after tonight?

MARTIN. I can't think beyond this point. (*Suddenly, loud.*) I've thought about this moment for *five years*! Leaving school.

MRS FORSYTHE. All the time.

MARTIN. I never stopped thinking about it – but I didn't ever get past this night in my mind. It just always stopped here. (*He smiles, animated.*) I always got up to the drink splashed all over the floor, and the girls dancing – lots of white bodies, curving all round you, and the coloured lights shining in your eyes, and your sister. And they're all here tonight. (*He looks up.*) Look, you can see the ceiling. Just!

MRS FORSYTHE (*looking up*). So you can.

MARTIN (*grinning*). Maybe it means that I'll never leave here. (*He stares up.*) Perhaps I should try to get a job here and they'd put you up on the premises as well, lots of rooms tucked away behind this. (*Pause.*) But there'll never ever be a job here. Anyway, I don't think tomorrow's going to happen. You never know. (*He grins.*) Who cares now? I may not wake.

MRS FORSYTHE. The amount you're drinking, that's almost certain.

MARTIN. Yes, I'll have such a headache, won't I? It will go on for six weeks probably. It'll stop me thinking of anything else. (*Suddenly.*) She isn't going to be long?

Audience applause and voice from distance . . .

VOICE. . . . Thank you Cathy – and in a moment we'll have Diana for you . . . she likes crispbread and choirboys and she'll be up here for you in a second . . .

MRS FORSYTHE. I ought to be with Mike. (*Moving up to him.*) You're quite bright, aren't you, in a way. Why do you let her make such a fool of you, then?

MARTIN (*sharp*). She is coming back, isn't she?

MRS FORSYTHE (*staring at him*). Is it your first time then? (*Smiles.*) Do people still have first times nowadays?

MARTIN. Don't be stupid. I was doing it in my cradle.

MARTIN *is unsettled. She softens.*

MRS FORSYTHE (*touching him*). I thought so. You really *have* cleaned yourself up for her. You're shining! Why's your shirt undone, though?

It's half undone. She does the buttons up slowly.

My first time was not far from here too. It was out of doors, nearly winter, in that miserable park round the Imperial War Museum in Kennington, amongst the litter and the big gun barrels sticking out there on the grass. I think he needed them for encouragement. I enjoyed it though. He became my husband, of course. I was terribly young, much too young to get married . . . about your age. (*She touches his cheek.*) But you look so old suddenly, like you've been alive fifty years. Something in your eyes. Why is that? And your friends too, when I passed them back there clustered together looking really bewildered, their faces swollen right up with drink.

MARTIN (*nervous*). That's right.

MRS FORSYTHE (*close to him*). You'll be coming here with your wife in a few years' time, no doubt – her night out, sitting in a corner watching the lights change colour. Girls are getting married much younger again – keeps them occupied. It's all right, just don't look at him.

MARTIN *has glanced over at* LAWSON. *She raises her voice.* I know what he's thinking . . . a mature frustrated woman feeling up a young boy – how sad, or whatever word he'd use. Because that's what it looks like, maybe that's what's happening. And I don't see why we should disappoint him . . . especially as he's probably noting it all down.

She kisses him, sexual kiss but gentle.

MARTIN. I . . . I'm . . .

MRS FORSYTHE. If you can't say anything you don't have to you know. You're quite a gentle boy really, in a messy way. Don't look so worried, this is not going to cost you extra, – if that's what you're worried about. This part is free.

MARTIN. I want . . . I just didn't . . . I'm . . .

MRS FORSYTHE. I'm just making up for what Christine is not going to give you . . . I'm probably doing exactly what she wanted, down to the last detail. But that's just too bad. And she's probably watching from some vantage point. I've never been watched by so many people doing anything. (*She kisses him again.*) You can unclench your teeth. That's allowed too. I won't bite your tongue off, though no doubt my daughter would.

MARTIN. Your daughter?

MRS FORSYTHE. You didn't hear that. You don't mind if I

stand like this. (*Her back to* LAWSON.) I know perfectly well that if I turn my head at all and see him watching me I'm going to faint from embarrassment, *literally*, so you keep looking straight. (*She holds his head, staring directly into his eyes.*) That's right, keep looking straight at me and don't move.

CHRISTINE *enters. She's holding a soft drink.*

CHRISTINE. What on earth are you doing, Mum?

MRS FORSYTHE (*turns and looks at her, then directly back at* MARTIN). She often calls me that for no reason at all.

CHRISTINE (*to* LAWSON). And what are you staring at?

MARTIN. Christine, shall we . . .?

VOICE (*over tannoy*). . . . Could we have Diana please . . . Diana, wherever she is in the building, could she come up here immediately. She is due on stage *now*. We'll be back with you very soon, ladies and gentlemen, with our non-stop dancing . . . we just seem to have mislaid Diana . . .

CHRISTINE (*gleefully*). They've lost one of their girls. When they've finished their act they go and hang them up on the coat rack in the Ladies, whole line of girls . . . you can see them hanging up there as you go in. Come on, Mum, this is for you. (*Gives her orange juice.*)

MARTIN. Why is she calling you that all the time?

MRS FORSYTHE. Probably because I'm her mother.

MARTIN (*astonished*). You're her mother. She's your daughter . . .

The TWO WOMEN *look at him.*

I think I've just got to go and see someone. It might take me a long time . . . I'll keep in touch. (*To* CHRISTINE.) I may not see you again, Christine.

He exits.

MRS FORSYTHE. I've never seen somebody change their mind so quickly.

She looks at LAWSON.

VOICE *on tannoy* . . . Diana will be with you any second. We are just checking the exits now . . .

CHRISTINE. If they want somebody, they can have me!

Suddenly she moves across the stage.

MRS FORSYTHE. Christine . . .?

CHRISTINE (*loud*). I'm over here.

The spot finds her – on raised bit of stage and the music starts.

MRS FORSYTHE (*turns to* LAWSON). Why don't you stop her?

CHRISTINE *is standing in the spotlight. Suddenly loud go-go music starts.*

CHRISTINE (*above music*). What do I do now?

She rocks gently backwards and forwards on her feet looking incredibly pale but also vibrant. She thinks hastily.

I could empty my pockets.

She picks up her bag and pulls out a string of Green Shield Stamps. Then she drops it.

MRS FORSYTHE. Oh God, I can't watch this, I really can't.

CHRISTINE (*grins*). You can't see me yet. I'm invisible because I've got my clothes on.

Suddenly, without warning she breaks into a highly efficient, aggressive, almost dazzling dance, which lasts for about a minute and then stops again as suddenly as it began. She grins.

CHRISTINE. A bit of the real thing.

She produces scissors out of her bag.

I can cut off most things with these.

CHRISTINE *slips blade into the top of her dress and cuts it, in small snips, only about two inches long. She holds the scissors there for a second. The go-go music stops as if bewildered.*

MRS FORSYTHE. What on earth is she doing?

CHRISTINE (*straightening with a smile*). There're a lot of people I know here tonight. I can see them quite clearly, hiding in corners smoking their lungs out, pretending not to be looking. (*Smiling.*) And I won't be here tomorrow so I'm . . .

MRS FORSYTHE. She's making a fool of herself now.

She moves across, catches hold of CHRISTINE *in the spot.*

Christine . . .

CHRISTINE *pulls her right into the spot.*

(*Confused, looking out front.*) Sorry, I'm just collecting my daughter, she's not one of the dancers. (*Suddenly nervous.*) Christ, in a spotlight. (*She moves to go but* CHRISTINE *hangs on to her.*)

CHRISTINE. Come back, have a look at them, the men of the district.

MRS FORSYTHE *stops in spotlight for a second.*

CHRISTINE. I'm her manager.

A VOICE *suddenly booms out, a different one from the one heard above. They both look up.* Neither of you are Diana, are you? Could you clear the stage, please? Could you please move? We're answerable to the authorities and unlicensed artistes cannot perform.

MRS FORSYTHE. It's the voice of the Brewery speaking.

VOICE *suddenly fierce.* Could you please clear the *floor,* now!

CHRISTINE (*turning on* MRS FORSYTHE *her manner suddenly outrageous*). You shouldn't have stopped me. I WILL NEVER HAVE SEX WITH YOU AGAIN! NEVER EVER – not even in the bath. Not even on Sundays.

MRS FORSYTHE (*shrieks*). Oh God, you little – bitch.

She pulls her out of spot and downstage left.

CHRISTINE. Never! I'm telling you. Not even oral sex.

MRS FORSYTHE (*really furious*). Is there absolutely nothing you won't stoop to, you evil girl.

She hits her across the face.

I've been longing to do that!

CHRISTINE (*really loud*). You've got a taste for it now. (*Her tone changes.*) Don't ever try to do that again.

MRS FORSYTHE. In front of all those people, saying that. They might think it's true. (*Looks at* LAWSON.) It's not true! They'll think we're some sort of circus freaks.

CHRISTINE. You shouldn't mind that.

MRS FORSYTHE. And stop waving those bloody scissors at me!

She moves to CHRISTINE.

CHRISTINE. Don't try to force me I warn you.

MRS FORSYTHE *tries to pull them away, they fight for a moment and the scissors drop between them on the floor, but they continue to fight for a few seconds.*

A fight to the death . . .

CHRISTINE *pushes* MRS FORSYTHE *up against the wall. Music is playing in distance, a much slower record.*

MRS FORSYTHE (*panting, glancing around*). People must think we're just two brawling drunken women.

CHRISTINE. And they'd be wrong.

> MRS FORSYTHE *smiles, pushes back her hair.* CHRISTINE *leans against the wall, looking strange, and for an instant fragile.*

MRS FORSYTHE. Christ, you're so strong, Christine. It's almost unnatural. And you seem to be getting stronger all the time.

> *She looks at* CHRISTINE.

And you said you weren't eating!

CHRISTINE. I think you may be getting above yourself, you know. It's really time for your fourth lesson.

MRS FORSYTHE. But that's already happened, hasn't it? (*Startled.*)

> CHRISTINE *shakes her head slowly, slow music playing.*

What does that shake of the head mean?

> *She pulls* CHRISTINE *to her.*

That dress smells of mothballs. Your eyes look very blue tonight. (*She laughs.*) I suppose they've always been that blue. I'm just seeing them again.

CHRISTINE (*smile*). I've got something to tell you. I'm not really your daughter at all – I adopted you, you're adopted.

MRS FORSYTHE. Stop it – just stand there, quiet.

> *She holds* CHRISTINE's *head for a moment.*

CHRISTINE. You can't touch.

MRS FORSYTHE. I remember when I took you out to the park when you were only three-and-a-half.

CHRISTINE (*quiet.*) You're not allowed to talk about the past.

MRS FORSYTHE. (*cuts her off*). Oh yes I can, and I lost you. You disappeared on purpose. You hid yourself so well it took me five hours to find you. And on the way home we passed a totally strange woman on the path, and you said straight out to her, just as she was passing. 'Hello Mum, I want you for a mum, you look a much better one.' You were only three-and-a-half.

CHRISTINE (*quiet, close*). Yes. Did I hurt coming out? I bet I did.

MRS FORSYTHE (*touching her hair*). I'm surprised you can't remember. You seem to remember the most unlikely things. You hurt like anything. Mike did. I ought to be with him now.

I don't know why I'm not. I can't think what you've done to make that happen. He could be worse . . . (*She touches* CHRISTINE's *hair.*) And you made such a lot of noise, Christine, when you were small. You were such work. You wore me out before I was twenty-one.

CHRISTINE (*quiet, allowing her to touch her*). That's right.

MRS FORSYTHE. And now you look so old. You look really old tonight.

CHRISTINE (*totally matter-of-fact*). And you look younger all the time.

MRS FORSYTHE. I'm going to wash your hair tomorrow and I'll get you some new shoes and maybe even a new dress. And cut your hair. (*She runs her hand through* CHRISTINE's *hair.*) It doesn't suit you like that. You can look much better. I don't want my daughter to look a total wreck.

CHRISTINE. Haven't you forgotten something? (*Pauses.*) I'm not going to be here tomorrow.

MRS FORSYTHE. What? We're not going to think about that. Something may happen. (*She holds onto* CHRISTINE's *arm tightly.*) *But you're mine for tonight.* (*She suddenly squeezes her arm really tightly.*) You're mine. I don't seem to have touched you for such a long time. I don't know why, not for ten years.

She touches CHRISTINE's *forehead with her lips.*

CHRISTINE (*quiet*). That hurts. *That's really hurting me,* you're holding so hard.

MRS FORSYTHE. Am I? (*She stops, surprised at herself.*) Yes. (*She looks at* CHRISTINE's *pale face.*) Why *are* you looking like that tonight, Christine?

CHRISTINE. Right. (*She moves.*) I'm going to get you a drink from the bar now, Marian.

She exits.

MRS FORSYTHE *doesn't pick up on the phrase. She leans against the wall.*

MRS FORSYTHE. I'm not surprised you're looking at me like that.

LAWSON. I'm not looking at anything or anybody. I've seen what I needed to see. I'm considering whether I've got the energy to lift myself out of this chair and get another drink – what do you think?

MRS FORSYTHE. I wouldn't know.

LAWSON (*his tone is acerbic, well lubricated but certainly not drunk*). I can hardly move now. I'm rather more than completely exhausted. I'm shattered. I don't think anyone from outside has even begun to realise how shattered we are at the end of term. In the last days you have moments when you feel your legs are going to buckle under you – quite literally.

MRS FORSYTHE (*preoccupied*). I hadn't realised.

LAWSON. When you start teaching of course, it's simple. You're full of ideas, some of them good ones, and energy. Nervous too, of course, it's not uncommon to be sick before you go and face a class in your first term. I was. But it's exciting. I used to lie awake at night nearly every night, in fact, pounding thoughts out in my mind. But if you go on doing that before every lesson, it kills you.

Music playing.

MRS FORSYTHE. Of course.

LAWSON. So you start to coast, first only a few lessons, and then a lot and suddenly it hits you that whatever you do doesn't make a blind fuck of difference because you can't make the buggers listen long enough. And that's when the greyness begins to set in. I fought it for a hell of a long time but it ensnares one. And they smell that you see, the girls especially, they smell it first, very quickly.

MRS FORSYTHE. I know. Of course.

LAWSON. And then I realised, and it quite amazed me, because I'm not that sort of person, that I had really begun to enjoy the stationery, the ordering of it, collecting it, filing it, looking through the catalogue for the latest types of staplers and felt-tipped pens. I really was getting pleasure out of that trivia – ludicrous. And I still am. It's comforting in an insane way. (*Looks at her.*) I don't know how you've managed to drink all that without showing more signs.

MRS FORSYTHE. I don't know either.

LAWSON. I don't like drunk women. I don't get drunk any more. It takes days for this ringing to go in one's ears. (*Looks at* MRS FORSYTHE.) I've taught *you* something now.

MRS FORSYTHE (*suddenly looks around*). I don't think she's coming back. (*She moves from* LAWSON.) She's probably gone. Oh, God . . . I can't stay here without her. (*Looks back at*

LAWSON.) I'm sorry, you must think this is strange but I can't be here without her – without my daughter. I . . . I . . . I'll . . . say good . . . (LAWSON *looks at her tolerantly.*) Oh Christ, I can feel things disappearing again. (*She glances around.*) How do you get out of here – out of the building? – which is the way out?

Blackout.

Scene Three

The sound of the Entertainments Pub – the loud music, dipping into total silence. Hospital bed, MIKE lying there. CHRISTINE enters, slowly and noiselessly. She stands for a second by the bed, then jolts it. Early morning sunlight. MIKE wakes up, truly startled, flinching as she jolts the bed, and sees her.

MIKE (*loud whisper*). Christine! What on earth are you doing here? It's much too early for visitors.

CHRISTINE (*speaking quietly*). I thought it was time you were awake.

MIKE. How did you get in here?

CHRISTINE. I walked in. They thought I was one of the patients. They told me 'they'd get round to me in a moment'. I look rather pale, so people tell me.

MIKE. Your make-up's all run.

CHRISTINE. I've been up all night, that's why. (*She rubs the smudged black lipstick on her lips.*) It's nasty stuff, anyway. I brought you a lemon. (*She produces one ordinary fresh lemon with its top cut off.*) Here – I couldn't get you any grapes.

MIKE (*watching her warily*). Thanks – but I think I'll do without it, if you don't mind.

CHRISTINE *lifts lemon to her mouth but does not suck it. Throughout the scene she keeps brushing it against her mouth without eating any of it.*

MIKE (*nervous of her*). Don't come too close!

CHRISTINE. You've dribbled on your pillow.

MIKE (*watchful*). Why are you here? They're bound to see you in a minute.

CHRISTINE. I know. (*Looking down at him.*) How are you then?

MIKE (*suspicious*). Why do you want to know? I've had to have nine stitches. It was worse than it seemed. I've got to keep completely still. (*He is lying propped up on pillow not moving his head either to left or right.*) Don't touch the bed, even the slightest knock hurts me.

CHRISTINE (*moving by bed but not touching*). Yes.

MIKE. And keep your voice down. (*He looks at her very warily.*) What do you want, Christine? Why've you come? And don't eat that lemon, it makes my mouth go all weird.

CHRISTINE (*suddenly*). I'm not eating it. Do you want to know what they say at the bottom of the bed here? (*She picks up chart at the end of the bed.*) Your name's crossed out, that means you're dead, doesn't it? They'll come to bury you, if you're not careful.

MIKE. What on earth are you going to do, Christine?

CHRISTINE. About what?

MIKE. You really are in terrible trouble this time and there's absolutely no way you can get out of it.

CHRISTINE. That's right, there isn't.

MIKE (*keeping completely still*). Whatever you try to do.

CHRISTINE. I'm going to have plastic surgery when I get to Borstal. Have my nose done rather than my knees. I've made the choice at last.

MIKE. Time's running out for you. There's never been much you've been good at is there? (*Lightly.*) I mean, what are you able to do, Christine? – not that there's anything for you to do. (*Slight smile.*) You'll have kids one day, if you're not in custody the whole time.

CHRISTINE. Naturally. (*She suddenly moves over.*) I'm going to try the bed now. (*She climbs onto the bed, lying beside him.*)

MIKE (*truly alarmed*). No! Christine – please don't. (*He flinches with pain as she climbs onto the bed.*) I'm not allowed to move! Don't you realise?

CHRISTINE *lies next to him on the bed.*

What on earth do you think you're doing?

CHRISTINE. Just trying it for size.

MIKE (*trying to keep his voice down*). You've got to get off here at once! What happens if a nurse comes past, you'll get me into terrible trouble. They'll think I've smuggled a woman in here.

CHRISTINE. You have. (*She looks up.*)

MIKE. Get down anyway. Put your head down.

CHRISTINE (*lying next to him*). I've never been in a hospital before, in my life. It's different to what I thought. It's all falling to bits.

MIKE (*uneasy next to her*). You were born here you know.

CHRISTINE. Was I?

MIKE. We both were.

CHRISTINE (*she smiles*). Yes, I remember it. You were born first.

MIKE. Of course.

He suddenly stares at her. His face is very close to her on the bed. His tone is truly shocked.

Christ! You really look strange, you know, Christine. Something about your face, it's all – what's happening to you? – it's like it's changed shape.

CHRISTINE (*lying next to him*). Has it?

MIKE. Can't you feel it? You look all different. No wonder they thought you were a patient. Have you really not been eating anything?

CHRISTINE. No – why doesn't anybody believe me?

MIKE. Why haven't you been?

CHRISTINE. I just stopped – and I really didn't see any point in starting again.

MIKE. Then what are you living off then?

CHRISTINE. Nothing. Absolutely nothing.

MIKE. What are you going to do about Mum?

CHRISTINE. Finish what I've done with her. Give her the last one.

MIKE. I haven't understood a word you've said to each other.

CHRISTINE *rolls on her stomach right up to him. He flinches as she moves.*

CHRISTINE. You've got freckles on the inside of your ear – I've never looked at you properly before, you know.

MIKE. You're going to get seen now.

CHRISTINE (*touching him*). They wanted a boy first. (*Smiles.*) Everybody does. And they got one. You were the special one, you were the favourite, weren't you? I didn't mind. I copied you in everything, do you know. (*She smiles as she touches him.*)

And that was what I was meant to do. I used to copy you *so much*, every day that I was small. You never noticed – you never even noticed me watching you. (*She smiles, touching him again.*) You need to shave . . . I'm going to squeeze this lemon down your throat – now.

She holds his arm tight, he flinches.

MIKE. Don't! (*Urgent.*) I think there's somebody coming! I can hear them . . .

CHRISTINE *gets up.*

The police could pick you up here so easily, you know.

CHRISTINE. Yes, nobody's come yet – surprised they haven't.

MIKE. They think I'm talking in my sleep, that's why. I've been having these terrible nightmares, really savage ones, at night. Each time I wake up I expect to find horrible things all over the pillow – and I feel like I've been slowly run over by a bulldozer.

CHRISTINE (*staring down at him in bed*). You know, I think you wanted to end up here. You should get up now, before it's too late. If you stay here long enough, you'll grow fat and you'll never get up again. *You'll just fall asleep for ever.*

MIKE. You could stay here, and not know what month it was, what year it was, even.

CHRISTINE (*urgent*). You should get up and walk out with me now. (*Louder.*) There's no reason for you not to.

MIKE. Isn't there?

CHRISTINE. You're a fucking idiot! (*Loud.*) Come on, get up!

Suddenly she kicks the bed really tremendously hard – MIKE lets out a stifled shriek of pain, then hastily glances over his shoulder at the rest of the ward.

Just get up, come on.

CHRISTINE *immediately kicks the bed again.*

MIKE. Careful, you fool! You'll rip open the stitches. Christine, please! Stop! Please. (*Loud.*) Nurse!

CHRISTINE *stops.*

CHRISTINE. I've stopped – for the moment.

MIKE. I'm going to have you moved.

CHRISTINE (*staring down at him*). You've got to leave here Mike, now!

MIKE (*keeping completely still*). But you don't understand. I *like* it here. I do – and I've got hundreds of books to read.

He indicates a pile of 'Disaster' books.

I've discovered something though, I've just proved it for myself.

Suddenly tone changes, more emotional and he lifts his head, slightly and rigidly.

I just can't read any more, you see. I stare at a page of a book and I say 'I will read it' – and I start. But suddenly, I find I'm looking away! MY EYES WON'T STAY ON THE WORDS. They just won't. I have to look away. I can't make myself get through a whole chapter now. It takes all my strength to finish a single page – and that's not reading every line. I'm not lazy. I did fight it. I thought it was because of distractions. It isn't. I know that now – lying here. I will never be able to get to the end of a book again . . .

CHRISTINE. It's not surprising. They're such terrible books you read.

MIKE. I know I'm clever. There're lots of things I could do.

CHRISTINE (*watching him*). You're lucky. You've at least got the confidence.

MIKE. I have ideas all the time – but I can't keep them in my head – everything just leaks away. I can feel it going, just disappearing, like there's holes all over my scalp. And it's as if somebody has put them there recently. Has made them happen without me knowing. (*Quiet.*) I think something has eaten my mind. (*Pause.*)

CHRISTINE. You shouldn't have let it! You could have fought it more.

MIKE (*lying back, staring at the ceiling, keeping still*). I don't really mind though. (*Smiles.*) Who knows, I may not be alive in three years' time. I feel something's going to happen soon. So it doesn't really matter what one does any more – in the end. That's what I think. (*Smiles to himself self-mocking.*) We could all be drowned very soon . . . or we could be poisoned by . . .

CHRISTINE (*very loud, cutting him off*). That's bollocks! You always sound so pleased.

She moves right up to the bed and stands over him. Very quiet.

I'm as clever as you are, Mike. I think.

Pause. He looks back at her. Suddenly she moves across.

I think you would have a heart attack if you managed to finish one of your books now.

MIKE (*nervous*). What are you doing?

CHRISTINE. I'm going to read you the end of one of these rubbishy books so there'll definitely be one book in the world you've finished!

MIKE. No you won't. I can't listen. I don't want you to.

CHRISTINE *picks up first book and starts to read incredibly fast. We get from her the meaning of the following passage without hearing every single word. As she reads MIKE lets out stifled shouts.*

MIKE (*during the reading*). Please stop, I can't listen – I don't want to be read to. I CAN'T LISTEN. Just stop! OK, stop it! Just give it here . . . (*He continues to shout all through the passage.*)

CHRISTINE (*reading fast*). 'Kline stood in front of his own front door. The cold compact handle of his Japanese F26 felt smooth and satisfyingly light in his hand. He started out across the street. Savage devastation greeted him wherever he looked. There were dead people everywhere, a lot of them were nude, lying strewn across the street with their mouths open. The road was beginning to crack up in the middle, paving stones were being hurled up in the air as the *black mud oozed on and on.* Kline noticed a beautiful naked blonde stone dead, her legs apart as the black mud covered her. It was beginning to creep into the basements of houses. The smell of sewage and putrifying bodies was completely overpowering.
Suddenly, with a vicious rapid burst, the police marksmen across the street opened up on a group of looters helping themselves from the corpses in the mud. The bullets ripped into them. *Kline knew this was it.* He was watching the end of civilisation as he knew it . . .'

MIKE (*lunges for the book*). Just stop it! Give it here, Christine.

He lunges for the book and falls sideways out of bed. As he does so he lets out an involuntary and very real shout of pain. Half of him still on the bed, the other half leaning towards floor.

MIKE. Oh God.

He holds his middle in real pain.

Look what you've done now.

CHRISTINE. Yes. (*She moves over to help him.*)

MIKE. They'll come now, I've made too much noise.

CHRISTINE. I know.

Comes right up to him.

MIKE (*seeing* CHRISTINE *about to help him, alarmed*). Don't try to help me, please . . .

CHRISTINE *tries to lift him. Her pale face reacts strangely. She pulls with all her strength – desperately trying to lift him.*

CHRISTINE. I don't think I can lift you. I should be able to . . .

She grits her teeth and really tries.

I can't. I can't lift you.

She lets him go and reels on her feet for a moment. She looks very peculiar and pale.

MIKE. They'll be here in a moment – you mustn't stay. (*He looks up at her.*) God, you look so strange, Christine! Something *is* happening to you. You'll have to hurry now.

CHRISTINE. You stupid boy. (*She flicks his hair.*) That's for you. You may not see me again, not for a very long time . . . maybe not ever.

She hesitates for a second then she suddenly bangs the button on the panel above bed, really hard. Music blares out.

MIKE. Christine, you'll bring everyone. (*Holds his side in pain.*)

CHRISTINE. You should have walked out of here – now with me. It was your last chance.

She moves to go. Music blares out. She stops and looks at him. He curls away from her.

Blackout.

Scene Four

Music continues and then silence. The room. CHRISTINE *enters through the door of the flat.* MRS FORSYTHE *is standing waiting for her, looking apprehensive.* CHRISTINE *stands in front of the door. She sways very slightly on her feet for a second. She is incredibly pale.*

CHRISTINE. Good you're waiting for me.

She takes off her shoulder bag slowly and very precisely.

MRS FORSYTHE (*nervous*). I didn't know where you were . . .

CHRISTINE *just stares at her.*

I didn't know if you were coming back or not.

CHRISTINE (*very precise and quiet*). Of course I was coming back.

She picks up the cut-off telephone receiver and twines the flex for a moment.

MRS FORSYTHE (*watching her, apprehensive*). How are you feeling? We haven't slept for two nights now, you know. Neither of us.

CHRISTINE (*very precise*). I'm fine.

She is standing directly in front of the door.

(*Slight smile.*) Of course, it might have been better for you if I hadn't come back.

Pause.

I'm going to give you your last lesson . . .

She stands in front of the door.

As you know, they're going to be coming to collect me this morning – to take me into their care. I will be leaving here. (*Her tone changes.*) And so you . . . (*She looks directly at her.*) . . . you're going *straight back* to what you were when I found you.

Slight pause.

You're not going to be able to go out. I'm going to put you back in this room again. You're going right back to what you were before. And this time you're going to stay that way. I'm going to make sure of that. I can turn you back just as easily as flicking a switch. And there's nothing you can do about it. You've got no choice.

MRS FORSYTHE. Haven't I . . .

CHRISTINE. Because I've starved myself. It was my protection.

She stares straight at her.

And I'm going to tell them you refused to feed me properly, refused to feed me at all! And so I'm not answerable for any of my actions.

MRS FORSYTHE (*very quiet*). I don't think they'll totally believe you.

CHRISTINE (*really sharp and strong*). Of course they will.

Because they've seen you behaving so extraordinarily over the last few days and they know you're capable of anything! You *lied* about me consistently to them on the phone. They've seen you *drinking* vast amounts in public and fighting. And you've gone around dressed in an odd way claiming to everyone that you're not my mother at all but my sister. You'll be lucky if they don't certify you – mad!

Pause.

MRS FORSYTHE (*staring back at her quiet but slight smile*). You horrible little girl. That's what you plan to do is it?

CHRISTINE. That's what I *am* doing – now. I'm going to brick you up again in here, for ever.

MRS FORSYTHE. You're trying to be very cruel, aren't you?

CHRISTINE. What are you smiling at?

MRS FORSYTHE. Because you've left it too late, Christine.

CHRISTINE. I still control you all the time.

MRS FORSYTHE. No. (*She looks straight at her.*) I'm no longer afraid of you. I was. But not now. Because you're very slightly too late. (*She smiles.*) You can't take back what you've done to me. (*Smile – calm.*) You can't stop it now. I'm going to get a job again.

CHRISTINE (*steely*). A job?

MRS FORSYTHE. And then a better one – and then a better one after that, if it's humanly possible. And even if it isn't.

CHRISTINE (*staring back*). You can't disobey me. It's useless to try. You should know that.

Suddenly shouts.

I'm not having you staying here as you are now, while they take me away. I'm *not* letting that happen.

MRS FORSYTHE. That's your own idiotic fault.

CHRISTINE (*savage*). I'm going to break you back again.

MRS FORSYTHE. You can scream as much as you like. It won't make any difference.

CHRISTINE. I made you like this, didn't I. I *created* you and now I'm putting you back amongst all this.

She indicates the magazines and Green Shield Stamps all over the floor.

MRS FORSYTHE (*smiles*). You've got the face of an old woman when you shout like that – really ugly.

CHRISTINE. I want to hurt you so much and I mean *really hurt*.

MRS FORSYTHE (*quiet smile*). You can tear small pieces off me. It won't make any difference.

CHRISTINE. You're not *staying* like this!

MRS FORSYTHE. You're much more dangerous, Christine, when you don't scream like that.

CHRISTINE (*suddenly her tone changes, really emotional and loud*). Don't you *understand*? Haven't you learnt anything at all?

She moves round room.

I've shown you everything. I've taken you out and shown you it all. (*Loud.*) And you've seen how horrible it is!

MRS FORSYTHE. No I haven't.

CHRISTINE. (*screams*). CAN'T YOU UNDERSTAND! I *hate* all this place. I hate all this muck they give us!

She kicks the magazines violently all over the floor.

They throw it at us. They try to drown us with it. (*Screams.*) And I hate all men!

MRS FORSYTHE. No you don't. Only some of them!

CHRISTINE (*shouting*). They only want one thing from me – ever. That's all I get from them – the way they've always looked at me. (*Shouts.*) And they've all gone to sleep! They have. They couldn't be bothered. They don't care about anything any more.

MRS FORSYTHE. You're much stronger than your brother, you know.

CHRISTINE (*carrying straight on, her voice reaching a pitch*). Don't you see there's nothing! Nothing any more! NOTH – ING. This is the worse time ever to be alive, *everybody* knows that!

MRS FORSYTHE smiles.

CHRISTINE (*shouting almost hysterically with real passion*). There's no point in me doing anything. There's nothing for me! Can't you see that? Can't you understand even that? I don't know why you're so stupid. (*She screams.*) You're so completely stupid!

Silence – pause.

Don't smile or I'll kill you.

MRS FORSYTHE. That doesn't work on me any longer.

Pause – CHRISTINE stares at her.

CHRISTINE. You've just been using me really, haven't you, the whole time.

Slight pause. Then she throws the keys at her.

Those are yours. You used what I had and at the same time just let me go ahead and do all those things.

MRS FORSYTHE. No I didn't. It was your own idiotic fault. (*Quiet smile.*) I could kill you when you spoil yourself like that.

CHRISTINE (*suddenly louder and more dangerous again*). You're not allowed . . .

She tries to lift a light ordinary chair to hurl at MRS FORSYTHE. She lifts it a few inches with incredible effort but can't get it further.

I can't . . . I can't bloody lift . . . I can't . . .

She really strains to try to lift it – it gives a few more inches and then she falls flat on her back on the floor. Total silence. CHRISTINE lies there. MRS FORSYTHE leans against the wall, doesn't move. CHRISTINE tries to lift herself but can't. She can hardly lift her head despite the effort that is going into it.

Pause.

I can't get up Mum.

Pause.

I can't get up now, Mum. I can't move . . .

MRS FORSYTHE *moves over to her after watching her for a moment – she stares down at her for a moment. CHRISTINE can hardly turn her head – tiny movement – her strength has gone.*

MRS FORSYTHE. You really haven't been eating, have you, you stupid child –

She kneels by her and looks across her body.

There's not much of you left, is there, Christine? You've shrunk. You should be dead, if you haven't eaten all this time.

She moves CHRISTINE's pale head.

What have you been living off?

CHRISTINE *just stares back at her, can't move her head.*

All that black rage that's just poured out of you? Is that what you were doing? Living off that?

She touches her.

I could pick you up with one hand now, easily.

She looks down at her, runs her head across CHRISTINE's *mouth and across her face.*

I never noticed that you had a slightly crooked nose. I must have forgotten. (*She smiles.*) Almost forgotten.

CHRISTINE *opens her mouth slightly but no sound comes out.*

You're such an idiotic girl – you just have to use all that power in there, (*She's just by* CHRISTINE's *body.*) locked in there. And there'd be no stopping you. Because you're so strong. Such a strong girl, aren't you?

CHRISTINE *runs her hand across her lips, opens her mouth.*

CHRISTINE. I've got no voice left either. It's disappeared.

MRS FORSYTHE (*carrying on*). And then you could reach anything you wanted. *Nobody at all* could stop you. (*Slight smile.*) If you kept out of trouble, of course.

CHRISTINE (*very quiet, hardly any sound coming out*). Don't . . .

MRS FORSYTHE. God, I can feel your ribs.

Runs hand along ribs.

If you'd kept this up much longer, you'd have disappeared completely, just your skin lying there.

She stares down at her, detached tone.

There really is very little of you left.

CHRISTINE (*louder, but still very quiet*). I hurt all over . . . I feel so strange.

MRS FORSYTHE. You nearly killed yourself, you know. When you stopped drinking. (*Quiet.*) You very nearly did, which would have been a pity.

CHRISTINE. I meant it. I was serious. It was a hunger strike. (*Slight smile.*) 'Young girls are the most dangerous now' – remember. IF I had, I really wouldn't have minded.

MRS FORSYTHE. Now you're talking like your brother. I hate you looking so pale and old. You're still shrinking. We've got to put you in some proper clothes for them, I suppose.

CHRISTINE. (*quiet, turning her head*). You could probably put your hand through me like through paper.

MRS FORSYTHE. Can you stand up? Come on.

She lifts CHRISTINE *up.* CHRISTINE *wobbles on her feet looking very fragile.*

MRS FORSYTHE. Can you?

She lets her go. CHRISTINE *steadies herself.*

(*Matter-of-fact.*) Are you going to reel about or can you stand?

CHRISTINE *leans against the wall and turns her head away. She begins to shake slightly and begins to make a noise.*

Are you crying, Christine?

CHRISTINE (*turns her head*). I would be if there was any water to come out – anything to come out at all.

She turns her head and suddenly begins to cry – it continues for a moment and stops as suddenly as it began.

I've stopped. It feels too strange.

MRS FORSYTHE. I haven't heard you do that since you were three-and-a-half.

CHRISTINE. You told me.

She leans against wall.

I'm not sure if it's a good thing or not.

She looks up at MRS FORSYTHE, *more forceful.*

I'm not going to write to you, you know.

MRS FORSYTHE. No, I know.

CHRISTINE. So don't expect it.

MRS FORSYTHE. I won't expect it (*Smile.*) I wasn't going to write to you.

CHRISTINE (*sharp*). There's going to be none of all that.

MRS FORSYTHE (*calmly watching her*). But you are going to start eating again, aren't you – wherever they put you.

CHRISTINE (*leaning against the wall holding pen, poking at the wall*). I still don't make any promises. I don't know. It depends on the cooking.

Pause.

I'll see . . . I'll see about a lot of things . . . I'm not sure if I'll be on this planet next year – or maybe the year after.

MRS FORSYTHE (*watching her*). Oh yes you will be.

CHRISTINE. Yes . . . maybe. You may never see me again, though.

MRS FORSYTHE (*staring at her*). I expect I will.

Staring at her, strong.

It depends if I'll want to.

CHRISTINE *looks up at her, the two women look at each other surprised. A moment's pause, then* CHRISTINE *turns back to the wall.*

CHRISTINE (*tracing the words out on the wall with biro but not really writing, faster than real writing*). Friday, 23rd, Mum and me are here – our last morning . . . people are just switching on their radios . . . I'm still alive, so it seems. The weather is terrible, of course.

Fade.

AMERICAN DAYS

American Days was premièred at the ICA, London on 12 June 1974, with the following cast:

TALLULAH	Toyah Willcox
GARY	Phil Daniels
LORRAINE	Caroline Embling
IAN	Jack Elliot
SHERMAN	Antony Sher
MURRAY	Mel Smith

Directed by John Chapman and Tim Fywell
Designed by Caroline Beaver

TALLULAH is seventeen years old, her hair is dyed a bright orange. Broad intelligent face, loud laugh. Birmingham accent.

GARY is eighteen years old, medium height, thin, mercurial manner, a charming smile, London accent.

LORRAINE is only about five feet high, seventeen years old, very pale sharp face, dark intelligent eyes, Sheffield accent.

IAN is twenty-nine years old, short hair, well-cut suit, but fashionable, bright green shoes; upper middle class accent, laconic self-mocking smile.

SHERMAN is in his late thirties, small stocky figure, enormous energy, dark piercing eyes, a very strong presence. His accent is classless, slight traces of a Midlands accent.

MURRAY is a very large man in his mid-thirties, grossly fat, long hair, huge blotchy face. Dressed in expensive clothes. Midlands accent.

The play is set in London on a day and night in July. The location is the Listening Room of an international record company – a large, very plush room, used for entertaining artistes, and covered from wall to wall in blue carpet. Among the accessories are a piano, a fridge and an aquarium.

ACT ONE

Scene One

The large Listening Room. Blue carpet. Gold discs on the walls. A sleek, long room with plants and an aquarium.
TALLULAH, *aged seventeen, is sitting at the piano. As the lights come up, she's plonking down on one note and then a second note, idly doodling on the piano. For a long moment we watch her bent over the piano.* GARY *enters, carrying a guitar.*

GARY. Don't mind me.

TALLULAH (*glances round at him, then back at the piano*). I wasn't.

GARY. Are you here for the same reason I am?

TALLULAH. I expect so. I don't know. (*She plays the note.*)

GARY (*sees fridge*). Why is there a fridge here? (*He pulls the fridge's door.*) It's locked. Wonder what's inside. (*Looks into aquarium.*) They've got snails in here. They must have eaten all the fish. (*Taps glass.*) (*Pause.*) Have you felt this carpet? It sort of oozes under your feet, doesn't it, feel it. It's down all the corridors, it's on the walls of some rooms. (*Pause.*)

TALLULAH. I was shown right in here.

GARY. I've come to see this important guy – I got an invitation.

IAN *enters – in his late twenties, fashionably dressed, he smiles a pleasant, professional smile.*

IAN. There you are. Now one of you is either very early or extremely late. In fact it's quite possible you're both late. (*He smiles.*) Which in the circumstances is quite helpful. So we'll forgive you. Anyway welcome to IBC – glad you could visit us, to sound a formal note for a moment. Hope it will prove profitable for all of us. This is what we call the Listening Room, newly decorated as you can see, which we use for all our interviews and discussions (*he smiles*) and the odd midnight session. (*Slight pause.*) You must be Gary and Tallulah then.

GARY. Yes, I'm Gary.

LORRAINE *enters.*

IAN (*calm but quite sharp*). Now what the hell are you doing here?

LORRAINE. I have an appointment.

IAN. Not any longer. You're Lorraine, right?

299

LORRAINE. Yes.

IAN. Didn't you get the telegram we sent? Your interview's been cancelled. (*Pause.*) We've had to cancel it.

LORRAINE. What, you mean you didn't want me to come after all?

IAN. Because time is shorter than I anticipated. Why didn't you get the telegram? I sent it personally.

LORRAINE (*quiet*). So you want me to go again.

Slight pause.

IAN. No – now you're here, you're here. Some squeezing will have to go on. (*Looking at them all.*) So first, here are some name badges if you can just fill them in, with your first name. (*Smiles.*) In capitals if possible, that saves us a lot of time.

GARY (*taking badge, quite polite tone*). Right, OK, are you him, then, the guy we're meeting?

IAN (*smiles*). Not quite, no. I'm the guy who spotted you. (*Looking at GARY.*) I tried to meet you for a drink afterwards I remember, but I don't think you showed. Now you're being seen by Don Sherman, which means you're in luck, because he's the top guy you can see.

TALLULAH. Good . . . great.

IAN (*carrying on*). I just hope he'll have time to see all of you – properly.

TALLULAH's *face immediately falls.*

IAN. I'm sure he will. People have waited five years to see him, and I'm not joking, but fortunately you're not in that position. He will have heard your tapes, so he's prepared, he knows something of your music. (*He smiles.*) When you see him it's important to keep him here, not waste his time, answer his questions, because once he leaves he just doesn't come back. Not a chance. You remember that – OK?

TALLULAH. Christ – I'm beginning to feel a bit peculiar.

IAN. There's no need for any of you to feel hostile about being here because though you may find the surroundings a bit alientating, we're very used to that. (*He smiles.*) And know how to handle it. So don't worry. (*Slight pause.*) Now if those of you that haven't done so could check in at security, picking your way over the alsatians, you can get your identity cards, then you'll be able to use our full facilities. Our restaurant – visitors' section – squash courts, television room and the bar, free of charge. (*He smiles.*) If you don't do that, you'll have to pay through the teeth. (*The loudspeaker phone rings.*)

SHERMAN'S VOICE. Ian . . . Ian.

IAN. Yes, I'm here.

SHERMAN. There you are. I've tried every room in the building. What on earth are you doing down there?

IAN. I didn't know you'd arrived.

SHERMAN. No, we just got in – come on up. It's rather nice and empty up here.

IAN. No, Don – I'm here with these kids, Don – the ones you're going to see, remember?

SHERMAN. What kids? I have no intention of seeing any kids.

IAN *looks embarrassed but keeps his cool.*

SHERMAN (*his voice continuing*). I have no kids on my schedule – Ian!

IAN (*to kids*). If you could all check in now with security.

GARY (*looking at loudspeaking telephone, grins*). Does that mean five years of our lives are going to go?

IAN. Go on.

GARY *exits with* LORRAINE, *both looking worried.*

TALLULAH (*doesn't move, she stands across the room looking at* IAN). I've already done that, checked in.

SHERMAN (*his voice has been continuing*). Ian, are you there . . . what are you doing?

IAN. Yes, I'm here. You remember the kids I wanted you to see, there are three of them.

SHERMAN'S VOICE. Three of them! I haven't conceivably got time to see three of them.

IAN. I know it's a bit difficult – and you've just got in. (*His voice suddenly sharp.*) But you've got to see them. (*He smiles.*) And it would be a real help to me, for obvious reasons.

SHERMAN'S VOICE. Not that again. I keep on telling you not to worry.

IAN. I know and I hope you're right – but you must see them, Don. (*Silence.*) Are you still there?

TALLULAH (*into loudspeaking telephone, right over it*). Come on

– come on down here, we're waiting.

SHERMAN'S VOICE. Who's that?

TALLULAH. Me.

IAN. That was one of the kids.

SHERMAN. Really. And you're waiting to see me?

TALLULAH. Yes – I'm here – in this Listening Room.

SHERMAN. And you want me to come down? (*Pause.*)

TALLULAH. Yeah. (*She is right up to telephone.*) Quickly.
   Pause.

SHERMAN. Good. Good. Fine. I shall try to make it.

TALLULAH (*by loudspeaker telephone*). Hello? Have you gone?
   Silence.

TALLULAH. He's coming now.

IAN (*leaning against wall, smiles*). That was close.
   Blackout.

Scene Two

GARY *is standing by the door, staring down the passage.*

GARY. He's coming. I can see him . . . (*He moves sharply away
   from the door and across the room.*) He's coming right now.
   Pause, nobody enters.

TALLULAH. Well, where is he then?

GARY (*remains across the room away from the door*). He must
   have stopped. Got stuck in the passage. (*Pause, watching the
   door.*) Maybe he caught himself on the radiator.

TALLULAH. Maybe he turned back.

LORRAINE. I don't believe he's out there. (*Glancing over to
   door.*) What does he look like?

GARY. Look like . . . ? He's sort of squat looking. A bit
   misshapen. Little chubby legs.

   SHERMAN *moves into the room as* GARY *is saying this last
   line.* LORRAINE *is standing against the far wall. Strong
   sunlight across room.* SHERMAN *stops for a split second as he
   enters the room, glances round, hardly seems to register the
   kids. He moves into the room. He is holding a bundle of letters,
   two of which he has already opened. He does not look at the
   kids at all, but moves across the room and puts the letters down*

on a small table. Stands looking down at the table. Silence.

SHERMAN (*not looking at them*). What day of the week is it?

The kids look at each other. He doesn't look at them.

GARY. Friday.

SHERMAN (*quiet*). Friday.

He undoes letter with paper knife, sharp movements.

SHERMAN (*smiling to himself, matter-of-fact*). I can't get people here to understand that I like opening my own letters. (*He is working his way through mail, summing up the contents of each letter with a very quick glance.*) If you try to pick a single envelope up, your secretaries grab it back at once. And they just won't let go. You have to tear it out of their hands. (*Flick of paper knife – fast.*) So I hijack my post on its way down the passage. (*He undoes letter, a wadge of bank notes comes out, he pushes it to one side.*) More wasted money. (*He opens another letter.*) During the worst of the bomb scares, this company had a special American come over to open all our mail. He was about nine feet tall. Blond. He opened every letter for a year. He used to wear white gloves. Artists get sent a lot of strange things. He's doing the same job now in our Rome office. He'll lose a hand soon. (*He looks up, but hardly seems to take in the kids.*) Terrific. (*He smiles.*) Smell of the new carpet – if anything it's stronger than last week.

TALLULAH (*quite loud*). Does he know we're here do you think?

Silence. SHERMAN ignores this, he moves over to the fridge.

GARY. He's got a key. (*He grins.*) They must be a group of special people that are allowed to get in.

The fridge is empty except for a bottle of milk.

SHERMAN (*suddenly loud*). *I don't believe this!* It's empty! It always happens in London. That's the second time in ten days! Each time I come back. They are meant to fill them up at the beginning of each week. I cannot believe that that is beyond them. (*Sharp smile.*) I can only operate with a full fridge. It makes anything I have to do in here bearable. (*He smiles.*) I have lived off the contents of one of these for a month. (*He smiles.*) Never needed to go out of the building.

He picks up the phone.

SHERMAN (*into phone*). No, which one are you? Sharon? Genista? Well, which are you? There's nothing in the fridge down here you realise. Yes, in the Listening Room. Except for a bottle of milk. No. I've just got in. Yes. Well *do* something *now*. And give me the new New York number. (*Smiles.*) No, you just have to say it once. (*He punches the number out on the phone.*) Hello, it's DS here. No, I just got in. Is Moss there? No, no. I'll let him finish, for once. I'll hold.

He puts down the receiver and lets it lie on the table. He has poured milk into a glass and is sipping it.

SHERMAN (*moving from table sipping milk*). I met three Germans on the plane. Young Germans. One of them was incredibly overweight. And you know what they were doing? They were going round the world without a break in fifty-six hours! They'd taken a bet to go round the world without stopping. Rushing from one plane to another. They'd flown to Tokyo, then to Sydney, then across to Brazil, then to Los Angeles, and now they were coming back to Frankfurt via London. The last leg of their trip. They were really extraordinary, they'd become completely hysterical. Giggling and bouncing up and down in their seats and leaning across and tugging at my arm. They were wearing little party hats, coloured paper hats, and they had no control over their actions at all. Tickling each other furiously and rolling out into the middle of the gangway and they were all red round the eyes — totally gummed up. (*He smiles.*) It was fantastic. All for a bet! They were going to win it too. (*He drinks the glass of milk.*)

GARY. Are we allowed to talk amongst ourselves while you're speaking?

Silence.

SHERMAN (*looks at them*). Two girls and a boy.

GARY (*half to himself*). At least he isn't blind.

TALLULAH. Do you know who we are? (*Pause.*) Have you listened to our tapes?

LORRAINE (*quiet*). We were asked here you know. Sent for.

GARY. Has he forgotten he's on the phone? (*Grins.*) You're on the phone to New York! (*Pause.*)

SHERMAN. Have you got name badges?

They have all taken theirs off.

GARY. You want to know our names.

SHERMAN. No, I want to see your name badges. I don't remember names. Could you put them on?

TALLULAH (*as she pins her name label on*). I'm Tallulah.

SHERMAN (*reads off* LORRAINE's *badge*). Lorraine.

GARY. I'm Gary.

SHERMAN (*as if he hasn't heard*). Have you got a name badge?
  GARY *puts it on*.

SHERMAN (*reads*). Gary. I need to see names.

GARY (*suddenly*). Christ, I wish you'd finish your phone call.

TALLULAH. I don't think it really is to New York. (*Pause.*) Are
  those noises from New York? (*Noises over loudspeaking
  telephone.*) You've had it lying there for five minutes you know.
  You'll get your phone cut off.

GARY. They probably get cheap rates because they use it so much
  – probably have their own private phone cable running under
  the Atlantic.

LORRAINE. Have you listened to our tapes yet? (*Pause.*) I don't
  think he knows why we're here.

TALLULAH. He doesn't seem to answer any questions at all.

SHERMAN (*who has been staring at them for the first time. He
  turns away*). I've listened to a lot of tapes today, already. And
  I've only been in the building forty-five minutes. We get 200
  tapes a week. People who have sent in little brown parcels of
  themselves singing. Often they're singing in the bath. (*Sharp.*) I
  mean it. That's because that's where they sing best. We hear the
  water sloshing around in the background and the tape often
  smells of Crazy Foam. They're all listened to.

  AMERICAN VOICE *comes stabbing out of the telephone and
  during* SHERMAN's *telephone conversation it often mumbles in
  the background.* SHERMAN *moves round the room as he talks
  very fast, his manner quickening, speedy, professional, a totally
  different tone from the one for the kids. He raises his voice
  when he is far from the phone, drops it lower when he is close.*

AMERICAN. Hello . . . are you there . . . hello . . .

SHERMAN. Moss, it's me. Yes . . . I just got in. (AMERICAN
  VOICE *mumbles.*) No – I arrive here just now – and there is
  nothing in the bloody fridge! (*Smiling.*) Nothing! No, a great
  yawning hole. Not even any ice, which takes some doing.

AMERICAN. It's different in Chicago.

SHERMAN (*speedy, laughing*). No, the best one is in Michigan.
  You just go through the door, and there are three

sixteen-year-old drum majorettes waiting curled up in the shower room, fast asleep. (*Straight on.*) You seen about Zat's single? As I said it topped quarter of a million in a week. (*He moves abruptly.*) No, it's peaked. It won't do more. No, there'll be the usual slight wobble in and out for the next month. He's definitely broken Europe now. I thought this would be the one. Even Holland. Holland was really holding out, but he's broken that too. Only Australia. He seems to be out to lunch in Australia. Out to lunch completely. Only 25,000. I know . . . three warehouses full of the single over there, it's pouring out of the windows apparently – they'll have to melt them. The promotion was wrong over there – they didn't listen as usual. (*His tone changes, harder.*) Now Moss, are you listening to me? I have recommended . . . on my recommendation . . . we are going to terminate that contract. Yes, the artist we discussed last week, subject X, since I'm being observed as I talk . . . No, it's been drying up for years for him. No, he was trailing badly even then. We have no reason to renew, I fall asleep when I hear anything of his now, we don't dare tour the schmuck any more. (*Louder, firmer.*) WE HAVE NO REASON TO RENEW. Yes, I remember that tour, of course. He looked wonderful. Yes, it's been settled. Now about the sleeve I was talking about – yes – No I phoned from the airport – the sleeve was rubbish. I didn't know what it was! No, I really didn't. I thought it was a lawnmower. I had to be told what it was. And the way she looked. She looked like an Arab shoplifter – incredibly shifty. Also if you hold it the wrong way up, upside down, it looks as if she's been cut in half. No, they should put her hands on the cover sleeve – no, I'm serious, the only bit of her that the camera likes, long bony hands, very white, very long fingers, like they belong to a dead person. Quite eerie. You should ask to see them next time. Yes – they can be holding something interesting . . . Right, no I'll phone Zurich myself. I'm catching the last flight out tonight. Maybe earlier. (*He suddenly glares up at the kids.*) It depends. Goodbye. (*He slams down the phone.*)

Silence. The kids have been watching this fast performance in stunned silence. They look at him.

SHERMAN (*smiles*). There's no need to be nervous.

TALLULAH. We're not.

SHERMAN. It seems to be a nice day.

He draws the blinds and curtains. The sunlight is entirely shut out, and the room is plunged into darkness.

SHERMAN. These curtains are already getting old.

TALLULAH. What are you doing?

The room is in almost total darkness.

SHERMAN (*as he finishes drawing the curtains*). I spoke to one of you before I came down.

TALLULAH *about to speak*, SHERMAN *has his back to them, he snaps.*

I *don't want* to know which one it was. (*He turns.*) It's no secret that I didn't want to see any of you today – so if you would rather leave . . .

TALLULAH (*loud*). No. (*Slight pause.*) We wouldn't.

SHERMAN (*steely*). Now, when I ask you to do something, whatever it happens to be, I want your co-operation.

GARY (*grinning*). Do we have to be careful what we say and do, from now on?

SHERMAN (*suddenly*). I'm afraid before I go any further, you'll have to take those boots off.

TALLULAH. Who are you talking to . . . !

SHERMAN. Could you please take those boots off?

GARY. He can't be serious can he?

TALLULAH *is wearing black gumboots.*

SHERMAN. They are just distracting – I'm afraid I can't work with them – they'll have to come off. They confuse me.

TALLULAH *slowly takes boots off.*

TALLULAH. You get a kick out of this do you?

SHERMAN (*sharp*). Small black gumboots, just like the Queen Mother; whenever people think of the Queen Mother they think of her gumboots. (*He smiles.*) I have seen statistics.

TALLULAH (*looking straight at him*). Is that all right or do you want me to take anything else off?

Pause.

SHERMAN (*matter-of-fact*). No. No, don't leave them where I can see them – put them in the fridge. (*Very sharp.*) What was your name?

GARY (*who has just taken his badge off*). Gary.

SHERMAN. Then put it back on. (*He stares at them for a brief moment, then moves away.*)

GARY (*half to himself*). Sadist.

SHERMAN (*swings round*). Who said that?

Slight pause.

GARY. Me. It was me.

SHERMAN (*slight smile*). You're quite wrong. That is not something I am.

GARY (*straight back*). That's all right then, they told us you just walk out without warning. Just like that. Bang. They said we've got to keep you here somehow otherwise we've blown it. Because you never come back ever.

SHERMAN (*slight smile*). You may get a warning.

Uneasy pause for a second.

LORRAINE. He's got yellow socks on – you know.

TALLULAH (*nervous smile*). Yellow socks – what does that mean about him?

SHERMAN. Could you go and stand against the far wall? All of you. Just go and stand against it . . . Look at me.

They are lined upon the far side of the stage against the wall. He looks across at them in a group. Long pause.

SHERMAN. Have any of you got a police record?

LORRAINE. What do you want to know that for?

GARY (*sharp grin*). Do we have to consider our answer carefully?

SHERMAN. I need to know. It makes a difference to the company attitude. Have any of you?

GARY (*half under his breath*). What the fuck is he doing?

LORRAINE (*quiet*). No – I have not.

TALLULAH. No, I have not. (*Mock.*) I swear on whatever you've got to swear on.

Pause. SHERMAN *looks at* GARY.

GARY (*deliberately slowly*). I do . . . not have one! He's giving us a shrewd look . . . see, a piercing look. (*Nervous grin.*) How are we doing so far then?

TALLULAH (*with mouth spray, raising it to her mouth*). I'm going to use this if I'm allowed to, it's for my throat, *my voice.* If I'm ever 'lucky' enough to perform for you. It contains eucalyptus and cocaine. Mint-flavoured cocaine.

GARY (*to* SHERMAN). Do you take drugs then?

Slight pause. SHERMAN *turns.*

Do you think he takes drugs?

TALLULAH. He must take enough speed for six people.

SHERMAN. I took *one* drug once, in San Francisco in the summer of 1970 with a needle. It was in the air then, that sort of thing. (*Smiles.*) And a necessary thing to know about.

TALLULAH *is holding her arm.* LORRAINE *has looked away.* SHERMAN *feels telephone receiver restlessly.*

SHERMAN (*his tone alters, business like*). Tallulah, come here, please.

He is in the middle of the stage; she has to cross to get to him. She hesitates.

No, come here.

TALLULAH. Come where?

SHERMAN (*staring at her*). Just here. Don't worry, just come here. Nothing is going to happen to you. I'm not going to do anything.

GARY. Don't get too close.

TALLULAH *stands in the middle of the floor opposite him.*

LORRAINE. He's going to interrogate you.

SHERMAN. Don't worry about the others. (*He is standing over her, he takes her by the hair, feeling her hair.*) Have you ever dyed your hair a different colour?

TALLULAH. Yes. Bright red.

SHERMAN. Bright red.

TALLULAH. Yes. (*Pause.*) I like violent colours.

SHERMAN. And what's its natural colour?

TALLULAH (*straight back at him*). It doesn't have one. I've forgotten what colour it was. Maybe it was white.

GARY. You have to be careful. It's the getting-to-know-you stage. (*He grins.*) Remember, people have waited five years to see him.

SHERMAN (*he moves her head sideways*). What would you look like with your hair long?

TALLULAH. Different probably . . . worse.

SHERMAN. Where did the name Tallulah come from? It's not your real name, is it?

TALLULAH. Off a railway bridge. It said 'Tallulah Lives' in

letters thirty feet high. I thought if I called myself that people would think it was about me – like an enormous free advertisement.

GARY (*grinning*). Careful, don't talk too long, he may get restless.

SHERMAN. Where do you come from?

TALLULAH. I come from Yardley. (*Sharp smile.*) Heard of it?

SHERMAN. Birmingham.

TALLULAH. Right first time.

SHERMAN. You live with your parents?

TALLULAH. You telling me or asking me?

SHERMAN (*slight smile*). Telling you. (*Pause.*) Do you work?

TALLULAH. In the evenings. In a pub. Washing up mugs.

SHERMAN. Mugs?

TALLULAH (*more out of nervousness than aggressiveness*). What else do you want to know? I've never sung in public – I've never performed live. I paid for my own tape out of my own money. When I perform live, I want to have a few really loud explosions go off and blood coming down the back wall.

GARY. What's he grinning for? Did you see his small grin; he made a sort of little sideways grin.

TALLULAH (*small smile*). Can I go back against the wall, please?

SHERMAN. Certainly.

GARY (*as she moves, jokingly*). How did she do then?

SHERMAN (*looking across at LORRAINE's name badge*). You've got it upside down. I can't read it.

LORRAINE. Lorraine. (*Quiet.*) It's my real name.

SHERMAN. Lorraine – could you come here, please?

LORRAINE *comes up to him. Stands by him.*

How old are you?

LORRAINE. I'm seventeen.

SHERMAN. Really? You don't look seventeen.

LORRAINE. So people tell me, all the time.

SHERMAN. How seventeen are you?

LORRAINE. Five months – and quite a few days.

Slight pause.

SHERMAN. If you're under sixteen – it doesn't matter you know. Particularly.

GARY. Yes it does, doesn't it?

SHERMAN. Just don't lie to me.

LORRAINE (*genuine*). I'm not lying to you . . . Why should I lie to you?

SHERMAN (*slight smile*). To make sure I don't throw you out.

LORRAINE (*quiet, a little nervous*). I didn't think you were going to. You didn't ask her her age.

SHERMAN. No. (*Not unpleasantly.*) Your teeth are pretty dirty. You should get somebody to clean them up for you.

LORRAINE (*quiet*). I'll remember.

SHERMAN. Where do you come from?

LORRAINE. Sheffield.

SHERMAN. Have you ever been in London before?

LORRAINE. No.

SHERMAN. How tall are you?

LORRAINE (*uncertain how to answer, because he can see she's very short*). Quite tall. Very tall . . . What do you expect me to say? You can see, can't you?

SHERMAN. Yes. You're not very substantial.

LORRAINE. That's right.

SHERMAN. Can you take that off?

She is wearing a sweater over a very flimsy T-shirt.

LORRAINE. What, now?

SHERMAN. Now, yes.

LORRAINE *slowly takes the sweater off, quite embarrassed being watched by the other kids, trying to make sure that the T-shirt does not ride up completely with the sweater.*

SHERMAN (*watching her with total detachment; the sweater comes off*). That's better. (*He turns sharply, speedily.*) Fine. (*Has back to them, with finality.*) Right.

GARY. What about me then? (*Realising he isn't going to get called.*) Aren't I going to get asked into the middle?

SHERMAN *has moved across the room.*

Hey! I haven't had my turn – my personal questions – you've missed me out.

SHERMAN (*quietly, pouring more milk*). I haven't missed anything out.

GARY (*charming smile*). I come from Isleworth . . .

SHERMAN. Isleworth?

GARY. I started wanting to be a musician during Mr Skinner's classes. He was completely bald, rather ugly in fact . . .

SHERMAN (*suddenly turns, loud, cutting him off*). What is all this talk about being a musician? It's completely ludicrous. None of you are musicians. You're just raw, totally inexperienced.

GARY. But we're here aren't we? (*Slight pause.*) You must want some young artists – fresh talent. You must need to sign some because you're seeing us aren't you?

Pause.

TALLULAH. You were careful, weren't you?

GARY. It's all right. He's not edging towards the door; we're OK.

SHERMAN (*slight smile*). What's your name?

GARY. Not this again, I don't believe it. (*He moves across.*) Here. Why don't you keep it in front of you, then you can keep checking, can't you?

GARY *is by the telephone as he puts his name tag down in front of* SHERMAN.

Can I call New York? I said I'd call about this time. Let them know how it's going.

TALLULAH (*worried at his boldness*). Ssssh . . .

SHERMAN (*tiny smile*). Would you like to go to New York?

GARY (*grins*). Are you making an offer?

TALLULAH (*grins*). He won't do, like that!

GARY. I've been already, anyway, to America, to New York.

SHERMAN (*smiles*). You've been? Good. When?

GARY (*surprised*). When? A few months ago.

SHERMAN (*still smiling*). And what was it like?

GARY. What do you mean?

SHERMAN. What's it like? Tell me about it. I want to know.

Pause.

(*evasive*). You want to know? OK. Everything . . .
open really late for a start. And I mean *everything*

. . . opticians, all-night opticians, vets, dentists – they only start to really get going about midnight! . . . Jewish movies, patisseries, agricultural machinery shops, piano-tuners, all-night window cleaning classes, that's when they teach you how to clean skyscrapers, they do! You can go and look up your birth certificate at two o'clock in the morning. Yes! And you can book in and have plastic surgery done, all-night zoos, double-glazing . . . you can go nude bathing in this department store at one o'clock in the morning. You can, all-night ballet in the parks – heliports – you can go into any café in the centre at three o'clock in the morning and it's full of helicopter pilots!

GARY *stops.*

SHERMAN (*unblinking*). Yes?

GARY. Yeah!

SHERMAN. Yes. And . . .

GARY. And the garbage disposal lorries are fucking enormous, with red lights all over them. They're fantastic . . . they . . . they have cigarettes this long – really long cigarettes about ten inches, and . . . tennis rackets, really hard metal tennis rackets. Can't buy any wooden tennis rackets any more – can cut people's head open with them if you lose a point. They're very bad losers, over there . . . er . . . the police are all rapists of course and *really crude* . . .

TALLULAH (*helping him out*). People making films in the streets all the time.

GARY. Yeah – and the hospitals. Got giant hospitals – which have their own cinemas, and their own porn shops and strip clubs, right inside the hospital. (*Carrying on fast.*) And you get houses with trees growing on their roofs, and of course pet alligators swimming in the baths and up your trouser leg.

TALLULAH. And you can get green chocolate now in the drug stores.

GARY (*sideways glance*). Have you been there? (*Looks back.*) And you pass old women of about seventy or eighty out in the street wearing see-through blouses, just walking along the pavement. You see I have been! And when it rains there, these really heavy drops come down – this big – the size of boiled sweets. They're quite dangerous! And there're dead people in the rubbish bins in the park of course, just dropped in there amongst the coke cans, with their legs hanging over the edge. (*He smiles.*) It's great there. Electric!

Silence.

SHERMAN. It would have been simpler, and saved time, if you had just said, no I haven't been.

The phone rings. SHERMAN *answers phone immediately, a voice only half audible blurts out occasionally during the following conversation.*

SHERMAN (*tone changes, indicating surprise for a fraction of a second as he is caught off his guard*). Hello – *Dave?* . . . It was clever of you to track me down . . . Yes, I've heard. Yes. No, I'm afraid that is what is happening. We cannot renew – we cannot renew your contract. . . . There is nothing we can discuss really. No, it wasn't – no – it was on *my* recommendation. (*Pause as he listens.* SHERMAN's *tone direct, unsoftened.*) I felt that you and the company hadn't got anything to offer each other any more. Or to put it more brutally, we cannot afford you. Sales just haven't been good enough. No, I know . . . but over all they've been on a continuous slide, for as long as I can remember . . . And that's how it works. (*Pause.*) No, I don't think we can see each other. No, I wouldn't like to meet, no. Because there is nothing we can talk about any more. No. If I thought a change in the image would work I would have suggested it. No, I had ideas. But you're just not that sort of artist. (*Sharp.*) What do you want me to say? I could say how sorry I am, but that wouldn't be true. I am *not pleased* of course, but I am not going to bullshit you. I think it just had to be done . . . No, I'm drinking milk . . . You wanted to talk to me and I'm telling you the truth. Yes, that's why I don't talk to people afterwards because I just upset them. No, I'm afraid it has to be final. My regards to your wife. (*Puts down phone. Immediately picks it up again – tone very animated, but not upset.*) Genista! I do not want anybody to be told where I am, and there are *no exceptions*. Is that clear? And I do not want any calls put through here, no matter what they are about. (*He glances up at the kids.*) Until I say otherwise . . .

The kids uneasy, a bit nervous about what they're just seen.

LORRAINE (*quiet*). He's just chopped somebody off.

SHERMAN *moves away from the phone. He moves across the room to the window seat and sits down. During the following exchange between the kids his head suddenly goes back, his eyes close, his body completely still.*

TALLULAH. How much do you get paid? (*She turns.*) How much do you think he gets paid?

GARY. About a quarter of a million . . . to start with.

LORRAINE. Look . . .

They look at him. He is sitting in the chair, his head back, eyes closed, totally still.

Silence – they stare at SHERMAN.

TALLULAH. What's the matter? What's happened to him?

No reaction from SHERMAN.

LORRAINE. He must be faking it – mustn't he?

GARY (*looking at him*). Faking what?

TALLULAH. Hello. (*Calls out to SHERMAN – uneasy smile.*) Hello.

GARY. Do you think he's still watching us – even though his eyes are shut?

TALLULAH (*moves up to him cautiously – looks at SHERMAN's face stretched back*). He'll look like that when he's dead.

LORRAINE (*uneasy smile*). Let's hope he hasn't had a heart attack.

TALLULAH. He's very well shaved – must have done it on the plane. (*She picks up milk.*) Shall I splash some of this over him, bring him round?

TALLULAH by him with milk about to flick some across his face – but as she moves to do so, his head jerks forward, and a second later he gets up sharply.

SHERMAN (*totally ignoring her, makes straight for the phone*). Right. (*He lifts receiver and bursts into confident and reasonably fluent French, ordering coffee and saying which room he is in. He is well into his third sentence and speaking fast, when he stops abruptly.*) Of course . . . I'm sorry – I thought I was in our Paris office for a moment, yes, the carpet is the same colour blue – and the furniture is in exactly the same position. (*Smiles.*) No, I think the aquarium may be different. No, some black coffee – for one. Thank you. (*Sharply puts down phone. He smiles.*) I feel terrific. (*Suddenly remembers he didn't ask on the phone.*) Which place is this anyway? (*Indicates phone.*) That girl had an American accent.

LORRAINE. I don't believe you don't know where you are.

GARY. He knows.

TALLULAH (*intrigued*). Yes – what city is out of the window?

SHERMAN (*swings round and stops by the closed blinds*). Out there . . . (*He stares for a second trying to think.*) It must be London – each city smells different.

Pause.

SHERMAN (*he focuses on them as if remembering. Very deliberately, with a smile on his face, says their names*). Lorraine . . . and Tallulah . . . and Gary.

GARY (*his eyes meet SHERMAN's, loud*). Christ – I've just realised something! (*To SHERMAN.*) What you're doing . . . I don't know what I've been thinking all this time – (*Straight at SHERMAN.*) You're only going to take one of us, aren't you . . . at the most. We're all in competition with one another, aren't we? (*Pause. Sharp.*) Aren't we?

SHERMAN (*surprised for a split second at GARY*). Not necessarily.

GARY (*sideways to LORRAINE*). Did you hear that! 'Not necessarily.' (*To SHERMAN.*) What sort of answer is that?

SHERMAN *smiles slightly.*

TALLULAH. Is that right, what he says?

GARY. He probably thought, right at the start, of maybe putting us together, seeing if there was the possibility of a group, he was making 'visual comparisons' or whatever they call it, but he's decided against it already – haven't you – when you put us up against the wall?

SHERMAN (*slight smile*). Are you asking me or telling me?

GARY. You're not meant to see us like this you know – you're meant to have us in one at a time, totally separate, and interview us.

SHERMAN (*loud, but with slight smile*). 'Meant to'! What on earth is this 'meant to'? There are no *methods* in this business, there's no green handbook with rules in it. Anybody telling you different is lying. I meet people from time to time – though I do my best to avoid them – who talk about 'nudging' artists and 'coaxing' artists. (*Straight at them, quiet.*) Well, I don't.

GARY. You *want* us to compete with one another, he really does, that's what he's setting up, you can't do that. (*To LORRAINE.*) He's exploiting us, isn't he?

SHERMAN (*suddenly loud, speedy*). Exploiting you! I'm *exploiting you*! Should have witnesses shouldn't I? I should ring for one of the five lawyers in this building. You're free to go whenever you like, aren't you? I don't believe you're being kept here by force. If you don't like the way we work here go to another label. Be one of the eight thousand other kids or whatever number it is each week, pestering people with their tapes, pushing them into one's face as one is trying to drink a cup of coffee. (*He moves, his voice changes.*) Exploiting . . . (*Dangerous.*) I don't want to hear the word again. (*Slight pause. He is by the window.*) If one was choosing athletes it would be simple. You just have to see which one runs the fastest – jumps the highest, but this is a little more complicated.

LORRAINE (*watching him*). So we *are* competing against each other.

No reaction.

TALLULAH. Have we got your assurance that we aren't going . . .

SHERMAN. I don't give assurances.

LORRAINE. Of course he's not going to give us an assurance.

SHERMAN. Any of you are free to leave this room now – if you are not happy. (*Slight smile.*) Taking on a large company isn't easy – nor should it be. I don't sign very many artists. (*Pause.*) A contract with us could obviously transform your lives. (*Pause.*)

GARY (*looking at TALLULAH and LORRAINE*). I don't think we should go along with this – being made to compete against each other. I really don't. (*Nervous grin.*) I think we should consult amongst ourselves. I mean for a start, what I'm doing is a lot different from what they're doing. (*To TALLULAH.*) I'm sure it's good – but with me, standing me up against walls you can't really tell . . .

GARY *leans against wall, close to* SHERMAN.

SHERMAN (*by window*). You worry too much.

GARY. Who?

SHERMAN. You. You're worrying too much about how you're doing.

GARY (*sharp grin*). I think it's a really shitty – fucking absurd way of doing things . . . if you ask me. (SHERMAN *turns, pause.* GARY, *a little surprised at himself, grins.*) So you want me to leave now? Right. Do you . . . (*Pause.*) I expect you want me to go now.

SHERMAN (*slight smile*). No. (*Pause.*) You're wrong.

SHERMAN *exits slowly*.

TALLULAH (*calls after him*). Wait . . . (TALLULAH *turns, furious.*) You've done it. That's it isn't it! He'll disappear now. We'll never get him back, won't even get near him again. You've blown it.

GARY. No I haven't. (*He moves.*) I don't think I have. (*Looks around him.*) They've probably got a few hidden microphones, we're being studied on our own.

TALLULAH. You handled him completely wrong, you know. You were really clumsy – really crude the way you did it.

LORRAINE. Yes, I don't think you did it at all right.

GARY. I don't trust him.

LORRAINE. I think he'll be all right. We don't *know* if he's only going to take one of us.

GARY. Of course he is. (*Smiles.*) Only one. Really weird – the way he went into that coma or whatever it was.

LORRAINE. If he comes back we've got to make him stay here.

TALLULAH (*loud*). He never comes back for *Chrissake*, remember. (*To* GARY.) Go and have a look for him.

GARY. Why me? (*Slight grin.*) I'll get lost! You go.

He begins to sing few bars of a song, as he moves nervously, one of his own songs. Strange, wistful lyrics.

TALLULAH. Shut up.

GARY *continues to sing*.

SHERMAN *re-enters with* IAN. SHERMAN *is holding paper cup of coffee that he drains completely with one abrupt movement during the next exchange. IAN is standing in a well-cut suit with notebook.*

TALLULAH. What's *he* doing here?

IAN *smiles, standing next to* SHERMAN.

LORRAINE. Where've you been?

SHERMAN. That needn't concern you.

GARY. He's got reinforced. (*To* SHERMAN, *indicating* IAN.) What's he going to do?

IAN. I have merely come to hover, and to help out if necessary . . . make a few notes.

SHERMAN (*slight smile*). He is here for your protection.

Kids are surprised.

LORRAINE. Or yours.

GARY (*mocking*). Come to help him *choose*.

IAN. Of course not.

SHERMAN. He is quite concerned you do well.

IAN (*slight smile*). Naturally. It is because of me that you are here.

GARY (*to* IAN). And if you want my opinion, I think he likes her (*indicates* TALLULAH), half likes her (*indicates* LORRAINE) and really loathes the sight of me.

They all look at SHERMAN, *he just smiles a slight smile, then moves sharply, his manner is flowing, moving back into top gear. More competitive feel between the kids.*

SHERMAN (*straight at* GARY). You play the guitar.

GARY. Yeah, that's right.

SHERMAN. Do you play the guitar?

TALLULAH. No. (*Then more competitive.*) I have played it once, one day last year I . . .

SHERMAN. Right. (*He looks at* LORRAINE.)

LORRAINE. No.

SHERMAN. Just checking. (*He moves, sharp.*) And the piano, do you play the piano?

GARY. No.

TALLULAH. No.

LORRAINE. Yes.

SHERMAN. Right. (*He moves away, as if about to ask something else, then he suddenly turns and looks straight at* LORRAINE.) OK, play it now. Play me a tune. You can play me anything you like. (*Moment's silence.*)

LORRAINE (*glances over*). On that piano?

SHERMAN. Where else?

LORRAINE. OK. (*She moves over to piano and briskly sits down at piano,* TALLULAH *and* GARY *are watching, fascinated.*)

IAN. You can take your time.

LORRAINE (*tenses herself by the piano*). This stool's a bit low for me . . . but I think I can manage. (LORRAINE *looks at the keyboard.*) The keys are dirty. (*She tries a note, a single note, presses it down.*) It's not in tune.

IAN (*watching her*). It's always kept in tune. (*He smiles.*) One of the rules of the house.

LORRAINE. You ought to get it fixed.

SHERMAN (*louder*). Play me a tune.

LORRAINE, *who has been behaving confidently up to this moment, is poised over the keyboard. For a second she sits there, and then plonks on the piano, a terrible racket, patently unable to play a note.*

IAN (*spontaneous exasperation*). She can't play.

LORRAINE *continues for a second after this, then stops. She sits by piano, waiting for the onslaught. Silence.*

SHERMAN (*steely, quiet*). You shouldn't lie to me – what *is* the point if you're going to lie? You might as well leave right now.

LORRAINE (*uncertain whether this means she's been sacked*). Do I . . .

SHERMAN (*loud*). Do you what?

Moment's pause, LORRAINE *a small figure standing by piano.*

LORRAINE (*very quiet*). Do you want me to go?

SHERMAN (*after a slight pause*). Go back and stand over there. (*Watching her.*) No – right back!

TALLULAH (*quiet as she rejoins them*). You shouldn't take risks.

IAN (*to* LORRAINE, *his voice sharp, exasperated by her*). That was a silly thing to do, if I may say so – wasn't it? How on earth did you think you were going to get away with that? It was obvious we'd ask you to play sooner or later. You don't want to waste Mr Sherman's time you realise. His time is worth more than anybody's in the building! You're quite lucky to be here at all.

SHERMAN (*swinging round*). He wants you to do well. (*He smiles.*) And he has his reasons.

IAN (*slight smile, trying to sound cool in front of the kids*). One or two, certainly.

SHERMAN (*slight smile*). He was willing you on just now.

TALLULAH. We're trying.

SHERMAN *is standing by* IAN.

SHERMAN (*to* IAN *in a quieter personal tone, not unpleasant, with a smile*). You shouldn't worry – you can usually tell if they are planning to do something, make a change – they stop replacing the equipment in your office. You don't get those large red drawing pins delivered to you any more, you just get given the plain ordinary ones and recycled envelopes. They start giving you the dregs.

Kids watching, uncertain what they're talking about.

IAN. That's not happening yet – I don't think it is . . .

SHERMAN (*moving, his adrenalin flowing*). Good, good . . . (*Suddenly to kids, indicating* IAN). You know what this man used to do – he used to tear up lawns with pneumatic drills, yes, at college and scrawl his name on chapel walls didn't you – and he wore his hair really long and walked barefoot over electric railway lines.

IAN (*brazening it out, trying not to look embarrassed*). Yes – and he's now wearing a suit that fits almost too well.

SHERMAN. And eagerly interested in how you're doing.

GARY (*to* IAN). You must be really worried then mustn't you?

IAN (*quiet*). Why?

GARY (*indicating* SHERMAN). Because he hasn't found out anything about us at all – or about what we want to do.

SHERMAN (*is by the window*). Hasn't he? (*He stares at* GARY.) Take you for example. I know almost everything I need to know already. (*Slight pause.*) I've also listened to your very muddy tape. (*Slight pause.*)

GARY. Yes . . . (*He glances at* LORRAINE, *half jokey.*) Christ, is this it? (*Pause.*) Is he going to do it?

SHERMAN (*tone direct, but not sneering*). You want to sing songs that are 'relevant' . . . the social angle . . . the lay-off-the-Blacks category. (*Matter-of-fact.*) That is what you want to do. (*He turns.*) I saw a group somewhere, some city, they were singing an anti-fascist song, and in the middle they completely forgot what they were singing about and started strutting around the stage masturbating with their microphones, thrusting their pelvis out. That's how much they were concentrating. Two lots of twins they were, with very pale baby-like faces. (*Quiet, to himself.*) They were almost interesting.

GARY. I thought we were talking about *me*.

SHERMAN (*staring straight at him again, sharp*). And to make that stuff sell now, it has to be really *unexpected*, done with a difference.

GARY. *But I can.* You have no idea what I'm like. When I play I can be all sorts of things, different things, can be really quiet, really subtle, so you hear every word, and I can be LOUD, really outrageous, I can shock . . .

SHERMAN. You can shock can you? (*Pause.*) How?

GARY. How? I just do.

SHERMAN (*suddenly*). OK. Do it – do the most outrageous thing you can think of. Shock us.

GARY (*startled grin*). Shock you – in here. No – I'm not going to start playing party games.

SHERMAN. I'm not asking you to. (*Slight smile.*) I thought you'd welcome the chance.

TALLULAH. Yeah.

GARY. You did – did you? (*He glances round.*) You serious?

SHERMAN. Of course. When I first arrived in London, I was amazed to see three little girls smoking on the underground. But you'll find it more difficult to shock me now.

GARY (*mocking, not believing him*). You want me to do something really outrageous – and then I'm going to get marks for it afterwards! (*Suddenly to* IAN.) What you think of this then? You think it's a good idea of his?

IAN (*smiles, stares straight back at him*). I'm looking forward to it.

GARY. He's looking forward to it! (*Suddenly.*) OK.

His hand goes down and pulls his flies down as a preliminary move while he's thinking.

SHERMAN. But no nudity.

GARY. What do you mean?

SHERMAN. Because it's so predictable.

TALLULAH. Could get him into trouble couldn't it?

GARY (*grins, mocking*). Perhaps we all ought to do it then. (*Glances at girls who are not budging.*) On my own?

SHERMAN. And what's more I can imagine it.

GARY. You better give me a list of all the 'shocking' things I'm allowed to do then.

SHERMAN (*quiet*). Everything else.

GARY (*suddenly realises from his tone he is serious*). Really? (*He moves purposely – grinning.*) You mean I'm allowed to wreck the furniture and everything. Right. (*He is grinning, looking for something. He picks up a chair and tosses it on to floor.*) How shocking do you want it to be, medium shocking – or really very shocking? (*He moves round room, he smiles.*) You really are a cunt, do you know that? You've been waiting to do this haven't you?

SHERMAN. You're not going to reduce us to quivering heaps like that. In fact I really doubt you'll manage it.

GARY (*fast, moving*). I could kill a few snails for a start. (*Taps aquarium hard.*) Melt a few of these down. (*He takes gold disc off wall and drops it on floor.*) And make you drink it. (*He moves a chair sharply, grins at them all as he moves.*) What are you hoping for? What's the favourite? (*He moves.*) I could piss, vomit, beat up a crippled nun. (*He stops.*) I think I'll cut one of my fingers off, do a bit of bleeding, that's always a good one, wounds, especially self-inflicted ones. (*Flicks out matches.*) I'll set light to the carpet . . . he thinks he knows what I'm going to do. (*He gently touches* LORRAINE's *face, looking at* SHERMAN, *aggressive towards him, not* LORRAINE. *Holds* LORRAINE's *head tightly.*) If I hurt her, damaged her, that would be really shocking because she hasn't done anything wrong. But I'm not going to. (*He moves near* IAN, *flicks* IAN's *biro out of his hand. Smiles.*) Or I could inconvenience him. (*Pause.*) Do you want to be? This'll all be in the company magazine you know.

TALLULAH. What you going to do, Gary? Because don't.

Moment's silence as GARY *moves again. He suddenly pulls* SHERMAN *close to him, holding him tightly and kisses him on the mouth. A very long and strong kiss.* SHERMAN *moves away when* GARY *lets him go, a split second of being surprised, then he resumes his normal manner. He dabs his mouth with a handkerchief.*

SHERMAN (*slight smile*). You really think that's still an outrageous thing to do? You seriously thought it would shock me?

GARY. Yeah.

SHERMAN. Why?

GARY. Somebody touching you.

Silence. SHERMAN smiles to himself, turns, and moves.

GARY. Did you see him do that? Give a tiny smile – I obviously gave the right answer!

TALLULAH. What does he taste like?

LORRAINE'*s head goes down, as if she's about to faint.*

SHERMAN. What's the matter with you?

Pause.

LORRAINE (*very quiet*). I just feel . . .

SHERMAN. Are you ill?

LORRAINE (*very quiet*). No . . . no, I don't think so.

SHERMAN *stares at her, trying to decide if she's just trying to get his attention.*

SHERMAN. Are you unwell or not?

Pause.

LORRAINE (*looks at him straight in the face*). No, I'm not.

SHERMAN *moves briskly to the piano, his tone business-like.*

SHERMAN. Ian, could you come here and work this thing? (*Indicating piano.*)

IAN (*self-mocking smile*). What I've been waiting for!

SHERMAN (*carrying on, business-like*). Lorraine, come here. (LORRAINE *moves.*) That's enough. (*She stops.*) Stay there. You're going to sing for me now. Just with the piano – so we'll be able to see the raw article. You know the words of 'Yesterday', I hope. (*Without waiting for her answer, although* LORRAINE *nods, he recites the lyrics of the first verse in a totally matter-of-fact voice, the words crisply distinct. Pulling a microphone from side and laying it down in front of him.*) If I think it would be worth it I may want one of you to use this.

IAN (*at piano, his manner professional*). Now you know what to do – take your time, I'm going to set a medium fast tempo – the key's 'f' – and I advise you to try.

IAN *plays opening bars,* LORRAINE *turns face away.*

SHERMAN (*loud*). What's the matter? Maybe it wasn't your voice on the tape you gave us. Maybe you can't do anything.

LORRAINE (*quiet back at him*). It *was* my voice. (*Pause.*) You just haven't given us any warning.

SHERMAN. Warning! Why should I give you a warning? What the hell are you here for?

LORRAINE *stands still. Silence.*

SHERMAN. Right now.

IAN. This speed OK?

He plays and she sings 'Yesterday', trying extremely hard, standing still, compact, a small sharp figure. Her voice is adequate. She finishes singing after the first verse; it hasn't taken long. Complete silence, everybody looking at SHERMAN, who is by window.

LORRAINE. He was going a little fast for me. (*Slight pause – SHERMAN doesn't look at her.*) Can I start again?

SHERMAN. No. (*He turns.*) Please just go back against the wall. Now you, please. (*Indicating GARY.*)

GARY *stands where LORRAINE was standing. The girls stand in silence next to each other, TALLULAH tense.*

GARY. Can I not sing that song – it's not the sort of thing I'm into.

IAN (*cutting him off*). No, just sing the same song, and try to relax, you sure you know the words?

GARY. We'll see won't we?

He starts to sing the song as IAN plays – a nervous but rather beautiful voice comes out, and putting everything he's got into it. SHERMAN turns and looks at him – interrupts him after a very short time.

SHERMAN. Can you stop moving around so much?

GARY. I usually have something in my hands. (*Glancing at microphone.*) Maybe if . . .

SHERMAN. No.

IAN *starts playing again,* GARY *misses his entrance.*

GARY. Wait a minute – I can't remember it. (*He becomes tense.*)

SHERMAN *repeats the opening two lines sharply. Piano starts.*

GARY. Christ . . . it's gone. Why did you interrupt . . . I can't do it at the moment. (*With real passion.*) You really shouldn't have stopped me. (*He looks up.*) Go on, you better say *next please,* like they're meant to. (*Moment's silence.* GARY *moves.*)

SHERMAN. I hope you're watching this, Ian.

IAN. I don't know what's the matter with them.

TALLULAH. I'm waiting.

SHERMAN. Tallulah, would you stand where Gary was standing?

IAN. Are you ready — are you really concentrating? Try to concentrate.

TALLULAH opens her mouth, she sings about a line and a half of 'Yesterday'.

SHERMAN. Stop! (*She stops.*) Just stop.

TALLULAH stares at him in disbelief and resentment.

SHERMAN. Here. Will you use this, please?

TALLULAH takes the microphone. She begins 'Yesterday', but suddenly switches into a contemporary song. She has a very good, strong voice, she moves round away from the central position as her confidence grows — she puts everything she can into it, not looking at him in case he stops her, using her voice, both loud and quiet, her face determined and eager, really exerts energy. She sings for about a minute and a half, growing really loud towards the end. She stops, panting and sweating. Silence, they all look at her.

SHERMAN. I said 'Yesterday'.

TALLULAH. You didn't stop me.

She hands him the microphone.

SHERMAN. Here's a handkerchief — wipe your face. You shouldn't wear clothes like that.

IAN (*quietly*). Well done.

GARY (*suddenly*). Christ, it must be really late — night-time by now.

SHERMAN (*moves over to the window with an abrupt movement*). You think so do you?

He lets up the window blind, sun pours into the room, bright evening sun. They look startled and blink in it. SHERMAN is by the window.

SHERMAN. When I accept people they don't usually say anything, not at first, just stand there chewing. (*Slight pause.*) When I turn people down sometimes they giggle and say 'I'm sorry, I didn't hear what you said, could you say it again', sometimes they thank you, taking so long they'll hope you'll change your mind. And sometimes they are abusive and shout and spit and kick chairs over.

LORRAINE. That's very helpful.

SHERMAN (*briskly exiting*). I'll see you tonight. (*He exits.*)

GARY (*looks round*). That means we're staying. We've all survived, that can't be right. (*Nervous.*) Have we all survived?

IAN. Thank you – that was good, excellent – you did well in the end . . . great . . . well done. (*He smiles.*) Good.

GARY (*not unpleasantly*). He's really pleased, look. How many of us is he going to take?

IAN (*looking round*). Just try to relax now.

GARY (*not unpleasantly*). Go on – run after him if you want to, we don't mind.

IAN. I'm not in the habit of running after people.

GARY (*he smiles at him*). Then we'll go together – because I'm going too! Come on. (*He catches* LORRAINE's *arm.*) You ought to come too. I'm going to have a real look round. (*He exits.*)

IAN. I'll see you tonight. (*He exits.*)

TALLULAH *and* LORRAINE *alone on stage together, the evening light.*

TALLULAH (*excited, smiling*). God, I feel sore all over. And really stiff. (*Lightly.*) I don't think he likes me, he looked sideways like that, when he saw me looking at him. I couldn't see what he was thinking.

LORRAINE (*quietly*). You did very well. He likes you . . . you're OK.

TALLULAH (*excited*). What the fuck anyway! We're here. I've missed my job tonight, you know. I only did half the shopping this morning. I always do it for the whole family on Fridays. (*Loud by the window.*) We should go out shouldn't we? It's so warm now! (*Smiling.*) What place is out there! (*Mimics* SHERMAN.) Where are we – which city? (*Moment's silence.*) I bet he knew all the time. We should go and see London, paint the town green. *Startle* people in bus queues – hijack a taxi, rape the driver on the back seat. (*She looks at* LORRAINE.) And all the other things people do here, should go together.

LORRAINE. Yeah, we could. Probably wouldn't let us back in here again though if we were late.

TALLULAH. Walking along with my hair like this, you and me, watching people *think* about picking us up, and we just walking straight past them. And then getting really drunk.

LORRAINE. Yeah, we could.

TALLULAH (*grins, excited*). Some other time though.

Music – classical music suddenly wells up, somewhere in the distance, but quite loud. TALLULAH looks around.

TALLULAH (*loud*). What the fuck is that?

Music continues, welling up from somewhere in the building.

LORRAINE. It must be their *classical* record division.

She looks towards the door, slight pause.

It's a big place.

They look at each other across the big room.

Fade.

ACT TWO

Scene One

The room as before, several hours later.
The blinds are down, and the curtains are drawn across them.
Lamps are on in the alcoves of the room, and the atmosphere is of mid-evening.
The lighting is sleek and very plush.
MURRAY is sitting in a chair, a very large man in his thirties, his hair is long, he is casually but quite expensively dressed. He is extremely fat. His manner is commanding and quite charismatic.
Distant music as from a cocktail party is coming from somewhere in the building.
The fridge door is open – and it is now full of food and drink.
IAN is standing in a red velvet jacket, evening clothes, mixing cocktails in long glasses, full of bits of lemon and fruit and various spirits. His manner is sharper than in the first act.

IAN (*staring down into the drinks and stirring them so the ice clinks around*). I've forgotten exactly what I've put in these – probably blow their insides apart . . . the kids . . . which would not be a good idea. I want them sober, otherwise they'll be useless. (*He smiles.*) The bastard probably did have time to see them separately after all. (*He slams the fridge door with surprising force and turns to MURRAY with a sharp smile.*) You have to slam it to keep it shut. (*He glances down at drink.*) Do you want one, Murray? (*For a second MURRAY does not react.*)

MURRAY. No – I don't like the drink here. They try to serve you American beer. (*He glances slowly round the plush room.*) The carpet's new. This room used to be a really filthy store-room.

IAN. I know, it's grown! The place is growing all the time.

Pause.

Does he know you're here?

MURRAY. Could be . . . could be.

IAN. It always surprises me how people know he's in town, so quickly. The news must be spread by some special system I don't know about.

MURRAY. It goes up in neon in Piccadilly Circus – the exact time of his arrival.

IAN. The phones start ringing for him as he walks through the glass doors, it's incredible. There's always somebody waiting to see him. They're prepared to wait for hours if necessary.

MURRAY. That's very unwise of them. (*Glances round.*) What's that fucking noise – that racket?

IAN. It's one of their tacky functions, there's nearly always one going on, every night. I think it's for a few senior reps. and P.R. men. Eliot V. Carver is over from Los Angeles, Henry Weisman, the infamous Conroy Anderson, Herman Graceberg Junior. (*He says the names with a smile. Hesitates.*) I've never been to one – the nearest I got was when I went into the room with the night cleaners, after they'd all gone, and I was quite shocked, the place was totally devastated, the table had been turned over and there was this thick gunge of squashed smoked salmon, broken ashtrays and spilt cocktails all over the carpet. Puddles of it!

MURRAY. Of course – every time.

IAN (*his manner sharply animated, sipping his drink*). Sherman is hosting tonight. All the assorted tsars are there. (*He smiles.*) Three weeks ago you know, I came upon them playing ping-pong at midnight in the Sports Area. These four executives in their blue and orange track-suits, their paunches sticking out; playing in such fierce silence – you've never heard anything like it – just the squeak of their specially made sneakers – and Christ they really *did mind* when they were losing – to put it mildly! I was completely hypnotised, I watched them for over an hour. (*Pause.*) It's the only time I've ever seen them.

MURRAY. You probably hallucinated it.

IAN. No, no, Sherman was refereeing.

MURRAY *lets out a sharp, mocking laugh.*

IAN. You here for any purpose, Murray, or . . .

MURRAY (*cutting him off authoritatively*). Both. (*Pause.*) I thought you'd be gone by now. You've managed to last seven, eight months is it?

IAN (*his tone is sharp, light*). Yes – I still don't know if I'm about to be asked to leave, my track record is a little 'spare', these kids tonight may or may not help. It's rather a fascinating feeling really wandering along corridors trying to find out if you've been sacked. You have these encounters in the lift. People start sentences and never finish them, like 'didn't I hear . . . ?' or 'I thought you . . . ?' and then snap shut. There's a special breed of lift language here. Secretaries give you this sort of really glum hostile look. They have this notice by the phone now – three things you're meant to say to unwanted callers, 'He's not in the country . . .', 'He's in a meeting' and

'He's in flight at the moment, I'm afraid' – little laugh. They have that written down, 'remember the little laugh'.

MURRAY. They'll soon only employ rows of answering machines, sitting on chairs in each office.

IAN. There's a wonderful idiocy about the whole thing really, you stare at the cashier in the cafeteria wondering if she knows something, because she hasn't smiled at you for a week. People start looking for Sherman-like signs too. They go into a panic because the lavatory paper hasn't been replaced anywhere on their floor.

MURRAY (slight smile). Good. That's good. Let them panic.

IAN. But it's not really a vicious, exhilarating paranoia here, more a sort of mild, solid, grey variety.

MURRAY. Fine. There are far too many people working here anyway. Should lose a few.

IAN. Sackings tend to be quite a long drawn out affair in the English office apparently and then suddenly this wind from the States blows down the corridor and people are just gone. There are a few reasonably exciting days when executives really gorge themselves on sackings. And then it's over. (Amused smile.) They actually have this phrase, 'He's still being scraped out of his office'. 'Still being scraped off the wall.'

MURRAY. The new Brutalism.

IAN. But, and this is a very important but, the mild sting is in the tail. (He smiles, moves round the room.) I think it is almost time to go on the offensive. Possibly. You're faced by the choice: either you trudge on fairly inconspicuously and get slowly weeded out, or you go on the offensive and try to rectify things, with, usually, the same results. But not always. (Slight smile. He looks at MURRAY). It's a matter of timing, picking the right moment, calculating the risk, and doing it in the right way, all that sort of thing. (Slight smile.) Something I don't understand at all . . . (Tastes the cocktail.) It's quite nice. It's an interesting time really . . .

GARY enters with LORRAINE. She is wearing a different coloured top to the one she was wearing before. It is a very bright red. Her eyes are heavily made up and she is wearing lipstick.

GARY. See – didn't I tell you – we're dead on time!

IAN. Good. (Indicating drinks.) These are for you . . . (Slight smile.) If you want some that is. Try not to spill any.

GARY. Special drinks. Isn't that overdoing it a bit? (*He looks down into drink.*) What on earth have you put in here?

LORRAINE. They're trying to get us drunk.

IAN (*sharp*). No, that is not the idea – quite the opposite in fact.

GARY (*takes a gulp of the drink, moving round the room, confidently*). I managed to get outside the building into London, into the fresh air – for about fifteen seconds. I got soaked – it's pouring with rain. (*Grins.*) All the litter's sticking to the pavement. (*Up to* LORRAINE.)

LORRAINE. Then why aren't you wet?

GARY (*smiling*). Because just walking down the passage – the blow-heaters are so strong they dry you off automatically. You sort of get skimmed along the passage. (*Pushes her hand on his sweater.*) Feel.

LORRAINE (*touching him, then pulling her hand away*). You're right. You're dry.

GARY. Why've you put that on? It doesn't suit you at all. (*He touches her scarlet top.*) It makes you look completely different – really weird.

LORRAINE. He asked me to change. This is all I brought with me, so I had to wear it. (*She moves away.*) He keeps staring at us, look.

They both look at MURRAY, *sitting in the chair – his huge shape.*

IAN. You don't have to worry about him.

GARY. Who do you think he is?

MURRAY. He's just passing.

GARY. He's not going to tell us.

LORRAINE (*staring at him hard*). He looks like a bodyguard.

GARY. Yeah – Sherman's bodyguard probably.

LORRAINE (*still staring at him*). He's the right shape anyway.

GARY. Yes – bulging with keys. (*He suddenly turns back to* LORRAINE, *pushing her slightly away from the others.*) I want to know something and you know what it is.

LORRAINE. No, I don't. What?

Slight pause. He grins. Touches her.

GARY. I want your phone number.

LORRAINE. You can't get me on the phone.

GARY (*slight smile*). Can't I – what about an address then? You've got an address haven't you?

LORRAINE. Yes. I live in Sheffield.

GARY. Good. That's easy. I'll drop in on you then. Afternoon tea. (*Smiles.*) I'll track you down you know. (*He smiles.*) I could if I wanted.

LORRAINE (*slight smile, straight at him*). I expect you will. Almost definitely. But I may not have time to see you.

GARY. Are you embarrassed – about them? They're not listening.

IAN (*watching them*). We aren't, no.

GARY (*touching her, grinning*). The thing about you is – I have to find the right button to press, to activate you. (*Grins.*) And I'm not quite sure where it is. (*Stares at her.*) But I'll find it.

LORRAINE *just looks straight back at him.*

I wonder if we'll ever see each other again after tonight!

LORRAINE. Depends what happens.

GARY. All the more reason for you to . . . (*He touches her, she moves away.*) Don't drink too much. Somebody of your size shouldn't.

TALLULAH *enters, music from the cocktail party very audible – as she comes through the door it wafts in after her. She stands in the doorway, in a different dress. A blaze of bright orange and brilliant green, incredibly bright – obviously prepared by her specially to make an impression.*

TALLULAH. I'm not late am I?

GARY. Christ!

They all look at her standing in the doorway. She moves slowly into the room.

GARY. If you looked at her through binoculars you'd be blinded. (*Watching her.*) You'll burn holes in the carpet. He asked you to change too, did he?

TALLULAH. Yes.

GARY. And you just happened to have brought that?

TALLULAH. Yeah – I just happened to. In case I went to a disco after – if he'd finished with me early. (*She turns.*) The discos in Yardley are terrible. Can I have one? (*She picks a drink, then laughs, as she stands in the middle of the room.*) Christ – you can feel the heat coming up through the floor. It's terrific. (*She looks at LORRAINE, dressed in her brilliant red, with brilliant red lips.*) Look at us! All dressed up for the evening. I hope he appreciates it.

IAN (*staring at the two girls up against the blue wall*). You both look very exotic . . . Extraordinary. (*Quiet.*) No, I mean it.

They stare back at him for a moment in their brilliant colours. The idea suddenly strikes GARY, he moves over to IAN.

GARY. Why haven't I been asked to change?

IAN. Just try to relax – OK?

GARY (*speedy, animated*). Relax! Like him you mean? (*He indicates MURRAY.*) He'll probably never get up out of that chair again. (*To IAN.*) You're not relaxed anyway. You're wobbling.

IAN (*dry smile*). I'm not. I'm surprisingly calm, in fact.

LORRAINE. Where is he – do you know?

IAN. Where that noise is coming from – from their little get together.

GARY. I wonder if he has any other 'young artistes' waiting for him at this moment – somewhere in this building, chained to the hot water pipes in the basement, and he's doing his rounds, seeing us all in turn – maybe there's even more competition.

TALLULAH (*smiles to herself*). I hope there isn't.

She turns to them, she is standing some distance from GARY.

GARY (*slight grin*). Who's going to take him on then? Sherman! Any offers? Which one of us is going to? (*Slight smile.*) Because it's got to be done.

The two girls stare back at him.

TALLULAH. I've been allocated a room, you know.

GARY. So've I. On the fourth floor.

TALLULAH. If we 'need' it, it says.

GARY. If we're still wanted that means.

LORRAINE (*worried*). Why haven't I been given a room?

She moves across to IAN.

I haven't been given one.

IAN. Don't worry . . . I'm sure it's just a mistake. It doesn't mean anything.

LORRAINE. You sure – is that official?

She leans away.

GARY (*looking over to* LORRAINE). She's keeping herself to herself, isn't she? Come on! Come over here.

TALLULAH (*moving up to* GARY, *their moods are all quite speedy, excited*). I think we should put this on him, don't you, Lorraine? (*She raises lipstick towards* GARY's *mouth.*) Make you look a bit more interesting, with green lips.

LORRAINE. Yes, I think so. Smudge it on. (*She holds on to* GARY *too.*)

GARY (*really worried*). Stop it – that could blow things for me you know. I don't want him getting the wrong idea.

As GARY *says the above she's putting it on. Explosion of energy –* GARY *trying to fight free of her, and* TALLULAH *very determined.* LORRAINE *breaks away and watches their fight from a detached distance.*

TALLULAH. Come on, it's good stuff this, very hard to get off.

GARY. Stop it – you've drawn blood, look – she's made me bleed! See!

TALLULAH. Then stop resisting. (*She stabs with make-up.*) And round the eyes – I once did this with my brother when he was very small. (*To* LORRAINE.) And why aren't you helping?

IAN. Now just try to calm down, save it, save it for later.

GARY (*fighting free, imitating* IAN). You heard him – 'he wants it saved for later'.

They hear SHERMAN's *laughter and voice calling someone down the passage: 'See you, Vernon' etc.*

IAN (*hastily to* MURRAY). Whatever you've come for, you won't take up too much of his time, will you? This evening's quite important.

LORRAINE (*staring at* MURRAY, *to* TALLULAH). He's a bodyguard.

GARY (*grins*). And he's ignoring us.

SHERMAN enters. He stops in the doorway, split-second pause -- as he notices MURRAY, *he looks surprised but it goes in an instant.* MURRAY *is still sitting in the same chair, big huge shape bulging out.* SHERMAN *moves into the room smiling, the noise of the music is still audible.* SHERMAN's *manner is one of quick-silver lightness to cover his unease.*

SHERMAN (*smiling*). What are you doing here? (*Then to* IAN.) The ghoul is here. (*Pleasantly.*) Who let him in?

MURRAY (*forceful*). Just thought I'd check and see if you were still alive.

SHERMAN. You've just caught me – if you'd been a few hours out either side, I would have been on a plane.

LORRAINE (*staring at* MURRAY). Who is he?

MURRAY. You always like working late, don't you? (*To the others.*) When it gets to about three o'clock he'll just be hitting his peak.

SHERMAN (*sharp*). I won't be here then. (*He glances at* MURRAY.) You're quite a size now, aren't you? (*Straight on to* IAN.) He's reached quite a size hasn't he?

IAN (*slightly embarrassed*). Yes. I think it suits him.

SHERMAN (*back to* MURRAY). You being here! I didn't expect it. (*Slight smile.*) You should have warned me.

MURRAY (*manner commanding*). You look exactly the same of course.

SHERMAN. I am the same.

MURRAY. The usual glazed look behind the eyes – the air-conditioned pastiness.

SHERMAN (*slight smile*). You ought to get your hair cut! Look at him. (*Indicating* GARY.) Does he have long hair? (*Feels* MURRAY's *hair.*) Yards of it now, isn't there. Should have it shaved off. It makes you look like a period piece.

MURRAY. You say the same thing each time I see you.

GARY. Who the hell is he?

SHERMAN. This is one of the first I ever signed, twelve . . . thirteen years ago, and a good one too . . . When I was on a very small label. (*Slight smile.*) One of the ones I brought with me.

LORRAINE (*quietly staring, fascinated*). Him – but he looks so horrible.

GARY. Like a giant sponge now.

SHERMAN. Hear that? When did I last see you?

MURRAY. About eight months ago.

SHERMAN. It's as long as that! It can't be. It seems like yesterday afternoon. But you've swelled up haven't you on all that health food? It was that that did it, all those bloody cashew nuts and vegetable cutlets and herbal tea. Just swollen up in your country retreat, drowning in apple blossom. (*Turns animated.*) I saw him from a taxi crossing Leicester Square, I didn't recognise him at all, until he shouted out. (*Pause.*) What's more he went to a gig of his old band, sat on the side of the stage and none of the audience recognised him. None.

MURRAY. Yeah – I really enjoyed that, I think. It was the second most enjoyable day of my life.

SHERMAN (*smiling*). You'll need special chairs built for you soon.

MURRAY (*catching* SHERMAN's *sleeve*). He can never stop talking. It's a disease. Just surges on.

SHERMAN. It's good to see you. I've missed you. (*Pause.*) I hear you've done a couple of tracks on the New Album – but only eight minutes of vinyl after all these months, we'll probably have to wait for 1985 for the rest. (*Slight pause. Smiles straight at him.*) We may not be able to wait that long of course.

MURRAY (*matter-of-fact*). I really couldn't care a fuck. That's how long it's going to take. You know I don't think you know a single lyric of one of my songs.

SHERMAN. Of course I do. (*A momentary pause.*) The trouble with him – is he became obscure! Too inward, too private, above people's heads.

MURRAY (*smiles*). People's heads grew smaller. I didn't change.

SHERMAN. He didn't keep moving.

MURRAY (*sharp*). Moving with what?

SHERMAN. Didn't take advice of course. (*Charming smile.*) And I'm serious. We may not be able to wait.

MURRAY (*abrupt, taking no notice, but quite friendly*). Come on, just stop talking for a moment. So I can get a word in.

SHERMAN (*innocently*). Was I stopping you? (*Pause.*) Why have you come to see me anyway?

MURRAY (*looks at* SHERMAN). I suddenly felt the need . . . extraordinary though that is . . . I must want another fix of you. (*Pause. Manner powerful, arrogant, not defeated.*) Have things to see you about. Come on . . .

TALLULAH. Oh no for Chrissake – they can't go out for a drink. He's leaving so soon.

LORRAINE. Yes, he is.

TALLULAH. And he won't come back then.

MURRAY (*sharp to the kids*). Just shut up a moment. (*Pause.*)

Other people are allowed in here to see him you know.

IAN. But I did ask you specially not to keep him long –

MURRAY. And you too – quiet.

SHERMAN. A lot of my early discoveries have been dropping in to see me recently for some reason.

MURRAY (*pulling at him*). You're coming with me. I need a drink now. This building really sucks it out of you. We have things to discuss.

SHERMAN. It would be nice! (*Referring to the kids.*) I can feel their eyes digging into my back.

LORRAINE. He's not going to leave us – he can't.

GARY. You asked us to stay here!

SHERMAN (*smiling*). You see you're taking up their time. They may do you an injury. What do you think of this lot? (*They look at the kids.*) Which one would you choose?

MURRAY (*staring hard*). Which one? (*Pause. He stares.*) Who found them?

IAN (*laconic smile*). I did, believe it or not.

LORRAINE. What's he staring at us like that for? (*Pause.*) I don't like it.

MURRAY (*in a chair staring at them. The kids are arranged along the wall*). When I first saw him. (*Indicates SHERMAN.*) This one here –

SHERMAN. No nostalgia! These kids don't even know the meaning of the word. Neither do I.

MURRAY (*carrying on*). In his little office – it was incredibly hot, and he was wearing shorts, Bermuda shorts, this kid who'd come out of advertising, first time in London, jabbering on about what I should do, from behind this desk that was much higher than he was, and his small brown knees sticking out.

SHERMAN (*staring down at him*). You were rather striking looking I remember, quite dynamic then. Sung for three hours without stopping on a small stool in the middle of the room. He had a nice tugging passionate voice. (*He grins at MURRAY.*) You can just see where the old face used to be, can't you? Just visible beneath the ripples. (*Indicates MURRAY's face. Silence – he looks at MURRAY's face for a moment.*)

MURRAY. Really? (*Dangerous smile.*) I can't. (*Stares back at SHERMAN.*)

SHERMAN (*sharply*). Do you hear that? (*The music is slightly louder than before.*) This place is meant to be sound-proofed! Is it not? Do you call that sound-proofing? (*Picks up the phone – speedy, annoyed.*) The secretaries have all left.

IAN (*smiles*). It is quite late you know – well after nine o'clock.

SHERMAN. They rush out at the first opportunity. I must remember to buy some chocolates for the secretaries in Cologne. (*He presses another dial.*) Yes. Give me the Eisenhower room. Yes . . . right, turn off the music please. Yes I know about the function, but it was time it was finished, they've had enough . . . The plane leaves then! Really . . . (*He puts down the phone.*)

MURRAY. He's always on a high when he knows he's flying out in an hour.

TALLULAH. As soon as that.

MURRAY. He'll be in a completely unstoppable mood as you will see. (*Pause. The music stops.*)

SHERMAN. I love flying. I even enjoy the turbulence. (*He turns, stares at MURRAY.*) Now these kids, can I . . .

MURRAY. You can have some time with them, I'll watch.

SHERMAN *turns and glances at the kids across the room. Silence.*

SHERMAN. Right. (*Slight pause.*) I'm afraid we have to lose one of you already, say goodbye to one of you – and that person is Tallulah.

Silence. It takes a second for TALLULAH to take in what she's heard, the other kids look at her in total surprise.

TALLULAH. Can you say that again, I don't think I heard what . . .

SHERMAN (*his tone is polite, not brusque*). Yes you did.

Slight pause.

TALLULAH. But I thought that you wanted me to . . .

SHERMAN (*stops her, smiling*). No, I've decided now, and I'm sorry there is no point you staying any longer.

TALLULAH. But . . .

SHERMAN (*carrying on calmly*). I won't insult you with all the usual 'thank you for coming' and 'it was nice to meet you' and the other absurd things people say.

GARY (*quiet to LORRAINE*). Just kick you out without them.

TALLULAH (*her manner disappointed, not tragic*). Why did you ask me to stay all this time and change and . . .?

SHERMAN. I wanted to see you in something else and to give you a moment's thought. (*Pause.*)

TALLULAH. And what was wrong then?

SHERMAN. What's wrong? (*He smiles.*) You've got a nice voice; but it's not just your singing, it's what the whole of you says.

TALLULAH (*slight smile back at him*). And what does it say?

SHERMAN (*quiet smile*). It doesn't add up. Look at your dress for instance, a bit of tomboy aggro, and a bit of femininity. Confused jumble of things, things you've seen on television and in newspapers.

TALLULAH (*exasperated*). I don't read the newspapers.

SHERMAN. And you've got them muddled up.

TALLULAH (*loud, urgent*). Anyway – this is what I feel. (*Indicating her dress.*) And it's what all the people I know are like . . . and I can sing.

GARY. You're doing very well, keep at him.

TALLULAH. So it was just because I put on the wrong clothes, was it?

SHERMAN. Of course not. I've tried to explain.

IAN (*to TALLULAH*). Please, there is no point in arguing with him, once he's decided, you could dance on the ceiling and it wouldn't do anything. (*Slight smile.*) That's it – you're out to lunch and you just have to accept it I'm afraid.

SHERMAN (*smiles*). There's no need to drown her with jargon.

MURRAY. He gets it all wrong anyway.

TALLULAH (*loudly*). I can be outrageous too, you know – really shock. I can do anything. (SHERMAN *gives a slight smile.*) I've made you smile anyway.

SHERMAN (*pleasantly*). I like bits of you, you know, your voice, your hands, your hair.

TALLULAH. Perhaps you should cut them off then and tie them all together. (*Silence, they all look at her. She turns, slight smile.*) Anyway, I think I want to play on the moon. I'll go there. That's where I really want to live. It'll be more interesting. (*She moves.*) OK then.

Silence.

SHERMAN. If you go to the security desk on the way out, they'll call a taxi for you and pay for it, believe it or not.

TALLULAH (*stares at him*). Are you married?

SHERMAN (*stares back at her*). Yes, I did get married.

Pause.

TALLULAH. Can I take my boots out of the fridge, please, or do you need them still?

SHERMAN. Of course you can.

She takes them out of the fridge.

IAN. I hope they're still useable – not too stiff.

SHERMAN (*watching her put them on*). Don't get frost-bite.

TALLULAH (*smiles*). Yeah – I'll try not to. (*She moves.*) I'll put them on the mantelpiece at home and my mum can use them for an ash-tray. (*To the other kids.*) Good luck.

She goes. Moment's stunned silence.

GARY (*quiet*). Christ – she's gone.

LORRAINE (*very quiet*). Yes.

MURRAY (*totally matter-of-fact*). One down, two to go.

LORRAINE (*looking at* MURRAY). Is he going to stay here?

SHERMAN. Now . . .

LORRAINE (*looking at* SHERMAN, *referring to* MURRAY). It makes me nervous even just to move in case I catch his eye.

GARY (*speedy, nervy*). You going to continue with the executions are you? Gun some more down. I'll make it really easy for you. (*Turns and faces the wall.*) OK, come on then if you're coming. (*He spreads his arms out, with his back to* SHERMAN *and remains there.*)

MURRAY. No, no, don't worry, he never does two immediately in a row. You're safe for a bit now. When he goes very still – it's always a danger sign.

SHERMAN *stops moving, he looks at* GARY.

SHERMAN. Gary.

GARY *has his arms out against the wall, he stays for a second, turns slowly.*

GARY. Yeah, what is it?

SHERMAN. I'd like you to play for me now. Properly.

GARY. Properly?

SHERMAN. And sing of course. Ian will give you a guitar.

IAN (*picking up guitar*). We do have a studio waiting you know, Don. It's just sitting there – with an engineer who . . .

SHERMAN (*snaps*). Not yet, maybe later.

IAN. But you're leaving later and . . .

SHERMAN (*sharp*). You must stop worrying, Ian.

IAN (*gives* GARY *the guitar*). Here. And try to relax.

SHERMAN. OK.

GARY, *about to play the guitar, looks up.*

GARY. What if the phone rings?

SHERMAN. It won't ring.

GARY. Why won't it?

SHERMAN. Because it knows I'm occupied.

GARY. Why don't you take it off the hook?

SHERMAN. Because I never do that – (*Slight smile.*) I can't work unless I'm near one.

Pause.

GARY. I'll be waiting for it now I've thought of it. It better not ring.

He suddenly starts to play, going into it without a break, before we expect him to. He sings two or three verses of his own song, in a strong, striking voice. The song is a powerful but confused 'relevant' song with phrases referring to Northern Ireland, the Blacks, the Common Market, nuclear warfare, all cropping up together. But he puts a lot into it. GARY stops playing as suddenly as he started. They look at him.

The phone looked like it was going to ring. I saw it vibrating.

Silence. GARY *looks at* SHERMAN, *they all look at* SHERMAN.

Well, what do you say?

Slight pause.

SHERMAN (*moving*). I liked it.

GARY. But? (*To* LORRAINE.) Just wait for the 'of course you're not quite . . .'

SHERMAN (*cutting him off*). No buts.

GARY (*grins, very surprised*). What, no buts at all? (*Grins.*) You're not suddenly going to throw in 'but of course you look totally wrong – your shoes are the wrong shape!'

SHERMAN. No. (*Moving by the window.*) You've got some energy; English kids seem to have some energy now. (*Smiles.*) And it is selling.

GARY. That's why you need us!

SHERMAN *indicates* MURRAY, *quick smile – an aside in passing.*

SHERMAN. He ran out of energy of course, the adrenalin just stopped, leaked out of him.

MURRAY (*sharp, smiles*). So that's what happened is it, Don?

SHERMAN (*ignoring this, to* GARY). No, I like you.

GARY. That's unexpected.

IAN. Good. Well done.

GARY *moves to the window, smiling.*

SHERMAN. What are you doing?

GARY (*excited smile*). Just seeing if it's still dark outside – checking you aren't going to do your little trick again, and show it's really still only five o'clock in the morning. (*Grinning by the curtain.*) Maybe the city's changed out there.

SHERMAN (*casually*). Of course the song's terrible.

GARY (*total surprise*). What song?

SHERMAN. Your song. And anything like it. We'll have to find you different material.

GARY. *There* – I knew he'd start! (*To* LORRAINE, *loud, grins.*) See! – 'the song is useless of course' – 'cos it's saying something!

SHERMAN (*his manner speeding up, supremely confident, smiling*). Of course it is – there isn't a market, can't you realise that? One song about the rights of the Blacks may sell, or about being a Happy Gay, but look at the sales of the next one! – even by the very same artist, we have to throw millions away, fill pot holes with them, give them to the Salvation Army! The kids don't want it. (*Smiles.*) There's no public demand for protest material.

GARY (*grinning*). Just listen to him, I knew he'd say it. How do you know anyway?

SHERMAN. Statistics of course.

GARY (*surprised*). Statistics?

SHERMAN (*ebullient, loud*). It's all fashion – everything's fashion and I know! I was trained in advertising. One follows fashions and sometimes one starts them, I have started fashions myself, pushed them into being.

GARY. You have?

SHERMAN (*loud at his peak, exuberant and powerful*). Of course! Where do you think they come from? Fall out of the sky onto the pavement, grow on the sides of buildings? One moves around, one sees what people are wearing and thinking, and then you pluck it out and broadcast it. I may just notice something very small, very tiny. I might see three girls walking down the street in virginal white – and if I think there is a feel for it, and there was a virginal sound to go with it, then it would be onto the television, radio and magazines, all over them, innocent white dresses, and it would spread like German measles.

GARY (*smiling*). Will you let me say something, please?

SHERMAN (*slight smile*). I don't think so, no.

GARY (*aggressive grin*). So what sort of music do you like then?

SHERMAN. I love the whole spectrum of course. I have no likes or dislikes. My favourite piece is 'My Fair Lady'. (*To* MURRAY.) He doesn't believe me!

MURRAY (*to* GARY). It's true.

SHERMAN (*smiling fast*). I have no prejudices, no politics, no allegiances and I haven't voted in twelve years.

GARY (*to* LORRAINE). Look, he's getting really excited! You're so fucking cynical aren't you?

SHERMAN. No one could call me cynical. I have a wide-eyed innocence!

IAN. Please don't argue with him Gary, you can't possibly win.

GARY (*opposite him, facing him*). He's like a mad electric dwarf!

SHERMAN (*smiling*). Insults won't make any difference at all They just slide off me. I have signed people that have urinated all over the studio floor in front of me.

GARY. I was only describing you – accurately.

IAN. Please, Gary, you're in with a good chance, just don't go too far.

GARY (*smiles*). Why not?

SHERMAN (*loud, controlled excitement*). Go to another label if you want. The really interesting question is why you are here at all – at a great company like this, an enormous multi-national, which you're meant to find so alienating and impersonal – and I'll tell you why.

GARY. Go on, tell me.

SHERMAN. Because you love it. (*Pause.*) You adore being here.

GARY (*grins*). Listen to him – he's crazy! (*Strong.*) I'm here because you invited me – (*Pause.*) I got an invitation. (*Pause, staring straight at him.*) Are you testing me again or something? (*Slight pause.*) Seeing if I can be moulded – transformed, pushed into a more commercial corner? Why are you smiling? (*He turns.*) So that's what you're doing is it? You are sort of testing me. I knew it.

GARY *moves round the room, picking up cheese puffs from the little cocktail bowls, and casually flicking them into his mouth.*

Shall I tell you something? (*Broad smile.*) You're the most dangerous man I've ever met.

SHERMAN (*slight smile*). Flattery won't get you very far, unfortunately.

GARY. I'm not going to sing any other sort of song. No other material, except my own. (*Slight nervous smile.*) Or something equally good.

IAN. Gary, careful, you've almost reached the studio.

GARY (*picking up another handful of cheese puffs, sharp grin*). Really? (*Looks at SHERMAN.*) I want to ask you a question – not that I'm hopeful of an answer. (*Looks straight at him.*) But are you going to take me on or not? (*Slight smile.*) Because I'm beginning to mind the suspense just a little.

IAN. Stop it, Gary.

GARY (*pointing at SHERMAN*). Look at him, sort of seeping into a corner. Are you going to take me on?

SHERMAN. I don't know yet.

GARY. Why not?

SHERMAN. I don't make many wrong decisions.

IAN. Gary, you can't force him like that, he's unforceable.

GARY. He's unforceable! (*Slight smile.*) I don't believe that. We'll see.

LORRAINE (*calls out warningly*). Gary!

He moves, then smiles at them.

GARY (*calmly*). I'm just going out for a moment. I have to have this constant injection of fresh air in this place. (*Moves towards door – glances back.*) Don't do anything you shouldn't. (*To SHERMAN.*) It'll give you a moment to think about it. (*Sharp.*) But I won't be long.

IAN (*looks at* SHERMAN). I'm not sure what he's trying to do but I think . . . he can be . . .

SHERMAN. Yes, what's he up to? (*Glances round at the cocktails.*) He's eaten most of the food in the room.

IAN. I'll fetch him straight back, Don – OK, I think he's got potential, don't you think? OK, I'll just get him! He's the only one.

He exits.

SHERMAN. Yes.

He turns, moves.

MURRAY (*suddenly gets hold of him by the arm*). If I hung on to you now, kept you right here and stopped you from leaving, I wonder what you would do.

SHERMAN (*sharp smile*). You wouldn't ever manage it. And you've been trying long enough.

MURRAY. Getting nearer though.

Their tone changes when speaking to each other, immediate familiarity, almost closeness, mingled with unease.

During the following exchanges, SHERMAN *twice glances quickly at* LORRAINE.

MURRAY (*dangerous smile*). You know I saw a guy have a heart attack the other day, in an airport, tumbled down the escalator. He was younger than you.

SHERMAN (*slight smile*). I've seen that too.

MURRAY (*pulling at his coat*). Maybe I should take you back with me, keep you tied up in the cowshed.

SHERMAN (*slight smile*). That would be terrifying. I hate the country. It's so noisy. A duck quacks half a mile away, and it sounds like a pistol shot. And I always get bitten to shreds by all those insects.

MURRAY. You're completely defenceless out there.

LORRAINE. Can I ask something?

Neither of them seem to hear her or take any notice of her.

SHERMAN. I'm going on a long drive tomorrow, to the new studio out there. There are some extraordinary roads there now. I like motorways, autobahns, big roads. I can't understand people who hate them. A really crisp new road is an exciting sight.

MURRAY. Do you still have pictures of them on your wall?

SHERMAN. I've been getting some very good dreams on them recently while being driven.

MURRAY (*sharp*). I can just see you – small shape squashed into the back seat, fast asleep.

SHERMAN. There is a certain state between sleeping and waking – you should know it well – when one gets particularly striking dreams. I wish there was a way of videoing one's dreams, getting them down on tape and then being able to play them back afterwards.

MURRAY. Your dreams would be unwatchable, Don – all cheap, bright colours, soft focus, like Martini ads.

SHERMAN (*very sharp smile*). Really? Not half as boring as yours! They would all be scratched and the reels would be in the wrong order.

MURRAY. Right, let's . . .

LORRAINE interrupts them. Noise of people banging up and down the stairs, laughing from the party, snatches of music.

LORRAINE. And what about me?

SHERMAN stops and looks at her, as if he has forgotten her existence. MURRAY stares at her.

SHERMAN (*slight smile*). What about you?

LORRAINE. What are you going to do with me?

SHERMAN. We can't use you, I would have thought I had made that clear.

LORRAINE. Can't use me? Is that all you're going to say?

SHERMAN. There, they did it again.

MURRAY. The moment of wounded disbelief.

MURRAY, who is standing next to SHERMAN, whispers in his ear.

LORRAINE. What's he whispering to you for? Is he giving advice?

SHERMAN (*slight smile*). Hardly.

LORRAINE. What's it got to do with *him*, can't he go *now*? Will you ask him to leave? I don't want him seeing this.

MURRAY (*staring at her, strong hostility between them*). I won't watch – I'll think of other things.

LORRAINE (*louder, urgent*). *Please* – I don't want him watching.

SHERMAN. I'm afraid you're going to have him watching, he's going to see everything.

MURRAY *and* SHERMAN *stand as a team together, watching* LORRAINE.

It won't work. Trying to throw people out of the room and get me on my own. As far as I'm concerned you're already on the Inter-City on the way back to Sheffield eating cold British Rail sandwiches.

LORRAINE (*straight back at him*). I don't ever eat on trains. (*Facing them both.*) You haven't worked with me yet you realise. You don't know anything about me.

SHERMAN. Your interview was cancelled today. You got a telegram saying so, and yet you still came.

LORRAINE (*loudly*). I didn't get the telegram, for Chrissake. Why doesn't anybody believe me? You'll want to search me next.

MURRAY (*slight smile*). Yes – where is it?

SHERMAN. Your singing is borderline to put it politely – in the extreme – and you're far too short, there's just a smudge of you, you'd totally disappear during any live appearance.

LORRAINE (*scornful, indicating* MURRAY). Is that what he thinks?

SHERMAN. I can't possibly recommend a shoddy product.

LORRAINE (*right back at him, her strong, small face opposite them*). If I am that – which I'm not – you ought to be able to do something about it, oughtn't you – if you really are some sort of Swengala like you think . . .

SHERMAN (*slight grin*). Some sort of what! What on earth did you say?

MURRAY. Swengala.

SHERMAN. Svengali – is that what you mean?

LORRAINE. Don't mock me. (*Pause – they stand together*

watching her.) You mould people don't you – change their image?

MURRAY. Why is she looking at me?

SHERMAN. A lot of artistes don't need it.

LORRAINE. So you could transform me couldn't you, if you wanted? Couldn't you? Now. (*She looks at him.*) Here – in this room.

SHERMAN (*sharp*). Yes . . . if there was something to work from, not just an empty space, a complete hole.

LORRAINE *turns and bursts into tears.*

LORRAINE. You aren't *allowed* . . .

She cries, MURRAY *moves slightly.*

LORRAINE (*to* MURRAY, *as she cries*). Go away. Please. Just go.

MURRAY *suddenly lurches out of the room – his big shape exits abruptly.*

SHERMAN (*watching her, matter-of-fact*). Please, could you stop crying? (*Pause.*) I'm afraid that will have no effect on me at all. (*Slight pause. She continues to cry. Matter-of-fact.*) Do you want a glass of –

LORRAINE (*turns, cuts him off*). I *don't* need anything.

She cuts out of the crying. Self-possessed – rubs her face, in her matter-of-fact way. Flicking tears off her face.

Christ, they're really salty – what comes out. They scratch your cheeks. Right. (*She moves purposefully.*) You asked me to put this on. I don't need to wear it now, do I? I'm going to change.

SHERMAN (*watching her move to her clothes*). Did you fake that – crying like that?

LORRAINE. No. (*She looks straight at him.*) I meant it at the time. I don't practise it if that's what you mean.

SHERMAN. I haven't ever seen somebody cry with such violence and then snap out of it so quickly.

LORRAINE. It's one of the talents I *have* got.

She turns her back and begins to replace her second-act top with her first-act top, standing barebacked to him as she changes, completely unbothered. She neither hurries nor lingers over it.

SHERMAN. Now we've come to the attempted seduction, have we?

LORRAINE. No. I'm not that stupid. (*Slight smile.*) I used to come third in class, you know – (*Very sharp.*) Equal *second* sometimes.

SHERMAN (*watching her*). You didn't need to change here.

LORRAINE (*throwing the red top aside*). I just wanted to get this off – get rid of it! (*She puts her other top on and turns to face him.*) I am not trying to seduce you. You can be quite sure of that.

SHERMAN. I almost believe you. (*Sharp smile.*) I've often had bribes thrown at me – girls spread out all over the floor, heaped up in hotel bedrooms. I don't think I ever touched one. (*Straight at her.*) But kids of your age don't seem to be that interested in sex any more.

LORRAINE. Speak for yourself.

SHERMAN. You have a sort of pale, lukewarm interest.

LORRAINE (*sharp*). What you mean is we don't have to shout about it all the time in public. Most men of your age still haven't got over the fact they're allowed to talk about it at all without hiding in corners, don't have to whisper behind locked toilet doors any more, drawing their little pictures. (*Looks at him.*) I'm not bothered. I can go without it for months if I want. (*Slight pause.*) And stop looking at me as if I'm some sort of specimen.

SHERMAN (*watching her*). Be interesting if when people didn't have sex for long periods of time, it began to show on their faces, like a kind of rash. I overheard somebody say that at a convention in Cleveland.

LORRAINE. Mine doesn't show. (*Urgent.*) I want you to hear me sing. To give me a test. Put me in the studio tonight.

SHERMAN. Being annoyingly persistent won't make any difference.

LORRAINE. You like insulting people, don't you?

SHERMAN (*dangerous smile*). Only when it's necessary.

LORRAINE (*strong and still*). I'm only doing what anybody would do in the same circumstances, anybody I know. I'm not going to just fantasise about it, sitting at home starry-eyed, reading the magazines, watching the tele, saving up for a little pile of records and then on Saturdays looking forward to 'going' out – going to sit on the stairs of the disco! I know there's a demand for kids of our age, I know what I can do, and I've got a bit of talent, and I can really work hard, *harder* than *you imagine*. I can work till I keel over in the street if necessary. (*Slight pause.*) And I want to get out of Sheffield of course. (*Stares straight at him.*) Maybe you know what I mean. And I need a bit of help from you now. (*Pause.*) And I won't ever be in this situation again of course. (*Slight pause; sharp.*) Do you see? (SHERMAN *smiles slightly. Loud.*) I never know whether you're listening or not . . .

SHERMAN. I have a plane to catch – so you'll have to try your methods with someone else.

LORRAINE. What 'methods'? They're not methods – I told you. (*Pause.*) Miss your plane.

SHERMAN. I never miss planes, I'm afraid.

LORRAINE. Maybe you should start.

SHERMAN (*gives a slight smile*). I think it might be time to call for assistance, I'll page the Security desk, and get you 'gently' evicted, bundled out of a side entrance.

He moves slightly.

LORRAINE (*sharp*). Don't.

He turns.

Don't . . . please. (*Pause. Suspiciously.*) Why you smiling?

Pause.

SHERMAN. Any decision that I might happen to reach tonight has to be ratified by at least one other executive.

LORRAINE. So it's not all up to you after all!

SHERMAN. Come here . . . come here a moment.

SHERMAN *takes something out of sideboard.*

LORRAINE. Why?

LORRAINE *hesitates and begins to move towards him.*

SHERMAN. Come on. (*Sharp.*) I just want to see something.

Suddenly LORRAINE *begins to back away, tremendously mistrustful, shouting at him across the whole width of the stage.*

LORRAINE. What are you going to do? (*Loud.*) I *want* to know.

SHERMAN (*matter-of-fact*). Don't worry, just come here.

LORRAINE (*moving sideways, keeping her distance*). Have you been waiting for this moment then?

SHERMAN. I thought you wanted to be worked with. Come on.

LORRAINE (*keeping her distance*). Yes. You can do whatever you like as long *as you* TELL ME FIRST *what* it's going to be. (*She watches him, sharp.*) Do you understand?

SHERMAN. What are you expecting?

LORRAINE *moves forward towards him very warily; when he moves to touch her, her head jolts back instinctively.*

To get hit?

LORRAINE (*very wary*). Are you going to tell me . . . ? I don't trust you particularly, not at all in fact.

Slight pause as noise of party-goers shouting down the stairs.

Going to let some of those drunks in, are you?

SHERMAN. Don't move.

LORRAINE. You've changed your mind. (*Slight pause.*) Have you?

SHERMAN *has produced a cloth, like a thick floor cloth, and begins to rub her face, to get the make-up off. His actions are firm and matter-of-fact without being vicious – neither are they particularly gentle.*

SHERMAN (*rubbing at her face*). All this stuff should come off of course; it's quite wrong.

LORRAINE. Careful, that hurt.

SHERMAN. You've pasted it on thick. (*He moves her head with a sharp movement.*) One of the few things you've got going for you – is your unbelievable paleness.

LORRAINE. That hurt, you realise. You're meant to use cream to do this.

SHERMAN. You should never let any colour get into your cheeks.

LORRAINE (*suddenly her voice rises in urgency – at first only half serious, but building into shouts of true pain*). Christ, do you have to do it like that, what is that you're wiping with, a bit of metal, you're scraping bits of me off, my skin – ough!

SHERMAN (*slight smile*). I don't make a habit of doing this.

LORRAINE. That really hurt – can't you . . . careful, I've got spots there for Chrissake. You're hurting me, please could you stop? (*Really loud, in real pain.*) YOU'RE HURTING ME. (*She breaks away. Moves several yards away from him holding her face – in real pain.*) God, it feels half my face has been rubbed off. You've split some spots open. (*She rubs her face.*)

SHERMAN (*slight smile*). That's a little better.

LORRAINE (*keeping her distance, sharp, straight at him*). You sure you've looked at me properly? You probably haven't even noticed the colour of my eyes.

SHERMAN. I haven't. (*Matter-of-fact.*) You've got a small birthmark on the back of your neck.

LORRAINE. Going to try to remove that as well are you? (*Slight pause. Staring straight at him.*) You've been interested in me all along – haven't you?

SHERMAN (*dangerous smile*). You reckon that's so, do you? (*He moves sharply efficiently.*) Change your top back. Go on – you shouldn't have taken it off. Come on.

LORRAINE *hesitates for a second.*

LORRAINE (*takes her top off – SHERMAN watches her unembarrassed*). Is this the way you get your pleasure then, like this. (*Pause.*) Gazing.

SHERMAN (*matter-of-fact*). I'm like a doctor with his patients. (*Slight smile.*) Purely clinical.

LORRAINE. Doesn't stop you looking.

Her top is on.

SHERMAN. Look at me. (*She looks up.*)

LORRAINE (*loud*). What are you trying to work out?

SHERMAN. Wear this, see what it looks like.

He hands her his own white jacket which she puts on.

LORRAINE. That? (*She puts it on – her face now totally white – standing in his jacket in front of him.*) You've taken everything out of the pockets.

SHERMAN (*to himself*). My plane's time must be checked.

LORRAINE. I'm surprised you can't make it wait for you on the runway.

SHERMAN. Look at me.

Pause.

LORRAINE (*suddenly*). I *know* why you've changed your mind, why you're going to let me go into the studio, you thought I wouldn't realise. (*Suddenly, getting really loud.*) You think I'm going to go down there and make a total idiot of myself – (*Sharp.*) Don't you? Humiliate myself. That's why. (*Loud.*) Isn't it? But that's not going to happen. (*Slight pause.*) I'm not going to let it.

IAN *enters sharply.*

IAN. Gary's here – I've found him. I've got him back. (*Slight smile.*) See –

GARY *enters.*

SHERMAN. So he is.

GARY. I said I would be.

MURRAY *enters with* GARY, *just behind him.*

LORRAINE. And him too. Have you been listening outside the door?

MURRAY. It could be heard clearly all over the building.

SHERMAN (*turns sharply*). I'm putting this kid in the studio – (*He indicates* LORRAINE *as he moves through the door.*) Just that one.

IAN (*amazed*). Her? You don't really mean her?

SHERMAN (*by the door as he exits*). Yes I do. Let Conroy know immediately.

IAN (*looking at* LORRAINE). He *was* serious. He was really talking about you.

LORRAINE. He was, yes. (*Then suddenly more nervous.*) I *hope* he's serious.

GARY (*slight smile*). Why shouldn't he be?

IAN (*still amazed, icily*). Then we better get you down there, before he changes his mind. You'd better do some rehearsing hadn't you?

LORRAINE (*moves sharply*). I'll find my own way down.

GARY (*nervous grin*). You might get lost, careful.

LORRAINE *glances at him for a split second.*

LORRAINE (*quiet*). Don't go away. Come and watch.

She exits.

GARY (*slight smile*). Why did you bring me back then? He was practically pulling me along the corridors to get me here.

IAN (*turning, sharp, animated*). For Chrissake, this is lunacy, this is complete madness.

MURRAY. That's putting it mildly.

IAN (*looking at* MURRAY). What are you leering like that for? He must be being purposely perverse tonight, I don't know what he's doing, he's not usually *spiteful*. I mean for Chrissake it wouldn't take that much longer for us to see both of them. To go with her! I mean he's mad.

MURRAY. Perhaps he really is overworking, finally got to him.

IAN. I found these bloody children after all. I sort of sensed this coming somehow, tonight –

MURRAY (*slight smile*). It could just be time to go on the offensive.

IAN. Exactly. (*Suddenly turns to* GARY.) Do you want to go down there?

GARY (*split-second pause*). OK – why not? If it's 'allowed'. If I'm not going to get security guards chasing me.

IAN (*speedy with the idea*). No, you won't . . .

GARY. With my own material though.

IAN (*moving*). Yes, naturally. We can sort all that out afterwards. (*Suddenly looks straight at him.*) And you'll perform properly won't you?

GARY. 'Properly' – how do you mean?

IAN. You'll put all you can into it.

GARY (*sharp, offended*). What else would I do?

IAN. Fine. (*Moving, speedy.*) I'll have to by-pass him, nothing else to do. I'll notify Conroy, straight away, get him paged, explain that Sherman's had a slight aberration. That he's completely wrong. (*He smiles.*) *Actually go behind his back*, a momentous occasion! Despite the Christian name and the green shoes this place is as hierarchical as Gulf-Oil. I mean for Chrissake there's nothing else I can do – it's me that gets affected by all this – *me*. (*Loud.*) We'll see you down there.

He suddenly exits.

GARY *and* MURRAY *alone on stage*, MURRAY *stares across at him*.

GARY (*quieter*). Haven't seen him like that.

Pause.

MURRAY. Neither has he probably. (*He stares across at him.*) You nervous?

GARY. I'm not sure.

MURRAY. You might need a drink.

GARY. Thanks.

MURRAY (*staring at him, slight smile*). So do I. (*Pause.*) You can buy them.

Blackout.

Scene Two

The studio is revealed, back wall rolls back, depending on space. The studio is a pool of light surrounded by darkness and the sheet glass of the box, through which the performers are watched, hanging directly behind them.
As the lights come up SHERMAN is standing on the podium by the microphone, by himself for a second.
He stands very still, he taps the microphone, it makes a loud popping noise, he flicks it off.
IAN enters from the side, his manner speedy, mercurial.
Both men are edgy, they stand in the pool of light in the middle of the stage.

SHERMAN (as soon as IAN *enters*). Why is it so hot in here? (SHERMAN's *manner is animated, confident.*) I can only exist in certain temperatures you realise. (*He moves from podium.*) I have never understood why the studios have to be so far underground. It's the same in New York. It's ridiculous. It's like they're expecting an atomic attack – and everyone will come scuttling down here.

IAN. Yes. This is studio F. There's an underground river running below here, I think.

SHERMAN. Why did they unlock *this* one?

IAN. Because it's after hours.

SHERMAN. There are piles of old synthesisers lying back there – you know – heaped up like old scrap aircraft.

IAN (*sharp*). Is Lorraine ready yet, is she here?

SHERMAN. Relax, Ian – you must try to relax. I told you to stop worrying.

IAN (*slight smile*). I am still trying.

SHERMAN (*produces a white envelope*). Here – I took a liberty, it was in your pigeon-hole – looks like your invitation for the Paris Convention. They've made the envelopes thicker so the inquisitive can't see through them. (*Slight smile.*) You've heard about the orange and pink card test of course. If you get the orange one you're going to be in the main hotel and on one of the top fifteen tables.

IAN (*laconic smile, taking envelope*). And if it's the pink card, one's in the annexe and almost certainly on the way out.

SHERMAN. And kept awake by the trains in the Gare du Nord.

IAN (*sharp smile*). Sometimes, you know, I'm really hoping I'm going to get the push, and other moments I'm extremely keen to stay. (*He looks sideways at* SHERMAN.) It's very interesting. (*He opens the envelope.*) This is exactly like getting one's exam results – trembling fingers opening the 'A' level envelopes. (*He smiles quite calmly as he opens it and draws out the green card. Staring down at it.*) And what does a green invitation mean?

SHERMAN. I have no idea. I haven't seen one before. They've obviously invented a new category for you.

IAN (*sharp smile*). Probably means I'll be kept in perpetual limbo for the rest of my time. (*Serious glance at* SHERMAN.) Unless things change.

Music in the distance, as if from the top of the building, coming down.

SHERMAN (*sharp, turns*). What's that? I thought I heard some music.

IAN. Yes – leaking out of somewhere. (*His voice is louder than usual, his whole manner more assertive.*) There's always someone working late. It's like a latter day Versailles here, isn't it? The place that never sleeps. Except of course there's not one but several monarchs, and the likes of me, constantly craning our necks to catch a glimpse of them.

SHERMAN. Really? It has never struck me as being like that. You've got a very whimsical imagination, Ian.

IAN (*carrying on, loud, smiling*). In years to come people will wonder at the baronial size these companies reached – like the age of the dinosaur! We're moving into our peak period now, with the coming explosion of the leisure industry.

SHERMAN (*sharp*). There is a recession to get through first!

IAN (*carrying straight on*). They'll be truly amazed that companies could sprout so many divisions, grow quite so bloated, they'll plod along these passages with guide-books in their hands! Looking at the scenery. (*Excited.*) You know, part of this company is making robots – yes – voice recognition robots. Every science-fiction film I ever saw as a kid had domestic robots, and now eventually, without much fuss, we've reached that point, it's a *fact*, we've got there. It's a funny feeling isn't it? And all this has grown from the first TV dynasty in the United States, from the first little TV network – the octopus grew. (*He smiles speedily,* SHERMAN *is staring at him.*) And it does have a certain tinny fascination, I'll admit, it *does*. The whole size of it all – (*He touches the wall, loud.*) But they can't even be bothered to see this building is built to last, underneath the blue carpet it's really so tacky, the walls are so thin . . .

SHERMAN. You seem to be in a rather excited state, Ian, what's the matter?

IAN (*sharp*). Nothing.

SHERMAN (*suddenly*) Don't worry, the girl's coming! Nothing to worry about. There's a phone. Good. I get withdrawal symptoms if I'm away from one for long.

SHERMAN *is eating out of a bag of peanuts.*

IAN (*suddenly*). I didn't know you were married, Don.

SHERMAN. Married? (*Slight, jokey smile.*) I think so. Yes! After a fashion. Once. We see each other quite often, still.

IAN (*loud*). I saw my girlfriend walking along the street the other day, quite by chance – near here. It was extraordinary, I watched her walking right by me, and I didn't call out to her, she was only about ten feet away – like that. (*He illustrates.*) I could have touched her – if I'd stretched out. But I didn't. I let her go by. (*Slight pause.*) And yet that evening we were as close as ever.

SHERMAN. That's nothing unusual. (*Moving.*) There should be more lights here. (*Suddenly louder.*) I wonder where that music is really coming from?

IAN (*sharp grin*). Ghosts! A collection of dead stars playing their old hits to each other.

SHERMAN (*snaps*). I hate nostalgia. It's a sleeping sickness. I can't understand it. I've never felt nostalgia for anything – that dull ache that some people feel.

IAN (*glances up towards music*). Must be somebody up there. I often think I should set off the fire-alarm and see who exactly is flushed out of the building. Probably whole nests of accountants would come crawling out, blinking in the light. It's funny to think of us standing here, at nearly midnight, waiting expectantly for these two kids to . . .

SHERMAN. One kid. (*Sharp.*) What is the matter with you, you've almost scrunched up your invitation?

IAN *hesitates nervously for a second, then takes the plunge.*

IAN. This is a little embarrassing – but it has to be said – because you'll discover any moment. I went to Conroy, and tactfully suggested you were completely wrong not to see Gary . . . so we're auditioning Gary too. I've been behind your back – emboldened by lack of sleep.

SHERMAN *stares at him, very slight pause.*

SHERMAN. You're a bloody idiot then. (*His manner is totally confident, totally dismissive.*) It won't make any difference. The boy's a waste of time. You've chosen the wrong one – and the wrong time – and the wrong tactics. (*Moving, sharp.*) You're a total fool!

IAN (*unfazed*). I had to. I thought you were wrong. The girl's nothing! I mean you were going to throw her out.

SHERMAN. I changed my mind. (*Dangerous.*) These decisions are mine.

IAN. But I couldn't just stand back and let things roll away from me, while you made . . .

SHERMAN. You're very disposable, you know, Ian.

IAN (*facing him*). I know.

Pause.

SHERMAN. And you're not very good – but I quite like you. (*He moves up to him.*) I can't stand all this university limpness, all the melancholic reflection, but I quite like you. (*Suddenly more dangerous.*) But you've chosen the wrong time.

IAN (*straight at him*). Have I? (*Very sharp.*) We'll see what Conroy thinks.

MURRAY *enters, stands some distance away, looking across the studio at them.*

MURRAY. What's the matter? Haven't they showed up?

SHERMAN. It's you. (*To* IAN.) His great shape lurking out of the darkness – I couldn't think what it was for a moment! You couldn't resist coming to see.

MURRAY. I have business to finish –

SHERMAN. I have never known you survive in London so long. You've usually escaped back to the cottage paradise by now.

MURRAY (*slight smile*). You'd prefer that. I used to come in here and the air reeked of drugs and coke, and beer was pouring out of everywhere, now there's just this chilly smell of disinfectant. (*Savage smile at* SHERMAN.) About sums it up. (*Sharp.*) By the way I saw that girl of yours, the small one, leaning up against a wall on the other side of the building.

SHERMAN (*surprised*). Did you show her the way here?

MURRAY. Of course not. I didn't like to disturb her. (MURRAY *moves round the studio.*) You know Conroy's here? (*Sharp smile.*) You're all in position.

SHERMAN *looks round, surprised.*

SHERMAN. Is he? (SHERMAN *turns round, and calls out loudly and not at all respectfully towards the box.*) Conroy? Are you there? (*We can't see into the box, since it's dimly lit, we only hear* CONROY's *voice. His voice is mid-Atlantic, his delivery harsh, and without* SHERMAN's *idiosyncratic quality, but authoritative.*)

CONROY. Yes, Don, I'm here. I've still got a few things to tie up tonight – so time is limited, almost more than usual . . . (*He unleashes words without waiting for a reaction, but obviously aiming it all at* SHERMAN, *for him neither* MURRAY *nor* IAN *exist.* SHERMAN *smiling to himself, his tone as to an equal, occasionally interrupts but* CONROY *doesn't wait.*) We're getting a lot of non-response out of publicity – we always seem to have this problem here – don't we? We need a clear-out.

SHERMAN (*sharp smile*). A bit of restructuring, what you're good at, Conroy . . .

CONROY (*without pausing*). . . . some readjustment anyway. (*Fast.*) I asked them today to check over some handouts, standard issue, going out to all UK record shops, new summer releases, it's already a month old – and you know, they tell me they haven't *sent them out yet*! First they said there was a

bottle-neck at the print-out – then that the machines had gone
and fucked up. The equipment they've had installed in there is
real third-rate shit, it's all IBM of course.

SHERMAN. Nothing works in the London office – it never has.
You must have realised that.

CONROY (*continuing without a pause*). I got very uncomfortable
last time I was here, there was cigarette smoke everywhere. The
extractors weren't working properly – they've probably never
been wired up, come to think of it. I could hardly see the band,
and they were real jerks whoever they were, thought it was all a
great joke, just here to fuck around, a complete waste of time,
never should have been allowed, you should have seen them!

SHERMAN (*glancing at IAN*). Sounds unpleasant, Conroy.

CONROY (*carrying straight on, his voice getting louder, harsher,
all the time rattling out*). I got trapped just now by somebody
from some regional office, somewhere I'd never heard of before,
he was going on about blank cassettes. I've heard *too* much
about blank cassettes this year, I said we're aware it's a problem.
(*Harsh laugh.* SHERMAN *is grinning sideways at* CONROY'*s
torrent.*) The problem that won't go away! . . . We are moving
towards a controlled strategy on it at last. It's taken some
getting. Otherwise there'll be more than just a slight wobble this
year . . . People have got EMI on the brain, you know – I don't
subscribe to that – (*Dry laugh.*) As if there was any comparison.
No way. It should do us quite a favour in fact . . . What did
you make of the awards last night then? I saw them on
playback. I thought the layout was an improvement this year,
much better balance, of course it . . .

MURRAY (*savage smile, really loud*). CONROY, JUST SHUT UP!
Total silence. MURRAY *standing centre stage. They all look at
box,* SHERMAN *smiling. Complete silence.*

MURRAY. Otherwise we'll have to come over and switch your
microphone off. (*To* SHERMAN.) He manages to make you
sound almost elegant. (*He stares towards the blackness in the
box.*) Has he lost all his hair yet? Got craters all over his scalp?

CONROY (*his voice totally unaffected, slow and harsh, full of
authority*). I'm waiting here, Don.

SHERMAN (*sharp*). The girl will be here any second – don't
worry. There's some beer in the box, why don't you drink some
of it, Conroy? (*Slight pause.*)

CONROY. I have one call to make – *then I'm ready.*

MURRAY *looking around him.*

MURRAY (*his tone acerbic*). You realise the city out there could be totally flattened – and we wouldn't even notice. Wouldn't hear a thing.

IAN. I heard some music just now actually.

MURRAY *glances at* IAN.

MURRAY. When we were in Los Angeles – I was with him. (*Indicating* SHERMAN.) The small one. We were working late in the studio through the night, doing one short track over and over, and we heard this sort of flurry of shouts and cries outside. (*Sharp to* SHERMAN.) Remember it! Voices calling out. And then we forgot all about it. Stopped listening to it. And when we came out in the morning, five-thirty in the morning, there were people lying everywhere, all over the pavement crying, in bundles. It had been the day Robert Kennedy had got shot, and they'd been shrieking and wailing outside this television station all night. It's where they gather in the States, and now they were too exhausted to go home. And there he was (*He points to* SHERMAN.) setting off immediately, *but* immediately, without a blink. (*Looks at him.*) Got this image of you picking your way over them on the pavement, trying your best not to tread on their heads, and not always succeeding, saying 'excuse me' . . . 'excuse me', clutching your little leather travelling bag . . .

SHERMAN (*staring at him*). You know, I can't remember that at all.

LORRAINE *enters wearing* SHERMAN's *jacket. She looks small, pale, and startling. She has wetted her hair back.*

SHERMAN (*his manner immediately changes, more aggressively animated*). Why weren't you here before?

LORRAINE. I'm not late. (*Looks around at the others.*) Am I?

SHERMAN. There's no need to ask them – you're late.

LORRAINE (*looks back at him*). I thought you liked working late anyway. (*To him.*) It's when you hit your peak isn't it?

SHERMAN (*moving*). Usually. It varies.

CONROY (*his microphone clicking on*). Is that the girl?

MURRAY (*sharp*). Well spotted, Conroy.

SHERMAN. That's the girl, yes.

CONROY (*harsh*). So one of them has *decided* to turn up, have they?

SHERMAN. This is the only one. (*Moving towards the podium.*

Brisk.) Her eyes look very bloodshot, like she's been up three nights in a row.

LORRAINE. Thank you.

MURRAY (*quiet*). That's how they all look.

SHERMAN. Have you bothered to rehearse?

LORRAINE (*sharp, responding to his aggression*). Bothered?

SHERMAN. Yes – did you make the effort?

LORRAINE. What else do you think I've been doing?

SHERMAN (*disbelieving her*). You really have?

LORRAINE. You should have seen enough of me to know I wouldn't lie about *that*.

SHERMAN (*sharp smile*). I don't think that follows at all. Quite the opposite. (*He moves.*) Go and stand up there.

He indicates the podium. LORRAINE *moves towards it.*

SHERMAN (*grins, sideways at* IAN). I told you the boy wouldn't come.

IAN. I'm not worried yet.

SHERMAN (*speedy*). I would be.

LORRAINE *is on the podium, with microphone in front of her – the harsh studio lights beating down, but the back of the studio is still in the darkness, with* IAN *and* MURRAY *watching her from the walls of the studio, and* SHERMAN *pacing near her.*

MURRAY (*staring at her small figure, hardly bigger than the microphone stand*). She probably keeps herself *artificially* small, you realise. Stops herself from growing by shovelling weed-killer down herself every morning, mouse poison.

LORRAINE (*sharp*). I stopped growing a long time ago, when I was ten. (*Suddenly to* SHERMAN.) He doesn't have to be here as well, does he?

SHERMAN. Of course, if he wishes it. (*Straight at her.*) Why shouldn't he be? (*He moves.*) We're going to do a voice test now, for levels.

IAN (*brisk, indicating*). Is that the right height for you?

LORRAINE (*suddenly nervous*). I don't know. Can I have a cigarette?

SHERMAN. She's decided she smokes now! (*Slight smile.*) A last request? Ian will give you a cigarette.

LORRAINE (*staring at* SHERMAN). I think you better have one too.

SHERMAN. Certainly not. I don't smoke.

IAN *lights her cigarette with his lighter.*

LORRAINE. It would stop you fidgeting – (*She tugs nervously at her cigarette.*) Are you videoing this? (*Staring around her.*) Is there a hidden camera somewhere, staring at me?

SHERMAN. No. We don't waste video like that.

LORRAINE (*straight back*). You can't waste video. You can use it again and again.

SHERMAN *stares at her. Slight smile.*

SHERMAN. Do you know how to use a microphone?

LORRAINE. Of course, it's not very difficult.

CONROY'S VOICE (*suddenly booming*). She looks like a school kid. You're sure she's not under age. Could get us into trouble working this late, Don.

SHERMAN. She says she's seventeen.

LORRAINE (*really loud*). I AM SEVENTEEN!

SHERMAN. We've no choice but to try to believe her.

LORRAINE. You don't believe anything I say, do you?

SHERMAN (*sharp*). Isn't your family worried about you, by now, out so late?

LORRAINE. My family? Of course not.

SHERMAN. She'll probably turn out to be thirteen and a half, and already have a litter of children.

LORRAINE (*stares at him*). Why do you have to be so rude to me?

SHERMAN. Just into the microphone, now – it's a voice test, for the engineer.

LORRAINE (*moving right up, suddenly*). Your jacket's too big for me.

SHERMAN. It wasn't designed for you.

LORRAINE. I think I'll . . .

SHERMAN (*authoritative*). No. Keep it on. A voice test.

LORRAINE. Now? (*Into microphone.*) Testing . . . testing . . . I'm standing here now about to . . . testing . . .

SHERMAN. No. Sing something. That's why we're here.

LORRAINE *half sings a few bars. Silence.*

SHERMAN. Were you trying that time, Lorraine?

LORRAINE (*really loud, back at him*). It was only a voice test, for Chrissake.

Pause. SHERMAN *moving around studio.*

SHERMAN. There are some people in this room, Lorraine, who don't think that you should be here. (*Slight smile.*) Everybody else present in fact.

LORRAINE. That's very encouraging to know. (*Straight at him.*) Why are you trying to put me off?

SHERMAN (*looks at* LORRAINE). They think you might cause trouble.

LORRAINE (*staring back at him*). How could anything I do cause trouble *to you?*

SHERMAN (*slight smile*). I'm wondering about that. (*Smiles, edgy in front of* CONROY.) Of course they may be right.

GARY *enters.*

IAN (*immediately*). He's here. For Chrissake where've you been?

GARY. Where do you think? (*Innocent smile.*) Been finding my way here, down four miles of passages.

LORRAINE (*quiet*). I didn't expect you to come too.

SHERMAN (*sharply*). It was a useless journey. (*Turns and moves directly towards the box, referring his remarks to* CONROY *with dismissive authority.*) This boy is a waste of time. There is no point in auditioning him.

CONROY. He's here now, Don, we might as well give him a chance.

SHERMAN (*sharp*). I did not consider this boy worth seeing.

He joins CONROY *in the box.* LORRAINE *gets down off the podium. The two of them stand next to each other as the* CONROY/SHERMAN *argument comes out over the speakers.*

IAN (*calling up to the box*). It would be absurd to send him away now.

CONROY. It won't take us that much longer to see them both, Don, it's easy to tell.

SHERMAN. I can't agree to this. The boy is a total waste of time –

CONROY. We'll just see what he can do.

SHERMAN. I see no purpose in that at all. It is completely obvious that he is the less interesting of the two, there is no arguing with that.

MURRAY. But people seem to be.

SHERMAN (*shouts*). Murray, could you clear the floor, please – if you want to watch come up to the box.

GARY (*innocent smile*). Can I say something?

The two are standing, looking pale and small in the light, as the voices boom around them. But GARY is smiling.

MURRAY (*as he moves into box*). Getting excited aren't you? (*Moving into box.*) I'm surprised there's room for me.

SHERMAN. There is nothing that boy can do that I don't know already.

GARY. Can I just . . .

CONROY. I can't agree with you there, Don, obviously we've *got* to see him now.

Slight pause.

SHERMAN (*icy*). A piece of late-night lunacy – but if you want to prove me right.

IAN (*sharp, who has remained with the kids by the podium*). Who's going first then?

GARY (*mimicking his eagerness*). Who's going first?

IAN (*impatient*). Yes! Who's going to have first try? Do you want to work that one out or shall I decide?

GARY. Can I just say . . .

IAN (*quick smile*). Actually, I think I'll decide – otherwise it could lead to argument. Gary, are you ready – could you get up to the mike?

GARY (*shouts into mike*). CAN I SAY SOMETHING, PLEASE?

And he takes microphone on its stand and hits downward on the podium floor so it makes an incredibly loud popping noise. He stops, silence.

SHERMAN (*icily matter-of-fact, over the mike*). I don't think so.

GARY takes mike off stand, and looks around him. Studio in silence. Him standing under the central light, LORRAINE near the podium, standing completely still, impassive.

GARY. Thank you. That's better. (*Slight pause. Manner is febrile.*) It's stopped raining outside you'll be pleased to know.

He hesitates for a second.

SHERMAN (*over speaker*). Good . . .

GARY (*swings round, holding hand mike, towards box*). He *thinks* he *knows* what I'm going to do. (*Loud.*) Don't you? The mad dwarf! Sitting behind glass now – all of you, like the tanks of fish in the other room – bubbles coming out of your mouths. You should stay there. It really suits you. You shouldn't ever come out again.

SHERMAN. Like the feel of the microphone, do you? Look at the way he's holding it, performing.

IAN. Gary . . .

SHERMAN. I know what he wants to do.

GARY. Do you? (*Loud.*) What I've been trying to say is – I have come here now – to collect my taxi FARE. (*Aggressive.*) Right?

IAN (*astonished*). What?

GARY. Being discharged, even if you do it yourself as I have just done, entitles me to the full taxi fare. (*Loud, animated.*) And it is all the way to Isleworth, which is twelve miles away. Could put you back twelve or fifteen quid, at least, and that's without the tip. I've got the taxi waiting, just outside the back entrance. (*Savage smile.*) So please could you give it to me?

IAN (*furious*). What on earth are you doing, Gary?

GARY. I would have thought that was fairly clear, isn't it?

SHERMAN (*his voice smiling*). Certainly. We'll give you the money. If you will kindly leave the studio now.

GARY. Chuck it down if you don't want to come out of your box, let them flutter down onto the floor here, then you'll be quite safe. (*Sharp smile.*) Won't get bitten.

SHERMAN. Fine. If you just go to the main entrance immediately . . .

GARY. Feed it through the crack in the glass!

IAN. Gary, I think you'd better just think about this and try . . .

SHERMAN (*cutting IAN off*). You can get the money from the Security desk. Could you now leave while we're still asking you politely? You're not required here.

GARY. Yes. (*He moves on podium, smiles.*) The only thing is – I'm not leaving by myself. (*Suddenly.*) I'm taking her with me now.

LORRAINE. Gary . . . ?

She stands impassively.

GARY. She's not staying here. And *yes*, I have *asked her*.

SHERMAN. Have you?

GARY. I can feel them getting worried, Lorraine, their time's money you see, the money, dribbling away as I stand here. He has to be transported somewhere soon, the dwarf, he shuts up like a shooting stick, you know, and they put him in a box and send him that way. (*Loud.*) They hadn't bargained for this! Had you?

SHERMAN (*really animated*). I knew it! I knew it! It just had to come, didn't it? It always does. I've seen it so often I've lost count.

GARY (*savagely*). Seen what?

SHERMAN. The canned rage, all this synthetic fury, turn the right knob and out it comes spurting, on demand. Cut-price aggression. You've all just about perfected it by now.

GARY (*loud*). But the difference is here, you're not going to acquire it this time, not going to get your hands . . .

SHERMAN (*cutting him off – over mike*). It's become so easy, so corrupted, hundreds of kids now, we get offered it every day of the year and usually a little better. It's become a whole efficient industry in itself . . .

GARY (*shouts*). But I've *withdrawn*, don't you REALISE that?

SHERMAN. And it doesn't fool me for a moment.

GARY. I'm not trying to. (*Savage.*) And my microphone's louder than yours.

SHERMAN. Just another performance. And what's even worse, you're still *hoping*, you still really want to get signed up. (*Loud.*) Aren't you?

GARY (*very strong*). You really think that, do you? *You don't believe anybody ever means anything!*

SHERMAN (*triumphant*). What did I tell you? Here it all comes galloping out . . . !

GARY. You really think I'm still panting for you to take me. (*Hits mike.*) Gobble . . . Gobble.

SHERMAN. You're making a total idiot of yourself now. Ian, could you please just . . .

GARY (*sudden flash of danger*). Maybe I should break the glass then, do you think? (*He rushes across the room right up to the glass.* SHERMAN *stares down at him through glass.*) Do you think, Lorraine, it shatters like a windscreen, leaving a clear hole just where his head is? (GARY *is right up to the glass, looking at* SHERMAN. *Silence. Slight smile.*) But I won't give you that satisfaction, of you having something on me. You really would like to bottle a bit of us, wouldn't you? Pump it out and store it for later. But you can't get me. Because *I've withdrawn.* (*He turns, moves back towards the podium. To* IAN.) I'm sorry, mate, but maybe you should do the same thing yourself – I mean it – (*Quiet.*) It's quite a nice feeling being still in one piece.

IAN (*icily*). Thanks, I'll try to remember.

CONROY (*booming*). Get rid of him for Chrissake, the boy's a nutter.

SHERMAN. Ian, could you please get rid of your discovery before he does anything else?

IAN. Come on, out.

GARY (*by* LORRAINE, *concerned*). Lorraine, you must leave with me.

LORRAINE (*impassive, firm small face*). It's all right, Gary.

GARY (*worried*). You'd be a real idiot if you stay here. You're not safe.

SHERMAN (*savage*). Will you stop trying to worry her?

GARY. I came back to fetch you.

LORRAINE (*impassive*). I know what I'm doing. (*She looks at him, quiet.*) It's all right.

GARY. Lorraine. Please . . .

IAN (*manhandling him*). Come on, you little bastard, you're going to have me 'escorting' you out.

IAN *takes him out.*

GARY (*turns at door, slight smile*). Last chance.

They exit.

SHERMAN. OK, we're ready.

CONROY. Ian didn't look in good shape, he lacks something that guy, he really does.

SHERMAN. Yes. But I think we should leave him where he is – anyone can make mistakes.

MURRAY. Except you of course.

SHERMAN. Of course.

Leaning forward, staring down at LORRAINE *who is alone on stage for the first time. Her small figure standing on the podium, wearing his jacket.*

The glass box behind her, harsh light above her head.

(*Voice sharp.*) Are you listening? We're going to do it now. The backing track will be coming up and it's quite loud. You know your entry, do you? (LORRAINE, *standing on podium, nods.*) Keep still – don't look at us, look straight ahead.

CONROY. Whose jacket is she wearing?

SHERMAN. She's wearing mine.

CONROY. Is she very nervous – she looks a bit nervous to me.

SHERMAN. She's just pale. (*Staring down at her.*) Her face really does look as if it's made out of formica, doesn't it? (*Loud.*) Don't look at us.

LORRAINE. If you're going to talk about me, could you switch your microphone off. (*Loud.*) Because I can hear every word you're saying.

SHERMAN. Look straight ahead. Are you ready, Lorraine? OK. It's yours now.

MURRAY (*acerbic*). We'll soon know, won't we, Don?

The backing track starts, SHERMAN's *directions coming booming over the speakers.*

SHERMAN. Wait for it, don't look at us, right . . .

Backing track getting louder. LORRAINE *remaining completely still, she doesn't open her mouth, makes no move to sing, her face completely impassive. She remains absolutely still,* SHERMAN *stares down at her from box.*

The backing track cuts out. Silence.

(*Voice steely.*) Lorraine – you missed your entry.

LORRAINE. Did I? (*She turns.*) I didn't hear it –

SHERMAN. You missed it. (*His voice really steely.*) I do hope you're not trying to imitate Gary. (LORRAINE *remains completely impassive.*) Concentrate for Chrissake – listen for it – you know when it comes. (*Pause,* LORRAINE *not moving.*) You've got to get it this time.

The backing track restarts very loud the same introduction. LORRAINE *impassive. Then* LORRAINE *begins to sing.*

Her voice is still borderline. But she has presence and strength, she begins to put the song over with extreme confidence and determination.

Her small figure alone on stage wearing his jacket. Sharp, almost dangerous, in her directness.

The song itself is a piece of straightforward pop, but her pale, determined figure makes it seem extraordinary.

Half-way through the song, as it begins to build to climax, SHERMAN's voice comes over the loud-speakers saying 'Lorraine', calling her name, trying to stop her throughout the rest of the song, but she ignores this, a really powerful determination comes out of her, as she clasps the microphone very tightly, absolutely furious concentration and willing herself to get it through to them.

The track finally cuts out. She stands for a second, very still, centre stage, her powerful small face staring out. Silence.

SHERMAN (*his voice*). Will you just stay there, please?

LORRAINE. Can I . . . ?

SHERMAN. Just stay exactly where you are, please.
Pause.

CONROY (*totally matter-of-fact*). Thanks very much, 'bye.

LORRAINE (*looking up at the box*). But how did I do? (*Pause.*) Where are you? (*Pause.*) Where have you gone?

Complete silence. She climbs off the podium, her head goes down for a second, the back of her hand against her lips with nerves, but she pulls herself through it in a second.

MURRAY enters. Moves slowly across to her across the darkened studio, LORRAINE staring at him, apprehensive, hostile.

(*Loud.*) What are you doing here . . . ?
Pause.

MURRAY (*slight smile, he looms over to her, his huge frame, and her small figure*). Came to see you.

LORRAINE. How did I do?

MURRAY. How do you think?

LORRAINE (*sharp*). What you mean? Why've you come? Is he just going to leave me here then – with you?

Pause. MURRAY very slight smile. LORRAINE staring straight at him.

Did you get what you wanted?

MURRAY. From whom?

LORRAINE. From him – you wanted to discuss some business with him – (*Pause.*) You wanted his attention. You've been waiting for it.

MURRAY. I had a few words, yes.

LORRAINE. Even though you don't like him – you still come to see him, don't you?

MURRAY. I'd noticed.

LORRAINE. And you will go on till he stops you probably.

MURRAY (*moving closer to her, sharp*). How old are you really?

LORRAINE. I told you.

MURRAY. Maybe you're a midget with a girl's head.

LORRAINE. I think you're jealous of me.

MURRAY (*surprised*). Jealous?

LORRAINE. But I don't mind. I'm used to it. There's a lot of it around at the moment –

MURRAY (*sharp*). Is there? (*He stares down at* LORRAINE.) I'm jealous of you? Hardly in the circumstances!

LORRAINE. What you mean? (*Suddenly worried, excited.*) You mean I haven't got through! (*Pause.*) Why aren't you telling me?

MURRAY. No.

LORRAINE (*shouts*). What you mean, no? No what?

MURRAY. The look on your face! (*Staring at her, the real panic, light smile.*) Complete terror at the thought!

LORRAINE. What do you mean? You're enjoying yourself aren't you? (*Moving back.*) And, please, I would rather you didn't touch me . . .

MURRAY (*staring down at her, quiet*). Jealous? (*His tone quiet but sharp, straight at her, just holding her arm.*) At the last concert I gave, a kid half-way down the hall stared at me the entire time, never moved his head, never seemed to blink, just stared straight at me with real loathing in his eyes, no other word for it. He didn't understand a single moment of what I was doing, like I was a different species. He just hated. I could feel the violence of it. He was about your age, maybe he was you with a wig on. Just staring straight at me as if he was trying to turn me to stone. Maybe he managed it.

LORRAINE (*quiet*). Could you let me go?

SHERMAN *enters, brusquely, hardly noticing MURRAY, his voice very sharp, dismissive.*

SHERMAN (*very sharp*). OK, Murray, see you when you're next around.

MURRAY *looks up.*

MURRAY. Could be . . . could be.

He exits.

LORRAINE. So how did I do then?

SHERMAN *stares at her for a moment, across the width of the darkened stage.*

SHERMAN. Do you want this? (*He moves slightly, stretches out a handkerchief towards her.*) Wipe your face.

LORRAINE. No.

SHERMAN. Go on, take it.

LORRAINE (*backing away*). No, it's what you gave to Tallulah. Does it mean you're going to try to do the same thing to me?

SHERMAN *moves to the back of the studio, his manner preoccupied.*

SHERMAN (*glancing at switches*). Somewhere.

The full lights come on, lights up the whole expanse of the stage, to the back wall. We see inside the empty glass box, with its piles of slightly ageing equipment, the fire notices up on the wall, instructions about electrical supplies, the grubby stains on the paint-work, and the dust round the edges.

This studio needs rebuilding.

LORRAINE (*swings round, blinking in the light*). What are you doing?

SHERMAN. Were you nervous?

LORRAINE. Of course I was.

SHERMAN. A great deal or a little?

LORRAINE. I don't know. (*Loud.*) Are you going to tell me how I did?

SHERMAN (*stronger*). You missed your entry.

LORRAINE. I know! For Chrissake why doesn't anybody give me a straight answer? Why are you being like this?

SHERMAN (*moment's pause, then sharp, he moves*). We are going to offer you a two-year contract.

LORRAINE. You are! (*Pause.*) So I did it?

SHERMAN. You just managed it, yes.

LORRAINE (*quiet*). I thought I had. (*Then sharp to him.*) You didn't think I would.

SHERMAN (*he moves, preoccupied*). I will assign a producer to you.

LORRAINE. When do I get the contract?

SHERMAN (*not looking at her*). You trust people even less than I do.

LORRAINE (*watching him*). I don't trust people, no.

SHERMAN's *mood is preoccupied.*

SHERMAN. But I have missed my plane because of this, you realise. Because of you. Which isn't good. I have never missed a plane before.

LORRAINE (*matter-of-fact*). You'll just have to get the next one.

SHERMAN (*whirls round suddenly, as if to a secretary*). Get me Reception.

Pointing to phone by wall.

LORRAINE. Me?

SHERMAN. Yes, just punch the button. (*Snaps.*) Punch nine for Reception. Go on! (LORRAINE *does so, holding the receiver and staring at him.* SHERMAN *moves.*) The heat seems to have switched itself off in here, it's noticeably colder.

LORRAINE. There's no answer.

SHERMAN (*fierce, as if to a secretary*). Keep holding – they take some time to answer. You just have to hold.

LORRAINE *stands by phone, staring at him.*

SHERMAN. If I'm still here you better have lunch with me tomorrow.

LORRAINE. No thank you.

SHERMAN (*looking at her*). I was only offering you lunch. (*Pause.*) A meal.

LORRAINE. I know. But I don't want to. (*Holding phone.*) I'm going to be by myself.

SHERMAN (*sharply, loud*). Put the receiver down and try again. Go on. Did you hit nine? It's nine . . . (LORRAINE *does so,*

staring at him all the time. SHERMAN *watching* LORRAINE.)
You're going to be given power to reach a large audience, you
know.

LORRAINE. I know. I'm not really interested in that side of it.
There's nothing particular I want to say to them.

SHERMAN. Of course that's assuming that you're a success. That
you don't go out like a light.

LORRAINE. I don't care if I do.

SHERMAN. That I don't believe.

LORRAINE. As long as I've lasted long enough to be safe, I've
made enough money to be secure, that's what I want. (*Sharp.
She moves from phone leaving it dangling there.*) And I'm
getting out of this place, out of England. I want to go to
America because it's easier there.

SHERMAN. To America! These determined English kids marching
into the States to make their fortune, the new ruthlessness,
probably trample over a few of the inhabitants.

LORRAINE (*straight at him*). But I don't want to come back. If I
really do sell there, I'm going to live there. I won't be coming
back to this country.

SHERMAN. You must want to in the end.

LORRAINE. Why?

SHERMAN. Because you were born here.

LORRAINE (*loud*). What's that got to do with anything? When
I'm away from my family, I have trouble remembering their faces.
They just fade away; you know what I mean. (*Really strong.*) I
don't feel part of anything and I'm not, not in the town where I
live or anywhere. (*Pause, straight at him, throwing back his own
words.*) I have no likes or dislikes, no allegiances.

SHERMAN. You'll change. You're just a kid, all kids feel . . .

LORRAINE (*loud, cutting him off*). I told you – I'm not going to
change. I'm hardly a child any more, I know what I mean. I'm
not going to suddenly wake up and start to feel differently. I
can promise you. (*Pause.*) Why do you look so surprised, like
that, there's nothing to be surprised about.

SHERMAN. I can almost touch the steel coming out of you. Go
back to the telephone. They may have answered.

LORRAINE (*not moving*). You keep on wanting to think of me as just some really hard-faced person, but I'm not. (*Crosses to phone, then back at him.*) I'm no different to anyone else. (*Picks up receiver.*) Nothing there.

SHERMAN. I wonder how long you'll last?

LORRAINE. As long as I do.

SHERMAN (*his manner progressively more agitated*). Nothing lasts now, absolutely nothing. I have watched a great many disposable things come and go – like you. It just needs one small gust of a new fashion, and a whole range of products and ideas are just wiped out. You have to be able to read the signs, in the ether, and I'm an artist at that, the only sort that matters . . . (*Sharp smile to himself.*) The only sort that lasts. (*Loud, suddenly swings round.*) For Chrissake, why is there no answer? This is ridiculous. (*Loud.*) I can't stay here! This city leaks . . . it gets cold at night . . . one missed connection and the whole house of cards of arrangements comes down. There isn't another flight tonight . . . (*Loud.*) What is the matter with this place? Dial out direct. (*Suddenly looks at her.*) What time is it in Los Angeles?

LORRAINE (*staring at him*). I don't know what time it is in Los Angeles.

SHERMAN (*half to himself*). And in New York . . . I can't remember – the different time zones get jumbled up . . . It's not late there I think. (*Pause, he moves.*) I have no more business here.

LORRAINE. I shouldn't worry about it.

SHERMAN (*he turns*). You don't realise.

LORRAINE. Don't I?

She moves, phone dangling down.

SHERMAN (*loud*). And don't walk away while I'm talking to you.

LORRAINE. Was I?

SHERMAN. Of course, you know you were!

LORRAINE (*straight at him*). It's a habit we share. And you do it more often than me.

She looks at him.

I don't see why it matters so much about your plane.

SHERMAN (*loud, his voice rising*). I would have thought that was obvious. (*Looks at her.*) Because I have to keep on the move, why else do you think? That's what makes it work, how

I function best, I always need to be moving . . . people are a constant blur, I can't survive in one place for long periods. If I see somebody is signed by a rival company then I act at once. I reduce the time that I sleep a bit more each week, I have streamlined my mind . . . you have to be able to ride the machine well . . . I have a hold over other departments that certainly can't go on for ever, it's volatile . . . have to keep up . . . there is a lot of competition in the air at the moment.

LORRAINE (*loud, agreeing*). I know! I know!

SHERMAN. People are worried. You meet it everywhere. Things are not slowing down at all, they change so fast. (*Savage.*) And if you stop, people in this company, ridiculous though it is, may forget you exist! You have to work – and work. (*Very loud, excited.*) *No time to spare any more at all.*

LORRAINE (*loud, excited*). There isn't! I know there isn't. (*At him.*) I *know*. (SHERMAN *staring at her.*) I understand that. I do!

SHERMAN. I thought you would – (*Glances around, towards the phone.*) Could you . . .

LORRAINE (*cutting him off, straight at him*). The difference is . . . I'm *better at it* than you are.

SHERMAN *looks up, totally startled.*

Aren't I? (*Slight pause.*) I don't have to sort of strain nearly so much after it. Make such a business out of it! (*Straight at him.*) I'm much better, aren't I? (*Straight at him, a steely smile.*) I want you to admit it. (*Pause.*) Go on, admit it.

Silence.

SHERMAN (*totally disconcerted*). I shouldn't have let you get through tonight.

LORRAINE. Why? Because I know what I want . . . or are you the only one allowed that?

SHERMAN *replaces the phone, turns.*

SHERMAN. I don't understand why there's no answer. (*Looks around him for a second – then at her.*) I'm just in that slightly curious state, when I'm stranded for a second – do you understand . . . I have made no arrangements. I have to wait . . . I'm caught. And it's not particularly pleasant. Do you see?

LORRAINE. Yes. (*Pause.*) But there's nothing I can do about it. (*Silence, her tone changes.*) Don't hurt me again, will you?

SHERMAN *is close to her.*

SHERMAN. Why should I hurt you?

LORRAINE. Because you want to.

SHERMAN. Do I? Why? (*Pause.*)

LORRAINE. Because I make you nervous – for some reason.

Silence.

SHERMAN (*detached tone, staring at her*). You've got a lot of spots on that side of your face. I can see them in this light.

LORRAINE. Yes . . . (*Slight smile.*) A *rash*.

SHERMAN (*matter-of-fact, professional*). But it's still very much better without the make-up.

LORRAINE *moves, then turns.*

LORRAINE (*detached tone*). You'll probably die in an airport eventually. (*She moves.*) I'm going to leave now – it must be really late. (*Pause.*) Do you want your jacket back?

SHERMAN. No. It doesn't look bad. You can keep it.

LORRAINE (*lightly*). You should sleep more than you do, you know. Your hair'll turn white if you don't. It could turn white overnight. (*Pause. She moves, stops by the door, totally matter-of-fact.*) I enjoyed meeting you today. 'Bye.

She leaves.

SHERMAN *turns abruptly, moves to phone, and punches out a very long number, he stops, and looks up, holding receiver, slight smile.*

SHERMAN. If I fall asleep, I'll forget again which city I'm in.

Fade.

STRAWBERRY FIELDS

Strawberry Fields was first staged by the National Theatre in the Cottesloe on 31 March 1977. The cast was as follows:

KEVIN	Stephen Rea
CHARLOTTE	Jane Asher
NICK	Kenneth Cranham
MRS ROBERTS	Anne Leon
TAYLOR	Frederick Warder
CLEANER	Maya Kemp
KID	Peter Hugo-Daly

Directed by Michael Apted
Designed by Di Seymour

The play is set in various locations up a motorway.

The time is the present.

ACT ONE

Scene One

Cafe, hot, dusty, edge of London, start of the motorway.
CHARLOTTE sitting at a table. Jukebox in the background
playing. She is 21. She is drinking orange juice. KEVIN, tall,
lanky, with long hair and dark glasses, stands watching her. He is
30. He moves closer as she drinks delicately through a straw. He
takes out his wallet, slight smile. He takes out of the wallet a
small green card, he puts it on the table and pushes it towards
her. CHARLOTTE looks up, she picks up the card, glances at
him, hands it back. He puts it back in the wallet. She smiles at
him. KEVIN sits down at the table glancing over his shoulder as
he does so.

KEVIN. I'm Kevin.

CHARLOTTE (*shy smile*). Yes.

KEVIN (*smiles*). Kevin.

   Pause.

   That's my real name as it happens.

CHARLOTTE. I know.

KEVIN. Good. (*Pause.*) Great then.

CHARLOTTE. And I'm Charlotte.

KEVIN. Yes . . . Great.

   Silence.

   I've got the van outside. Waiting!

CHARLOTTE. Yes. (*She sips her orange juice.*)

KEVIN. Yes. She's completely ready. Tuned up. I've tuned her
   up. She'll give us a fantastic ride. Yes – we'll be really safe
   inside her.

CHARLOTTE. Good. (*Very delicately.*) Do you think I could
   have another straw, this one's got a little dirty . . .

KEVIN. A dirty straw! They're probably all really dirty straws in
   a place like this, probably been used several times before. (*He
   reaches for a glass of straws, knocks it over.*)

KEVIN (*smiles*). That tends to happen.

   CHARLOTTE *picks it up quickly and takes a straw.*

   Have you got a straw?

381

CHARLOTTE (*shyly*). Yes. Thank you very much. (*She starts to drink again out of the new straw.*)

KEVIN (*staring at her drinking*). Got a straw now, have you?

CHARLOTTE (*surprised*). Yes!

KEVIN. Great.

Pause.

I'm very early aren't I?

CHARLOTTE. No, you're exactly on time, I think.

KEVIN (*grins*). Am I? Looking forward to it are you?

CHARLOTTE. Yes, in a way.

KEVIN. Yeah. So am I. Where are we going first?

CHARLOTTE. Hertfordshire.

KEVIN. Great. I've got the 'literature' and everything. It's all ready – it looks really good, really clear, I'm quite proud of it. yes! They're all expecting us, are they?

CHARLOTTE. Yes, of course.

KEVIN. Great.

Pause.

Got the list and everything, have you?

CHARLOTTE. Yes. (*She taps her bag.*) In here.

KEVIN. Great. (*He smiles at her.*) Guard it carefully, won't you?

CHARLOTTE. Of course. (*Shy smile.*) Naturally.

KEVIN. I've got hundreds of maps – yes, the whole country! Every inch, M1, M6, M18 *all the roads*. Want a cup cake? (*He fishes into his pockets.*) I've got some somewhere. One chocolate, two banana flavour . . . (*Smiles.*) Where are they? May have melted, of course, in this weather. (*Grins.*) Maybe I'll find they've run down my trouser leg. Sorry.

CHARLOTTE. No, thank you anyway.

KEVIN (*looking at her*). Nervous, are you?

CHARLOTTE. Slightly, I think. I don't know . . . a little.

KEVIN. Your first time is it?

CHARLOTTE. Yes.

KEVIN. Mine too. No need to be nervous, no need at all. (*He smiles.*) Perhaps we ought to go for a swim instead, much better. One of those days your arse, your bottom sticks to the leather of the seat, isn't it! You'll like the smell of leather in the van, you know, that smell of really old leather, it's a great smell, gets you like a drug, old wooden dashboard too, fantastic, really ace one, with an extraordinarily roomy glove compartment, enormous! Like a tunnel. You can reach for miles, up to your armpit.

Pause. He smiles.

Sorry.

CHARLOTTE. We ought to leave in four minutes. (*She takes out a yoghurt, begins to eat.*)

KEVIN. Soon as that? (*He watches her.*) What you got there in your hand?

CHARLOTTE (*looks surprised*). It's my yoghurt. (*She stares at him.*) You ought to wear real spectacles, I think.

KEVIN (*broad smile*). Yeah – I only wish I could.

Silence. CHARLOTTE watches him.

CHARLOTTE. We've met before once, haven't we?

KEVIN. Yes – at the winter meeting, I think. I sat on the radiator. And you may have seen me duplicating.

CHARLOTTE (*staring right at him*). You're the one that has trouble with his eyes.

KEVIN. That's right. I've trouble with my eyes. Yes – a little.

CHARLOTTE. But you can see all right, can't you . . . I mean.

KEVIN. Oh yes, yes, I can see all right.

Pause.

But I'm going blind . . . maybe.

CHARLOTTE. Blind? (*CHARLOTTE is calm; she stares at him.*) I'm sorry to hear that.

KEVIN (*genuine smile*). So was I. It's a disease you know – of the retina. So all could be blackness up here – (*He taps his eyes.*) – quite soon.

CHARLOTTE. I'm sorry.

KEVIN (*smiles*). No, no need to be. We ought to have a coffee now – sharpen us up for it.

CHARLOTTE. No, thank you very much, but I don't drink coffee.

KEVIN. The thing is . . . what's worrying me, about our journey

. . . is, my driving licence is a bit out of date. Two years out of date.

CHARLOTTE. Why? (*Astonished.*) Why didn't you have it renewed?

Pause.

KEVIN. I forgot.

CHARLOTTE. And anyway, one's not really meant to drive at all if one can't see. (*She looks at* KEVIN.) Is one?

KEVIN. You're right about that . . .

CHARLOTTE. Then what happens if we're stopped . . .

KEVIN. Stopped by whom?

CHARLOTTE. The police, of course.

KEVIN. They won't stop us. (*He smiles.*) They won't now I can't see, will they? I'm a very safe driver, I am in fact – I just keep going in a straight line.

CHARLOTTE. I'll drive, I think.

KEVIN. You can drive?

CHARLOTTE. Yes – a little.

KEVIN. A little.

CHARLOTTE. Enough . . .

KEVIN. OK then. Why not? (*He pulls out the keys, holds them.*) But the whole *point* of me *being here* was to drive the van.

CHARLOTTE. I know. (*She smiles.*) But we don't want to get killed, do we?

KEVIN. No. You're right, of course. Here. (*He hands her the keys.*)

CHARLOTTE. I hope you don't mind me asking, but it's important . . . I mean, what can you see?

KEVIN. Well, I can see you . . .

CHARLOTTE. Good, that's a start.

KEVIN. You've got black hair, haven't you? (CHARLOTTE *is blonde.*) Short cropped black hair.

Pause. KEVIN *gives a broad smile.*

Actually you haven't. Don't worry. I know you haven't. Only a joke, it's apricot, a sort of apricot.

CHARLOTTE (*staring hard*). Yes. I've just had it cut, actually.

Pause.

KEVIN (*suddenly looks nervously over his shoulder then back at her*). Sorry – just having a look, that feeling gets to you, doesn't it, a sort of buzz down here. (*He feels the pit of his stomach.*) Christ! (*He suddenly smiles.*) Any moment we'll be speeding along, actually starting on it. I've got a camera with me. *And* some film. Be able to record it all. It's great weather for it anyway.

CHARLOTTE. You're very warmly dressed for it, aren't you?

KEVIN. Am I? (*He smiles.*) I don't like taking clothes off in public. I even sunbathe in a mackintosh.

CHARLOTTE. Do you really?

He glances at her.

KEVIN. You're not wearing sandals anyway.

CHARLOTTE. How do you know I'm not wearing sandals?

KEVIN. I can feel under the table.

CHARLOTTE. Yes. (*She smiles.*) I don't usually wear sandals.

KEVIN (*suddenly*). I saw a film once, it was only half an hour, but it was all of feet, feet crawling, feet eating, feet running over marshy ground and things, even over hot coals, getting burnt, that wasn't so nice. Just gone through my mind, you see. (*He smiles.*) Sorry, those pre-journey nerves again. (*Suddenly, a shrewd look.*) You're a little keyed-up, aren't you, but not showing it. Don't worry about it. (*He moves.*)
(*Fast.*) Yeah. I used to go to the movies a lot you see, more than just a lot really. I went every day for two years. Almost. You know, see all the movies – (*He indicates his eyes.*) – before these run out . . .

CHARLOTTE *gives a slight, amused smile.*

Go ahead. I don't mind people laughing . . .

CHARLOTTE. I wasn't. I wouldn't laugh at something like that.

KEVIN. No, honestly, I don't mind people laughing, it's no skin off my elbow. (*Friendly smile.*) It really isn't. (*He looks at the table.*) Filthy here, isn't it, in this cafe, start of the road! A bit of fried egg here on the table – full of stains.

CHARLOTTE. Yes it is.

KEVIN. Imagine when the holocaust comes and these places are all deserted and there are thistles growing on the motorway . . . and there's grass growing over the jukebox . . . and honeysuckle coming out of the expresso, yeah . . . and tadpoles swimming in the ladies.

CHARLOTTE (*amused smile*). Yes – I can imagine.

KEVIN. And of course there'll be a new sort of beast that hatches its eggs in the remains of the stale chips, yeah, in the chip trays, it lays its small blue eggs everywhere, all over, this new beast, and suddenly . . . and then suddenly it emerges from the fryers, this monster covered in batter, whole body in batter, and it goes after the last humans, catching and eating them. (*He smiles.*) We'd be among the survivors of course.

CHARLOTTE. Yes, of course.

KEVIN. Great scenario isn't it, for a B movie. Scenario de Bergerac.

CHARLOTTE. Yes. It's time now.

KEVIN. Sorry. I'm sorry – I'm talking shit, don't usually talk as much as this, must be annoying you.

CHARLOTTE. No. It's not.

KEVIN. It's just nerves you know. (*Self-mocking smile.*) Not that I'm nervous, of course.

CHARLOTTE. No.

KEVIN (*brushing himself*). It's just so dusty in here.

CHARLOTTE. I have a few of these if you like, moistened tissues.

CHARLOTTE *passes a tissue to* KEVIN.

KEVIN. Thanks, yeah. (*He wipes his face.*) Great things these. Now I feel ready for anything. We ought to get you some dark glasses too, oughtn't we, for the journey?

CHARLOTTE (*smiles*). Then we'd certainly get stopped, wouldn't we . . .

KEVIN. Yes, maybe. We mustn't get stopped . . . (*He grins.*) Not a good idea.

CHARLOTTE. Shall we . . .

KEVIN (*jumps up*). Yes! (*He moves over to the jukebox.*) I think we'd just better have a record for the road, don't you? Get us in the mood. (*He crosses over.*) Get us travelling well – speeding along . . . we're going the whole way . . . (*He selects a nostalgic Beach Boys standard.*)

(KEVIN *picks up his bag.*) Nice! It brings back memories, doesn't it? Let's leave. (*He doesn't move.*) Gets one, doesn't it

. . . No, come on – let's leave!

CHARLOTTE *leaves a tip on the table and picks up her bag.*

(KEVIN *is staring about him with feeling.*) This cafe could be anywhere, couldn't it? This view – this smell, the traffic out there – not just London – we could be anywhere on earth.

CHARLOTTE (*glancing round*). No it couldn't.

KEVIN (*quiet*). No. (*Then he grins.*) Ready? Prepared?

CHARLOTTE. Yes.

KEVIN. Great!

Blackout.

Scene Two

The verge. NICK, *blond hair, in his early twenties, stands staring down at them. Sound of traffic very loud, then quieter dying in and out of scene.* KEVIN *and* CHARLOTTE *are sitting with their picnic basket, and a small vat of ice-cream, a bottle of mineral water, a camera, an umbrella, and a book lying beside the picnic basket.*

KEVIN (*staring at the ice-cream*). We better have it now, don't you think or it'll melt.

CHARLOTTE (*glances round at him*). You're always wanting to eat, aren't you?

KEVIN (*smiling*). No. No I'm not. But I bought this specially. See, mocha almond fudge, lots of it. (*He lifts the lid slightly.*)

NICK (*calls down at them*). Hey!

KEVIN. We don't have to have it now, if you don't want. Save it till later. Easy. (*He moves the vat of ice-cream.*) It's nice and cold anyway.

CHARLOTTE (*quietly to herself*). I've got to phone home at some point. I mustn't forget. I've got to phone mother. (*She glances at him.*) Why don't you eat it if you want some – go on!

KEVIN (*lifts the lid of the ice-cream*). I don't know . . .

NICK (*very loud*). Hey!

They turn and see him.

KEVIN. Yes?

NICK *moves closer.*

NICK. I . . . (*He smiles.*) I saw you get out of that van just now, the old one back there.

KEVIN. Yes, that's the one – she's just being filled up.

NICK. And I just wondered – (*He smiles, looks from one to the other.*) – which way you're going?

KEVIN. Which way we're going? (*He glances at* CHARLOTTE.)

NICK. Are you going north by any chance . . .?

KEVIN. You mean up the motorway?

NICK. Yes – are you?

KEVIN. Yes, I think we are. We're going that way. (*He indicates.*)

NICK. That's north.

CHARLOTTE (*sharp*). Yes we know.

KEVIN *opens the lid of the ice-cream.*

KEVIN. I think we'll have the ice-cream now don't you, get it open, before it disappears.

NICK. And I was wondering – (*He smiles.*) – just wondering if you had any room?

KEVIN (*looking up*). Any room?

NICK (*irritated*). Yes.

KEVIN. You mean in the van?

NICK. Yes, for a lift.

KEVIN. No, we don't have any room at all. I'm sorry, we're full up.

NICK (*quieter, smiles*). With what?

CHARLOTTE (*suddenly sharp*). We're full. (*She's drinking out of a bottle, but with a straw, delicately.*)

NICK. Sorry, OK, thanks. (*He moves slightly, then stops.*)

CHARLOTTE. Is there anything else you want . . .?

NICK. No.

KEVIN (*looking towards* CHARLOTTE). We don't mean to be

rude, we're just full up. Want an egg? Got hundreds of boiled eggs here?

NICK. OK. (*He smiles.*) Thanks very much.

KEVIN. I'll peel it for you. (*He begins to peel it very slowly.*) This heat's so heavy isn't it, hottest summer there's ever been. (*He glances behind him.*) Can hardly see the pylon back there – through the haze.

CHARLOTTE. Hardly, no.

KEVIN. The road may melt, of course, in a moment. No, seriously, roads are melting now, traffic, slushing around in hot black tar. Just look at it, you can smell it from here, it's already starting to bubble a little. (*Pause.*) Not a pretty sight. Great setting for a modern-day Western wouldn't it?

NICK (*smiles, amused*). Yes I suppose it would be. (*He glances with an amused grin.*) People galloping along the freeway, keeping to their different lanes, lassooing everything. (*He smiles.*) Yes . . .

KEVIN (*smiles at him*). Yeah . . . sorry we couldn't help you.

NICK. That's OK.

KEVIN *puts the egg he was peeling for* NICK *into his own mouth.*

CHARLOTTE. Careful Kevin – it's still got the shell on.

KEVIN. OK thanks – I thought I'd got it all off. (*He looks at* NICK.) I was doing it for you, wasn't I, anyway. Here do one for yourself. (*He stretches to give* NICK *an egg and knocks over the mineral-water bottle;* NICK *catches it.*)

NICK. There!

KEVIN. Thanks.

NICK. Lucky it had the top on, isn't it.

KEVIN. I'll try the ice-cream shall I – hope for more success. (*He scoops at the ice-cream.*)

NICK (*watching them*). Where you going?

CHARLOTTE. Scotland.

NICK. That's nice. (*He smiles, watching them.*) I'm going to Scotland too actually, as it happens.

KEVIN (*hardly listening*). And back. We going there and back.

NICK. Visiting relatives you see.

KEVIN (*ignoring him*). Great. That's great. Here try that. Mocha almond fudge. (*He holds out a cone with ice-cream.*) Should be OK.

NICK. Thanks. (*He takes the cone and licks it.*)

KEVIN. How is it?

NICK. Yes, fine. (*He takes another cautious lick.*) Tastes a little of petrol but it's fine.

KEVIN. Petrol?

NICK. Yes – just a little.

KEVIN. Can't taste of petrol can it?

NICK *squats, picks up the book.*

CHARLOTTE. Careful of the ants – they're everywhere.

NICK. Yes, of course I will.

He flicks the pages of the book; CHARLOTTE *is tense.*

KEVIN. Must be my hands if it tastes of it. Nasty stuff petrol . . . occupational hazard you know.

NICK (*amused*). I quite understand. (*He licks the ice-cream.*) It's very nice really.

CHARLOTTE (*she picks up a piece of litter*). Careful of mess.

KEVIN. Yeah. (*Suddenly pushing his hand into the ground.*) I wonder what's underneath here, under the ground, probably a drainage system, a whole network of shafts, five hundred, a thousand feet deep, going right into the heart of it. Maybe something in them as well. All the rubbish. Tons of it. bound to be. Dead animals and things, maybe a dead body even. One never knows what's underneath the earth, does one?

NICK (*puzzled*). No . . .

KEVIN. Could be anything.

The roar of a jet overhead – really loud and screeching; they all look up and shade their eyes.

KEVIN. See it! Can you see it!

NICK. Yes! It's very low.

CHARLOTTE. It's a really large one.

KEVIN (*suddenly shouts*). Get away! Go on!
You want to stretch out your hand, don't you – pull it down, put it out of the sky. We *would be* eating under a flight path.
The noise begins to die.

KEVIN. I once went to a concert near here. I used to travel round

England a lot you see. Great concert round here somewhere, you know outdoors, years ago.

NICK (*smiles lightly*). Yes, I can remember all that too.

KEVIN. I don't remember the planes though. Sorry – nostalgia corner there! Take a picture shall I – (*He jumps up, picks up the camera.*) – of this haze. Better use the camera since it's here. (*He lifts the camera.*) A landscape. (*He clicks, moves his position.*) There! Easy! A landscape with road! (*He clicks again.*) Great shots.

NICK. Yes!

KEVIN. It's good to keep a record. See what's happening in the countryside. Yeah, be great to put a camera in the truck, keep filming as we move, whole lot of images moving along the road, filming everything.

NICK. Don't forget to wind on the film.

CHARLOTTE. That's right, did you wind it on Kevin?

KEVIN. I have now. (*He does so.*) Take one of you Charlotte, shall I?

CHARLOTTE. No, thank you.

KEVIN. Come on, don't be shy.

CHARLOTTE. I am shy – I'm not at all photogenic. People are always teasing me.

KEVIN. No, come on, it'll be great. Just one picture. Come on, now keep still.

CHARLOTTE. Please Kevin – I'm asking you, I *don't want* my picture taken. And you're embarrassing me in front of strangers.

NICK. I'll turn my back – (*He smiles.*) I'm not watching. (*But he doesn't move.*)

KEVIN. One, two, three, nothing to be afraid of.

He snaps; CHARLOTTE jolts.

You moved!

NICK (*watching, amused smile*). Why you going to Scotland?

KEVIN (*winding on the film*). What?

NICK. Why you going?

KEVIN. Business.

CHARLOTTE. And a very short holiday.

NICK. What . . . if you don't mind me asking . . . what sort of business?

KEVIN. What sort? Just business, that sort.

NICK. I see. (*He smiles, glances at the book he's holding.*)

CHARLOTTE. Are you reading that book, because if not . . .

NICK (*smiling*). No – does it look like it?

Awkward atmosphere. They watch him.

I mean, sorry to be curious, what's the van full of?

KEVIN. Packages.

NICK. Packages of what?

They look at him.

Sorry, I'm just interested.

CHARLOTTE. Packages of leaflets.

NICK (*flicks one out of the book, from a wadge which is between its pages*). Is this one of them?

KEVIN. What's that?

NICK. They're lots in this book.

KEVIN. Yeah – that's one of them. (*He looks at CHARLOTTE.*) There's no reason why he shouldn't know is there? Don't muck it up will you?

NICK. Can I read it?

CHARLOTTE. If you have to . . . if you're really interested.

NICK *glances at the leaflet.*

KEVIN. They're nicely printed this time aren't they?

CHARLOTTE. Yes.

NICK (*surprised*). The English People's Party!!

KEVIN. Yes – that's what we are.

NICK. (*grins*). What? All two of you.

Silence.

I'm afraid I haven't heard of it. Is it new?

CHARLOTTE. Not all that new, no.

NICK (*begins to read the leaflet, they watch him intently*). I see . . . (*He suddenly laughs.*) Fucking hell! (*He reads, skipping through the leaflet.*) Have you thought about England lately, England now . . . the ordinary, long-suffering English people. *Pollution* . . . the length and breadth of England polluted, every river, every *field*! Pollution on a gigantic scale. *Urban Wastelands* – (*He smiles.*) – the sad urban wastelands, disaster of our city centres . . . too many people crammed together like mice. (*He grins.*) LIKE MICE! . . . leading to distressing violence, criminal town and population planning. *Impersonal Government* – ordinary people offered no chance or choice, crushed by impersonal government. *The Mauling of the Countryside* – the countryside has been mauled . . . disastrous series of mistakes . . . the worship of the motor car . . . internal combustion engine eating away the fabric of the country, the very fabric of ordinary people's lives destroyed. Preserve . . . exclamation mark . . . Preserve. (*He turns the page.*) Preserve!

Silence. He smiles.

This is pretty heavy isn't it? Are you really distributing this?

CHARLOTTE. Yes.

NICK (*amused*). You two . . . Both of you together.

KEVIN. That's right.

NICK. Going up the road, handing these out.

CHARLOTTE. Yes. What's the matter?

NICK (*smiling*). It's just a little surprising finding you two picnicking by the motorway . . . and doing this. (*He looks at the leaflet with a broad smile.*) So it's conservation, and kill the motor car.

CHARLOTTE (*looking* at KEVIN). He's not really interested.

NICK. Of course I am. Can I keep this?

CHARLOTTE. Only if you're really interested.

KEVIN. I think we better clear up, hadn't we?

CHARLOTTE. Yes, we're five minutes behind schedule.

NICK. Schedule! (*He grins.*) You've got a schedule?

CHARLOTTE. Yes, thank you. Do you think you could pick that up? (*She points to the ice-cream cone he's left lying; NICK picks it up.*) It's just litter's not very nice, is it?

KEVIN. Even by a motorway. Right. I'll take the picnic basket, shall I? (*He picks it up.*) Nice meeting you, mate. Have a good trip. Good luck. (*He goes.*)

NICK (*picks up another piece of litter, puts it in her plastic litter bag*). There.

CHARLOTTE. That's right. Could you pass me the mineral water, please.

NICK. There.

CHARLOTTE *sits, methodically rolls back her sleeve.*

CHARLOTTE. The sun doesn't do me any good.

NICK (*watching, smiles*). It looks as if you're going to give yourself an injection.

CHARLOTTE. Don't be stupid. Please don't talk like that. (*She lifts the mineral water, suddenly splashes it over her arm.*) That's better.

NICK. Are you – (*He laughs.*) Are you really on this English People's Party trip?

CHARLOTTE. We told you, yes.

NICK (*smiles*). I don't quite believe you.

CHARLOTTE *picks up the litter.*

CHARLOTTE (*detached*). And what do you do?

NICK. I'm trying to be a teacher.

CHARLOTTE. Good. (*Not unpleasant.*) I hope you find work.

NICK. And you're going all the way up the country?

CHARLOTTE. Yes.

NICK. I'm going that way myself.

CHARLOTTE. So we gathered.

NICK (*picks up another piece of litter, big smile*). There.

CHARLOTTE. Thank you. Do you always try to force yourself on people for free lifts?

NICK. Yes. Quite often. Yes.

CHARLOTTE (*not unpleasant*). Must make you popular, mustn't it. (*Holding her bag.*) Do you want the eggs? No. You can have them. We'll give them to you.

NICK (*laughing, amused*). No, thank you.

KEVIN *enters.*

KEVIN. There! Ready? Prepared?

CHARLOTTE. Yes.

KEVIN. I must find my shoes. (*He glances round.*)

NICK. Here they are! They're here. (*He finds them for* KEVIN.)

KEVIN. Great. Thanks. Knock the insects out. (*He does so.*)

NICK. How about as far as Nottingham?

Slight pause.

CHARLOTTE. I don't think so.

They move to go.

NICK. Won't you be needing these?

They turn.

Your car keys. (*He holds them up.*)

KEVIN. Oh great – thanks. We ought to have those. Yeah.

NICK. You would have left them behind wouldn't you? (*He holds them.*) Do I get a lift now, just as far as Nottingham.

Pause.

Come on, why not? It won't cost you anything.

KEVIN. No . . . but . . .

NICK. Why not. I won't be in the way of anything, will I.

KEVIN (*casual*). No . . . but . . .

NICK. And you could always try to convert me, couldn't you?

KEVIN. Are you really interested?

NICK. In a way.

Pause.

KEVIN. OK. Why not. To Nottingham then.

NICK (*smiles*). Here.

NICK *tosses the keys,* KEVIN *completely misses them.* CHARLOTTE *stops, looking for them.*

There . . . to your left.

KEVIN *goes to his right.*

No, to your left.

KEVIN. Yes. (*He picks them up. They stare at* NICK.) Great.

Blackout.

Scene Three

The sun lounge. Muzak rising and falling. CHARLOTTE *and* KEVIN. MRS ROBERTS *sitting, nervously flicking through a magazine; she's in her late thirties, good-looking. She's surrounded by shopping bags.*

CHARLOTTE. (*staring behind her*). Has he come up? (*She turns to* KEVIN.) Has he?

KEVIN. Yes, he's just behind you.

CHARLOTTE *swings round as* NICK *enters*.

CHARLOTTE. We said Bedford, didn't we. You'd leave at Bedford.

NICK (*grins*). I know.

CHARLOTTE (*moving down to* KEVIN). I wish he'd go away.

KEVIN. It'll be all right – he'll leave.

CHARLOTTE (*staring down at* MRS ROBERTS). There she is, anyway.

KEVIN. Where?

CHARLOTTE. Over there.

KEVIN. You sure that's her?

CHARLOTTE. Yes.

KEVIN. The one on the list?

CHARLOTTE. Yes. (*She turns towards* NICK.) If you have to be here, please be polite.

NICK. Of course.

They approach MRS ROBERTS.

CHARLOTTE. Hello, Mrs Roberts.

MRS ROBERTS *flicks round and stares up at her*.

It is Mrs Roberts?

MRS ROBERTS. Yes, yes it is.

CHARLOTTE. I'm terribly sorry we're so late.

KEVIN. We had a bit of a picnic you see.

NICK (*staring behind him*). God, it's enormous back there, isn't it?

MRS ROBERTS. That's perfectly all right of course. How do you do . . .?

CHARLOTTE (*they shake hands*). I'm Charlotte. We met very briefly before. The February meeting.

MRS ROBERTS. That's right – yes.

CHARLOTTE. This is Kevin Gellot.

KEVIN. Hello. Great to meet you.

MRS ROBERTS. Yes. (*She glances towards* NICK *who is standing some distance away.*)

CHARLOTTE. He's nobody. He managed to cadge a free lift off us; we'll be dropping him off.

MRS ROBERTS. Yes, I thought meeting on the road was best, so you didn't have to leave the motorway. And it's always empty, here in the sun lounge.

NICK (*smiles*). The sun lounge . . .

The muzak cuts out. An announcement comes over the speakers: 'The coach to Newcastle will be leaving in three minutes, please take your seats.'

MRS ROBERTS (*looks round at the speakers*). I have to listen out . . . For my coach. Do you want anything? Some tea? Some chocolate? I could go and fetch some.

CHARLOTTE. That's awfully kind – no thank you.

MRS ROBERTS. Do sit down . . . please.

CHARLOTTE. Thank you.

MRS ROBERTS *looks anxiously at* NICK.

NICK. I'll stand, thank you. I'm only here to watch.

KEVIN (*staring out*). It's incredible here – the glass is thick. Can hardly hear the traffic, just watch it.

MRS ROBERTS. I know, there was an accident last time I was here and nobody heard it. It was extraordinary really.

NICK (*smiles*). It's just like an airport in here isn't it?

KEVIN (*serious, staring out*). Yeah . . .

MRS ROBERTS (*glancing up*). It's all right for you here is it. (*She smiles.*) I do hope it's all right. We can manage here I think, do what we have to do. I mean it's quite nice here, have you seen the pictures on the walls, the pictures of England everywhere, some beautiful views, and on *all* the ashtrays and the mats. See, (*She indicates the mats.*) and brochures too. (*She shows* CHARLOTTE.) Even in the passageways and the toilets. (*She smiles.*) Quite fun really, isn't it? And there's lots of sun for you today.

CHARLOTTE. Of course. It's perfect. (*She laughs a short laugh. She picks up a mat.*) They're lovely, that's one of home I think, the North Downs.

KEVIN (*staring down*). See, look at that one, so bulging with oil, hardly can get round the bend.

NICK. You don't like traffic, do you?

Over the speakers: 'The coach to Newcastle will depart in one minute. Take your seats.'

MRS ROBERTS (*suddenly urgent*). I mustn't miss the coach back. That would be terrible – I have to fetch the children.

CHARLOTTE. Yes, how are they?

MRS ROBERTS. They're well thank you. A lot of bother of course. The eldest, Barbara, she's always going off, she's a lot of bother, I hardly ever see her. The baby's very well. The other two – (*She smiles.*) – they're becoming a little difficult too of course . . . oh yes. They're very well. (*She looks at the speakers.*) But I know you want to get down to business. I know you're very short of time . . . and so am I. We must do it. (*She looks at* NICK.)

  NICK (*smiles*). Yes . . . I'll – (*He grins.*) I'll make myself scarce, shall I? I'll play the machines. That's OK is it? I have a habit of winning on these. (*He moves over to two fruit machines standing side by side.*)

CHARLOTTE. Don't worry about him.

MRS ROBERTS. Yes, this is a quiet corner anyway – it's so big here. There's always a corner where you can be unnoticed. And there're hardly any black waiters, or black waitresses, which is extraordinary isn't it. (*She smiles nicely.*) But they don't seem to have them here. (*She suddenly turns in her seat.*) Sorry, I'm a little worried about missing my coach.

A loud buzz is heard through the muzak, then a voice: 'The coach to Newcastle has left, the coach to Newcastle has now left.'

MRS ROBERTS (*glancing at* CHARLOTTE). There's not much time to go you know.

KEVIN (*suddenly, still staring out*). I went to a concert near here.

MRS ROBERTS (*to herself*). Oh yes.

KEVIN. An open air concert, a long time ago now. It was a festival. A huge one. And at the end, the last evening we walked back along here, down the motorway, right down here, brought the whole road to a standstill. There were jugglers, people lighting bonfires along the way, sword swallowers, a whole fayre. It was three miles long, a great sight, a huge column, and a whole colourful army of it.

NICK. Three lemons and a cherry. Fourteen! Fourteen! You see I always win.

KEVIN. Can almost see it now. And hear it. Then fade back, fade back to the road, the roar of the traffic, back to . . . now. We're going all the way up that road.

The loudspeakers. 'The coach to Crewe will leave in three minutes. The coach to Crewe will leave in three minutes. Please take your seats.'

MRS ROBERTS (*looking towards* KEVIN). We ought to get on.

CHARLOTTE. Why don't you join him, Kevin, just for a moment. Play the machine.

NICK (*calling*). Yes, come and try to win!

KEVIN. Great! Of course.

CHARLOTTE (*to* MRS ROBERTS, *as* KEVIN *goes to the machines*). There's our latest circular for you to read. The membership's rising you know, through word of mouth, and our advertisements have been successful. They've done very well.

MRS ROBERTS (*takes the circular*). Thank you.

KEVIN. I used to know somebody that could get these machines to pay up, just by tickling them. Like tickling fish. Yeah, they loved it, it was great, they coughed up like anything, they loved it. (*He rubs the handle of the machine in masturbatory fashion.*)

NICK (*laughs*). Hey! What you doing?

KEVIN (*grins*). Sorry about that, bit of crudity for you there.

MRS ROBERTS (*having glanced at the circular*). Thank you. That's good news. I came here last week as well you know, on party business.

CHARLOTTE. Did you?

MRS ROBERTS. It's good to get out of town for once. It was my husband's night out. I took the coach, full of people shouting and screaming, as you can imagine.

CHARLOTTE. Yes.

MRS ROBERTS. I got Eileen from next door, she's a very excitable girl, but she came round to mind the kids.

NICK. Four strawberries. Sixteen! Sixteen!
Don't do that Kevin.

KEVIN (*wrenching at the handle*). I never win.

MRS ROBERTS. I came here to meet a schoolmaster, a Mr Godfrey. He's a very nice man, very well-mannered. You wouldn't know him but . . .

The speaker. 'The coach to Crewe will depart in one minute. The coach to Crewe will depart in one minute. Take your seats.'

MRS ROBERTS (*swings round as the announcement is made*). Sorry, I just mustn't miss my coach. We have so little time, but I must tell you this, may I, quickly (*Fast.*) . . . Mr Godfrey, you see, I came here to meet him. He's a teacher at the comprehensive. He teaches Geography and French, I think it is, he's a very clever man, he feels things strongly. There's a few of them at that school who do. It's nice isn't it, to meet somebody that feels things strongly, instead of just muddle.

CHARLOTTE. Of course.

NICK. Four cherries. There we go – another eight!

KEVIN. Don't know how you do it.

MRS ROBERTS. I came here to meet him. *But he didn't turn up.* I don't know why – maybe he couldn't get away. I was here, in this very seat, for hours and hours waiting. It was night, you get some rather strange people about at that time you know, their faces coming up to you.

KEVIN (*by the machine*). I never win anything.

MRS ROBERTS (*fast*). I went and asked them to call him over the speakers. Call Mr Godfrey, see if he was somewhere in this huge place, in a corner somewhere. But they wouldn't. (*Urgent.*) I tried to phone him too – tell you this too, if there's time . . . it's good to talk to you, you know – I tried to phone him. There're eighteen telephones back there, I don't know if you can see them, I went to call him, and fourteen of them, no fifteen of the phones were out of order. You lifted them up and they made this really terrible whining noise, nearly blows your head off you know – (*She smiles.*) – like a scream almost. You know what I mean. Fifteen of them. I left all the receivers off, one by one, let them make the noise, to draw attention to it. I think it was worth doing.

CHARLOTTE. Yes, of course.

MRS ROBERTS. There's so little time, I know . . . (*She glances over her shoulder.*) – but can I tell you this too, I think I can. (*She looks at the loudspeakers.*) You see I had rather a strange experience when I was here then . . .

NICK *and* KEVIN *return.*

NICK (*grins*). I won over a pound.

KEVIN. He's really lucky – really really lucky. They just poured out for him.

NICK (*smiles*). I'm always lucky.

CHARLOTTE (*to* NICK). Ssssh . . . Mrs Roberts.

MRS ROBERTS. Don't you want to sit down? . . . I was telling Charlotte . . .

The speakers. 'The coach to Crewe has left. The coach to Crewe has now left.'

(*Louder.*) Yes! I had to wait such a long time here last week and I had . . . I'll show you – (*She gets up.*) – if you excuse me . . .

NICK *moves out of the way.*

You don't mind me showing you. (*She moves over to the radiator.*) I was alone here you see, by myself, by this radiator, and then I saw a little smoke coming out of it. I smelled this strange heat, and saw this piece of smoke. (*She smiles.*) It was coming out, you see. (*She shows with her hand.*) And I saw here – (*She feels in the radiator.*) – there was this long plastic thing lying in the radiator smoking. (*Lightly.*) I thought it was a bomb put there. Of course I shouted. They came – after a long time.
They said it wasn't a bomb, I didn't know whether to believe them, whether they were just saying that. It was frightening of course. They scraped it away, scraped it off. (*She feels with her hand, then pulls it back.*) I think there's some there now, a little left. Yes. (*She smiles.*) Whatever it is. (*She smiles at them.*) I've told you now.

CHARLOTTE. Yes, it must have been unpleasant.

KEVIN. Oh yes.

MRS ROBERTS. I think, I really think people who do that, leave bombs and think up these terrible hoaxes, have to be really dealt with now. I think they have to be shot really. (*She smiles.*) Don't they? Shot on sight.

The speakers. 'The coach to London will leave in two minutes. The coach to London will leave in two minutes. Please take your seats.'

MRS ROBERTS. It's not my coach, but the next one will be. I

have to get that one, can't let the kids get the school bus —
they're all so violent on a Friday, all the kids, aren't they?
Come on quickly, where's my bag? (*She scrambles with her
bags.*) We must do it now, mustn't we, quickly I know. It's all
in here. (*She opens a large bag.*) This is just . . . just a book of
cuttings, I thought you'd like to see. (*It is a book like a child's
album.*)

NICK (*smiles*). A book of cuttings?

CHARLOTTE (*to* NICK). Don't you want to play those
machines again?

NICK. No, not now.

MRS ROBERTS I stick things in here, to keep a record, so I
remember what's happening in the world. It's not very complete
I'm afraid.

KEVIN. Great! Look she's stuck everything in there.

MRS ROBERTS. (*opening the scrapbook*). There's Mr Relph of
course, the Relph case, you know, the case of his board, his
notice, 'NO BLACKS ALLOWED TO BUY THIS HOUSE', you
know about that of course. Then there's the piece about trouble
at the comprehensive. A stabbing a black boy did there. It's
extraordinary what goes on, isn't it? I mean you notice it all the
time, I'm not that particular, but you can't walk down the street
without them running into you, hitting you and things, on
Saturdays especially. (*She smiles.*) Mostly black boys of course —
but not all by any means I'm afraid. I got bruised three times
last week. (*She begins to roll her sleeve back.*) Bruised rather
badly. I'm sorry to go on, but I better show you, if there's time,
I'm not sure there is, but . . .

*The speakers. 'The coach to London has now left.' She finishes
rolling her sleeve up.*

You can see them down my arm, right down my arm I'm
afraid.

CHARLOTTE. Yes, that's horrible.

MRS ROBERTS (*smiles*). And I'm afraid it does hurt. It does
really hurt rather a lot. (*Louder.*) It still does!

KEVIN (*looking at her arm*). Yes, that must do.

NICK (*staring at her*). Are you a member of the National Front?

MRS ROBERTS (*looks up*). Yes, yes I am.

NICK. Christ (*He stares at* CHARLOTTE.) Did you hear that?

MRS ROBERTS (*rolling down her sleeve*). Sorry I know I

shouldn't have bothered you with that. I just wanted to tell you, you see. My coach is coming now, any moment they'll call it. So here! Before it comes, here it all is. (*She rummages in her bag.*) The things I've got . . . I don't know if they'll come in useful. This is – (*She pulls out a crumpled parcel.*) . . . this is an eletroset, that's what the name is isn't it. It was going so cheap, I thought you might want it.

CHARLOTTE. Thank you, that's marvellous, isn't that good Kevin?

KEVIN. Yes, that's great.

MRS ROBERTS. And this is – (*She pulls it out of her bag.*) . . . here's some wire, a large roll, see, strong wire. I don't know if it'll come in useful. But it's very strong.

NICK (*astonished*). Wire! What's that for?

CHARLOTTE. Thank you very much. That's wonderful.

MRS ROBERTS. And here we are now, here it is. There. (*She pulls out of the bag a wadge of bank notes wrapped in the sort of paper cheese is wrapped in.*) There's £83 and 40 pence. I'm very sorry, I thought it was going to be more. I thought we were going to manage at least £110, but it's only £83. Do you want to count it, you better do it quickly, I expect you do, don't you?

CHARLOTTE. No, that's all right thank you.

MRS ROBERTS. Not nearly as much as we hoped. It's so difficult to get people to keep their word isn't it? I hope you're not too disappointed. I know I was terribly.

CHARLOTTE. No, of course we're not. (*With the money.*) That's wonderful, isn't it Kevin?

KEVIN. Yes that's great. It's a lot.

MRS ROBERTS. I don't feel that it's nearly enough really.

NICK (*suddenly*). Why are you a member of two organisations Mrs Roberts?

MRS ROBERTS. What? (*She looks up at him.*) What did you say?

The speakers. 'The coach to Preston will depart in one minute. The coach in Preston will depart in one minute. Take your seats.'

MRS ROBERTS. That's it now! That's my coach. Why have they only given us one minute now?

CHARLOTTE. Here's the receipt for the money.

MRS ROBERTS. Of course thank you – if I miss the coach – I don't know what will happen about the kids.

CHARLOTTE. Kevin, maybe you could help Mrs Roberts?

KEVIN. Of course. Here, I'll take those, no trouble at all.

MRS ROBERTS. Thank you. It's always such a rush now isn't it? Everything just one long rush. So nice seeing you, being able to talk, even for so short a time. I'm sorry I didn't have more for you.

KEVIN moves off.

Bye bye. (*As she leaves.*) It is like an airport here, like he says.

Silence.

NICK. Christ! (*He smiles.*) And I thought she was almost normal at first.

CHARLOTTE (*turns*). What?

NICK. She wasn't obviously cranky.

CHARLOTTE (*sharp*). Why should she be cranky? She's no more cranky than you or me.

NICK. I'm sorry. Of course all this is perfectly normal! The usual goings-on in the sun lounge! I suppose she's lonely.

CHARLOTTE. No. I don't think she's lonely. (*Matter-of-fact.*) There are a lot more people like her.

NICK. She *was* a little paranoid, wasn't she?

CHARLOTTE *has moved over to the radiator. Over the speakers we hear.* 'The coach to Preston has now left. The coach to Preston has now departed.'

NICK. There. She's gone anyway. One of your more extreme members I take it – is she?

CHARLOTTE (*by the radiator*). I don't know.

NICK (*sharp*). Why is she a member of two organisations?

CHARLOTTE. It's her choice.

NICK. Making sure she's fully covered for when the holocaust comes.

Pause.

Charlotte.

She turns.

You don't mind me calling you that I presume.

CHARLOTTE. It doesn't worry me, no.

NICK (*suddenly*). So you're the sort of conservation wing of the National Front . . . are you?

CHARLOTTE. No, we certainly are not!

NICK (*moving nearer her*). I mean the National Front's no joke any more, Charlotte.

CHARLOTTE. Of course not. It never has been.

NICK. Are you connected with it in any way?

CHARLOTTE. No we are not! Why should we be? They're aware of our existence. But you're not really interested anyway.

NICK. Oh yes I am! Very! (*Getting near her*.) I mean where do you stand in all this, Charlotte?

CHARLOTTE (*facing him*). Stand in what?

NICK. I mean she was saying some pretty hideous things.

CHARLOTTE. She has her views . . . and I have mine.

NICK. And what are they?

CHARLOTTE. You know what they are. You read the leaflet.

NICK. I want to hear you say them. (*He grins*.) Explain them to me, Charlotte.

CHARLOTTE (*firm*). No. You'd only mock wouldn't you? (*She feels the radiator*.)

NICK. Is there anything there?

CHARLOTTE (*she feels very carefully then pulls her hand away suddenly*). I don't know – I don't think so.

NICK (*grins*). Of course not.

CHARLOTTE. Why of course?

NICK. She's the sort of person that thinks there are bombs and landmines in every litter bin, illegal immigrants everywhere, drugs in the lining of every car, isn't she? Why did you take that wire off her?

CHARLOTTE. I had to take it, didn't I? She would have been offended otherwise. If it's no use we'll probably use it for our Christmas decorations.

NICK (*smiles, amused*). I see!

CHARLOTTE. We can't get rid of you here I suppose. You'd only go straight down and sit in the van, wouldn't you? You leave finally at Doncaster.

NICK. That's right. I promise.

KEVIN *enters, smiles at them*.

KEVIN. Ready? Ready to hit the high road are you?

CHARLOTTE *moves away from* NICK.

CHARLOTTE. Yes . . . we're ready.

Blackout.

Scene Four

Cinema posters and stills on one side of the stage. Hot dog van in the middle. The van is empty. The smell of onions. Sausages piled up. Fanta orange machines and Coke machines in the hot dog van. A pocket television flickering at the side of the van. Night. Stark lighting. KEVIN *and* CHARLOTTE *standing waiting nervously.*

KEVIN. How long?

CHARLOTTE. He said ten o'clock. He should be here very soon. (*She looks about her.*) I don't even know what he looks like, but he'll be here. (*She takes out a handkerchief, wipes her face.*)

KEVIN. This is the right place, is it? You've looked on the list?

CHARLOTTE. (*sharp*). I told you, yes.

KEVIN. You all right, Charlotte?

CHARLOTTE. Yes, I'm fine. I could have done without the company we had on the journey.

KEVIN. Nick?

CHARLOTTE. Yes, we've done very well otherwise, haven't we? We're ahead of schedule. (*Pause. She glances around.*) I just feel a little exposed standing out here.

KEVIN *drinks from a wine bottle.*

Don't drink too much, Kevin.

KEVIN. No, of course not. (*He takes another drink, nervously rubs hand across the wall.*) It's pretty filthy round here isn't it?

A police siren in the distance.

KEVIN. (*flicks round*). What's that?

CHARLOTTE. It's all right – (*But she tenses slightly too.*) I saw a fire engine dash up a street in London not so long ago. It was two, three in the morning. All the streets were deserted, but it was roaring up them, screaming its head off, its siren was screaming. It came to this square, and started going round and round in circles, making this extraordinary noise. I think they were just having a bit of fun, trying to wake people up. But nobody stirred. Nobody shouted. Nobody moved at all.

NICK *enters,* CHARLOTTE *looks up in surprise.*

CHARLOTTE. What?

NICK *stares at her, slight smile.*

CHARLOTTE. Why are you here?

NICK. I followed you.

CHARLOTTE. So I see. Why?

NICK. I don't know really. Just an impulse, an instinct, I hope you don't mind.

CHARLOTTE. We *had said goodbye.*

NICK. I know.

KEVIN. Yes, we had Nick.

CHARLOTTE. You don't intend to stay here I hope.

NICK. What? (*Worried by the tension in the air.*) I thought you'd be pleased to see me. (*Pause.*) What's happening here anyway?

KEVIN (*suddenly looks up*). Yes, where is he?

NICK. Who? (*He turns, stares at* CHARLOTTE.) Who you waiting for Charlotte?

CHARLOTTE. We're just . . . waiting for someone, that's all.

NICK. Who? (*He stares at the hot dog stand.*) Not him? (*He looks at the hot dog stand.*) The little man from behind here?

CHARLOTTE (*very quiet, controlled nerves*). We're waiting . . . for a hamburger.

KEVIN. See here – it's just closed down.

NICK (*swings round nervously*). What?

KEVIN. The cinema! Last week – it's closed down, it's finished.

NICK (*swings back again*). The hot dog man. You're waiting for the hot dog man!

CHARLOTTE (*very quiet*). I didn't say that.

NICK (*excited*). I don't believe it. I can't believe it! You mean he! (*He points.*) Him! The guy who stuffs sausages into these. (*He holds up a fistful of onions.*) He's *one* of you – is he?

CHARLOTTE (*very quiet*). Is he what?

NICK (*shouts*). One of you? A member. Another member!

She is sitting on a step, completely still. No reply.

(NICK *smiles.*) He is? (*Moving round.*) And you've come to collect off him – have you?

Pause.

What's he going to give you?

CHARLOTTE (*very quiet*). That's our business, I think.

NICK (*delighted*). So he is going to give you something. (*Loud.*) Come on! What you going to get off him? (*Fast.*) What secret goodies is he bringing? What's he bringing?

KEVIN. Same as before.

NICK (*swings round*). Same as before. I see. Then why you so nervous?

CHARLOTTE. Nervous?

KEVIN (*trying to lessen the tension*). Here, want a fag? Help you calm down. (*He gives him a cigarette.*) When I start rolling one – I like rolling seven or eight.

NICK. You're not going to get arms off him are you, Charlotte?

CHARLOTTE *remains still.*

CHARLOTTE (*puzzled tone, quiet*). Arms?

NICK (*smiling, mocking*). I mean he's not . . . (*He laughs.*) He is not going to produce a few grenades out of the sausages and hand them over 15 pence a time. Do they come with onions, or do you go out to a dark country lane with him and get them there. (*He moves over to the hamburger stand, stares at it.*) Fortunately for you, I don't believe it's possible. I mean that is just a little too unlikely, just a tiny bit too fantastic. I mean it's been a strange day, but not that strange.

CHARLOTTE. Please, just go.

NICK *flicks through the buns on the stall.*

NICK. Is it just from this one charming little stall or will any do – are there hundreds dotted over everywhere, the whole country?

Silence.

(*Loud*). Charlotte? (*With nervous energy, trying to get a reaction.*) I mean, the terrible thing about grenades these days is they all come covered with tomato juice and mustard already on them, whether you like it or not, not like the good old English grenade. I mean there's absolutely no freedom of choice any more is there? You can go into a nice ordinary hamburger house – can I have a grenade please, and it comes in 20 seconds, totally packaged in this nasty box, and smothered in all kinds of filth, hardly recognisable. It's the terrible American influence isn't it?

Silence.

(*Aggressive.*) Not funny? NO.

Silence.

KEVIN. You realise we're in the middle.

NICK. Middle of what?

KEVIN. Middle of England. Middle of Britain. The heart as it were. We're standing on it. Now!

NICK (*ignoring him, looking at* CHARLOTTE). Isn't this all a trifle dangerous for you, out in the open air?

CHARLOTTE (*calmly but strongly*). Why don't you just go, Nick? Leave us alone.

NICK. No, I'm keeping you company aren't I? (*He smiles.*) I'm here to stay.

CHARLOTTE *looks away.*

KEVIN. I'm very thirsty now.

NICK. Why don't you help yourself? (*He indicates the hamburger stand.*)

CHARLOTTE. No, that would be breaking the law, wouldn't it.

NICK (*smiles, mocking*). Of course! The law. You're completely law-abiding, I forgot.

CHARLOTTE. Yes, of course.

NICK (*loud*). Why's Kevin so nervous then?

KEVIN. I'm not nervous. Not at all . . . (*Staring at a poster.*) There's the last poster see, for the cinema, already fading fast.

NICK (*reading, smiling*). 'The Killer Elite'.

KEVIN. Yeah. We can't even keep our cinemas open any more, in this country, can we? Used to be the centre of the community didn't it?

NICK (*in a teasing tone*). Are you a movie freak then, Kevin?

CHARLOTTE. Do you have to shout all the time?

KEVIN. Just a bit. You see my eyes have a little difficulty, as you may have noticed. I'm probably going blind.

NICK (*stunned, only half believing*). Blind?

KEVIN. No, don't worry – I've got a disease up here, in these orbs. No real stopping it.

NICK. I'm sorry. I didn't realise.

KEVIN. No need to be. Doesn't worry me.

NICK. That explains a lot.

CHARLOTTE. I thought you'd make a remark like that.

KEVIN. So I went to the movies. I saw everything that they poured out. I went twice a day when I could afford it.

NICK. You should get them on the National Health, shouldn't you? The movies, I mean.

KEVIN. No, I've stopped going. Didn't want to take any more.

NICK (*loud*). So you've been living off films have you, Kevin?

KEVIN. That's right. Me and a few others. Hey! Imagine going in there now, into the empty cinema, there's a whole cinema there behind us, just waiting, with a bare screen, probably going brown now, being chewed up. Imagine going in there now.

NICK. Yes! Why not.

KEVIN. And you could sit me down, my head's full of pictures you see, you could sit me down, point me straight at the screen, give me one small hit on the head, or something like that, and we'd be away. I could pour it out onto the screen. All of it! Onto that empty screen. All that I've seen.

NICK. Yes, you could, Kevin.

KEVIN. No, I mean it. I've seen it all. Seen some great skin pictures.

NICK. Yes, you must have seen some pretty dirty things.

CHARLOTTE (*warning*). Kevin . . .

KEVIN. Yeah – I've seen some really filthy things, yeah and also some pretty weird ones, oh yes, spikes, big spikes, on metal gloves, and all over cars, and on people's tongues, yes! Saw a few forests, that was nice, and a few deserts, one all covered in tar, and a lot of needles too – (*He grins.*) – they all run into each other, you see! Yes! And some pretty, you know, unpleasant things too, heads split open, running free.

NICK. Really?

KEVIN. And killings. Hundreds of killings, of course. In different colours, different ways, fast and slow, falling past you, and women's feet in bear traps. (*Loud.*) Yeah! There're these car thieves, you see, a big gang, they steal cars and smash them up, in America, and blow them up all over the city. They wear stocking masks. Yes! And they always go back to this one great car park at night, forty stories high! And the police can't catch them, so this head guard, he puts down mantraps in the dark, he does! And this girl's leg goes into the metal man-trap, and it's bitten off her, the teeth goes in, and it bites it off, (*He flicks his hand.*) just like that! YOU SEE IT.

CHARLOTTE. Kevin . . .

KEVIN (*carrying straight on, fast, louder and louder*). And the head guard, he's got a withered arm – from Vietnam – with steel finger-nails – and he goes mad, you see, to catch this gang, and he goes round all the traps at dawn, collecting the feet in each one, he has a sackful of feet. *You see them!* Squashed in together, in a pile.

NICK *is grinning, drinking, watching* KEVIN.

CHARLOTTE. Please, Kevin, I don't want to hear . . .

KEVIN (*carrying straight on – oblivious, loud, fast*). And he hangs them above his bed, the feet! From his mantelpiece. You see them on this kitchen wire, dangling there, he plays with them! They stay there the whole film going bad. Slowly. They do!

NICK (*loud, grinning*). All right Kevin! We get the . . .

KEVIN (*carrying straight on*). And he gets caught in *one of his own traps* at the end, because he's put down so many, hundreds! And he tears himself out, and *it really hurts him!* You see it! It's *not nice.* And he crawls over the whole town with one leg, on his belly along the pavement, with a machine-gun, hunting them across these concrete walls, and across bridges, you see him crawling, and leaving a trail of blood and things behind him . . .

CHARLOTTE. Kevin, please, sssh.

KEVIN (*really loud*). And he gets face to face with the leader of the gang, and he blows his head off, and it bursts open, it bursts right open, splashes over all of them!

NICK (*grins*). Kevin, stop!

KEVIN (*very loud*). Then the rest of the gang get HIM, the guard, and they throw him into a dust-cart shredder, you know, and he's squashed, and eaten, and shredded up, you know, by the spikes, screaming his head off, screaming so loudly, really loudly, and they pick up little raw bits of him, they do, collect him in their hands. (*He screams.*) RAW PIECES OF HIM. YOU SAW IT.

Pause.

You see! (*Quieter.*) *That's* the last movie I saw, it's just run through my head, *unfortunately*.

NICK. Not very nice, no!

KEVIN. Could see how mad they were getting. Weirder and weirder. You began to feel a bit funny down here – (*He feels his stomach.*) -- in your insides, as you went into the dark, before it started.

NICK. Did you, Kevin? You shouldn't have gone then . . .

KEVIN. Mad, mad images, they reflect things more than you imagine. Oh yes! You can see what's happening all right in the world, if you think, *if you really think about what you've seen,* when you come out of the dark, the attitudes in it, the sort of madness, you can see the whole sickness.

NICK (*loud.*) No, you can't. They're only films, Kevin – *just films,* and they release things in some people.

KEVIN. No! No! I ought to run them for you now, while we wait, then you'll see. *Give a free show.*

NICK. OK then! Yes! run them for me, now. Give me a playback. Run them now . . .

KEVIN (*grins*). No, sorry, no, I'm talking shit.

CHARLOTTE. Calm down both of you, that's enough.

NICK. No come on, run them for me . . . come on! You said you would! Splash them all over the walls of Doncaster.

CHARLOTTE. Stop it!

NICK (*pulling KEVIN – excited*). There's a wall. That one. About the size of a screen. It'll do perfectly.

KEVIN. No, look I'm talking shit, forget it. (*Loud.*) I mean how can I run them on that *wall*, it's absurd, isn't it?

NICK. (*very animated*). No, run them, come on, I want to see.

CHARLOTTE. Just ignore him, Kevin.

KEVIN. No, look it was terrible shit. Forget I spoke.

NICK (*loud*). No! Kevin . . .

KEVIN. Always the best policy.

NICK (*pulling him up*). Come on do it! Run them. Let's see it

Kevin! Do you want me to start it! (*He points* KEVIN's *head straight ahead. Very loud.*) There! Right *Kevin*. Run them, now. (*Even louder.*) NOW!

KEVIN (*standing facing the wall, standing very straight, arms by his side*). OK then . . . if you *really* want it.

CHARLOTTE. Just leave him alone, you've got him drunk.

KEVIN. No, he hasn't. (*He takes off his dark glasses; slight smile, then loud.*) A LOT OF STRANGE MUCK WILL COME OUT, OF COURSE. Here goes then! (*His arm stiffens by his side – slight pause.*) My eyes should light up, shouldn't they really, and film come out of my ears and round into my mouth for the full effect. (*He stiffens.*) Here it comes then! (*He stands very straight, eyes wide, a noise like a projector beginning to come out of him, which turns into a high-pitched whine, which grows louder and louder, and really piercing.*)

NICK (*suddenly breaking away*). You're both completely crazy, do you know that? Complete nuts, look at you, a freak and an overgrown schoolgirl on this ludicrous trip through England! One of you thinks you're a film projector –

KEVIN. That's only a joke, mate . . .

NICK (*carrying straight on*). The other sits by a hot dog stand, expecting it to cough up rifles. (*He smiles.*) You're both completely gone – fortunately for the rest of us. Just a couple of little cranks.

CHARLOTTE. You're very drunk too, aren't you? Far too drunk.

NICK. Am I? (*He moves away.*) Oh no, I'm not. (*Moving further away.*) You realise of course I could expose the whole organisation now if I wanted, the whole tiny network, the whole cobweb of shabby semi-fascist study groups, little grubby fanatics whispering about England in corners. Could expose the lot if I wanted. Couldn't I? 'Bye now. I've got to piss. Nice knowing you – or was it? (*About to go.*) But I may be back. (*He goes.*).

The stage cross-fades to semi-darkness, the sound of urinals flushing, sputter of water. Lavatory atmosphere, although all we see is NICK *in the half light, back to the audience, relieving himself.*
For a moment he's alone, shaking his head slightly.

CHARLOTTE *enters behind him.*

CHARLOTTE. Are you there?

Nick turns.

NICK. You shouldn't be in a Gentlemen's lavatory –

CHARLOTTE. But I am – there's nobody about anyway.

NICK. Yes – why is that? (*He swings round.*) Why is the whole fucking place deserted? The hot dog stand, the urinals, it's a fucking ghost town, the whole place has stopped breathing. Where is everybody?

CHARLOTTE (*staring straight at him*). They're all indoors watching television probably. (*At him.*) Aren't they?

NICK. Except you two! It's very dark, Charlotte – isn't it?

CHARLOTTE. I'm sure it's meant to be closed, Nick. It's hot even here!

Pause. CHARLOTTE *is looking at him.*

NICK. You know I haven't seen you sweat yet.

CHARLOTTE. Haven't you? (*She looks over her shoulder.*) I ought to spend a penny myself actually.

NICK (*amused smile*). Spend a penny?

CHARLOTTE. That's right, yes.

CHARLOTTE *moves into darkness, suddenly she stops, having trodden on something. She stoops, picks up smashed toy, an 'action man' model, mangled, its head battered, filthy, pushed into a hole in the floor.*

CHARLOTTE (*to herself*). Look at that.

The sound of cisterns flushing in the darkness.

NICK. Yes!

CHARLOTTE (*handling it carefully*). It's very dirty! Who would have done that, mangled it? Children I suppose, fighting. The savagery of what they do – it's torn to pieces.

NICK. It's not savagery at all – just energy.

CHARLOTTE (*turning*). How can you possibly know?

NICK. Because I do!

Pause.

Because I'm good with kids, believe it or not.

Pause.

Which you won't! It's what I like doing actually, playgrounds, community projects, (*Defiant.*) that sort of thing, Charlotte!

CHARLOTTE *glances into shadows.*

What? Nobody? Some people probably still feel forced to meet here — leaving messages on walls.

CHARLOTTE. They're worse than rats those sort of people. (*She drops the model onto the floor.*)

NICK (*disbelief*). What did you say . . .?

CHARLOTTE. They're worse than . . .

NICK. Yes, I heard. Extraordinary thing to say. Come here Charlotte. (*He catches hold of her arms; the cisterns flush.*) They flush a lot those cisterns. Perhaps they've gone mad like everything else tonight, can't stop flushing. (*Up close to her.*) Do you think there's somebody in one of the cubicles now, a special sort of fascist dwarf, that comes out at night, never sees daylight at all, comes out when it catches your scent, when it knows you're in town. (*Aggressive.*) We are not amused are we? (*Loud, confident.*) You're unnerving me, Charlotte!

CHARLOTTE. Am I? You've been drinking too much.

NICK. No I haven't.

CHARLOTTE. I've come to tell you I want you to be on your way.

NICK. Yes. (*He smiles.*) Yes!

CHARLOTTE. I mean it.

NICK. Of course you do.

CHARLOTTE. Right.

She moves to try to go, but he blocks her, moves in on her.

NICK. I'm not sure about you, Charlotte, you know.

CHARLOTTE. Aren't you? Why not?

NICK (*smiles*). I mean, I can understand about Kevin thinking like he does. I mean, he's one of those sixties' leftovers, isn't he really, a great many of them about at the moment, an epidemic, I meet them everywhere. Lost in his own pool of exciting memories isn't he? Especially when summer comes. I mean, he's quite a nice guy in his way, with his eyes and all his movies. Got some imagination too, hasn't he, a spark . . . It's just a little unfortunate isn't it, when the Easy Rider bit goes badly sour, a little sad. He's just a crank now.

CHARLOTTE (*turning on him*). He *is* not a crank. I have told you. No more than you, probably considerably less. Why do people always have to be cranky to feel things strongly? (*She moves.*) Now can I get out.

NICK (*barring her way, smiling*). Yes! But you Charlotte, you're not quite so simple are you?

CHARLOTTE. Kevin's not simple. Can I . . .?

NICK (*ignoring her*). I mean, most extreme right wing *cranks*, I mean the actual activists, are usually bandy-legged little tin soldiers, isn't that right? You know those typical slightly manic faces, the pictures of them, their eyes staring out at you, full of the usual English sort of hatreds, Charlotte, (*Watching her closely.*) foreigners . . . sex . . . change, all that, desperately trying to whip it all up now. (*Loud.*) Right? You can recognise them a mile off; *I know.* We used to live near one of them when I was a kid, who's now quite famous, he used to sing to himself, in the street when he saw somebody coloured. Yes sing! 'Black Beetle, Black Beetle, stick him with a needle'. He did. Not loudly. But you could hear him.

CHARLOTTE. They're pathetic nonentities.

NICK. Who?

CHARLOTTE. The leaders of the National Front. They're ridiculous . . . useless.

The lavatories flush.

NICK. (*up close to her*). But I mean you, Charlotte, you're not bandy-legged, are you?

CHARLOTTE. No?

NICK. At least it doesn't appear so, or balding. (*He smiles.*) I mean, you probably approach being a normal healthy girl. Quite attractive in a schoolmistressy, English-rose sort of way. You don't seem to be suffering from a hatred of your body, disgust at the bodily functions.

CHARLOTTE (*quiet*). No . . . I'm not.

NICK. Probably enjoy an energetic screw as much as most people.

CHARLOTTE. Sometimes, yes . . . with the right person.

NICK (*suddenly up to her, loud*). So what do you really believe in, Charlotte? (*Urgent.*) Come on. What?

CHARLOTTE. I told you, it's in the leaflet. That's all you need to know. (*By him.*) I want you to leave.

NICK (*smiles*). I am.

CHARLOTTE. Good.

CHARLOTTE *moves as if relieved,* NICK *suddenly catches her.*

NICK. But first, Charlotte. Come here. (*He pulls her close – quite roughly.*) We're in an underground toilet, in the middle of Doncaster, the entire population is watching telly, there is an abandoned hot dog stand outside – and you're going to tell me all the *rest's a joke.*

CHARLOTTE *stares.*

Hamburgers and arms.

CHARLOTTE. You mentioned those, didn't you?

NICK. I know.

Pause.

CHARLOTTE. All the rest's a bit of a joke, yes. (*She smiles very slightly.*)

NICK. That's better. At last! (*He is still barring her way.*) You're all goose-pimply suddenly. (*He touches her offhandedly.*)

CHARLOTTE. That's because I don't particularly like being touched by you.

NICK. No, of course not.

CHARLOTTE. Like all stupid people, you're very clumsy, aren't you?

The cisterns flush.

I don't like men's lavatories very much, they must be the ugliest places in the world. But that's quite appropriate isn't it? (*She touches his crotch in a detached way.*)

NICK. Yes, Charlotte. (*He grins.*) That's right.

CHARLOTTE (*moving her hand away*). Just think if there was a whole mass consisting of holes like these, suddenly there they were, they'd grown up, side by side, back to back, like all those screaming echoing subways you walk through at night. If you woke up in the morning, and that's all there was everywhere . . . everywhere you breathed was *like this* stench, tasted like this.

NICK (*loud*). But that's not what everything's like, (*Aggressive.*) is it?

CHARLOTTE. What would you do, Nick?

NICK. If it happened, I'd get out.

CHARLOTTE. No, you wouldn't, because there's nowhere to go.

NICK (*amused smile*). No, of course not, nowhere.

CHARLOTTE (*suddenly loud*). There isn't.

NICK (*grins*). No.

CHARLOTTE. That's right, that's better.

NICK (*amused smile*). Yes, Charlotte. (*He touches her again.*) The goose-pimples have gone now, almost a throb going through you.

CHARLOTTE. Is there? . . . Yes. (*Suddenly she turns.*) No. I've had enough now. It's time to get back to work. (*She moves.*) Can I . . .? (*She brushes past him and out.*)

Lights up on the whole stage. The hamburger van, KEVIN sitting there.

NICK (*suddenly mocking, excited tone*). Nobody's come? See!

KEVIN. No.

CHARLOTTE. Have you been watching?

NICK. Of course he has.

KEVIN. Yes.

CHARLOTTE (*sharp*). *Have* you been watching?

KEVIN. Yes, Charlotte . . . I told you, been watching everything.

NICK. What he can see, that is.

CHARLOTTE (*quiet*). Why isn't he here?

NICK. Why indeed?

CHARLOTTE (*turns on him*). You're going now, Nick . . . NOW!

NICK (*grins*). In a moment, not now. I want to see how long you're going to keep this up. It's getting late you know. Are you going to camp on the building-site over there then Charlotte? Among the scaffolding and the cement-mixers. Not quite what you're used to, is it? Or maybe inside Kevin's rotting cinema. Pitch your tent in the middle of that.

CHARLOTTE. I told you. Just go.

KEVIN. I'm thirsty anyway. (*He gets up and looks towards the hamburger van.*)

CHARLOTTE. I told you not to touch that . . . it's against the law.

NICK. She must be joking, Kevin — mustn't she? Who on earth's going to know?

KEVIN. Yes. (*Looking at the van.*)

CHARLOTTE. I told you not to.

KEVIN. But I've got to drink something in this heat.

CHARLOTTE. You've drunk enough.

NICK. Come on, let's defy her shall we, Kevin?

They suddenly rush over to the van.

How do we get in? (*He pulls the door open.*)

KEVIN (*pulls at the lever of the Fanta machine*). This doesn't work!

NICK. It must work.

CHARLOTTE. You're being immensely stupid.

KEVIN. Give them a good pull.

NICK. Pull! Pull! Tiny trickle out of this one! Come on. Like milking a metal cow isn't it?

KEVIN (*taking the lid off*). Only onion-flavoured water in here – can pour that out. Packet of uncooked sausages. (*He tosses them onto the ground.*) No good to us. (*He suddenly splashes the onion water out – great splashes.*)

KEVIN. Come on get it!

The whole van begins to shake violently; NICK is tugging on the handle.

NICK. It's coming! Coming!

CHARLOTTE. *Stop it . . .*

TAYLOR, *a young police constable, enters. They all look up.*

TAYLOR. All right – let's have you over here.

They stand still.

I said let's have you out here, over here.

NICK (*smiles*). That would happen, wouldn't it? (*He doesn't notice* CHARLOTTE's *tense face.*)

TAYLOR (*to* NICK). What were you doing with that machine?

CHARLOTTE (*sharp*). They were just getting a drink.

TAYLOR (*glances at* CHARLOTTE). I was speaking to the gentlemen. (*To* NICK *and* KEVIN.) Helping yourself, were you, that the idea? All right. (*He takes out his notebook.*)

NICK. He's very young, isn't he? Do you realise he's probably younger than me?

TAYLOR. You all together, you three?

NICK. No.

CHARLOTTE. Yes, we are.

TAYLOR (*looking at them*). So you're all together. What were you doing out here anyway?

KEVIN. Waiting . . .

TAYLOR. Waiting for what? (*Pause.*) All right. (*To* KEVIN.) Could you open that bag please – (*He turns to* CHARLOTTE.) – and yours too.

CHARLOTTE. Why?

TAYLOR. Open that bag please – routine check.

NICK (*grins*). He's sweating – it's a very thick uniform.

TAYLOR. Come on, I haven't got all night. I've got a bed to go to, let's have those bags open.

KEVIN *lowers his bag, opens it to show inside.* TAYLOR *moves across to it.* CHARLOTTE *shoots him from a gun in her handbag. Very loud explosion. He falls on his face.* NICK *makes a noise of spontaneous shock as the explosion happens.* CHARLOTTE *crosses over to* TAYLOR, *stands by him for a moment, her dress brushing his body. She empties the gun into him.*

Silence.

Fast fade down.

On the soundtrack a loud electric buzz lasting 50 seconds in the blackout.

End of Act One.

ACT TWO

Scene One

The noise heard at end of Act One returns at full volume.
After ten seconds of this an explosion of bright neon light. The
motorway cafe, stark, dirty, very late at night. The neons are
overpowering.
KEVIN, NICK and CHARLOTTE are standing at the edge of the
cafe area, with NICK in the middle of the three.
Upstage there's a trolley laden with food remains and dirty plates.
The WOMAN CLEANER, about thirty-four, overtired,
bedraggled appearance, is stacking plates on the trolley, back to
audience, seemingly oblivious of the three of them. They stand
there, for a split second, a still moment as CHARLOTTE glances
over the tables. KEVIN lifts a milk bottle that he's holding,
throws back his head, takes a long drink, wipes his mouth.
CHARLOTTE glances towards the CLEANER, who glances back
at her then away. KEVIN takes another drink of milk.

CHARLOTTE (*moving down to one of the tables*). Here'll do.
  Come on.

KEVIN (*not moving*). What?

CHARLOTTE. Here. (*She puts her handbag on the table, the*
  carrier bag by the chair.) That's better. Sit down, Nick – there.

  NICK moves slowly, but obediently sits opposite her.

NICK (*quiet*). Yes.

KEVIN (*very quiet, also sits slowly, glancing round him*). There's
  a comb in this ashtray. (*He pulls the ashtray towards him.*) See,
  there's a comb here. (*He drinks out of the milk bottle.*)

CHARLOTTE. Can I? (*She takes the milk bottle; keeping her eye*
  very firmly on NICK and her handbag out of reach, she takes a
  long drink of milk.)

KEVIN (*indicating milk*). It's very warm I'm afraid. (*Nervous.*) It's
  almost bubbling.

CHARLOTTE. Yes. (*She holds out the milk bottle to NICK.*) Do
  you want some?

NICK. No. (*Very quiet.*) No I don't.

CHARLOTTE. Sure? Then would you pass one of those? The
  napkins.

  She is pointing to the paper napkins – NICK moves slowly.

(*Sharp.*) Come on. (*He passes them – she wipes her mouth.*)
We've got to get something to eat quickly. We have to fetch it.

KEVIN (*glancing up*). We're high up here. Can you keep a watch
out. The light's very bright isn't it? You can't look straight at
them at all can you. Can't we . . .

CHARLOTTE (*firm*). Kevin . . . sssshh!

The CLEANER *comes up to the table.* KEVIN *tenses.*

CLEANER (*slight smile*). It's hot tonight isn't it?

KEVIN (*sharp*). Yes it is.

CLEANER. So what you going to have?

They look up.

I'm not meant to serve you as you know, but it makes a change.
So what do you want? Plaice and chips. Chicken Maryland. The
Chicken Maryland's not bad.

CHARLOTTE (*sharp*). Thank you – that's kind of you. (*She looks
at the men.*) We've got to eat. We'll have three Chicken
Marylands.

NICK. Not for me. (*He looks up.*) I don't want any, Charlotte.

CHARLOTTE. He'll have a coffee then.

KEVIN. And some milk . . . can we have some more milk?

CLEANER (*smiles*). I better get that down. Do it properly. (*She
takes a napkin off the table, and a pen out of the pocket in her
tunic. She tries to write.*) It doesn't work! (*She wets the tip of
the pen.*) It's not writing.

KEVIN (*loud*). It's all right, we can get it . . . We'll get it now!

CLEANER. No. I'll remember it. Two Marylands, coffee, glass of
milk.

KEVIN. No, could we – I want a jug of milk. (*He glances at*
CHARLOTTE.) A jug – a large jug. (*Loud.*) And it's got to be
cold, ice cold.

CLEANER (*hesitating*). I don't know if there is a jug here.

CHARLOTTE. If you're going to fetch our food – could we have
it *very quickly.*

CLEANER (*surprised*). Yes – it's over there already. It's just lying
there. (*She moves off.*)

Silence.

KEVIN (*glances over his shoulder*). We ought to have gone and
got it – ourselves.

CHARLOTTE. No. (*She looks at* NICK.) You should have something to eat.

NICK (*looks up, very quiet*). Should I?

CHARLOTTE (*forceful*). Yes, you should.

NICK (*very quiet*). Of course.

Silence – they sit still.

KEVIN (*suddenly loud*). How long do we have to sit here – under these lights here?

CHARLOTTE. Not long.

KEVIN (*fast words tumbling out*). Be a great place for a film too – wouldn't it? Chickens slowly going round on their spits . . . in their lockers.

CHARLOTTE (*tense*). It's all right, Kevin.

KEVIN. See them, behind glass getting brown slowly. Could have other things going round – cats.

Pause.

Don't know why I said that.

The CLEANER *enters with a tray of food.*

CLEANER. There you are. Two Marylands, *jug* of milk.

KEVIN *takes the jug of milk immediately, and drinks out of it, large gulping drink.*

You're very thirsty aren't you?

KEVIN. Yes! (*He holds jug, feeling the cold.*) I am.

CLEANER (*she stands by table – smiles*). You going far?

CHARLOTTE (*looks up*). Yes, we are, quite a way.

The television noise dips.

CLEANER (*picking up a paper napkin from the table, folding it*). We're not that busy tonight. (*She smiles – slowly.*) My husband comes out here sometimes. Occasionally. Suddenly you look up, and there he is; you get the shock of your life. But he can only come out a very few nights. It's quite a way you see.

CHARLOTTE. Yes, I see. How much do we owe you?

CLEANER. You can't pay me – you pay over there.

CHARLOTTE (*sharp*). I want to pay now – I'm going to pay you.

CLEANER (*slight smile*). Could get sacked for that.

CHARLOTTE. How much?

CLEANER. Two pounds thirty.

KEVIN (*tense*). Right. We'll give you the money.

CLEANER (*standing at the table – just as* CHARLOTTE *gets out her purse*). It gets busier again later. Right in the early hours. You get some funny types then.

CHARLOTTE (*getting the money out of her purse*). I'm sure.

CLEANER (*carrying straight on*). Few nights ago this lorry driver came in, I looked up and there he was standing just over there – (*She indicates.*) – and he had – (*She laughs.*) – his trousers were round his ankles, no I swear it, right round his ankles, and his pants – (*She laughs.*) – they were down too, right down, I swear, he was standing just here.

CHARLOTTE (*holding money, getting tense*). Yes, I see.

CLEANER. He was so drunk, he couldn't see a foot in front of him and he sat down, sort of singing quiet to himself, he had a high voice, and all the time he was doing it down his leg . . . you know. He was quite good-looking you know, but he couldn't really move at all.

CHARLOTTE. Yes. Here's the money.

KEVIN. OK.

CLEANER. Yes. (*She takes the money, holds it in her hand.*) Where do you come from?

CHARLOTTE. We've come from London . . .

CLEANER. I come from round here. I can remember when the road was being built – yes – I saw it being dug out, watched it. And I walked along it before it was open too. Yes. Right down the middle – where all that is moving now. (*She indicates the traffic.*)

NICK (*quiet, looking straight at* CHARLOTTE). I don't feel very well, I think . . .

CHARLOTTE (*staring straight back at him*). Then you better eat something – here. (*She pulls a bit of food off her plate.*)

NICK (*a little louder*). I don't want to eat.

CLEANER. Do you want me to get you anything else?

CHARLOTTE (*really terse*). No, thank you. We're all right now . . .

CLEANER (*smiles at them, wiping the corner of the table automatically as she talks*). It's funny you know, people look at you in here, they're amazed you can talk; you should see the surprise on their faces, that you *can* actually tell them things, yes, that there's something going on in your head after all.

KEVIN (*beginning to get extraordinarily tense*). Right, I see. It must be . . .

CLEANER (*carrying on, smiling to herself*). Not all of them of course, you know, the Army came through here one night – some soldiers, going somewhere in a truck. They livened things up all right. They were very young, about ten of them you see. Jumping all round here, on the tables. Sent us all mad. It was about a couple of months ago now . . .

KEVIN (*bursting out*). OK. Could you just leave us now? All right. (*Pause.*) Thanks, but could you go . . . Right, sorry – but we're in a hurry.

CHARLOTTE (*watching her*). Yes.

CLEANER. Yes. (*She stares back at them.*) I've got to go to the kitchens now anyway.

She goes. CHARLOTTE *stares at the food.*

CHARLOTTE. OK – just eat now. (*To* NICK.) Drink your coffee. (*She turns the Chicken Maryland round on her plate.*) I'm going to take all the batter off this . . . scrape it off.

She does so. Silence.

NICK (*picks up his coffee – then puts it down staring at her*). Look – you're eating it.

CHARLOTTE (*looking up*). What?

NICK. You're eating it – see. (*Pause.*) See – she's . . .

CHARLOTTE. Yes. (*She puts the piece down, her face tense.*) But it doesn't taste of anything. You ought to eat too, I told you . . . (*She suddenly turns to* KEVIN's *plate.*) Mind Kevin, there's something in yours – (*She picks at it.*) A hair, I think . . .

NICK (*still staring straight at* CHARLOTTE, *fiddling with the sugar bowl*). You know she – (*He looks down at the table – stirring the sugar round.*) You know Charlotte's got blood all down her dress don't you . . .

CHARLOTTE *continues to eat – she doesn't look at him.*

Do you realise she's sitting there with it down her, all down that side.

CHARLOTTE (*suddenly looks up*). Don't do that, Nick. (*Tense, pale.*) Please . . .

NICK. You can feel it. You can feel it under the table.

CHARLOTTE (*looking straight at him*). Can you?

NICK (*quieter*). Yes.

She takes a napkin, picks up her chicken leg.

CHARLOTTE. I'm keeping this for later. I didn't particularly want anything fried. (*She gets up.*) I'm going to change. (*She hands KEVIN her handbag.*) Just finish your food. I'll be back very quickly. (*She moves towards the exit.*)

NICK (*suddenly calls out in a very loud voice, ringing out over whole cafeteria*). CHARLOTTE? WHERE'S CHARLOTTE GOING – WHERE'S SHE GOING?

CHARLOTTE stops, turns. Pause.

(*Still shouting.*) What's she going to do . . .

CHARLOTTE (*clenched*). Stop it, Nick.

NICK (*still loud*). Where's Charlotte going . . . ?

Silence. CHARLOTTE crosses back to the table, right up to NICK.

CHARLOTTE (*clipped, right by NICK*). You better both come out too then, hadn't you?

Cross fade to the foyer.

The same powerful neon lighting.

Amusement machines lined up – 'On Safari' (shooting at elephants). Distant music seeping through speakers, litter on the floor.

They enter. CHARLOTTE moves across the foyer.

CHARLOTTE. Kevin – stay here with him.

KEVIN (*mechanically*). Stay here with him.

CHARLOTTE. Yes. (*She moves to go.*)

NICK (*loud*). Charlotte!

CHARLOTTE turns.

CHARLOTTE. I'm just going to change.

NICK suddenly crosses the foyer, presses right up to her by a machine.

NICK (*nervous, hostile*). Going to change out of your working clothes then . . . ?

KEVIN (*coming up close*). Leave her –

CHARLOTTE (*up against the machine*). Nick . . . Stop it!

KEVIN (*moving up, takes* NICK's *arm*). Leave off her, mate . . . don't try . . .

NICK. Going to change?

CHARLOTTE. Yes.

NICK. It's wet. (*His arm touches the side of her dress.*)

KEVIN. I told you – leave her alone. (*He pulls him off forcibly.*) Come on . . .

KEVIN *holds* NICK. CHARLOTTE *stares at* NICK *across the foyer.*

CHARLOTTE. You were hurting me.

NICK (*loud*). Was I?

KEVIN. Sssssh!

CHARLOTTE. Leave this to me – it's all right.

NICK (*still loud, staring across at* CHARLOTTE's *dress*). Could feel it down the back of your leg –

CHARLOTTE (*steely*). Just calm down, Nick.

KEVIN. Charlotte – shall I . . .

CHARLOTTE. No, Kevin – it's all right. (*Staring straight at* NICK's *eyes.*) You're going to control yourself, Nick . . .

NICK (*loud*). That's right!

CHARLOTTE (*dangerous*). Do you understand me?

NICK. Yes.

   Pause.

   (*He suddenly shouts.*) I am nothing to do with these two. I have nothing . . .

KEVIN (*loud, jumps*). Stop it! Just stop it. We're armed, you know.

   Pause.

CHARLOTTE (*her tone slightly gentler*). Don't raise your voice again.

NICK (*his arm held by* KEVIN – *staring at* CHARLOTTE). I'm going now.

CHARLOTTE. You can't.

KEVIN. Listen, mate . . .

CHARLOTTE (*cutting in*). You're not going anywhere. I've

already told you. You're staying with us and doing what you're told. And then it'll be all right. You're safer with us.

NICK (*quieter, bit defiant*). Yes.

KEVIN (*still*). Where would you go anyway?

NICK (*totally bewildered*). What do you mean where would I go?

KEVIN. *Where* would you go? It's hundreds of yards to the road. There's nowhere to go – see.

NICK (*glances up*). Yes.

They watch him.

CHARLOTTE (*firm*). Now control yourself.

NICK. Yes. (*For a split second he looks at her; then suddenly.*) Shall we go into the shop? (*Louder.*) We'll go into the souvenir shop, shall we?

CHARLOTTE (*very steely*). It's closed.

NICK. I want to buy something. OK. You going to stop me, Charlotte?

CHARLOTTE (*staring straight at him*). It's closed, Nick.

NICK (*trying to raise his voice again – but it doesn't come out so loud*). These people are preventing me from going in there . . .

KEVIN (*loud, aggressive*). No, we aren't . . . !

CHARLOTTE. Nobody's listening to you at all. Look, nobody's watching – see!

KEVIN. They'll think you're drunk anyway.

NICK (*same tone*). These people are preventing me from leav . . .

KEVIN (*jumps*). Charlotte!

CHARLOTTE (*staring straight at him*). It's all right, he's going to pull himself together, isn't he . . . ?

NICK. These people are stopping me . . .

CHARLOTTE (*dangerous*). Nick, for the last time . . .

NICK (*gazing straight at her*). So you see I'm off now!

CHARLOTTE (*really savage*). JUST SHUT UP, NICK!

NICK *goes quiet.*

Silence.

CHARLOTTE. Thank you. That's better.

NICK (*quiet, clenched*). Right . . .

CHARLOTTE. You see that's better, isn't it – now.

KEVIN. And keep it like that.

NICK. Yes. (*He puts his hand into his pocket, pulls out a fistful of coins – then looks up at* CHARLOTTE.) I think I'm just going to make a phone call. (*Louder.*) I've got a lot of 2p's here. (*He holds out a fistful.*) Never had so many.

KEVIN (*by him still*). Christ, will you stop?

CHARLOTTE (*calmer*). Now, don't start it again, Nick.

NICK. No. I'm just going to make a quick call. Right! (*He looks straight at her.*) When *you've* gone, Charlotte.

Suddenly he moves abruptly, a step away from KEVIN – *and the coins drop all over the floor – spin everywhere.*

Silence.

NICK (*quiet – staring at them*). Oh Christ.

CHARLOTTE. What a mess. Why did you do that? Pick them up! I said pick them up!

NICK *doesn't move.* CHARLOTTE *picks up the coins.*

God the dust here, it's inches thick – and the smell.

KEVIN. There's one over here, I think. Can't see.

CHARLOTTE (*still by* NICK). Lot of muck here, all over the place. There's one here. (*She picks it up.*) We'll leave the rest, that's enough. We can't waste any more time. I'll be back in a moment. (*She goes.*)

KEVIN *moves across to the other side of the foyer, opposite* NICK, *who is by the 'safari' machine.*

KEVIN. Gone to change.

NICK (*hardly audible*). Yes.

KEVIN. Stay there, right.

He pulls the bottle of wine out of his pocket with an abrupt movement, then glances down at his clothes, then immediately looks up at NICK. *Muzak playing.* KEVIN *has the bag with the gun.*

I haven't got anything on me, have I?

NICK. What?

KEVIN (*glances down at his sleeve, then up at* NICK *again*). Haven't got anything on me? Don't think I have . . .

NICK. I don't know. (*He glances towards* KEVIN.) Yes, you have.

KEVIN, *keeping an eye on* NICK, *feels his clothes.*

No, you haven't.

KEVIN (*loud*). Got to see!

NICK (*suddenly loud*). For Christ's sake!

KEVIN *stops feeling his clothes.*

You're all right.

KEVIN. Thanks. (*He thrusts the bottle forward.*) Have some of this.

NICK. No, thanks.

KEVIN (*loud*). HAVE SOME!

Silence.

Look, I know what's happened. It's . . . (*Suddenly loud.*) WELL, IT'S HAPPENED, SEE! (*He drinks, watching* NICK, *quieter, feeling the shock.*) It's happened . . .

NICK (*staring down at the floor*). Yes.

KEVIN. Charlotte won't be long. Don't worry, she won't be long. (*He is staring at* NICK, *and holding the bottle.*) It's hard for you, of course it is! (*Loud.*) We do realise that, you know. (*Gentle tone.*) But you're all right. You're with us. Just keep still. (*He drinks.*) This stuff works quickly, doesn't it – goes down you like razor blades. (*He thrusts it forward again.*) Have some!

NICK. No, thanks.

KEVIN (*opposite him, across the foyer*). You feel you're falling fast – (*He wipes his hair back.*) – head buzzing, want to lie down almost, you know, melt into it! You know, just lie down here, let the sounds drown it all out, put your head on the grass out there – you know, the green grass. (*Suddenly loud.*) Nick!

NICK (*looks up*). Yes . . .

KEVIN (*fast, jumpy*). Got to keep talking! Makes it better. Easier for you. (*Louder.*) It does!

NICK (*mechanically*). Easier?

KEVIN (*fast, straight at* NICK). I was at Glastonbury, you know. Yes! The Great Free Festival. (*Straight at him, loud, urgent.*) LISTEN TO THIS, NICK! One morning, it was Sunday morning. It was five o'clock. Dawn. Everybody asleep, and everything peaceful. There was this wonderful feeling in the air. It was so strong! You could almost touch it. There was a young singer on stage, just singing to himself, nobody was listening. It was David Bowie – Yes! I was the only one up, almost; later, I was wandering about, in amongst all the people asleep, and I saw on the stage this *small white boy*, yes! All alone you know, about seven, standing with sun on his hair, smiling, really smiling you know, it was like the future, I just remembered it! That kid up there. (*Savage at* NICK.) But things didn't go on like that, did they . . . ?

NICK. No. (*Not looking at* KEVIN.) Not for you, Kevin, no.

KEVIN (*really loud*). FOR NOBODY. FOR NOBODY AT ALL! (*Pause. To himself.*) Not so loud.

The noise of some vehicle arriving close by.

KEVIN (*glancing out, then at* NICK). What's that? Did you see? What is it?

NICK. A coach arriving . . .

KEVIN. Here! Arriving here?

NICK (*louder*). I don't know.

KEVIN. At the motel! Be at the motel. It's all right. (*Then urgent.*) We shouldn't be out here so long! (*He moves slightly, glances behind him for a split second.*) Charlotte'll be back in a moment. She knows what she's doing.

NICK (*mechanically*). Yes.

KEVIN. She does. It's going to be OK.

NICK (*quiet*). Yes, of course.

KEVIN (*loud*). It is you know!

NICK (*quiet, clenched*). Do you think he will count to ten – and then get up again, because it was only playing? (*Clenched, staring at the ground.*) Is that it?

KEVIN (*back at him*). People get killed on that road all the time. They do! Accidents. Probably one happening right at this moment. NOW. Often it's a type of murder, because there are too many cars out there. (*Straight at* NICK.) Aren't there?

NICK (*quiet, clenched*). Of course. It makes sense now.

KEVIN (*loud, straight at him*). Well, aren't there?

NICK. Yes – of course there are.

KEVIN (*straight at him*). You don't know how much is at stake, do you?

NICK. No, I don't.

KEVIN (*snaps*). Keep still, I told you. I suppose you think it's because of this trouble, my eye trouble, that I think the things I do, feel what I do.

NICK (*quiet, clenched*). I don't know.

Pause. Muzak playing.

I don't know *what* you feel.

KEVIN. You can think what you like. But you're wrong, you know.

NICK. Yes, of course I am.

KEVIN (*serious*). Yes.

NICK (*clenched*). I'm not even sure how bad your eyes really are.

KEVIN. People always want superficial reasons for things. (*To* NICK.) They do, don't they? *So then they can dismiss them.* They want easy, obvious reasons for things. (*Loud, urgent.*) *Listen to this, Nick.* You really ought to, you know! But you see I've felt these things for a long time. Oh yes. Like a lot of people now. Know this place, this country *belongs to them.* Know it has to be protected.

NICK (*bewildered*). Protected . . .

KEVIN. It's not just a question of race – it's a question of England.

NICK (*clenched*). I'm not listening to this . . . (*Loud.*) I'm just not listening to this, Kevin, so you can . . .

KEVIN (*very sharp*). Quiet, keep it quiet . . . (*He lowers his own voice, but it's really urgent, almost passionate.*) You've *got to listen, you see.* Maybe this trouble has made me realise things a little earlier, because it sharpens things, you know, thoughts, maybe I'm six months ahead, but only six months. I *know* a lot of people who feel this, people of my *age.* All sorts. From young bankers to people like me. You don't believe me, of course, do you?

NICK. No.

KEVIN. But you *ought to.* I would show you the list, the list we're carrying, our contacts, but I'm not allowed to. Can't show that. That's why we *did* it. That's why it happened back there . . . we've got members all over the country. People full of disappointment . . . or whatever you call it.

NICK. Disappointment?

KEVIN. Or whatever you'd call it. (*Suddenly* KEVIN *whips round, looks over his shoulder.*) Where's Charlotte now? For Chrissake! Why is she being so long . . . ?

NICK (*quiet, clenched*). She had to clean herself up, didn't she?

KEVIN. Nothing can have happened, can it . . . ?

NICK. Of course not.

KEVIN. Then where is she? (*Intensely nervous, he calls out loud.*) Charlotte? (*He still keeps an eye on* NICK.) She didn't say she would be so long. (*Loud.*) Charlotte? (*He turns.*) She'll be back in a moment.

NICK. Yes.

KEVIN (*urgent*). We got to move from here! (*He stares straight at* NICK.) You know this now – this could be the beginning of a chase. (*Sharp.*) It probably is! A huge chase. We being hounded along the road. (*He looks at* NICK.) And if the police do catch up with us, *which they might do quite soon*, do you realise what that means?

NICK (*quiet, not looking at* KEVIN). Yes.

KEVIN (*staring straight at* NICK). Do you? I don't think you do. It means we stand a chance of becoming famous tonight, me and Charlotte, of becoming a sort of myth.

NICK (*clenched*). Kevin . . .

KEVIN. I know it sounds weird standing here, by this pathetic souvenir shop, in this dust, and this music, but you'll see on the radio, maybe soon; it might just be the beginning of a bit of a legend . . . something that will haunt people, young people. Following our route up here.

NICK (*louder, clenched*). Kevin – will you stop, just . . .

KEVIN. It may not happen – of course. *I really don't know.* (*Loud, sharp.*) We'll see, won't we! It could all be small and nasty. But *there is* a chance, if we get cornered and caught. (*Pause. Loud.*) BECOMING A MYTH TONIGHT! (*He stands staring at* NICK.) Yes! (*He swings round.* CHARLOTTE *is coming back in.*) Charlotte! She's back, it's all right.

CHARLOTTE *is wearing a clean new skirt and blouse. Pink or white, tight against her breasts. She is carrying the bag.*

CHARLOTTE. Right! Thank God that's done now.

NICK (*who is staring at her intently*). Yes! Feeling better are you?

CHARLOTTE. Yes I am. I've had a wash. (*Aggressive at* NICK.) I think you bruised my back just now – but I'm all right.

KEVIN (*concerned*). Do you want me to drive now, Charlotte?

CHARLOTTE. No, I'm fine. I can do it.

KEVIN. You must be very tired. I'll drive if you want, I will . . .

CHARLOTTE (*sharp*). No, I'm fine. Come on now.

NICK (*suddenly moving from the machine*). You've put scent on haven't you, I can smell it.

CHARLOTTE (*determined to control him*). That's right.

NICK (*louder*). Put scent over it have you? All over it.

CHARLOTTE (*sharp*). Nick . . .

NICK (*up to her*). The dress is in the bag is it? (*Glancing down at it.*) Yes it is – stuffed in there.

KEVIN (*dangerous*). Leave her alone now for Chrissake. (*Warning.*) I told you . . .

NICK (*aggressive*). Why didn't you leave it in a basin? Just lying there.

CHARLOTTE (*firm*). Now don't start again will you . . .

NICK. Put scent all over – have you!

CHARLOTTE (*controlled*). Stop it, Nick.

He is silent.

Right. (*She glances round, tenses slightly.*) We'll go out the way we came. Quickly. Walk straight to the van. We'll get as far as we can with the petrol we've got.

KEVIN. Yes, can't fill up here. (*Straight at* NICK.) Been here long enough.

CHARLOTTE (*staring at the exit*). Yes we have.

KEVIN *hands her handbag back.* CHARLOTTE *takes it, tenses, straightens.*

(*Sharp.*) I'm ready then. (*She glances at the two men.*) Are both of you?

KEVIN. Yes.

CHARLOTTE *looks straight at* NICK – *pause.*

NICK. Yes.

CHARLOTTE. Good.

Blackout.

Scene Two

In the blackout we hear a disc-jockey on a late-night show chatting away . . . mentioning 'trouble on the road, bother in

Doncaster, but for all of us that are safely tucked up, doing whatever you do when you're safely tucked up, on this hot night — yes, it is a bit hot for that, even for me! And that's saying a lot, here's . . .' He fades in a blast of music. The lights come on an area outside the kitchens of another motorway café. Huge rubbish vats in the background; in the foreground a tarpaulin stretches over some crates, completely covering them. Lights streaming from the kitchen doors.

KEVIN, CHARLOTTE *and* NICK *by the tarpaulin.*

KEVIN *squatting by the radio moving the dials; blast of noise.*

CHARLOTTE. Not so loud . . .

KEVIN (*moving the dials*). It's all the late shows.

CHARLOTTE (*staring down at the radio*). Yes.

KEVIN. All the night shows — yattering. Listen to them. (*He lets the disc-jockey pour out.*)

CHARLOTTE. Yes. Come on. (*She glances up.*) There's nobody in those lorries over there? (*She stares.*) No.

NICK (*suddenly, staring down at the radio*). There isn't anything about it there! There isn't anything!

CHARLOTTE. Not so loud.

KEVIN (*moving the dials, exasperated — as commercials ring out*). It's just all of this pouring out.

Suddenly KEVIN finds it. The fanfare for a news item.* They tense. Then the News comes out — the item announces a policeman has been found shot dead in Doncaster. It gives the exact location and 'two men and a woman were seen leaving the area'; they listen to it in silence.

KEVIN (*as the first words of news item are read out*). There! (*Then he goes silent.*)

CHARLOTTE. Somebody saw us then. (*She moves away from the radio; the news has moved on to other things.*)

KEVIN squats by the radio, he's holding a torch, he moves the dial.

NICK. Yes! It seems they did.

KEVIN. They're out searching now . . .

---

* For news items see page 462.

CHARLOTTE. We must be eighty miles away.

KEVIN. A night search. Patrols, road blocks, spreading out in wider and wider circles. (*Quiet.*) I wonder if there's any more. (*He flicks the dials some more.*)

CHARLOTTE. Not so loud!

KEVIN. Listen. There's some more. (*He hits the end of another news item about it. He moves the dial, and again we hear the end of a news item. KEVIN is quiet, staring at the radio.*) It's everywhere, the whole machine is full of it. Totally crammed with it. (*He looks up at NICK.*) You see.

NICK (*quiet*). I see . . . A huge chase . . .

CHARLOTTE (*moves briskly*). I ought to phone Harrowby Street, but if the phones *are* tapped there . . . it's not worth the risk, is it?

KEVIN. No, it isn't.

She is keeping a close watch on NICK. KEVIN moves up to her, close, confidential.

KEVIN. Are you cold now, Charlotte?

CHARLOTTE. Cold? No?

KEVIN. Good.

CHARLOTTE. Stay still, Nick.

KEVIN (*close, confidential, only half audible*). It's strange hearing it. You begin to feel it hasn't happened, a blank – but it has.

NICK (*loud, concerned*). What's he saying? What's he saying to you, Charlotte?

CHARLOTTE moves.

What was he saying to you?

CHARLOTTE. It's all right. Switch it off, Kevin. Go on.

KEVIN goes over to switch the radio off; as he squats by the radio, the KID enters.

KEVIN. There! (*He switches it off.*)

KID. Hey . . .

They look up. The KID is about seventeen, looks older, messy dazed appearance, nervy manner; he has obviously been through a lot of drugs.

CHARLOTTE (*stiffens*). Yes – what is it?

KID. Have any of you got a light?

CHARLOTTE. I don't think we have. Has someone got a light for him?

Pause, nobody moves.

KID. I just want a light. (*Nobody moves.*) Come on! Somebody must have a light.

NICK (*suddenly*). Yes! Here.

KEVIN (*butting in*). No, I've got one. Here . . . (*He throws box of matches at KID.*)

KID. Ta.

CHARLOTTE. Right.

The KID half moves, then turns.

CHARLOTTE *is leaning by the tarpaulin. Through this sequence KEVIN moves close to NICK.*

KID. Can you – can you give me something for the juke-box, get some music, get the place back there going . . . wake it up.

CHARLOTTE. No. I'm afraid not . . .

KID. No, come on! The windows are open. You'll hear it too. Easily. So come on now. You can even choose the records if you like. Yuh . . . Have our own request programme.

CHARLOTTE. No.

KID (*moving towards her*). Can I join you then . . .?

CHARLOTTE (*sharp*). No, you can't.

KID (*stopping*). You're wearing perfume, aren't you? Got perfume on.

NICK. Yes, she has . . .

KID. All over – I can smell it. (*To all of them.*) What you doing then?

CHARLOTTE (*very sharp and loud*). Nothing. We're just travelling!

KID (*turning to KEVIN and NICK*). You're going to give me something for the juke-box aren't you? Get some real dancing going . . .

KEVIN (*tense*). Look, we can't. OK . . . .

KID. You're not meant to dance in these cafes. Indecent behaviour they call it. But I know a black chick that dances all night by herself in one of these places, should see the things she does. Christ! But she doesn't let anyone near her.

He suddenly looks at CHARLOTTE.

She doesn't believe me.

KEVIN. She believes you. Right!

CHARLOTTE. Yes, you're talking about some black girl, could you just –

KID. Which way you going? Maybe I'm going that way myself. (*Broad grin.*) You never know – you might be lucky!

CHARLOTTE (*dipping into her bag*). There's the money, you can have it now . . .

KID. Ta! Great! (*He takes the money.*) Have I seen you round here before?

KEVIN (*very tense*). Why should you have . . . You couldn't have . . . so just . . .

NICK. Just take it. Go on.

KID (*straight on*). No reason. Sometimes I know people. I go hitching backwards along the road you see. I get to one end . . . do a few things then come straight back again.

KEVIN. Right. OK!

KID (*carrying straight on, moving around*). I know the road well now. And all the cafes! Been doing it for weeks. Some others do it too. It's catching on. But we don't tend to see each other much. You understand?

CHARLOTTE. Yes I do. Could you . . .

KID. It's great. Been in all sorts! Lorries, tankers, a Rolls-Royce. Christ! Yeah! . . . you get that sort on weekends, coming back from the country, where they go and stay.

KEVIN. OK! – Look mate, we're in a hurry, so . . .

KID (*carrying straight on, ignoring him, fast*). I got a big Jaguar you see. And the back seat was completely covered in daffodils, and rhododendrons and things, thick with it, piled up, and right on top was a dead duck. Honest! Always look on the back seat. You see some really weird things.

CHARLOTTE. Could you leave us?

NICK. Just take it.

KID (*carrying on*). I got one car – this bloke kept looking at me all the time, then when I said I wanted to get out, he wouldn't stop the car you see. No! He said I looked like President Kennedy when he was young, the same expression; yeah, he had a huge hand. It came straight down on my trousers. Like a crane. Jaws! (*Suddenly.*) Are you listening? Are you listening to me?

CHARLOTTE. Yes. We are. But . . .

KID (*cutting her off*). What was I saying then?

Pause.

What was I saying? See – she doesn't know . . . I sleep in these places too, you know. Have my own bench here, I call it my own. Crash out here.

KEVIN *is glancing at* CHARLOTTE.

CHARLOTTE. Listen – could you just leave us now?

KID. Christ, the dreams you get doing that! You have no idea. Really incredible dreams. Every quarter of an hour you get woken up. You can dream a hundred different things at night . . .

KEVIN (*really tense*). Look mate, we told you – we're in a hurry, so . . . just . . .

Suddenly KID *up to* CHARLOTTE, *by her.*

KID. Sometimes you know you're really dreaming of a nice body you know, like this one here, up against her, and she's doing things, Christ! The feeling! It *really is good*, really strong.

CHARLOTTE (*tense*). Is it?

KID. And you wake up at five o'clock in the morning, and you know the whole place by then is full of people, on every seat. Curled up! Wish I could wake up with her, that would be good, wouldn't it?

CHARLOTTE (*sharp, moving*). Look, I think we'll move on now, OK . . .

KID (*catching hold of her*). NO, you don't . . . NO. (*He grins.*) You want to see my tracks then. (*He begins to roll up his sleeve.*) You want to see them? You believed me! (*He shows arms.*) Actually, they don't show any more. Not much. (*Up by* CHARLOTTE.) Want to see them?

KEVIN (*suddenly loud*). Don't talk about that sort of thing. That muck! Right – just stop it!

KID (*grins, unabashed*). OK – she doesn't know what I'm talking about anyway.

CHARLOTTE (*really tense*). Unfortunately, I do.

KID (*up to her*). I saw an accident the other day, near here. I was really close. It was smashed all over the road. That was all right. She didn't like that, did she? (*Nervous grin.*) I don't blame her.

CHARLOTTE. Please would you leave us alone – could you just . . .

KID. It's great going up and down the road. You ought to do it. I might try London. It didn't work out for me before. I came down to London but it didn't work out.

CHARLOTTE (*clenched*). Please, just leave us alone, will you?

KID. Didn't get much to eat, you see . . .

CHARLOTTE (*really tense*). Look, you've got the money haven't you? *Would you go now?*

KID. I'm allowed to be here.

CHARLOTTE. But I'm asking you to leave. I find your being here – I don't find it very pleasant.

The KID *is pressed up next to her on the tarpaulin.*

KID. You can't stop me being here.

CHARLOTTE (*to* KEVIN). Are you going to get rid of him, please?

KEVIN. Yeah – come on, move.

KEVIN *is standing by* NICK.

KID. I'm all right here, aren't I?

CHARLOTTE (*beginning to get desperate*). Are you going to go? (*She turns to the men.*) Come on, one of you, make him go away. (*Suddenly she screams.*) DON'T YOU UNDERSTAND, I CAN'T STAND HIM BEING NEAR ME – *DON'T YOU UNDERSTAND?*

KID. Listen, I'm only . . .

CHARLOTTE. You're filthy, you revolt me. (*She shouts.*) Go away, can't you! I can't stand him near me. I can't stand him near me.

KID. Are you nutty or something?

CHARLOTTE. MOVE HIM! (*Screaming.*) GO ON. JUST GO AWAY. (*Screaming.*) JUST GET AWAY FROM ME. GET OUT.

The KID, *stunned by her savagery, moves away.*

KID. Is she crazy or something – (*Loud.*) – is she?

CHARLOTTE (*very, very quiet*). I can't take this now.

KEVIN (*loud*). JUST GET AWAY FROM HERE. GET OUT.

KID (*aggressive*). I was just being here, wasn't I . . . I was just talking. Not allowed any more, is it? Not allowed! (*He moves to the exit.*) Well, you've got it coming to you – you fucking have.

The KID *exits.*

Silence.

CHARLOTTE. He was filthy. I couldn't take it.

CHARLOTTE starts to cry. Silence. Just her crying.

KEVIN. Charlotte.

Pause. Just her crying.

NICK (*startled, only half hostile*). Charlotte . . .

CHARLOTTE. He was so disgusting. (*She cries. They watch. Suddenly, she clenches herself, pulls herself together.*) I'm sorry to make an exhibition of myself. I shouldn't have shouted. He was just so filthy. (*Her head flicks round.*) Don't move, Nick.

KEVIN (*moving around, abrupt, nervous*). Do you – Charlotte – do you want anything?

CHARLOTTE. No. (*Suddenly it hits her they haven't done anything. Urgent.*) Come on. We've got to get on. Got to get the van filled up. Quickly, we can't stay here. They'll be coming down the road. (*Sharp to* KEVIN.) I said quickly.

KEVIN. Yes. I'll get her filled up now. (*He glances at* NICK.) I'll be back as quick as I can, Charlotte. (*He goes.*)

CHARLOTTE *is lying on the tarpaulin facing* NICK.

CHARLOTTE (*sharp*). I'm all right now. Stay there.

Pause.

NICK (*fiddling nervously with the torch*). You realise! If a lorry comes out of the car park now, passes us now – he'd look down from his cab, and he'd see these people lying here, and he'll probably just think we're a couple of midnight picnickers or something – or even a couple of lovers lying by the kitchens, looking so normal. The pair of us. (*Aggressive.*) You're going to get seen any moment, you know.

CHARLOTTE. Are we!

Silence.

NICK (*staring at her*). You cried.

CHARLOTTE (*looking at him*). Yes, I did. That's right.

*Music starts from the juke-box, continues through whole scene
– the records changing.*

CHARLOTTE. That kid . . . Listen to him.

NICK. Why are you lying down like that?

CHARLOTTE. Because you bruised my back when you pushed
me, and it's hurting now.

NICK (*moves*). Is it?

CHARLOTTE (*really steely*). I told you not to move.

NICK. I know you did.

CHARLOTTE. Then don't. I've explained, haven't I, it's going to
be all right if you do what we say. And if it suits us to be
caught when the time comes, you could be a lot of use to us. So
you really ought to believe me.

NICK (*quiet but strong*). I'm not that stupid, Charlotte.

CHARLOTTE. It's your own choice anyway. We don't want you
to get hurt. Do you think we want to hurt. Just for the fun,
seeing . . .

NICK (*sharp*). I wouldn't know about that, would I?

CHARLOTTE (*steely*). You think we enjoyed what happened
back there, do you . . . Is that what you think, you bastard?
That's what you believe, is it?

NICK (*watching her*). I don't know.

CHARLOTTE (*steely*). Is it?

NICK. No.

CHARLOTTE (*quieter*). That's better. Then keep still, will you?
(*Watching him.*) Have you broken that torch?

NICK. What?

CHARLOTTE. Have you broken it?

NICK. What does it matter? It doesn't work now.

CHARLOTTE. Then would you mend it?

NICK (*quiet*). Mend it!

CHARLOTTE. We may need it.

NICK (*pulls it to pieces*). My hand's shaking.

CHARLOTTE. I keep expecting to hear a siren any moment . . . I
hope Kevin's going to be all right.

NICK (*loud*). Why shouldn't he be all right?

CHARLOTTE (*anxious*). I wonder how long he'll be . . . I hardly knew him before today, strange isn't it . . . I hope he hurries!

NICK (*loud*). Why are you talking about Kevin all the time for Chrissake. I'm here, and you're going to talk to me now, yes, whether you want to or not.

She looks at him.

Right. (*He looks down.*) I don't know what I'm doing with this torch. It's in pieces, the spring's gone.

CHARLOTTE. Give it here then – come on, give it to me.

NICK *lifts the torch.*

Just hand it to me.

NICK *leans forward and hands it to her, and in doing so, moves closer.*

NICK. My hands are so sticky, I couldn't grip it.

CHARLOTTE *fiddles with torch; we see her nerves.*

CHARLOTTE. There. (*She flicks the torch, it works; she shines it in his face.*) I've done it.

NICK (*aggressive*). You're nervous now, aren't you – aren't you?

CHARLOTTE. Of course.

NICK (*charged*). Have you got brothers and sisters?

Pause.

Come on, have you got brothers and sisters?

CHARLOTTE. Brothers and sisters!

NICK. Don't just repeat it.

CHARLOTTE. A young brother.

Music playing.

NICK (*sharp*). And your parents?

CHARLOTTE. Yes?

NICK. Are you close to your parents?

CHARLOTTE. Close?

NICK (*very loud*). DON'T just repeat it.

CHARLOTTE. Quite close really.

NICK. Yes. Go on. You're going to talk. Go on . . .

CHARLOTTE. How long will he be do you think?

NICK. Forget about Kevin. Go on . . . Charlotte. (*He moves nearer.*)

CHARLOTTE. Don't move. I told you. I don't want you any closer. (CHARLOTTE *moves herself up on the tarpaulin.*) You *really* did hurt my back. It's shooting through me now. (*Real determination.*) But I'm going to make it go. I can! (*She is lying propped up – staring down at* NICK.) When I was small, I once went swimming in a lake near us in the country. In Kent, quite a lovely part really.

NICK. Yes. Go on . . . Go on!

CHARLOTTE. It's not like that any more of course. Completely ruined. The middle of the fruit country. The water was very thick with mud and oil and things, filthy and very hot . . . How far are we from the road? (*She stops.*)

NICK. Go on.

CHARLOTTE. And I thought if I could bring myself to swim underwater in this filth I can do anything. I can do just about anything. And I did do it! You see. I went under – yes. I couldn't see anything except a sort of horrid muzzy darkness. It went all over me and in me. Over my mouth like a mud gag. (*Suddenly.*) It feels like that now doesn't it, all the time. (*Watching him.*) Doesn't it? Put your hand over your mouth and hold it there – go on, put your hand over your mouth.

NICK (*half raises his hand*). No –

CHARLOTTE. That's what it felt like – feels like – all the time, for a lot of people.

Pause.

NICK. Go on . . . Go on.

CHARLOTTE. I got out and walked for miles down the path through *our* fields, I was working things out. I was only fourteen. I wouldn't do that now. I was a ridiculous child in many ways. But I thought a lot – when I was on my own. (*She shifts slightly and winces in pain.*)

Music playing. Pause.

NICK (*sharp, staring at her*). Go on! The things going on in your head, Charlotte . . .

CHARLOTTE. You don't know anything about that. (*Straight at him.*) You don't know what's going on at all.

NICK (*leaning towards her, forceful, not hysterical*). Oh yes . . . the girl from the country estate, a beautiful house, who had everything she wanted, always, right, didn't she?

CHARLOTTE (*loud*). Don't move.

NICK (*carrying straight on*). No! Worried about what's happening to England, worried that things might get worse for her, so blame it on the Blacks, so round them up, ship them off, of course, ship them away, out to sea – (*Shouting.*) – and then, of course, anything else that's offensive, remove that as well.

CHARLOTTE (*loud*). STOP IT, NICK – I mean it.

Pause. He is nearer her.

You won't ever shout at me again.

NICK (*defiant*). NO!

Pause.

Go on – Go on, Charlotte – (*He stares straight at her.*) Tell me *everything* now – tell me about the English People's Party –

CHARLOTTE. I've told you all you're going to know. (*She glances round.*) Why is he being so long? Where is he?

NICK (*forceful*). Forget him! (*He leans towards her on the tarpaulin.*) Why were you carrying a gun, Charlotte? Come on, tell me –

CHARLOTTE. To protect myself.

NICK. Protect yourself against what?

CHARLOTTE. Against all the leftist groups that know what we're doing.

NICK. What leftist groups?

CHARLOTTE (*steely*). All of them. They're armed too. They've been acquiring arms all the time . . .

NICK. You really believe that?

CHARLOTTE (*fierce*). It's not a question of *believing* . . .

NICK (*louder, closer*). You really believe there are hundreds of armed people moving all over the country *tonight* . . .

CHARLOTTE. Yes. It's increasing all the time. Don't come any closer, Nick . . . I mean it.

Pause. Music playing.

A lot of people may experience it soon.

NICK. Experience what?

CHARLOTTE. Where is he? He should be back.

NICK (*loud*). Experience what –

Pause.

CHARLOTTE. Having to kill someone. Seeing them fall. (*She looks straight at him. Loud.*) You have no idea what's happening – none at all, have you? You believe nothing's really going on at all – don't you? (*Sudden, straight at him.*) There's a civil war coming . . . in eighteen months, in two years. I don't want it to happen, but we can see it coming . . .

NICK (*forceful*). So that's what you're trying to do is it? Whipping people up. Making people believe all this . . .

CHARLOTTE. There'll be guerrilla-style clashes to begin with.

NICK (*strong*). But you won't manage it, Charlotte, unless you're allowed to.

CHARLOTTE (*suddenly letting it pour out*). And they'll escalate – and keep on escalating. It's already nearly happening. The Left disrupting meetings, like they disrupt everything, preventing freedom of speech all the time. Running down England, bringing this country to its knees, killing it, you just have to read their press, to see what they're intending to do.

NICK (*quiet, forceful*). Charlotte, you don't really –

CHARLOTTE (*straight back*). YES, I do.

Pause.

(*She's now worked up.*) When did you last feel happy about the future? (*Loud.*) When? Tell me.

NICK. Often. (*Loud.*) I often –

CHARLOTTE (*straight back*). When? When did you? Five years ago? Ten years ago? When you left school? All those wasted years, letting the country be overrun – people who just don't belong.

NICK (*clenched*). You don't know what you're saying, Charlotte . . .

CHARLOTTE. Where has it got anybody, anybody at all, everything sliding, sliding so fast! And they're powerless to stop it. Everything been grey for so long, and the mess, everywhere, just totally grey. (*She looks at him, quieter.*) Like you . . .

NICK (*defiant*). Like me? –

Silence.

CHARLOTTE (*with controlled passion*). Look at this – look at it, here. (*She gazes out across the landscape.*) This sprawling mess, those lights up there, that savage light, have you ever seen something so horrible? Anything so inhuman, more disgusting,

it's just degrading. It presses down on us all. (*Loud.*) Do you
know what used to be here – where we are now. DO YOU? A
valley and fields. It did. How can people live with a dread of
the future all the time? How can you bring people up like that –
just offer them that all the time. Tell me. Somebody's got to do
something.

*Silence. With an abrupt movement, NICK gets onto the bottom
of the tarpaulin, much nearer CHARLOTTE. She flinches away
– a few feet between them, dangerous, holding the bag with the
gun.*

CHARLOTTE (*fierce*). DON'T!

Pause. He lies there.

(*Steely calm.*) You shouldn't have done that, Nick.

NICK. No. (*Pause. Near her.*) No, I know I shouldn't. (*Quiet.*)
Do you think about him at all?

CHARLOTTE. Who?

NICK (*louder*). And maybe his family – are you thinking about
it . . .

CHARLOTTE (*steely*). Didn't I tell you not to raise your voice?
And you've moved even closer – haven't you –

Pause.

Don't try to touch me.

NICK. No.

The music finishes.

CHARLOTTE (*her head flicks slightly*). The music's stopped.
(*Pause – suddenly loud.*) Where is he? Where's Kevin? (*Really
urgent.*) WHERE'S KEVIN – ?

NICK. He's not come back –

CHARLOTTE. No.

NICK *stretches out his hand slightly, but only tentatively.*

(*Calm.*) Don't do that . . .

NICK (*quiet*). Your cardigan's soaked . . . look at it, it's
completely soaked in sweat.

CHARLOTTE. It's because it's hot, isn't it? It's an old cardigan.

NICK (*quiet*). An old one . . . it's probably one of your mother's
– isn't it? You could wring it out – it's so wet.

CHARLOTTE. I told you not to try to touch me.

NICK (*quiet, straight at her*). You really must be in pain, mustn't you?

CHARLOTTE. Don't tell me what I'm feeling.

NICK. Yes – your eyes are watering. I can see it.

CHARLOTTE. And if I am. Whose fault is that?

NICK (*quiet*). That's right . . . yes. And you're lying on some oil, it's all over you.

CHARLOTTE. I'm all right. It's only a bruise after all.

She suddenly sits up bolt upright on the tarpaulin, flinches with the pain, then straightens. NICK moves back instinctively.

There. (*She straightens her back with effort.*) It's gone. See – it's gone.

NICK. Yes. The oil's all over your back, Charlotte . . .

CHARLOTTE (*staring straight at him*). I know.

NICK. You realise, Charlotte, we're about the same age, you and me.

CHARLOTTE. Yes.

NICK (*suddenly loud*). What are you really expecting to happen – tonight – (*Pause.*) What you expecting?

CHARLOTTE. I don't know. We were *seen*, that's all we know. (*She looks at him across the tarpaulin.*) Are you going to move of your own accord, Nick?

They face each other.

NICK. No. You're very thin, aren't you, Charlotte?

CHARLOTTE. Yes.

NICK (*staring at her*). I don't see – I just don't . . . You're not even a very intelligent girl, are you? You aren't. Not deep inside there. Not even very bright. You've no ideas at all, nothing, except shabby, vicious, second-hand thoughts. (*Forceful.*) Why am I still here, Charlotte? I could have easily . . .

CHARLOTTE. No. You couldn't.

NICK (*forceful*). I really don't know why I didn't . . .

CHARLOTTE (*quiet, staring at him*). Because until now you were being sensible, weren't you . . . and it was all right.

NICK (*quiet, firm*). Was I? I'm not moving from here Charlotte. I warn you – I'm not moving.

KEVIN enters.

CHARLOTTE. He's here.

   KEVIN *stands staring at him.*

KEVIN. Go on – leave her.

   NICK *doesn't move.*

   I said LEAVE HER.

NICK. NO!

   Pause. Silence.

   I'm not moving, Kevin.

   A moment's pause, as NICK *lies by* CHARLOTTE *on the tarpaulin –* CHARLOTTE *then, with a sudden movement, gets up, moves off the tarpaulin.*

KEVIN. Yes! Are you all right, Charlotte . . .

CHARLOTTE (*sharp*). I'm fine now. Absolutely fine.

KEVIN (*loud*). I've done it. And paid! I thought I was going to be short – I thought I didn't have enough, I thought I'd have to come back. But I did have enough!

CHARLOTTE. Right.

KEVIN (*loud*). We've got enough to go the whole way . . .

   The KID *enters.*

CHARLOTTE. Oh God . . .

KID. Hello –

KEVIN (*dangerous*). What do you want?

KID. I was wondering since you're still here, and just filled your van up – how about a lift —

KEVIN (*tense*). A lift –

KID. Yeah – I've been here eight hours.

CHARLOTTE (*steely*). Have you . . . ?

NICK (*nervous*). Christ . . .

KID. And can't get a lift. I want to be moving, can't stay here any longer. I've been here eight hours! Got to get away. Come on – give me a lift –

CHARLOTTE. NO.

NICK. Just leave, go on – I'm telling you – leave –

KID. Just to the next cafe – come on – you're going to give me a lift.

CHARLOTTE. Get rid of him –

KEVIN. We told you once.

KID. I want a lift. It won't hurt you.

NICK. Just get out will you –

KID. No. I'm going to get a lift.

KEVIN (*dangerous*). Are you going to go?

KID. No.

> KEVIN *throws himself at the* KID, *shouting 'Just get out'. The* KID *fights back really viciously* – NICK *suddenly follows* KEVIN, *catching hold of the* KID's *head, shouting 'Just leave'. The* KID *breaks away from* KEVIN, *and* NICK *catches hold of him. A siren is heard faintly in the distance.*

CHARLOTTE. For Chrissake – (*As the fight goes on.*) Just get rid of him – that's all.

> *The* KID *fights viciously with* NICK; KEVIN *goes for him too;* NICK *drags the* KID *away.*

NICK. Just go. Right. (*He lets the* KID *go.*)

KID (*stunned*). I don't . . . (*Very quiet, dazed.*) What's the matter with you? (*He goes.*)

> NICK *stares at* CHARLOTTE, *then at* KEVIN. CHARLOTTE *looks at both of them.*

CHARLOTTE (*quiet*). Thank you.

> *The siren suddenly starts again, approaching fast.*
>
> *They stand still, as it approaches.*
>
> *The siren increases, really loud, getting incredibly close – then it roars past.*

CHARLOTTE (*as soon it passes while it's still dying*). Gone past.

KEVIN (*big grin of relief*). Yes!

CHARLOTTE. Come on – pick the things up. We've got to be moving.

> *Blackout.*

Scene Three

The hillside. Dark. Blankets and thermos spread out. KEVIN, CHARLOTTE, NICK, *leaning up against a low stone wall or a grassy bank.*

In the blackout a strong radio bulletin is heard about the night
search, which cuts into the radio on stage. At end of bulletin
CHARLOTTE gets up, moves across abruptly to the radio and
switches it off.*

CHARLOTTE (*sharp*). Right! (*She crosses over and sits down, she
has some crumpled writing paper with her, and a biro, puts
them on her lap.*)

Silence. They all stare out.

KEVIN (*matter-of-fact*). Christ it's quiet. (*Pause.*) Terrifyingly
quiet suddenly. (*Loud to* NICK.) Isn't it?

NICK. Yes.

NICK is nervously tying the lace on his desert boots.

KEVIN (*feeling the bank with the palm of his hand*). And the
ground's so hard, baked hard. (*Loud.*) This heat – it really does
feel as if it's before *something enormous.*

CHARLOTTE (*scribbling on the paper*). Yes.

KEVIN (*staring out*). You can just see the edge of the road –
curling round. (*Loud.*) See it! Cutting through!

CHARLOTTE. Yes. Not so loud.

KEVIN (*mechanically*). Not so loud.

CHARLOTTE. And keep your heads down both of you.

KEVIN. Yes. (*Pause.*) What you writing all the time,
Charlotte?

CHARLOTTE. It's all right . . . (*Very tense.*) I've nearly finished. I
can't concentrate now, though, the pen keeps slipping – all the
time. (*She suddenly looks up at* NICK; *unnaturally loud.*) Stop
that! The lace is broken, Nick.

NICK. Yes, I know. I know it is.

KEVIN. Going to stand up.

CHARLOTTE. Why?

KEVIN. I want to . . . They can't see . . . (*But he keeps upstage.
Staring out.*) Do you think they're out there now, slipping
silently into place? Cars driving across the fields . . .

CHARLOTTE (*quiet*). I don't know . . .

---

* For news items see page 463.

KEVIN. Moving through the long grass – encircling the whole hillside. They could well be doing that. (*Suddenly loud.*) Yes – there's a light, I think. See –

CHARLOTTE. Where? Where is it?

KEVIN. You see it? I think . . . no, it's gone. (*Pause.*) I can't see, can you?

CHARLOTTE. It's gone.

Siren sounds in the distance. CHARLOTTE *glances round, tense.*

There they are anyway.

KEVIN. Yes. (*Glancing behind them.*) Out there somewhere.

CHARLOTTE. It's quite a way off still.

KEVIN. Yes. It is.

Siren playing around in the distance.

Getting nearer though.

CHARLOTTE. Slowly, yes.

The siren dies.

NICK (*sharp but quiet*). Looking forward to it, are you . . . ?

CHARLOTTE. I don't know. (*She glances down at the paper, matter-of-fact.*) I don't know what I feel . . .

NICK (*louder*). Looking forward to it, are you . . . ?

CHARLOTTE (*stares straight at him*). Just don't begin that again.

KEVIN (*quiet, moving downstage slightly*). You realise we would just have to fire first. We just have to fire the first shot – to unleash a whole stream from out there. A complete onslaught.

NICK (*sharp*). Kevin.

KEVIN. They shoot to kill . . . they do in fact.

NICK. Kevin, don't you . . .

KEVIN (*quiet, cutting him off*). It's the truth. Haven't you read the papers . . . They shoot to kill . . . (*Pause.*) Whole burst from there. They'll smash straight into us.

NICK (*quiet, aggressive*). Smash into you?

Silence.

CHARLOTTE (*with the thermos, quiet*). Have some. (*She holds it out to* KEVIN.) Come on, I don't want any but you have some.

KEVIN *takes the thermos, takes a short drink.*

NICK (*suddenly loud*). Christ . . . What do you want now, Charlotte?

CHARLOTTE. I don't know. (*She takes the thermos from KEVIN.*) It's all right . . . (*Then to NICK, as she holds out the thermos.*) Have some?

NICK. No.

CHARLOTTE *puts the thermos down beside her.*

What you hoping for then? (*Pause.*) Charlotte Pearson and Kevin Gellot . . . (*Pause, nervous but controlling it.*) See that – written on the streets?

KEVIN (*staring out*). Yes . . .

NICK. Is that what you want . . . ? Staring out of all the hoardings, Charlotte and Kevin . . . up there, huge . . . blow by blow account . . . all this . . . blow by blow . . .

CHARLOTTE (*calm*). Quieter . . .

NICK. In the papers . . . in the supplements too, pages about you.

KEVIN. Yes.

NICK (*loud*). What do you mean, Yes? (*Louder.*) What do you mean . . . ?

CHARLOTTE. Don't move around . . . I told you.

Pause.

NICK (*looking down, pulling at the grass, short abrupt movements*). Yes . . . up on people's walls, above their beds, life-size . . . is that what you want? The martyrs . . . for those school kids whose minds you hope to poison. Hope to *infect*.

CHARLOTTE. Just try to keep still.

Siren – same distance as before.

There it is . . . same distance, isn't it? . . . circling still . . .

KEVIN. Yes. It is.

Pause, as the siren plays around.

Bound to find us sooner or later, England's such a small country . . .

The siren dies.

NICK. You've knocked the thermos over – it's spilling. (*Sharp.*) Pick it up . . .

CHARLOTTE. Yes. (*She does so.*)

Pause.

NICK (*pulling at the grass, looking down*). You can see that, can't you . . . the faces in the dock. Staring out. Both of you. Pale faces. Your hair cut short. And the headlines . . . all that muck . . . the hundreds of headlines. Charlotte Pearson – the girl . . . and Kevin Gellot – the half-blind companion . . . (*Pause – still looking down.*) Yes, you can see the pictures. Just for a moment you can see them. Clearly . . . (*Loud.*) But it's not going to happen like you want. (*Loud.*) It isn't you know . . . (*Pause. Pulling at the grass, to himself.*) It hasn't happened yet . . .

KEVIN (*staring out*). Maybe not . . .

NICK. Because you're alone.

CHARLOTTE (*moving her position slightly, against bank*). I haven't slept for twenty-four hours, you know. I've never been without sleep for so long. It's an extraordinary feeling. (*She brushes her hair back with her hand.*)

KEVIN. No, nor have I. (*He goes over to* CHARLOTTE, *quiet, close, confidential.*) I hardly slept at all the night before. Before this one. Because I was thinking about this trip – this journey of ours. I couldn't have slept for more than an hour. (*He is right beside her.*) Not more than an hour, Charlotte.

CHARLOTTE. No.

KEVIN. How's your back?

NICK. What you saying to her?

CHARLOTTE. It's better now. It's fine.

NICK (*loud*). What you saying to each other?

CHARLOTTE. It's all right, Nick. Stay there. (*Tense.*) We'll know very soon. It gets light very quick, see . . . it comes up so swiftly at this time of year. Just have to prepare ourselves.

KEVIN (*by her, quiet, matter-of-fact*). Yes, I know.

CHARLOTTE (*looking at* KEVIN, *gently but matter-of-fact*). Quiet . . . that's right, that's better.

KEVIN. Not much time now . . .

CHARLOTTE. No, I've written it down. Everything . . . What we stand for. I couldn't finish it . . . I've just scrawled it down . . . I don't want to show it, it's not how I'd like to have put it. But it's almost all there – everything.

NICK (*louder*). Charlotte?

CHARLOTTE. Just stay there.

NICK (*loud, aggressive*). Tell me as well then . . .

CHARLOTTE. I am telling you . . . (*She glances down at the paper.*) So it's down there now.

KEVIN *suddenly gets up, moves downstage.*

Where you going?

KEVIN. Show myself.

CHARLOTTE. Why?

KEVIN *stands downstage.*

KEVIN (*loud*). It's all right! Nothing so far! We're in a good position for it, aren't we? In a really good position – the best we could have. (*Suddenly.*) You know what happened here? You know what happened on this hillside, that valley? It's a battlefield – an old battlefield. No, it's true. I know about it. The Wars of the Roses, right here, by these gorse bushes, in these fields. Under the ground, under this earth, there're pieces of England, lying right under the surface, under this grass. Scrape it away, scrape away the top, and you'll find it, it'll be staring up at you, out of the ground! The whole history of the place. (*Suddenly really loud.*) AND YOU CAN'T CHANGE THAT!

CHARLOTTE (*quiet, firm*). NO.

KEVIN. There should be a monument here. 150 feet high. Thick, granite! Unmovable, yes, up on top of this hill. I know all about it, because we came up here, years ago now, it seems, that's why I knew we had to stop here. Because I saw it! I recognised it! (*He smiles.*) There was a lot of us that came up, a whole lot of us round here then, in Northumberland. It was like our own village, all of us together, here, building things, making things, living under this sky. Peacefully. It was incredible. Spread over here. Fifty of us – you should have seen it, the colour and the feeling then! And it lasted all that year. (*Loud.*) I passed through that wood just now, coming up. I saw the remains of it all, the bits of it lying there. The bits we built, rotting and covered in wire, and sawn into pieces, broken up! Old nails sticking out – you could tear yourself on it now, rip your leg open, get diseased. You could. And the pool where we used to swim. Dried up, of course, rusted up, and filled in, full of filth, where we used to be all the time . . . (*Loud, fast, suddenly letting rip.*) WHAT'S HAPPENED TO THEM? Tell me that. What's happened to them all?

NICK (*tensing*). Kevin . . .

KEVIN (*carrying straight on*). I see a face in the street sometimes.

I hardly recognise it, it's changed so much. Exhausted, eaten into. Without a job, of course, they always are, or just about to lose one, limping along, unable to do anything, almost broken, no life for anything. Shadows. (*Loud.*) Just shadows, of course. But that is changing now. It is.

CHARLOTTE. Yes. It is.

NICK (*tensing*). Charlotte . . .

KEVIN (*carrying straight on*). People have had enough now – they have! This summer is different. Under the heat, it's all changing.

CHARLOTTE. Yes . . .

The light is increasing, getting brighter all the time.

KEVIN. A kind of turning point, yes! This is going to be quite a famous summer, it really is. It's the end of an era – end of this appalling era, isn't it, yes. (*Really loud.*) And if we're the first, the first of our age, to become really known, show what's happening, *then we're the first!* And there it is!

CHARLOTTE. Yes.

NICK (*loud*). Charlotte . . .

KEVIN (*loud*). Just look at this! This is one of the most beautiful parts of England. This here! See it now. It's totally unspoiled – untouched. It's ours still. You just have to open your mouth here, and it'll roll over five counties, it will. There's nothing in the way. *They haven't ruined it yet.*

CHARLOTTE (*sharp*). And it's going to stay that way.

KEVIN. Yes. It is. It's not full of people that don't belong.

NICK (*dangerous*). Stop it, Kevin – are you going to stop?

KEVIN. That just shouldn't be here! That never ought to have been allowed to come – they've got to be sent back now! Back to where they came from. Yes! Even the kids in school are beginning to feel it, feel their Englishness, know this place belongs to them . . .

NICK (*jumps up, grabs KEVIN*). Kevin, just stop it! Do you hear? STOP IT!

CHARLOTTE (*shouts*). Let him go . . .

KEVIN. Get off me . . .

NICK (*shaking him really hard*). Just stop that, once and for all. Stop it.

KEVIN. Let go of me . . . (*Pause.*) Go on – let go.

Silence. NICK lets go of his arm.

CHARLOTTE. That's right.

NICK (*staring at* KEVIN). Kevin . . . Racing with it, aren't you
. . . (*He glances at* CHARLOTTE.) Look at him . . . still racing
through him . . .

Pause.

KEVIN (*quiet*). You don't feel anything, do you? You have no
idea what to do at all.

The siren starts again, much nearer.

CHARLOTTE. Sit down, both of you. (*Dangerous.*) Sit down –

KEVIN. It's much nearer.

The siren is approaching, but is not on top of them yet.

Isn't it? They're going to get to us now.

CHARLOTTE (*really tense*). Maybe. Move back. Against this.

They move against the bank, tense.

Right back.

NICK (*loud, strong*). Charlotte?

KEVIN (*nervous*). It's gone quiet again. (*He glances behind him.*)
Where are they now?

NICK (*his voice strong, bold*). Charlotte – look at me a moment.

*The lights are coming up to full brightness during the exchange
between* NICK *and* CHARLOTTE.

(NICK *is suddenly really authoritative.*) *Charlotte?*

CHARLOTTE (*really sharp*). Don't move . . . Just sit there . . .

NICK (*loud, angry, very strong*). Look at me, Charlotte.

CHARLOTTE *turns her head, and looks at him.*

That's better. You look different this morning.

CHARLOTTE. Do I?

NICK. Yes you do . . . messy.

She turns.

No! Look at me now. (*Quietly powerful.*) So you believe all this
obscene muck, do you . . . ?

CHARLOTTE (*not understanding*). What?

NICK. You heard me. All this obscene muck.

She looks down.

(*Very strong.*) No, keep looking, keep looking at me. (*Really loud.*) Look at me, Charlotte . . .

CHARLOTTE (*turns her head*). Yes?

NICK. You believe all that, do you – ALL OF IT?

CHARLOTTE (*quiet*). You've been told.

NICK. I mean, Kevin's finished now, completely finished.

KEVIN (*dangerous*). That's right.

NICK (*strong, staring at her*). But you – with you, there's a crack, isn't there, just a crack, but it's there. (*Really loud.*) Isn't there?

CHARLOTTE (*quiet, tone distant*). I don't know what you're talking about.

NICK. Just a slight one – but it's there, after this night. Yes! (*Strong.*) Because you don't believe quite all of it, do you? Not deep down. Not the *whole lot.* You can't believe quite all of it can you, Charlotte?

CHARLOTTE. I don't understand what he's saying. (*She glances towards* KEVIN.)

NICK. Don't look at him – he won't help – look at me, Charlotte!

KEVIN. What's he saying – what's he talking about?

CHARLOTTE (*distant, uncomprehending*). I don't know what he's saying.

NICK (*loud*). Yes you do – you can't quite believe *everything*, can you? And you know you're completely alone, too. (*Forceful.*) Come on, Charlotte. You know what I mean – you know exactly what I'm saying. (*Strong.*) Come on –

CHARLOTTE. I've told you everything. (*Quiet.*) It's not worth the effort to try any more.

NICK. Come on – that's not good enough, is it, Charlotte? That just won't do – will it?

CHARLOTTE. If he doesn't understand now – he never will –

NICK. Won't he? BUT I DO UNDERSTAND.

CHARLOTTE (*staring right back*). Do you?

KEVIN (*staring out*). I'm not sure if there's anyone out there . . .

NICK (*loud, passionate*). And I'm going to get it out of you, Charlotte. I AM –

KEVIN. What's he saying to you?

CHARLOTTE (*very distant*). I don't know. I really don't know.

KEVIN. Just leave her.

NICK (*watching her*): NO. Not now –

CHARLOTTE. I've told you everything.

NICK (*really loud*). I told you – that won't do, Charlotte – *I know*. I know, deep down, inside there, right in there you don't believe it all, and I'm going to prise it out of you, Charlotte. You're going to say it, you are.

Pause.

(*Urgent.*) Now, come on. Tell me. Tell me.

CHARLOTTE (*very distant, calm*). Will you stop this now? I don't understand at all.

NICK (*suddenly catching hold of her arm*). I mean for Chrissake you're almost a normal girl, aren't you, I mean in other circumstances people wouldn't look twice, normal little rich girl, I mean, lots more like you – (*By her face.*) There's nothing special there at all. Is there? NOTHING.

Pause.

(*Strong.*) So come on now – tell me, Charlotte –

CHARLOTTE. Just leave me alone. I don't understand.

KEVIN. Leave her.

NICK. I'm talking to you, Charlotte, aren't I? Come on, tell me. (*Suddenly really shouting, emotional, tightening his grip on her arm.*) You're wrong. And you know you're wrong. You do. And you're going to say it. You are! Even if I have to break that head open . . . Come on Charlotte . . . Come on! (*Slightly quieter.*) You really know you are . . . You do.

Pause.

(*Much quieter.*) Come on.

CHARLOTTE (*quieter, matter-of-fact*). You've still no idea at all, have you?

NICK (*quieter, but still quite forceful*). Haven't I?

CHARLOTTE (*quiet*). No idea at all.

NICK (*quieter*). I see . . .

Pause.

(*Quiet, matter-of-fact.*) Come on . . . tell me.

The lights are now up to full.

KEVIN (*suddenly loud*). There isn't anyone out there! Look, there isn't!

CHARLOTTE (*looks out*). No, there isn't.

KEVIN (*loud*). They've gone past –

CHARLOTTE (*slight smile*). I thought they might.

KEVIN (*loud*). They've gone by again! Right by! (*He smiles.*) We're alone up here.

CHARLOTTE. Yes. Just the tractor down there. God, my clothes feel rough . . .

KEVIN (*staring out*). Three hundred feet down to there. Look. A dewy morning. There's no wind at all, is there – completely still –

CHARLOTTE. Come on – we must leave at once. Right now – they'll be back very soon. Pick everything up, Kevin – (*She snaps.*) Quick.

KEVIN *moves with speed.*

We're moving on now, Nick – (*To* KEVIN.) Come on, quickly, that blanket as well – (CHARLOTTE *folds the blanket.*) – take them to the van.

KEVIN. That's everything – (*He takes his dark glasses off.*)

CHARLOTTE. Yes, Kevin –

KEVIN. Goodbye then, mate.

NICK. Goodbye.

KEVIN *hesitates for a split second.*

CHARLOTTE. Go on, Kevin, quickly. I'll bring these.

KEVIN *goes;* CHARLOTTE *finishes folding the blanket.*

NICK. You're going now?

CHARLOTTE. Yes.

NICK (*quiet*). Good.

CHARLOTTE. Yes. (*Matter-of-fact.*) Finish the trip. (*She puts the blanket on top of the big bag, and picks up the thermos.*)

NICK (*staring out, not at* CHARLOTTE). I see. (*Quiet.*) If someone was standing right over there, we'd just be two small dots on a hillside, you realise. (*Quiet, he moves his head slightly.*) God, it's still, isn't it? Suddenly there's no wind at all. He's right. Just quiet.

CHARLOTTE. Yes. Don't turn round now, Nick.

NICK. What?

He turns, she's holding the gun. Split second between them.

Charlotte?

She shoots him – very close range.

She picks up the bag and the thermos and leaves.

On the soundtrack we hear the sound of traffic news on the wireless getting louder and louder, brash, jarring names of by-passes and road intersections blasting out fiercely. Then total silence.

Fade.

FIRST NEWSCAST
(Scene Six)

Fanfare for news.

ANNOUNCER. Independent Radio News, at one o'clock. This is
David Williams.
A police constable was shot dead in Doncaster tonight. His
body was found in the North West of the city at about 10.30.
Police are not revealing his identity until relatives have been
informed. Here is Ken Lewis in Doncaster.

KEN LEWIS. At around ten o'clock tonight a young police
constable, out on his normal beat, was shot dead at point blank
range here in Clive Road, in the North West of Doncaster. He
was found out on the pavement here, by the side of the old
Granada Cinema. He had been shot four times. This is a fairly
deserted area of the city, the cinema like most of the
surrounding area is awaiting demolition, and the police are
urgently requesting anybody that may have seen some people
leaving the area hurriedly at about ten tonight to come forward.
They already believe that more than one person was involved, and
are interviewing witnesses who heard the sound of the shots.
Road blocks have been set up all around the city and in
surrounding areas. And the whole of the Yorkshire force has
been alerted. There is no sign as yet of what motivated this
particularly brutal murder. This is Ken Lewis I.R.N. Doncaster.

DAVID WILLIAMS. In the House of Commons tonight, the
Leader of the Opposition, Margaret Thatcher, launched one of
her most bitter attacks yet on the Government in what is seen
as a further indication that an early General Election is a
possibility . . .

SECOND ANNOUNCER. A policeman has been shot dead
tonight in Doncaster. His body was found in Clive Road, by a
deserted Cinema in the Northern part of the city, he had been
shot several times.

THIRD ANNOUNCER. . . . was shot dead tonight in Doncaster.
He was a young police constable out on his usual beat. He was
found lying outside a deserted Cinema. He had been shot four
times at point blank range.

FOURTH ANNOUNCER. . . . in an alleyway by a Cinema. His
identity has not as yet been released. Police are anxious to talk
to anyone who was in or near Clive Road between 9.30 and
10.30 tonight . . .

SECOND NEWSCAST
(Scene Seven)

Begins in blackout before the scene. No fanfare. Half-way through, it cuts to the radio onstage as the lights come up.

DAVID WILLIAMS (*or perhaps another announcer*). Following the shooting of a Police Constable in Doncaster, police are mounting a full scale manhunt, North of Newcastle. Here is Ron Allen in Newcastle.

RON ALLEN. After eye witness accounts that two men and a woman, thought to be in their twenties, were seen leaving the area of the killing in a van, Police here in Northumberland are mounting one of the most massive manhunts ever seen in the North East. Men have been drafted in from surrounding forces and Scottish Police have also been alerted. The three young people are believed to be somewhere either in the hills in the Border country, or just across the Border; police are combing the lonely country roads in that area and checking on outlying farmhouses.

Helicopters are standing by for an aerial search at sunrise. Police are regarding the suspects as potentially extremely dangerous, and both detectives and many uniformed police have been issued with firearms as they attempt to encircle the whole area in one large Police cordon.

This is Ron Allen I.R.N. Newcastle.

Methuen World Classics *and*
Methuen Contemporary Dramatists

Aeschylus (two volumes)
Jean Anouilh
John Arden (two volumes)
Arden & D'Arcy
Aristophanes (two volumes)
Aristophanes & Menander
Peter Barnes (three volumes)
Brendan Behan
Aphra Behn
Edward Bond (four volumes)
Bertolt Brecht
 (five volumes)
Howard Brenton
 (two volumes)
Büchner
Bulgakov
Calderón
Jim Cartwright
Anton Chekhov
Caryl Churchill
 (two volumes)
Noël Coward (five volumes)
Sarah Daniels (two volumes)
Eduardo De Filippo
David Edgar (three volumes)
Euripides (three volumes)
Dario Fo (two volumes)
Michael Frayn (two volumes)
Max Frisch
Gorky
Harley Granville Barker
 (two volumes)
Henrik Ibsen (six volumes)
Terry Johnson

Lorca (three volumes)
David Mamet (three volumes)
Marivaux
Mustapha Matura
David Mercer (two volumes)
Arthur Miller
 (five volumes)
Anthony Minghella
Molière
Tom Murphy
 (three volumes)
Musset
Peter Nichols (two volumes)
Clifford Odets
Joe Orton
Louise Page
A. W. Pinero
Luigi Pirandello
Stephen Poliakoff
 (two volumes)
Terence Rattigan
Willy Russell
Ntozake Shange
Sam Shepard (two volumes)
Sophocles (two volumes)
Wole Soyinka
David Storey (two volumes)
August Strindberg
 (three volumes)
J. M. Synge
Sue Townsend
Ramón del Valle-Inclán
Frank Wedekind
Oscar Wilde